THE ART AND CRAFT OF ASIAN STORIES

Bloomsbury Writer's Guides and Anthologies

Bloomsbury Writer's Guides and Anthologies offer established and aspiring creative writers an introduction to the art and craft of writing in a variety of forms, from poetry to environmental and nature writing. Each book is part craft-guide, with writing prompts and exercises, and part anthology, with relevant works by major authors.

Series Editors:
Sean Prentiss, Norwich University, USA
Joe Wilkins, Linfield College, USA

Titles in the Series:
Environmental and Nature Writing, Sean Prentiss and Joe Wilkins
Poetry, Amorak Huey and W. Todd Kaneko
Short-Form Creative Writing, H. K. Hummel and Stephanie Lennox
Creating Comics, Chris Gavaler and Leigh Ann Beavers
Advanced Creative Nonfiction, Sean Prentiss and Jessica Hendry Nelson

Forthcoming Titles:
Fantasy Fiction, Jennifer Pullen
Advanced Fiction, Amy E. Weldon
Advanced Poetry, Kathryn Nuernberger and Maya Jewell Zeller
Experimental Writing, Lawrence Lenhart and William Cordeiro

THE ART AND CRAFT OF ASIAN STORIES

A WRITER'S GUIDE AND ANTHOLOGY

Robin Hemley and Xu Xi

BLOOMSBURY ACADEMIC
LONDON • NEW YORK • OXFORD • NEW DELHI • SYDNEY

BLOOMSBURY ACADEMIC
Bloomsbury Publishing Plc
50 Bedford Square, London, WC1B 3DP, UK
1385 Broadway, New York, NY 10018, USA
29 Earlsfort Terrace, Dublin 2, Ireland

BLOOMSBURY, BLOOMSBURY ACADEMIC and the Diana logo are trademarks of
Bloomsbury Publishing Plc

First published in Great Britain 2021

Copyright © Robin Hemley and Xu Xi, 2021

Robin Hemley and Xu Xi have asserted their right under the Copyright, Designs and
Patents Act, 1988, to be identified as Authors of this work.

For legal purposes the Credits and Permissions on p. vii constitute an extension of this
copyright page.

Cover Design: Eleanor Rose
Cover image © Xu Xi

All rights reserved. No part of this publication may be reproduced or transmitted in any form or by
any means, electronic or mechanical, including photocopying, recording, or any information storage
or retrieval system, without prior permission in writing from the publishers.

Bloomsbury Publishing Plc does not have any control over, or responsibility for, any third-party
websites referred to or in this book. All internet addresses given in this book were correct at
the time of going to press. The author and publisher regret any inconvenience caused if
addresses have changed or sites have ceased to exist, but can accept no responsibility
for any such changes.

A catalogue record for this book is available from the British Library.

A catalog record for this book is available from the Library of Congress.

ISBN: HB: 978-1-3500-7655-6
PB: 978-1-3500-7654-9
ePDF: 978-1-3500-7657-0
eBook: 978-1-3500-7656-3

Series: Bloomsbury Writer's Guides and Anthologies

Typeset by Deanta Global Publishing Services, Chennai, India

To find out more about our authors and books visit www.bloomsbury.com and sign up
for our newsletters.

CONTENTS

Credits and Permissions — vii

Introduction — 1

1 Family Matters — 5
1 "The Brothers" *by Lysley Tenorio (USA)* — 5
2 "My Mother Pattu" *by Saras Manickam (Malaysia)* — 18

2 Attraction — 29
1 "Convince Me" *by Jiang Yitan (China) Translated from Chinese (Mandarin) by Philip Hand* — 31
2 "No Toes" *by Michael Mohammed Ahmad (Australia)* — 37

3 Routines — 45
1 "We That Summer" *by Han Yujoo (Korea) Translated from Korean by Janet Hong* — 45
2 "Birds" *by Deepak Unnikrishnan (UAE)* — 57

4 Little Fish — 69
1 "A Clerk's Story" *by Dilip Kumar (India) Translated from Tamil by Padma Narayanan* — 70
2 "National Day" *by Jeremy Tiang (Singapore)* — 81
3 "An Errand" *by Angelo Lacuesta (Philippines)* — 88

5 Shedding Skins — 97
1 "All About Skin" *by Xu Xi (USA)* — 99
2 "Dragon Menu" *by Zhang Xinxin (China) Translated from Chinese (Mandarin) by Helen Wang* — 107

6 Invaders — 115
1 "Farangs" *by Rattawut Lapcharoensap (USA)* — 116
2 "Boondocks" *by Robin Hemley (USA)* — 127

7 Diasporas — 131
1 "The Boat" *by Nam Le (Australia)* — 133
2 "Dreams in English" *by Noelle Q. de Jesus (Philippines/Singapore)* — 159

Contents

8 Mysteries — 173
1. "The Door" *by Dorothy Tse (Hong Kong) Translated from Chinese (Cantonese) by Natascha Bruce* — 173
2. "Where Did I Lose You" *by Fan Xiaoqing (China) Translated from Chinese (Mandarin) by Paul Harris* — 186

9 Taboos — 197
1. "The Quilt" *by Ismat Chughtai Translated from Urdu by Gopika Jadeja* — 198
2. "Video" *by Meera Nair (USA)* — 205
3. "Prayer in Training" *by Ploi Pirapokin (USA)* — 218

10 Histories — 223
1. "Bee Honey" *by Yoshimoto Banana (Japan) Translated from Japanese by Michael Emmerich* — 224
2. "Lee Kuan Yew Is Not Always the Answer" *by Inez Tan (Singapore)* — 229

11 Future Tense — 239
1. "Pink" *by Hoshino Tomoyuki (Japan) Translated from Japanese by Brian Bergstrom* — 240
2. "Learning Curve" *by Yeung Chak Yan (Hong Kong)* — 255

Index — 263

CREDITS AND PERMISSIONS

Note: In many Asian cultures, the surname or last name is placed before the first name, in particular in North Asia such as Korea, Japan, and China; however, some authors do Anglicize their names and the Western convention of first name before the surname or last name is used in those cases. With that in mind, this list is alphabetical by the author's surname or last name.

"No Toes" by Michael Mohammed Ahmad. Originally published in *Best of Meanjin 2017: Fiction*, Australia, and subsequently in *Best Summer Stories*, Black Inc., Australia, 2018. Used by permission of the author.

"The Quilt" by Ismat Chughtai published with the permission of Ashish Sawhny, copyright holder of the author's estate and of translator Gopika Jadeja for the unpublished translation from Urdu, 2019.

"Dreams in English" by Noelle Q. de Jesus. Originally published in *Witness*, Vol. XXXI No. 3, Winter 2018 and subsequently in the author's collection *Cursed and Other Stories*, Penguin, October 2019. Used by permission of the author.

"Where Did I Lose You" by Fan Xiaoqing. Originally published in *Paper Republic: Chinese Literature in Translation*, November 2016, translated from Chinese (Mandarin) by Paul Harris. Used by permission of the author and translator.

"We That Summer" by Han Yujoo. Originally published in *Brick 102*, posted December 12, 2018, translated from Korean by Janet Hong. Used by permission of the author and translator.

"Boondocks" by Robin Hemley. Originally published in *Iowa Review*, Spring 2018. Used by permission of the author.

"Pink" by Hoshino Tomoyuki. Originally published in *Granta 127: Japan*, 2014, translated from Japanese by Brian Bergstrom. Used by permission of the author and translator.

"Convince Me" by Jiang Yitan. Originally published in *Paper Republic: Chinese Literature in Translation*, November 2017, translated from Chinese (Mandarin) by Philip Hand (Alexander Clifford). Used by permission of the author and translator.

"A Clerk's Story" by Dilip Kumar. Originally published in *The Caravan Magazine*, August 2012, translated from Tamil by Padma Narayanan. Used by permission of the author and translator.

"An Errand" by Angelo Lacuesta. An earlier version appeared in the author's collection *Coral Cove and Other Stories*, UST Publishing House, Manila, Philippines, 2017. Used by permission of the author.

"Farangs" by Rattawut Lapcharoensap. Originally published in the author's collection *Sightseeing*, Grove Press, 2005. Used by permission of the author.

"The Boat" by Nam Le from *The Boat* by Nam Le, copyright ©2008 by Nam Le. Used by permission (North America) of Alfred A. Knopf, an imprint of the Knopf Doubleday Publishing Group, a division of Random House, LLC. All rights reserved. Also used by permission (UK and Commonwealth excluding Canada, Australia, and New Zealand) by Canongate for volume and ebook rights.

Credits and Permissions

"My Mother Pattu" by Saras Manickam (Saraswathy M. Manickam). Originally published in *Granta*, The Online Edition, June 10, 2019. Used by permission of the author.

"Video" by Meera Nair. Originally published in the author's collection *Video*, Pantheon, 2002. Used by permission of the author.

"Prayer in Training" by Ploi Pirapokin. Originally published in *Fiction International: Taboo*, Issue 49, November 2016. Used by permission of the author.

"Lee Kuan Yew Is Not Always the Answer." Originally published in the author's collection *This Is Where I Won't Be Alone*, Epigram Books, 2018, pp 43-58. Used by permission of Epigram Books Pte Ltd., Singapore.

"The Brothers" by Lysley Tenorio. Originally published in a slightly different form in the author's collection *Monstress*, Ecco, 2012. Used by permission of the author.

"National Day" by Jeremy Tiang. Originally published in the author's collection *It Never Rains on National Day*, Epigram Books, 2015, pp 151-66. Used by permission of Epigram Books Pte Ltd., Singapore.

"The Door" by Dorothy Tse. Originally published in *Mascara Literary Review*, posted June 8, 2018, translated from Chinese (Cantonese) by Natascha Bruce. Used by permission of the author and translator.

"Birds" by Deepak Unnikrishnan. Originally published in the author's novel *Temporary People*, Restless Books, 2017. Used by permission of Restless Books, Brooklyn, New York.

"All About Skin" by Xu Xi. Originally published in a slightly different form in *KR Online*, Spring 2012 and subsequently in the present form in the author's collection *Insignificance*, Signal 8, 2018. Used by permission of the author.

"Learning Curve" by Yeung Chak Yan. Originally published in *Bellingham Review*, Issue 72, Spring 2016. Used by permission of the author.

"Bee Honey" by Yoshimoto Banana. Originally published as "Hachi Honey" by Banana YOSHIMOTO, Copyright ©2000 by Banana Yoshimoto, Japanese original of the work appeared in the book *Furin to Nanbei*, Gentosha, Inc., 2000. English translation rights arranged with Banana Yoshimoto through ZIPANGO. Used by permission of Zipango, S.L., Spain. Subsequently published in *The Penguin Book of Japanese Short Stories*, Penguin Random House UK, 2018 as "Bee Honey" translated from Japanese by Michael Emmerich. Used by permission of the translator.

"Dragon Menu" by Zhang Xinxin. Originally published as "Dragonworld" in *Paper Republic: Chinese Literature in Translation*, November 2016 translated from Chinese (Mandarin) by Helen Wang. Used by permission of the author and translator.

INTRODUCTION

In some fundamental ways, this is not your parents' guide to writing fiction. The first, most obvious difference between this and all other guides to writing fiction is that this is the first guide in which all the stories included have a connection to Asia, though our selection of stories is in no way meant to be representative of all of Asia. If we tried to do so, the anthology would have to include at least forty-eight countries or territories and would be so expensive and mammoth that simply lugging it around would be considered an accomplishment. We should also admit right here that we have not read every Asian story ever published to come up with our selections—let's liken it to fishing in a very big sea. Some fish we caught and kept, some we threw back, and undoubtedly many fine fish swam unnoticed underneath our boat. And before we begin in earnest, we should also mention that this anthology is not at all meant for Asian students and Asian students only. Our aim here is not one of isolating stories by Asians for Asians, but quite the opposite. Our aim is to widen the field of models for students of any background from any country. Your own stories can reflect who you are and where you live, or not, depending on your passions as a writer and your abilities. Our aim is to open up a world of stories you might not otherwise come across and to glean from these stories' techniques and approaches, some of which you might find in your typical fiction writing text and some that you likely wouldn't find.

On that last point: you'll notice that we don't break up the chapters into the traditional elements of the short story: character, voice, point of view, setting, and so on. One of our aims in this book is to integrate these elements organically into our discussions of the stories at hand. We want to let the stories we've chosen teach you their techniques, and rather than trying to isolate them, we want to discuss the various teachable elements of each story as a whole. Our exercises at the end of each chapter will isolate some of these techniques so that you can practice them after reading the chapter. Certainly, your instructor can supplement our points with their own experience and store of knowledge. You'll also notice that the chapters are arranged thematically—the stories we chose led us to uncover these themes, which not only seemed appropriate to the stories themselves but also suggested to us rich ways to conceive of stories, no matter where you come from. We hope that you will agree that the stories we've chosen, the way we discuss them, and the exercises we suggest will breathe life and vigor into your own stories.

From the outset, we understood some of the basic challenges of writing such a text. We didn't want this to be a book that siloed off Asian writing for Asian writers. The aim of the book was, in part, to demonstrate that the world of the short story is a global phenomenon, and that North American writers, writers in the UK, Australia, and elsewhere could glean as much from Asian stories as writers in Asia could glean from North American models. After all, there's a long history of writers from various continents cross pollenating as it were, from the early twentieth-century writer Lu Xun, finding inspiration in Virginia Woolf, to the mid-twentieth-century poet Ezra Pound, finding inspiration in poetry from the Tang dynasty. More recently, a generation of Western readers and writers have been captivated and certainly influenced by writers such as Murakami, and two Chinese writers have won the Nobel Prize in Literature within relatively recent years, Gao Xingjian (2000) and Mo Yan (2012).

While we have included a couple of stories that are older, such as "The Quilt," by Indian writer Ismat Chughtai, which was written in 1942, the majority of stories are contemporary. Many of the stories we've included are by lesser-known writers, at least outside of their home countries, and deal with circumstances that, if not universal, are ones that we thought might appeal to a contemporary audience.

We should note too that Asian stories don't always follow the conventional models laid out in many Western textbooks. Some do, but not all. Of course, a number of Western stories don't necessarily follow traditional convention either. For this reason, we thought it might be a good idea to forego the typical fiction text structure and allow the stories we chose to teach us themselves about their forms. That doesn't mean we will avoid discussing standard craft issues such as point of view, dialogue, setting, and so forth. It just means that these discussions will arise somewhat organically in our discussions of the stories we're using as models.

Consequently, we have chosen the stories we wanted to include and have written the chapters around them. Each chapter is organized around two or three model stories, and the exercises at the end of each chapter build off the themes and techniques discussed in the chapter. The first chapter, you'll note, deals with family. Most of us have memories of our birth families, and the writer Flannery O'Connor once said that by the age of eighteen you have enough stories to last a lifetime. We've arranged the chapters from less challenging to more challenging concepts. This is why "Taboos" appears near the end of the book, as well as the two companion stories that some might find difficult in terms of subject matter. But writers often cross lines and invite controversy, whether intended or not. "The Quilt," for instance, while a charming story, deals with sexuality in a way that a lot of people in India weren't ready for in 1942, when it was first published. In fact, the author, Ismat Chughtai was made to face an obscenity trial when she published the story and was asked to apologize. She didn't apologize and she won the case. Stories make people uncomfortable sometimes for a lot of reasons, including political reasons. This is why so many writers are jailed and why they sometimes use metaphor to criticize oppressive or chauvinistic political regimes. Consider as you read some of these stories if there are inherent criticisms in them of the conventional narratives pushed by church and state. Writers are dangerous, and we take pride in this—even when we write fantasy, we are often revealing truths that make the powerful and the complacent uncomfortable. As Albert Camus famously wrote, "Fiction is the lie through which we tell the truth."

Originally, we thought that we would limit the authors in the anthology to writers from Asia who live in Asia, but this cut out a lot of wonderful stories, and also ignores the fact that there are many émigré and diasporic writers of Asian descent. People do not stay put and they never have, and a story about a Filipino father visiting his dying daughter in a Boston hospital (Noelle Q. de Jesus's "Dreams in English") says something just as important about notions of migration as a story about refugees from Vietnam trying to survive a perilous sea voyage to Australia (Nam Le's "The Boat"). And so you will find writers who live or were born in Australia, the United Kingdom, the United States, and elsewhere. You will also find writers in translation who lived or have lived all their lives in India, China, and Korea. And writers from the Philippines, Hong Kong, Thailand, and elsewhere who write solely in English.

You'll notice, too, that we aren't including a history of the short story in Asia as part of this text. That's a conscious decision as this is not that type of book. We reason that most of our selections are contemporary stories and that, as such, Western and Asian literary traditions mix freely. To define an Asian type of writing would in some ways defeat what we are trying to do here, which isn't to claim that Asian stories are appreciably different from Western stories. Instead, it's our intention to present a selection of writers and writing from Asia and the Asian diaspora that present an alternative to the typical anthologies that focus on a developing contemporary Western canon. Our aim is to showcase the wide array of talented and unusual voices who write in a form that is often considered "American," starting with Edgar Allen Poe's definitions of the short story, but that have been adopted and hybridized in contexts well outside of the American landscape.

In fact, it is principally content that makes the stories included "Asian," in the sense that the setting is often in Asia and most of the characters are Asian. About the most "Asian" characteristic we can offer as a general observation is that the stories selected for this anthology often do address political or historical issues—both country-specific and global—as well issues of intercultural conflict. This might less likely be the case if we were compiling an anthology about writing featuring only stories by North American writers. We suspect this might *in part* be due to the landscape many Asian writers must negotiate—colonialism, military or authoritarian rule, cultural traditions that still dominate contemporary life, specific historical or racial or religious issues. By contrast, much of North American life is suburban and middle class, where some of these issues simply wouldn't apply, and where many writers might be focused more on personal stories. By presenting stories from across Asia, our choices leaned toward those that showcased the political, historical, or cultural landscapes many Asian writers choose to write about that might be less familiar to English-language readers. Likewise, for those stories written in English, and not translated, there is the additional linguistic issue of writing a literature that is not necessarily the country's "native language." Yet in contemporary Asia, English is often the lingua franca for education, commerce, travel, much of ordinary life, and, depending on the political or geographic entity, English might even be the "official" one alongside one or several other Asian languages. Singapore, Hong Kong, and India are three examples. However, we are aware that all the stories selected could easily find a comparable in short stories by American or English writers when it comes to content generally. After all, the short story is the ideal form to examine what in life forces us to sit up and pay attention.

But in the end, if you believe you can discern what makes an Asian short story "Asian" besides its setting and/or author, forgive us if we're a bit skeptical. Asia is not a monolith, and there is no singular identity of say, Thais, Chinese, or Filipinos.

We hope that you will find this book as a useful guide to the writing of fiction. We're proud that the book is the first of its kind, and a contribution that we think is long overdue.

CHAPTER 1
FAMILY MATTERS

You hardly need to look further than your family to find some of your best possibilities for writing stories. In some ways, a family is a collection of stories handed down (or sometimes suppressed) by the generations. But there's a big difference between the stories that a family tells about itself, the story it *wants* told (We're all perfect and nothing ever goes wrong!), and the *real* story that the writer in the family knows and understands (We're a bit of a train wreck, aren't we?). Of course, we're exaggerating. Most families have success stories and failure stories and failure stories that are really success stories and success stories that are really failures, and stories that fit neither of these judgmental terms, but are open for interpretation. Ambiguous stories. But one thing indisputable about families is that they have conflicts, and conflict is often considered the backbone of storytelling.

Does it make you uncomfortable thinking about your own family stories, the ones that your parents probably don't want you to reveal to the world outside the family? If so, good. Stories don't only create tension in the reader, but they also can create tension in the writer. What might come as a surprise is that stories rarely resolve the tension they create in the reader. Novels quite often have endings that resolve all the loose ends, but stories tend to leave the tension unresolved. There might be movement *toward* a resolution, but not in any grand or final way. Stories that end neatly in ways that release the tension rarely feel satisfying, but feel quite the opposite. Take, for example, the classic, trick ending. She woke up—it had all been a dream. While there are certainly famous narratives that resolve in just such a fashion ("Oh, Auntie Em, it's you!"), short stories tend to leave the reader feeling pretty disappointed if the author makes too much of an effort to resolve the tension. That's likely because the reader will see such an effort as inauthentic. We know that most moments of tension are not fully resolved, but are deferred, sublimated, partially forgiven but not forgotten, overcome for the most part but still haunting, reduced to a nagging voice, and so on.

Let's go ahead then and take a look at conflict and the building of tension in one of our model stories for this chapter. Go ahead and read "The Brothers" by Lysley Tenorio first, before continuing:

1 "The Brothers"

by Lysley Tenorio (USA)

Lysley Tenorio is the author of the novel *The Son of Good Fortune* and the story collection *Monstress*, which was named Book of the Year by the *San Francisco Chronicle*. Born in the Philippines, he lives in San Francisco, and is a professor at Saint Mary's College of California.

My brother went on *Ricki Lake* to prove he was a woman. The episode had a title that kept flashing at the bottom of the television screen: is she a he? is he a she? you decide! The show went like this: a guest would come out onstage, and the audience would vote on whether or not she was the real thing.

They came out one at a time, these big-haired and bright-lipped women, most of them taller than the average man. They worked the stage like strippers, bumping and grinding to the techno beat of the background music. The audience was on its feet, whistling and hooting, cheering them on.

Then came Eric.

My brother was different from the others. He was shorter, the only Filipino among them. He wore a denim skirt and a T-shirt, a pair of Doc Martens. His hair, a few strands streaked blond, fell to his bony shoulders. He was slow across the stage, wooing the audience with a shy girl's face, flirtatious, sweet. But he wasn't woman enough for them: they booed my brother, gave him the thumbs-down. So Eric fought back. He stood at the edge of the stage, fists on his hips and feet shoulder-width apart, like he was ready to take on anyone who crossed him. "Dare me?" he said, and I saw his hands move slowly to the bottom of his T-shirt. "You dare me?"

They did, and up it went. The crowd screamed with approval, gave him the thumbs-up. Someone threw a bra onstage and Eric picked it up, twirled it over his head like a lasso, then flung it back into the audience.

I looked over at Ma. It was like someone had hit her in the face.

He put his shirt down, lifted his arms in triumph, blew kisses to the audience, then took a seat with the others. He told the audience that his name was Erica.

He'd left a message the night before it aired, telling me to watch Channel 4 at seven o'clock that night. He said it would be important, that Ma should see it too. When I told Ma she looked hopeful. "Maybe he's singing," she said, "playing the piano?" She was thinking of Eric from long before, when he took music lessons and sang in the high school choir.

I reached for the remote, thinking, *That bastard set us up.*

I turned off the TV.

That was the last time I saw Eric. Now he's lying on a table, a sheet pulled to his shoulders. The coroner doesn't rush me, but I answer him quickly. "Yes," I say. "That's my brother."

Eric's life was no secret though we often wished it was: we knew about the boyfriends, the makeup and dresses. He told me about his job at the HoozHoo, a bar in downtown San Francisco where the waitresses were drag queens and transsexual women. But a year and a half ago, on Thanksgiving night, when Eric announced that he was going to proceed with a surgery ("Starting here" he said, patting his chest with his right hand), Ma left the table and told Eric that he was dead to her.

It's 6:22 p.m. He's been dead for six hours.

"We need to call people," I tell Ma. But she just sits there at the kitchen table, still in her waitress's uniform, whispering things to herself, rubbing her thumb along the curve of Eric's baby spoon. Next week she turns sixty-one. For the first time, she looks older than she is. "We have to tell people what's happened."

She puts down the spoon, finally looks at me. "What will I say? How can I tell it?"

"Tell them what the coroner told me. That's all." He had an asthma attack, rare and fatal. He was sitting on a bench in Golden Gate Park when his airways swelled so quickly, so completely, no air could get in or out. As a kid, Eric's asthma was a problem; I can still hear the squeal of his panic. *Can't breathe, can't breathe,* he'd say, and I'd rub his back and chest like I was giving him life. But as an adult, the attacks became less frequent, easier to manage, and he deemed his inhaler a thing of the past. "The severity of this attack was unusual," the coroner explained. "No way he could have prepared for it." He was dead by the time a pair of ten-year-olds on Rollerblades found him.

The look on her face makes me feel like I'm a liar. "He couldn't breathe," I say. "It's the truth." I go through cupboards, open drawers, not sure what I'm looking for, so I settle for a mug and fill it with water and though I'm not thirsty I drink it anyway. "He couldn't breathe. And then he died. When people ask, that's what you say."

Ma picks up the spoon again, and now I understand: "*Ang bunso ko,*" she's been saying. My baby boy, over and over. Like Eric died as a child and she realized it only now.

The morning after the show, my brother called me at work. When I picked up, he said, "Well . . . ?" like we were in mid-conversation, though we hadn't spoken in six months.

"You grew your hair out," I said. "It's blond now."

"Extensions," he said.

"They look real."

"They're not." He took a deep breath. "But the rest of me is."

It was a little after seven. I was the only one in the office. Not even the tech guys were in yet. I turned and looked out my window, down at the street, which was empty too.

"Goddamnit, Edmond," my brother said. "Say something."

I didn't, so he did. He said he was sorry if it hurt Ma and me, but this was a once-in-a-lifetime opportunity. "I showed the world what I'm made of." He said this slowly, like it was a line he'd been rehearsing for months. "What do you think of that?"

"I saw nothing," I said. "What?"

"I saw nothing." It was the truth. When Eric lifted his shirt, they didn't simply cover his breasts with a black rectangle. They didn't cut to commercial or pan the camera to a shocked face in the audience. Instead, they blurred him out, head to toe. It looked like he was disintegrating, molecule by molecule. "They blurred you out," I said.

I could hear him pace his apartment. I'd never visited, but I knew he was living in the Tenderloin in downtown San Francisco. The few times he called, there were always things happening on his end—cars honking, sirens, people shouting and laughing. But that morning, there was just the sound of us breathing, one, then the other, like we were taking turns. I imagined a pair of divers at the bottom of the ocean, sharing the same supply of air.

"You there?" I finally said. "Eric, are you there?"

"No," he said, then hung up.

And that's how it ended, for Eric and me.

I go to my apartment to get clothes, but stay the night at Ma's. My old bed is still in my old room upstairs, but I take the living room couch. I don't sleep, not for a minute. Before light comes, I call Delia in Chicago, but her fiancé picks up. I ask for my wife, which irritates him. But technically, I'm right: the divorce isn't final, not yet. I'm still her husband, and I won't let that go, not until I have to.

"No message," I tell him, then hang up.

Somehow, I'm wide awake all morning. Driving to the funeral home in North Oakland, I don't even yawn.

Loomis, the man who handled Dad's funeral eleven years ago, waits for us in a small square of shade outside the main office. He's heavier now, his hair thinner, all white. Back then he walked with a limp; today he walks with a cane.

"Do you remember me?" It's the first thing Ma says to him. "And my husband?" She pulls a picture from her wallet, an old black-and-white of Dad back in his Navy days. He's wearing fatigues, looking cocky. His arms hang at his sides, but his fists are clenched, like he's ready for a fight. "Dominguez. First name Teodoro." Loomis takes the photo, holds it eye level, squints. "I do remember him," he says, though he saw my father only as a corpse. "And I remember you too." He looks at me, shakes my hand. "The boy who never left his mother's side that whole time."

That was Eric. Ma knows it too. We don't correct him. The funeral doesn't take long to plan: Ma makes it similar to Dad's, ordering the same floral arrangements, the same prayer cards, the same music. Only the casket is different: Dad's was bronze, which best preserves the body. Eric's will be mahogany, a more economical choice. "It's all we can afford," Ma says.

Later, Loomis drives us through the cemetery to find a plot for Eric. We head to the north end, pull up at the bottom of a small hill where Dad is buried. But his grave is already surrounded, crowded with the more recent dead. "There," Ma says, walking uphill toward a small eucalyptus. She puts her hand on a low, thin branch, rubs a budding leaf between her fingers. "It's growing." She gives a quick survey of the area, decides this is the place.

"But your knee." I point out the steepness of the hill, warn her that years from now, when she's older, getting to Eric will be difficult.

"Then you help me," Ma says, starting toward the car. "You help me get to him."

Back home, Ma calls the people we couldn't reach last night, and each conversation is the same: she greets them warmly, pauses, but can't catch herself before she gives in to tears. Meanwhile, I get the house ready, vacuuming upstairs and down, wiping dirty window screens with wet rags, re-arranging furniture to accommodate the foot traffic of all the guests who will pray for my brother's soul. This will be the first of nine nights like this.

"I hate the way Filipinos die," Eric once said. It was the week of Dad's funeral. "Nine nights of praying on our knees, lousy Chinese food, and hundred-year-old women keep asking me where my girlfriend is." The businessmen were worse. On the last night of Dad's novena, one guy—he said he was related to us but couldn't explain how—tried selling life insurance to Eric and me. He quoted figures on what we could get for injury, dismemberment, death, and even took out a pocket calculator to prove how valuable our lives were. "Promise me, Edmond," Eric had said, "when I die, take one night to remember me. That's all. No old people. No kung pao chicken. No assholes telling you how much you'll get for my severed leg." He came close to crying, but then he managed a smile. "And make sure Village People is playing in the background."

"'YMCA'?"

"'Macho Man,'" he said. "Play it twice."

He started laughing. I started laughing. The house was full of mourners but we stood our ground in the corner of the room, matching in our Sears-bought two-piece suits, joking like the closest of brothers. But now I know we were wrong to talk like that, as though I would automatically outlive him. I was five years older than Eric, and he was only twenty-six.

Brothers are supposed to die in the correct order. I keep thinking: *Tonight should be for me.*

By six, the house fills with visitors. A dozen or so at first. Soon it's fifty. I stop counting at seventy-five.

Strangers keep telling me they're family. They try to simplify the intricate ways we're related: suddenly they're cousins, aunts and uncles, the godchildren of my grandparents. None of these people have seen Eric in years, have no idea of the ways he's changed. All they know about my brother is that he's dead.

Twice, an old woman calls me Eric by mistake.

When a neighbor asks, "Where's Delia?" Ma answers before I can. She's embarrassed by the idea of divorce, so she says that Delia is on the East Coast for business, but will be here as soon as possible. I wish it were true: I keep checking the door, thinking Delia might walk in any moment, that somehow she found out what happened and took the next flight out to be with me. Eric's death would have been our breakthrough, our turning point. I try not to think of tonight as a lost opportunity for Delia and me.

At seven, we get to our knees, pray before the religious shrine Ma's set up on top of the TV—a few porcelain figurines of Jesus Christ and the Virgin Mary, laminated prayer cards in wood frames, plastic rosaries. On the floor, an arm's reach from me, in front of the TV screen, stands an infant-sized ceramic statuette of Santo Niño, the baby Jesus Christ. All good Filipino Catholic families have one, but I haven't seen ours in years. He still looks weird to me, with his red velvet cape trimmed in gold thread and a crown to match, silver robes, brown corn silk hair curling down his face past his shoulders, the plastic flower in his hand.

When Eric was small, he thought Santo Niño was a girl: I caught him in his bedroom kneeling on the floor, and Santo Niño was naked, his cape, robes, and crown in a small, neat pile by Eric's foot. For the first time, I saw how he was made: only the hands and face had been painted to look like skin; everywhere else was unglazed white, chipped in spots. "See," Eric said, his finger in the empty space between Santo Niño's legs, "he's a girl." I called him an idiot, tried to get it through his head that he was just a statue, a ceramic body that meant nothing. "Santo Niño is a boy," I said. "Say it." He wouldn't, so I took the Santo Niño from Eric, held him above my head. Eric jumped, reached, tried to get him back, knocked him out of my hands.

Ma heard the crash, ran upstairs and found pieces of Santo Niño scattered at our feet. Before she could speak, I pointed at the pile of clothes on the floor, told her what Eric had done and said.

I tried putting Santo Niño back together in my room and listened to Eric getting hit.

But my brother had a point. This second Santo Niño, the one Ma bought to replace the one we broke, does look like a girl, with glass-blue eyes, long black lashes, a red-lipped smile, offering a rose. When everyone's eyes are shut tight in prayer, I reach out, try to take it. It's glued to his fist.

What started as praying is now a dinner party. Ma makes sure the egg rolls stay warm, that there's enough soy sauce in the chow mein. I hear her swap recent gossip with neighbors who moved away long before, watch her hold the babies of women who grew up on our street. In the Philippines, my parents threw three to four parties a year, and Ma boasted how her wedding was the grandest her province had ever seen. She promised equally grand weddings for us. But I was twenty-one when Delia and I eloped, and she gave up on Eric long ago. Funerals and novenas, I think, are all Ma has left.

People keep coming. I try to stay close to familiar faces: I comfort Mrs. Gonzalez, Eric's second-grade teacher, who's brought the crayon portraits Eric drew for her on paper sacks. I talk with Isaac Chavez, Eric's best friend from grade school and the first boy, Eric confessed to me later, he ever loved. He never told Isaac; maybe I should. But when Isaac introduces me to his new wife, I see no need to complicate his night.

Later, when the Mendoza brothers walk in, I stay away. A long time ago, at a Fourth of July picnic, they found Eric under the slide by himself, making daisy chains, singing love songs at the top of his lungs. I watched as they called him a girl, a sissy, a faggot. "That's what you get for playing with flowers," I told Eric later.

Ma catches me in the kitchen. "We're out of ice," she says. Beside her is a Filipino woman rattling melting ice cubes in her plastic cup. She looks like she came to dance instead of pray: her black hair falls in waves past her shoulders, and her tight black dress is cut above the knee. In her high-heeled boots, she's taller than almost everyone here.

"No problem." I take the cooler from the kitchen, step outside. The freezer is in the backyard, and its low hum is the only sign of life out here. The grass is weeds. Ma's roses are gone. And the four stalks of sugarcane Dad planted when he bought the house—one for each of us—have been dead sticks for years.

I take out a blue bag of ice, pound it against the concrete, breaking it up. Behind me the glass door slides open: it's the woman in the tight black dress. "This okay?" she asks. She means the cigarette between her fingers.

I slide the door shut. "It is now." "I'm Raquel."

"Edmond." We shake hands.

"The brother." She lets go. "Cold."

Icy flakes stick to my fingers. I wipe them on my pants. "You're friends with Eric?"

"Sisters. That's what we call ourselves, anyway." She lights the cigarette, takes a drag, then lets out a long breath of smoke. "I have no family here. They're all back in Manila, pissed at me for leaving. So she became my sister. Sweet, huh?" *Sisters. She.* I feel like I'm being tested on what I know and don't know about my brother.

"Eric always wanted a sister."

"Well, if we're sisters, then that makes you my kuya Edmond, right?"

"*Kuya?*"

"That's Tagalog for 'big brother.'" Without asking, she unfolds a lawn chair and sits down. She crosses her legs, rests an elbow on her knee, her chin on her hand, looks at me closely. "How are you?"

Not even the coroner asked me that, even after I saw the body. "Fine." I squat down, smash more ice. "Holding up."

"Not me. Last night, when you left that message at the bar, I wanted to erase it. I was thinking, *I don't know anyone named Eric, and I don't know an Eric's brother.* But I knew who you meant."

She describes the rest of the night: how they closed the HoozHoo early, gathered the waitresses and the regulars together, drank and wept and sang songs until morning. Before everyone went home, they stood in a circle on the dance floor, held hands and said a prayer, music off but lights on, disco ball spinning above them. "It looked like heaven," she says. "All the girls wanted to come tonight, but I told them no. It should just be me. Out of respect for your mother."

It's like the start of a joke: *a dozen drag queens walk in on eighty Filipinos praying on their knees* . . . And I can picture the rest of it: six-foot-tall women in six-inch heels, glittering in a crowd of people dressed in black. I can see the stares, hear the whispers, Ma in the middle of it all, wishing them away. But maybe everyone would have been fooled, taken them as the very girlfriends that old ladies had pestered Eric about. Right away I knew what Raquel was, but so much of her looks real, like she was born into the body she's made.

"You're staring at my tits, hon."

The ice slips from my hand, slides across the cement onto the dirt.

She manages a smile, shrugs. "People look all the time."

She glances at them herself. "Four years ago, when I came to the States"—she gestures at her breasts, like she's trying to display them—"there's nothing here. Just flat. All empty. So now, if people want to look, I let them. They're mine, right?" She puts out her cigarette, lights another. "It's the same thing with Erica. Hers turned out really nice, really—" "More ice?" I reach for another blue bag. "There's ice." She reaches out, puts her hand on my shoulder. "I've embarrassed you. Sorry. That wasn't Coke in my cup." Raquel pulls a silver flask from her purse, unscrews the top, and holds it upside down. "All gone," she sighs. "I should be gone too." She gets up, but she's off balance. "Walk me to the door?" She puts her hands on my wrist, holds it tight. I don't know that I have a choice.

We step inside, work our way through the crowds in the kitchen, the living room. People look but they don't stare, and I think we can slip out quietly. But then I see the Mendoza brothers on the couch, eyeing Raquel, smirking at one another. My guess is that they've gone from childhood bullies to the kind of men who would follow a girl to her car with whistles and catcalls.

I help Raquel with her coat. "I'll walk you to your car."

"I'm at the end of the street." We step outside, walk down the driveway. Raquel takes my arm again, her hold tighter this time.

"Maybe you should've had Coke after all," I say.

"No," she says. "I need to be this way tonight."

We get to her car, a beat-up Honda dented all over, with a missing back window replaced with plastic and duct tape.

"Time for you to go back home," she says, leaning against the door. She searches her purse for her keys, not realizing she's holding them in her left hand.

Then she says, "Oh, shit."

I see it: on the corner, seven women, tall and big as Raquel, empty out of a minivan and head toward Ma's house, their heels clicking loudly against the sidewalk.

"I told them they shouldn't come," Raquel says. She takes a step toward them but I don't let her go. "It's not our problem," I say, then take the keys from between her fingers, walk her to the passenger's door. I unlock it for her, then get into the driver's seat.

"What about your guests?" Raquel asks.

"I don't have any." I start the car, watch the women enter Ma's house one by one. "Where to?"

"San Francisco."

I drive down Telegraph Avenue, head for the bridge. "You're a nice man, Kuya Edmond." Raquel reclines her seat, turns toward the window, like she's watching the moon. "Can I call you that? Kuya?"

"Why not." No one else will, and Eric never did.

It's less than ten minutes from Ma's house to the bridge, and yet I never cross it. Yesterday, when I drove to ID the body, was the first time in years that I'd been to San Francisco.

The time before that was when Ma kicked Eric out. He was seventeen. She found him in his bedroom, made up as a girl, in bed with a guy. She told them to leave, and told Eric not to come back. "For good this time," Eric said on the phone. "But there's nowhere for me to go." He was breathing fast and heavy, fighting not to cry.

Delia and I were living in Richmond, a good half hour away. But who else was going to help my brother? "Find a place," I said, "and I'll drive you there."

When I got to the house, Eric was sitting on the curb, a suitcase and an orange sleeping bag at his feet. He looked up at me, and what I thought were bruises was just makeup smeared together. "She tried wiping it off with a dishrag," he explained. "I look awful, don't I?"

"Get in the car," I said, then went inside to check on Ma. She was sitting at the top of the stairs, still in her Denny's uniform, Dad's terrycloth robe draped over her lap. She had just gotten home from a late shift when she found Eric. "I brought home a sandwich for him," she said. "He doesn't want to take it. If you're hungry—"

"I'm not," I said.

She nodded, went to her room. I heard her lock the door. I went back outside, got in the car. Eric was in the passenger's seat, putting on lipstick. I grabbed his wrist, squeezed so hard he dropped it. "Didn't I tell you," I was shouting now, "you don't do this here. You want to play dress-up, that's fine. But not in Ma's house. You keep it to yourself."

"I'm not playing dress-up," Eric said.

I started driving. "Just tell me where to go."

Eric gave directions, and before I realized it I was on the Bay Bridge, bound for the city. He had a friend with a spare couch who lived in the Mission neighborhood. I headed down South Van Ness, turned onto a dark street that got darker the farther down we went. "Stop at the next house," Eric said. I pulled up in front of an old peeling Victorian. "Here," I said, and I put four twenty-dollar bills in his hand. He gave one of them back, reminded me that Mother's Day was coming up, and asked if I could get flowers for Ma.

He got out of the car, but before he closed the door he leaned in. "It was the first perfect night I ever had," he said. "Know what I mean?"

I didn't. "Call me in a few days," I said.

Eric walked toward the front door, dragging his things behind him. At the top of the driveway, he turned around. We looked at each other, as though neither of us knew who should be the first to go.

What I wished then I'm wishing now: that I'd reached over and opened the passenger door. Maybe then we could have made our way back to Ma's, or to a place neither of us had been to before. An all-night diner off the freeway. A road that dead-ended with a view of the city. If we'd had more time, I could have taken him home. Maybe then, things could have stayed the same.

It took me hours to find my way back to the bridge.

Ma finally spoke to Eric a year later, just in time for his high school graduation. But she never invited him to live in the house again, and he never asked to come back. Eric's room is storage space now, but mine she left as is: my childhood bed against the window, my blue desk beside it, Dad's wicker rocking chair still in the corner. It's like she knew Eric was never coming back, and I always would.

I tap Raquel on her shoulder. "We're here," I say. "Tell me where to go."

For now, Raquel is homeless; a pipe burst in her apartment building three weeks before, flooding every unit. She'd been staying with Eric ever since. Had she said this before I got in her car, I'm not sure I would have driven her home.

It takes forty minutes to find parking, and when we do, it's blocks away from Eric's building. Walking, we pass drunken college boys negotiating with prostitutes, homeless kids sharing a bottle, cops who seem oblivious to everything around them. "I get scared at night," Raquel says. I let her keep hold of my arm.

Eric's building is on Polk Street. Two teenage girls sit on the front steps, smoking cigarettes. "New boyfriend, Miss Raquel?" one says.

"Ask me again in the morning and I'll tell you." Raquel laughs, high-fives both girls.

We take the stairs to the third floor, head down a narrow hallway lit by fading fluorescent lights. Eric's apartment number is 310. The door is white, like all the rest. "I'd meant to visit," I say. Raquel says nothing.

She takes the keys, lets me in. "After you, Kuya." I don't know how I'm getting home.

Those times I spoke to Eric, I imagined him sitting on his windowsill, and what his apartment might look like: wigs and dresses piled on a red leather couch, Christmas lights framing every window, drooping down from the ceiling. It was the kind of place where I would stand in the middle with my arms folded against my chest, careful not to touch anything; I'd keep an eye on the door, ready to escape at any moment. But when I step inside, everything is muted—there's a metal desk, a cream-colored futon, a cinderblock bookshelf with a stack of newspapers and magazines. On the windowsill are two framed pictures: one is of Ma and Dad in Long Beach, when they first came to the States, and the other is of me, from a time I don't remember. I'm just a kid, four or five, looking unbelievably happy. I don't know why or how. It seems impossible to me that anyone could be that pleased with life.

Raquel offers a tissue. I tell her I'm fine.

She goes into the tiny refrigerator beneath the desk, takes out a Mountain Dew and a small bottle of vodka. She mixes them in a paper cup, stirs it with her finger.

Then she takes out a bottle of pills from her purse. "Headache?" I ask.

"Nothing's wrong with my head." She pops a pill in her mouth, sips her drink, makes a face when she swallows, like it hurts. "Hormones," she says, "no pain no gain." She takes another sip.

"There's pain."

"Figure of speech, Kuya. It goes down easy."

"There must be pain. There has to be." I think of Eric on a table, surgeons cutting into his body, needles vanishing into his skin. I think of that studio audience giving him the thumbs-down, like a jury deciding his fate. I think of Ma telling Eric he was dead. "The things you do. To prove yourself. We loved him as is. That should have been enough."

Raquel walks over, stands in front of me eye-to-eye. "You think that's why we do this? To prove a point to you? Listen, Kuya Edmond. All of this"—she unfolds her arms, takes my hand by the wrist and puts it on the center of her chest—"I did for me." She keeps it there, presses it into herself like I'm supposed to check for a heartbeat, but she lets me go before I can feel anything.

"I should get back," I say. She nods, walks me to the door. I make a tentative plan to stop by next week, to pick up some of Eric's things, though I'm not sure what I can rightfully claim. She says yes, of course, anytime, like she doesn't believe that I'll ever return here.

Just as I walk out the door, she hands me forty dollars for the cab ride back to Oakland, and refuses to take it back. "You brought me home," she says. "If you didn't, I could be dead too." She starts crying, then puts her hand on my face. I don't come closer, but I don't pull away either. "She loves you," she whispers, "okay?" Then she holds me, her body pressing against mine. I wonder if this is how Eric felt after he changed, if the new flesh made him feel closer to the person he held. I won't ever know, but I wish I could stay this way a little longer, listen to Raquel whisper about my brother the way she just did, in the present tense, like he's still going on.

The next morning Ma is sitting at the bottom of the stairs, a vinyl garment bag over her lap. Eric's body is being prepared for tonight's viewing. We need to deliver his clothes.

She says nothing about the girls from the HoozHoo, doesn't ask me where I went. But on the way to the funeral home, I can feel her staring at me, like she's waiting for me to confess to something I didn't do.

Loomis is waiting in the lobby. "We've set up a room, Mrs. Dominguez," he says. We follow him through the lobby, but pass his office and continue down the hallway. "There's a phone inside, if you need anything." We stop in front of a metal door. He looks serious, like he's worried for us. "It's not too late to change your mind."

Ma shakes her head.

Loomis takes a breath, nods. "All right then." He turns to me. "It's good that you're here," he says, then leaves us.

Ma opens the door. I close it behind us. Eric lies on a metal table with wheels, a gray sheet covering him from the neck down. A strand of his hair hangs just over the edge, the darkest thing in this white room. I can see the incision on his neck, the thread keeping his lips shut.

Ma takes the garment bag from my hands. She goes to Eric. I stay by the door. "They have staff who can do this," I tell her.

She hangs the bag on a hook on the wall, unzips it. It's a suit. One of Dad's. "We have to change him." Ma puts her hand on Eric's right arm, rubs it up and down, the sheet still between them. She bends over, whispers *"Ang bunso ko"* between kisses to his cheek, his forehead, his cheek again, weeping. For a moment I mistake this for tenderness, her gesture of amends, a last chance to dress him the way she did when he was a boy.

Then she stands up straight, wipes her eyes, breathes in deep, and pulls several rolls of ACE bandages from her purse. Now I understand.

She lifts the sheet, folds it neatly down to his abdomen. For the first time, we see them, his breasts. They look cold and hard and dead as the rest of him, like they have always belonged to his body. If this was how he wanted to live, then this was how he wanted to die.

"Lift his arms," Ma says.

I don't move.

"This will work. I saw it on TV. Women who try to look like men. This is what they do."

"You can't."

"Everyone will see him tonight," Ma says, unrolling a bandage.

I tell her to forget tradition and custom, to keep the casket closed. "You picked out a nice casket for him. Beautiful flowers." I keep my voice calm and move toward her slowly, like a person trying to save someone from jumping off the ledge of a skyscraper. "They won't see," I say, "they won't know."

"I will," she says.

I reach for her arm but she pulls back. She steps around, stands behind Eric's head, slips her hands beneath his shoulders, manages to raise Eric a few inches from the table, but he slips from her. Ma tries again, her arms shaking from the weight of him, but she's just not strong enough. "Please," she says, looking at me. One way or another, she means to do this, and she'll only hurt herself in the end.

I walk over to the body. The light in here is different than it was in the morgue. Yesterday, the room seemed lit by a gray haze, and it took me only a second to recognize my brother. Today, the light makes shadows on his face, and I notice the sharpness of his cheekbones, the thin arch of his eyebrows. His lips are fuller than I remember, his neck more narrow. "It's still him," I say, but Ma doesn't believe me.

His body is hard from the embalming fluid, and he is heavier than I expected. To hold him up, I have to slip my arms beneath his, fold them across his chest. I can feel him, and I don't care how we look: we are together and we should stay this way, for all the moments we can. We have been apart for so long; soon he'll be gone for good. "Leave him alone," I say, but she doesn't listen, and then her hands separate me from my brother as she works the bandage round and round his breasts. I kiss the back of his neck, just once, in love and in apology.

Ma keeps going, another bandage and then one more, so tight the breasts vanish back into him, like they never existed. If my brother were alive, he wouldn't be able to breathe.

I say nothing to ma on the way back to her house, and I let her off at the bottom of the driveway. Then I make my way to Telegraph Avenue, heading for the bridge.

I find my way to the Tenderloin, and as if it was meant to be, find a parking spot right in front of Eric's building. I hurry inside, pass the same two girls on the doorstep from last night, run up the three flights of stairs, down the hall to the end. I knock on the door.

"Who is it?" Raquel says.

"Edmond," I say. "The brother."

And she opens to me.

Now that you've read this story, identify the conflicts and whom the conflicts are between. A story can have a number of conflicts, though they tend to be connected. Are the conflicts external, psychological, or a combination of both? The conflicts in this story overlap one another:

- The conflict between Edmond and Erica.
- The conflict between Erica and her mother.
- The conflict between Edmond and his soon-to-be ex-wife.
- The conflict between the truth of Erica's life and the lie the mother would like her friends to believe.
- The conflict between Edmond's respecting Erica's wishes versus their mother's wishes.
- The conflict between the way Edmond acted toward Erica and the way he wished he'd acted.

Go ahead and add other conflicts or restate the ones in the list. There might be others, depending on your own interpretations of the story.

Most of us in an academic setting are accustomed at some point to analyzing pieces of literature such as this in terms of theme, symbolism, and the like. But let's put all that aside and think about this story and the stories to follow not as literary critics but as fellow writers trying to understand how to bring the reader most fully into the experience so that they experience the conflicts along with the characters. No matter one's views on the subject matter of this story, it would be difficult to read "The Brothers" and not feel in some way moved by it. That's largely due to Tenorio's ability to create scenes that demonstrate through the building blocks of characterization (*dialogue, description, action, and thoughts*) what the characters are experiencing. The story, told through Edmond's *point of view*, is necessarily limited, just as we are limited to our own consciousness in real life, but we can still understand how the other characters feel by the ways they express themselves, or don't.

Consider the feuds in your own family, especially the long-simmering ones and those that are driven by different religious or political beliefs, by gender, by class. We are often told by our families that we should never air our dirty laundry (to use a cliché) and that two subjects one should never discuss are politics and religion. Maybe that's so in life, but in art, there's no such thing as an off-limit subject. For the writer, what's important is how you write, how you draw the reader in, not the subject matter itself. Short story writers, such as Tenorio, more often create a tension that is never fully released. Consider again the feuds in your family. Are any of these conflicts resolved? Hardly ever. If anything, cease fires are declared and held shakily for a while.

"The Brothers" starts rather dramatically with Edmond recounting how he and his mother watched his sibling Eric/Erica on national TV flash the audience "to prove he was a woman," in Edmond's words. While that's dramatic enough as an episode, it serves mainly to introduce the characters and the tensions between them. Edmond's tone is bitter as he relates how he and his mother were "set up" by Eric, who had not revealed why he was going to be on national TV, just that Edmond and their mother should watch. The language he uses to describe the reaction of his mother, a conservative Catholic, shows her horror. "It was like someone hit her in the face."

This establishing action could be the crux of the story if Tenorio wished. He could tell the story of Edmond's confrontation with Eric, their mutual recriminations, but wouldn't that be a kind of predictable path to take? What are the options? They either reconcile or they don't, the mother perhaps finally acting as the peacemaker, learning to accept that she has an LGBTQ+ child. Yeah, okay, maybe that's satisfying emotionally because we want to see everyone getting along. In life, we want to avoid tension. But Tenorio smartly decides not to go down that path, which might either end in an unbelievable and sentimental fashion or let his characters scream at one another until the mom falls down dead of a heart attack. Could happen, but killing off a character in order to resolve a story tends to fall flat. Such a move doesn't resolve tension so much as execute it. The same does not apply if you kill the character at the beginning of the story, as Tenorio does. We learn at the end of the second page that that TV show was the last time Edmond saw his sibling. Now they're lying dead in a morgue.

Often stories deal with the aftermath of crisis. Where a lesser writer might end with Eric/Erica taking their own life, Tenorio kills her right away, and in the most undramatic fashion. She dies of an asthma attack. What Tenorio is doing here so brilliantly is taking away any sensational elements he can to keep the focus where it belongs, on the family tensions between Erica, Edmond, and their mother. If they took their own life or were killed by a homophobic stranger (all things that are unfortunately believable enough), the story would be overwhelmed by these tragic events and the focus would be less on the characters and more on the tragic deaths. Death by asthma is so divorced from Erica's trans identity that it doesn't take away from a more nuanced (and more difficult) exploration of the family dynamics of this trio. This demands a deeper knowledge of his characters than might otherwise occur if Tenorio allowed sensational events to carry the weight of the story. He has to be intimately familiar with every aspect of his characters' lives. We happen to know that this is not an autobiographical story, though it possesses the authenticity of lived experience. That's because Tenorio has done his homework. He has given each character a believable history—émigrés from the Philippines living in San Francisco, the father dead, and a glimpse into their histories with one another and apart. This is essential if you want to create a story that reads authentically.

We won't go through the story point by point, but it would be useful for you to look at the points of tension in the story and track them yourself. Note how Tenorio steadfastly increases the psychological tension between the characters rather than allowing the lessening of that tension. Even the ending keeps the tension high rather than providing some kind of easy, sentimental resolution. Indulge us for a second as we explore a possible alternate sentimental resolution (with sincere apologies to Lysley Tenorio):

Edmond stays his mother's hand as she's binding Erica's breasts.
   "No, Ma, don't. This is not what Eric, I mean, Erica, would have wanted."
   Shock and then anger register on her face [actually, there's nowhere else on a person where shock and anger can register besides a face, but never mind]. She raises a hand. "Don't think you're too old for me to take over my knee. Paluin kita!" ["I'm going to spank you," in Tagalog]
   She looks at him, blinks and falls weeping into his arms.
   "Oh my son, Eric! Oh, my daughter, Erica!"

Yuck, right?

It's sentimental, unrealistic, and melodramatic, a great trifecta of problematic resolutions to conflict. Such an ending is too easy a solution, and while you might think your audience wants a happy ending, more important is an ending that feels believable. Family feuds rarely end in anything but a draw at best. If the resolution is no resolution but instead makes you feel even more tense, you're probably onto something, especially in regard to family tensions.

What actually happens is this: Edmond, who you might expect to defy his mother after he fled the wake when Erica's friends showed up (showing some disdain for his mother's sense of respectability), instead becomes complicit in an act that he knows would have horrified Eric/Erica. In other words, he betrays her. Instead of ending there, we see Edmond drive back to Erica's apartment where Raquel opens the door to him.

Has the conflict been resolved? Has the tension been resolved? No. But we know that things are changing inside Edmond, though we don't know exactly how. Why do you think he's driven back there? What's his motivation? What do you think would happen next if the scene were to continue?

When we think about the causes for family conflict, we could probably break them down into a few basic conflicts:

- Opposing belief systems;
- A physical or mental challenge and overcoming or succumbing to it;
- A betrayal;
- An emotional/physical/sexually violent parent/sibling/grandparent;
- Sibling or parental jealousy;
- An act of defiance;
- An eccentric/irresponsible parent or sibling or other relative;
- A family secret/skeleton in the closet;
- A smothering/controlling parent; and
- A stolen inheritance.

There are likely more ways to sort such conflicts, but the point is that despite these basic breakdowns, each family acts out their conflicts in their unique fashion. Also, conflicts can overlap. Betrayal and physical violence can easily be one and the same, but all betrayals aren't necessarily physical. Look over the previous list and consider how many of these conflicts you can identify in "The Brothers."

Different writer. Different family, different conflict. In "My Mother Pattu," Saras Manickam tells the story of a mother/daughter relationship in tatters. The mother in this story is almost an outsized villain, though not quite. It's hard to have any sympathy for her at all until the end, when we glimpse what precipitated her rage and hatred toward her daughter, or more precisely, the life that her daughter is able to lead. Go ahead and read it now.

2 "My Mother Pattu"

by Saras Manickam (Malaysia)

Saras Manickam won the 2019 Commonwealth Short Story Prize in the Asia category for "My Mother Pattu." She is a Malaysian freelance writer, language and creative writing teacher, and co-author of three English-language textbooks for schools. Originally from Teluk Intan in Perak, she now lives and works in Kuala Lumpur.

My mother Pattu graced our lives largely with her absence, for which my father and I and, to a lesser extent, grandma were profoundly grateful. She descended upon us once a month to collect her allowance from grandma, loot the pantry, curse my father and cuff me on the ear. We breathed a collective sigh of relief when she went away, except for grandma, who wept in secret for the daughter she could not stand to live with.

When there was no Pattu, there was light. There was fun: cycling to the food stalls near the market with my mates for the best *kuay teow* ever in Mambang; playing badminton in the cemented patch in front of Ahmad's house; walking home with Rubiah after a party, together with the boys—Wong Seng Chye, Manoharan, Raju and Abdullah, who all fancied me like crazy; meeting up with the "gang" in the porch in Mr. Goh's house, talking, laughing, eating *kuaci* and drinking orange crush. It meant twice-weekly Carnatic singing classes with Auntie Sundari, a few doors away from home. Pattu tried unsuccessfully to stop my classes claiming they would give me ideas above my station for "after all, you *are* going to marry a beggar." Aunt Sundari's was one of the few houses in town to which Pattu was never invited.

When there was no Pattu, I could wear my bra from the shop instead of the tight-fitting scratchy camisole tops grandma ran up on her sewing machine. They flattened my breasts and I hated them with a passion matched only by Pattu's insistence that I wore them.

There is a single framed black-and-white photograph of my parents in the cupboard in Grandma's room. It was taken after their marriage in 1950. A Chinese man and an Indian woman in Indian wedding dress; my father looked like a bit player in a promotional shoot for some cheap movie where the budget did not run to hiring a real actor. With a slight build and delicately beautiful despite a ravaged expression, my father sat rigid, facing the camera. His already white hair was brushed back from his forehead, settling just above his shoulders. He wore thick gold studs in his ears, white shirt, white veshti, black leather shoes. He was not smiling. Pattu stood beside him, her sculpted features marred by the insolence in her eyes and a sneer tipping her lips. The heavy Kanjipuram silk sari that she wore could not hide the swelling of her belly. One hand rested on her hip. The other, more brazen, she placed on her husband's shoulder. Even the photo resonated with her energy, her restlessness. She looked all woman, not fourteen.

* * *

In 1965, twenty years after the Japanese Occupation ended in Malaysia, my father remained in thrall to the specter of the past which haunted him as his constant companion, memory breathing into his sleep, where his body thrashed his bed, filling the room with screams and then whimpering cries for mercy. When this happened, grandma and I would rush to his room and grandma would apply the sacred ash on his forehead and his chest. She said he was remembering the time he worked on the Siamese death railway during the war. At such times, he struggled between sleep and wakefulness, trapped in a hell-hole, unable to cross over to sanity, his body drenched with sweat, fat globs of water oozing from the pores of his soul as he begged the Japanese soldiers to kill him, once and for all, in the name of God. Till the day he died, he could not bear to look at a Japanese man, not even in a photograph in the newspapers.

When the war was over, my Indian grandpa found him wandering in the streets, a young half-dead, skeletal-thin Chinese man with a tortured face and grey white hair, who refused to speak of his life before the war. Grandpa took him home and looked after him as if he were a baby. Except for a three-month strain, the men were devoted to each other until grandpa passed away eight years later.

Frail, yet with a cigarette constantly on his lips, my father safeguarded his Chinese identity as an entity separate from his life with grandma and me. He ate Chinese dinners cooked and delivered by Cheong Kee Restaurant in town. He wore striped pajamas tailored by Nam Fook Tailors in Jalan Bandar. He listened to the Chinese channel on the radio, drank Chinese tea, read Chinese newspapers and the Straits Times and steadfastly refused to talk of anything from the time before he became my father. "Why do you want to know what is no longer important," he would ask, not looking at me. I was abjectly devoted to him, terrified of saying anything that could bring down the shutters on his face.

* * *

When I was ten, I asked Pattu if she loved me. "Love you, Lalita?" She drawled. "Stupid question. As stupid and ugly as you. I was fourteen when I had you—that big horrid thing that swelled my stomach, gave me heartburn and cost me my life."

"Oh come now, Pattu, surely . . ." Grandma's voice tapered off.

"She cost me my life, amma," Pattu insisted. "Everything came to an end with you, idiot girl. And don't forget, ten hours of pain before you were born."

"It was a very short labor. Even the doctor was surprised," Grandma said.

"No, ten hours. So much pain. God, I was sick of you already." Pattu boxed my ears and turned away.

I was shocked at first that a mother would not automatically love her baby but it was a secret relief to hear her words. I was free then to hate Pattu without guilt.

Pattu was the bile that I retched out after each of her visits. She was the screaming in my head whenever I could not answer her quickly enough, receiving a sharp slap as reward. She was the poison leaching my blood, my bones, and that was the real nightmare for if you discounted a few details like my hair, skin color or eyes, I was a dead ringer for her. I could not bear the horror of it. There was nothing of my father in me, nothing, for he was not my father. Everyone knew that story. I knew it soon enough, in the way children absorb stories almost through osmosis, though papa never spoke of it, nor did grandma.

I knew how Pattu silently pointed to papa when her parents discovered she was pregnant. I knew how grandpa beat him with his fists, yelling the pain that rose from his stomach: "I saved your life, you Chinese bastard, I saved your bloody life and you do this to me?" I know that papa did not fight back. He merely repeated: "I have never touched her."

I heard how grandpa clutched my father's feet and wept when I was born: I had green eyes and hair the color of wheat.

* * *

I never called her *amma*. She was always Pattu right from the time she ran away with a travelling salesman, two weeks after the thirty-day lying-in after giving birth. But before running away, she helped herself to cash from grandpa's strongbox and several gold chains. Six months later, she returned, sans money or gold or salesman, a seething brittle creature who, the neighbors said, pinched me black and blue when she thought no one was looking. After that, it was a series of ding-dongs, run away with somebody or other, with whatever valuables she could lay her hands on, come back empty-handed, run away, come back again, each time quicker to anger, feverish discontent biting at her ankles until grandpa gave up and bought her a house ten miles from Mambang where she could live alone and do as she pleased.

There were no secrets to be had in our home, in our neighborhood. Everything was out in the open—who drank on the sly (Auntie Judith, who wrapped her daily beer bottle in a newspaper and sneaked it home); who demanded money under the table for doing his job as a clerk in the government (Abdullah, Hassan and Chandran); who beat his wife (that list was too long) and straying husband (Fauziah, whose husband was eying a third wife); and who was Pattu's latest lover. There were no secrets, true, but none was paraded in the open. In public, we were deeply conservative and so staunchly upright you could balance a spoon on us. All except Pattu.

There's a story that has turned into local legend: when Pattu was at the market one day, she overheard a man-about-town making unfortunate remarks about her morals. Pattu tucked her sari into her waist, strode up to the man, grabbed his shirt, and thrashed him. "Oh, how he tried to run, Lalita," said Auntie Jansi, a neighbor, when she related the story to grandma and me. "Like a whirling demon she was, she punched him and tore off his clothes and she stomped on him and described his manhood with choice profanities." I looked bewildered. "Bad words, girl," she explained. "Pattu is many things, but you know what, that day, when she beat up that miserable bugger, it was like all the wife-beaters and all the snarky men got a taste of their own medicine. My heart glowed."

I must have scowled for she continued. "Pattu—Pattu is just Pattu. She'll give us her last dollar without a thought . . ."

"Then she'll come home and give me a slap," I said. "But no more. Papa said . . ."

"Hush, Lalita," Grandma stopped me, her eyes pleading.

"Even the beggars adore her. She's welcome everywhere except over there . . ." Auntie Jansi flicked her head at the general direction of Aunt Sundari's house.

"Pattu is a generous woman," Grandma agreed. "She's good in the heart. She loves everyone. It's just her family she can't stand."

"No grandma," I said. "It's just papa and me she can't stand."

Grandma sighed. "She craves the things she can't get. But I won't let her hit you anymore, Lalita. No, enough already. I mean it."

"Why does she do it?" I asked. Grandma looked away. "Think back to last Friday," Aunt Jansi said.

We had been walking back from temple that evening, a group of us from the neighborhood. Papa was away in Kuala Lumpur. The women were draped in saris; I wore my silk pavadai. We wore flowers in our hair, bangles on our wrists. Grandma's gold jimikis glittered in my ears. In the temple, at least three boys kept looking at me when they were supposed to be praying. My cheeks flushed, my eyes shining, I felt high as a kite.

As we crossed the street from the temple, we saw Pattu talking to a man, in the shadowed doorway of a shophouse. We could not see their faces clearly but Pattu was leaning against the doorway, her hand glancing light on his shoulder. I knew though I could not see, that she would have arched her eyebrows, a smile playing on her lips, laughter waiting impatient at her throat. After all, I knew my mother. I did not know the man though. There was a dignity about him, uncommon in most of Pattu's men friends.

"Let's take another route," I said at the same time grandma called out: "Pattu!" Pattu turned and her eyes narrowed when she zeroed in on me. My heart dropped like a stone.

"Namaskaram," the man greeted us. "Who is the child?"

"My granddaughter, Lalita," grandma said, her voice uneasy, recognizing too late, the expression in Pattu's eyes.

"Beautiful child," he said, "like the goddess Lalita herself."

"What are you all waiting for? Go home," Pattu's voice was a machete slicing me wide open, spilling blood. We straggled home in silence. Once inside the house, grandma and I waited. I began to sob. "Maybe she won't come, Lalita," grandma said. "Maybe she has already gone back. It's late."

She came, her hands fueled with bitter rage. I did not make a sound. Grandma shrieked, "Aiyoh, aiyoh, aiyoh!" tears falling down her cheeks. Afterwards, she tried to rub some ointment on my body but I pushed her away. "You didn't stop her," I railed. "I wish she would die. Just die, you understand? Just die and leave us in peace."

Papa's face was white when he saw the bruises. "If you let her touch my daughter again, we will both leave this house and you will never see us." Grandma wrung her hands and cried. For the first time in my life, I didn't believe a word papa said. Didn't he know Pattu hit me every single time she visited? Did he think spending his days at work and his evenings in the Chinese Recreation Club gave him reason not to know?

* * *

A week later, *The Sound of Music* was finally playing in our town. The excitement among my friends—gosh, it was like a fever. We knew all the words to all the songs. We sang them during recess in school and in between classes. We were going to catch the afternoon matinee on Friday since school finished early. Rubiah had bought the tickets. I was to cycle to her house and then together we would go to Meena's where three other girls would be waiting. After the movie, it was to be ice *kacang* at Uncle Wong's stall in time-honored tradition. Papa was in Kuala Lumpur again, this time for a medical appointment with a specialist. He would be away for five days but had already given me money for the cinema ticket plus a bit extra. My heart would not stop singing that day, I was that delirious.

I rushed home after school on Friday to change out of my uniform. Pattu was there. She was at the dining table, with our neighbors, Auntie Jansi and Auntie Leela, waited on by grandma who, I noticed, had made her daughter's favorite dishes. They had finished their lunch. Pattu took out a wad of cash from inside her blouse, peeled off a few notes and handed them to Auntie Leela. "Here, Leela, buy something for yourself and for God's sake, hide the damn money from that drunken lout of yours." Auntie Leela's face shone. Pattu smiled, looked up, saw me and her face changed. "What are you looking at, sour face?" I had told myself I would never let Pattu beat me again but when I saw her, my insides shrank and my heart thudded so violently I thought they would be able to hear it. My hands shook so I had to hold my schoolbag tight to hide the trembling.

"Gr-grandma, I-I'm g-going to take my shower n-now."

"Oh yes, child," grandma smiled. "You're going to see the film today, right?" Too late, she clamped her mouth shut.

"What film?" Pattu wanted to know.

"Nothing, Pattu. I made a mistake," grandma said. "What film, amma?"

Auntie Jansi stepped in. "It's an English movie, Pattu. The Sound of Music. Very famous movie. Every kid is singing the songs. Everybody wants to see the movie including me, my children and even my mother-in-law. That's all. It's nothing to get uptight about." She looked at me. "You go bathe, child."

"Oh ho! Going to see an English film. Going to dress up nicely is it, this English missy, to go out with boys to watch an English film?" Pattu drawled. "Go, child, go and bathe and get ready." Pattu's mouth curved into a small smile even as her eyes turned hard and I knew then that she had known all the time about me going to see the film.

"Grandma!" My throat choked.

"Go and get ready," grandma said. As I walked up the stairs, my legs felt like lead. I heard grandma cajoling. "Please Pattu, the child has been talking of nothing else but this film for weeks. Don't ruin it for her."

I bathed and wore my newest outfit. Papa had bought it in Kuala Lumpur—a thin, delicate peacock blue pleated skirt, daringly three inches above the knee and a white blouse with a lace collar. I looked in the mirror and saw my face, pale, puffed up. Eyes dulled. Perhaps I could hide in the room until Pattu left, I thought. I could still catch the movie another day. I looked in the mirror again and saw my face mutating into my grandma's. Even as I dithered, a strange sensation, blazing white with cold ferocity swept over me.

"We'll see if she dares to go," Pattu was saying softly as I came downstairs. "When I'm done with that missy . . ."

"I am going." There, I said it, though my voice wobbled a bit.

"Ho-ho, the worm turns!" Pattu looked me up and down. "Look at the skirt, so short, you can see her arse. Why bother to wear it, huh?"

In a second, she was in front of me. Her hand grabbed my skirt. There was a ripping sound. She raised her hand again. My hands caught it in mid-air and I pushed her away. Her other hand swung up and yanked my hair hard.

I felt no pain, nothing but that white cold anger that coursed through my body. I sensed rather than saw, Auntie Jansi and Auntie Leela pulling a cursing, shrieking Pattu away and sticking her on a chair. "Have you gone mad, Pattu?" Auntie Jansi. I sensed grandma wailing, "Aiyoh, aiyoh, aiyoh," hitting her head with hands. I sensed it in slow motion like someone in a fog for my vision wasn't very clear all at once. I knew though, what I wanted to do. I took my father's walking stick and I stood above Pattu and I raised it high with both hands. I did not say a word but there were noises growling at my throat. Grandma flung herself at Pattu and shouted: "No, Lalita!"

The stick remained in my hands. "Don't become like her!" Grandma said.

The stick was stuck to my hands. I could not lower it. Pattu's voice in the background: "She wants to hit me? I'll kill her." And Auntie Jansi: "Shut up, Pattu."

"You're not Pattu, you understand? Lali?" Grandma said.

It took me some time before I threw the stick down. Grandma turned to Pattu. "What is the matter with you? You want to kill your own daughter?"

"I'm not her daughter." I said, rubbing my head. It throbbed with shooting pains.

"No, you're just a bloody whore who took away my life. You and your father."

Grandma said, "Pattu, not this again . . ."

"Whore, I say. Whore!" Pattu used *theyvadiye*, a Tamil word for whore that was unspeakable, a word that once uttered meant there was no going back for speaker and listener. Spittle sprayed from her lips as the women looked at her in horror. Grandma pressed her hand against Pattu's mouth

"I'm not the whore here, Pattu." My voice was level.

"Pattu, from the time you were twelve," Grandma knelt before her daughter, her face wet. "I could do nothing with you. No tears or threats or begging could shift the lies. Telling your father you were doing needlework with Judith when you were partying with her and the white sailors. I tried locking you in your room . . ."

". . . but I just climbed out of the window." Pattu rocked herself: "It was a prison, amma. Don't do this, don't do that. Don't go there. Don't talk to boys. Don't dress like that."

"It's the Indian Handbook on Bringing up Girls, Pattu," Auntie Jansi said. "Every Indian family had it."

"I just wanted some bloody fun, Jansi. What's wrong with that? Instead, I got the family honor constantly shoved down my throat. Couldn't breathe." Pattu took a deep breath. "Still can't," she said as if to herself.

Grandma said, "I hid everything from your father. He never knew. Not about the white sailors who plied you with chocolates or the times you slipped away from home to go to the cinema with some boy . . ."

"Don't talk to me about my father. That man stopped me from going to school. School, Jansi, can you believe it?"

Grandma was about to say something but Pattu waved at her to be quiet. "The nuns actually came to my house and begged him to let me continue. Said I was the best student in the class—that I could amount to something. But he—"

"You had reached puberty, Pattu. Your father was old-fashioned," Grandma said.

Pattu shrugged. "Those white men were a different world. You know what, if one of them had said, 'Come away with me, girl' I'd have gone, without a thought. Like that." She snapped her fingers.

I did not want to listen anymore. I felt wiped out, emptied, without any thought or sensation. Except, one small part of me kept going back to that young girl, a little younger than me, who tried to escape from her cage only to find it growing bigger and bigger. I walked to my room to change my clothes.

Auntie Leela's voice floated over: "Pattu, you are the most generous friend I have, but when you curse and beat Lalita, it's not right . . ."

There was silence. Then Pattu said, "She's living the life I wanted."

I paused on the stairs. Pattu said, "I won't have it, I tell you. I won't let her." There was silence for a bit and then she laughed. "She'll marry a bloody beggar, I'll make sure of that. You just wait and see."

I selected a bright green skirt, folding up the waist several times so that it was five inches above my knees. I cycled with my friends to the cinema to watch *The Sound of Music*. I could not remember a single scene from the movie.

This story has the flavor of a memoir in some ways in that it's told retrospectively, the protagonist looking back on her childhood and the time she wanted to see *The Sound of Music* with her friends. We can't assume that it *is* something that really happened to the author, and even if it did, that doesn't matter. We can assume that no matter how autobiographical the story might or might not be, the author has liberally changed whatever details she deemed necessary in order to tell the strongest story possible. The aim is to make the story read authentically and believably, not autobiographically. If the author is making you wonder, that's good. It means they're doing their job.

The way in which the author of this story explores the family dynamics and conflicts is strikingly different from "The Brothers." If we think of the tension like a volume knob, where ten is the highest volume and one the lowest, where would you gauge the tension in each story? Go ahead and write down the respective volumes. What's your rationale for marking one higher than the other? Perhaps you see the tension as virtually the same. If so, then you're stating that the tension is similar, but differently expressed. How so? What creates tension in each story and what diffuses it?

In the case of "My Mother Pattu," Pattu is clearly the *antagonist* and Lalita is the *protagonist*, but that doesn't mean she's a stock villain (Think: James Bond, the villain, who wants to do evil simply because it's fun to blow stuff up). She's definitely twisted emotionally and psychologically and she's physically and emotionally abusive. It's hard, if not nearly impossible, to like her, but it's the writer's job to make us at least understand why she behaves as she does. If you have a character in a story such as Pattu, it's usually a good idea to let us understand her motivations. It can be difficult to do so without being too heavy-handed or relying too heavily on exposition. How does Saras Manickam give us the necessary background on Pattu? When you have as difficult a character as Pattu you need to undercut her bad qualities with some good ones. Manickam mitigates Pattu's horrible behavior toward her daughter by making her well-liked, kind, and generous to everyone else. Does this seem believable to you? If not, consider the members of your own family. Do they always act in public the way they do in private? Can you imagine the behavior of a family member that might surprise or even shock outsiders if they saw it manifested? Perhaps your family is perfect (cough, cough), but ours aren't. One of the fundamental truths of human behavior is that we tend to project our worst traits onto others. Our shared histories sometimes produce a sense of contempt, or at the very least, we're unnecessarily impatient and/or rude or even downright nasty to the people closest to us. These patterns develop early and it's nearly impossible to break free of them. While it doesn't seem as though Pattu is someone who feels much more than self-pity, can you imagine that perhaps in the solitude of her own home, she might feel some remorse for how she treats her daughter? And what is the grandmother's role in all of this? She's a crucial figure in this dynamic of mutual hatred between Pattu and Lalita. Instead of solving anything, she invariably makes things worse. She says she's going to protect Lalita. Does she? She calls out rather thoughtlessly to Pattu on the street when she's with a man, when she should know that any meeting between Pattu and Lalita is bound to end badly for Lalita. Then she lets slip that Lalita is going to the movies. What *is* it with her? No, really, think about this. Making her so careless shows how torn she is in her loyalties. By showing the contradictions in a character's personality, an author is able to make that character complex. This is nearly all you need to know about people: know that they are a mass of contradictions. If you can show that on the page through their actions, thoughts, dialogue, and description, chances are that you've succeeded in creating a character who seems believable. In her case, she's quite clearly torn between her helpless love and perhaps guilt toward Pattu and her love and desire to protect Lalita. She seems to have a pretty big blind spot when it comes to Pattu, almost as though she keeps forgetting that Pattu is a maniac when it comes to her daughter. That's rather regrettable for Lalita, but it's good for the building of tension in the story. Without the grandmother playing the role of bringing the two together, Lalita might simply spend all her time successfully avoiding her mother.

Consider, too, the role of the minor characters in the story. How do they add to or diminish the familial tension. Likewise, what role does *The Sound of Music* play? Conflict is one of the building blocks of fiction, but sometimes writers will make the mistake of creating protagonists who are passive rather than active. It's much more compelling for a story to have a main character who actively wants something and sets about trying to achieve it, or conversely, who doesn't want something and goes about trying to avoid it. In "My Mother Pattu," we have a protagonist who wants both to avoid her mother and wants to see *The Sound of Music.* And for those lit majors among you who love to look for symbolism, let's note that the family portrayed in *The Sound of Music* is just about the polar opposite of Lalita's in terms of their love and respect for one another. In the movie, everyone has to avoid the Nazis. In Manickam's story, Pattu takes on the role of the Nazis single-handedly.

Lalita, for her part, is consistently unsuccessful in avoiding Pattu and is ultimately successful in seeing her movie, though in some ways, it's Pattu who wins in the end as Lalita doesn't remember anything of the movie she watched. And that's not an easy movie to forget.

What about "The Brothers"? Can you identify what Edmond wants and what he wants to avoid? What are the roadblocks put up in front of him, and how does he succeed or fail in the end?

Novice writers, influenced by drama as portrayed on film and television, sometimes think that conflict is like a punch in the nose, or the unloading of a round from an AK-47, a car chase, or a death star destroying the planet Andoxia. But conflict in a short story is generally a much more nuanced matter, for a couple of good reasons. The canvas of the short story is much smaller than that of a visual drama on the big or small screen. Drama of the movie variety tends to overwhelm the characters of a short story quite rapidly, to the point where we have no idea who is chasing or trying to kill whom, and we don't much care because we haven't had a chance to get to know them. It's not what happens, but to whom it happens that's important in a short story, the emphasis being on character *motivation*. For this reason, some creative writing teachers forbid their students to kill off their characters in their stories. Why? Because, as mentioned at the beginning of this chapter, it's the easy way out of a story—you can't figure out what comes next after Jacob refuses the marriage proposal of Ming Xi? So you decide that Ming Xi has to shoot Jacob. That might be shocking, but most often such action seems simply gratuitous, disappointing, and/or unbelievable. If Lalita had brought down the stick on her mother's head, what would that have done to the story?

So now maybe you're ready to begin writing your own family stories, and by that we mean stories about family written by you, not necessarily stories actually about your family. The source of your ideas can come from anywhere, even something someone told you once about their own family and that's haunted you ever since, or something completely made up, or something semi-autobiographical. It's not so much the source of the idea that's important but what you do with it, how successfully you create the family dynamic and ultimately how believable it is in its execution and resolution (or lack of one).

Exercises

Note: With all of these exercises remember to make ample use of dialogue, description, action, and thoughts (or at least some combination of these).

1. Continue "The Brothers" from the moment Raquel opens the door to Edmond.
2. Think of your own family's dynamics and start writing a semi-autobiographical story based on at least one of the conflicts we listed in this chapter. This shouldn't be completely autobiographical. Change some of the basic details that make it autobiographical. Change it enough so that you feel free to alter what really happened to make it what might have happened.
3. Write a family conflict story that isn't autobiographical at all, but use real details from your life or the lives of people you know well to make the story seem as though it's authentic.
4. Flip the situation of "My Mother Pattu" and write a story in which the daughter is exceedingly cruel to her mother, or a son exceedingly cruel to his father, or any combination of these. Your task is not to make the daughter into a super villain but to give us an idea of what made her the way she is.
5. Write a story from the point of view of a relative of yours who you understand least and/or would least like to be, or whose beliefs you find most difficult. Your task is to try to understand what motivates him/her and to make the character understandable, if not completely sympathetic.

CHAPTER 2
ATTRACTION

In Chapter 1, we focused on the tension and conflict caused by family members clashing. A somewhat different sort of tension is created by the attraction (or lack of) between two people. The two stories we will examine in this chapter, one from China and the other from Australia, show different ways in which this tension can play out. Is the attraction mutual or is it unrequited? Even if the attraction is mutual, there might still be a lot of roadblocks and tension. Think: *Romeo and Juliet.* We're not going to focus exclusively on tension, but more on the ways in which the central images of the story enhance the tension surrounding the tension or conflict of the story. Both "Convince Me" and "No Toes" use striking imagery to create stories that at first glance might seem simple, but that are actually quite complex in the ways they are crafted as well as what we take away from them as readers.

When we were young and just starting out as writers, we thought that all of our writing had to have hidden meanings and be "deep." We're not going to share any of the poetry we wrote when we were sixteen, but if we did, we're afraid you might find it anything but deep and its meanings rather obvious. We filled our poems with images that we thought would symbolize heavy subjects, such as death and, well, more death because we were kind of morbid teens. There were crows that symbolized death, open graves, trees with barren branches blowing in the howling wind, maybe a grim reaper or two, and some mocking skulls in the mirror (always a nice touch, those mocking skulls). The point is that these were the opposite of meaningful images—they were stock images, clichés. If a symbol in a story, or the story itself, has only one possible meaning, then it will most likely elicit a groan and an eye roll. The idea that inserting symbols into your work like vitamin supplements is misguided but understandable because in analyzing works of literature we've been taught to extract and try to understand those symbols. So when it's our turn to write a poem or a story, we imagine that we need to start off with a few symbols from The Big Grab Bag of Symbolism in order to impress our audience with our brilliance and sensitivity. Actually, the process is quite the opposite—when we're writing a story, we don't start by thinking, *I'm going to write a story about mortality and so I'm going to need a few death symbols.* That's going about it backward, starting with a grand theme and narrowing to the specific when, typically, we start our stories with specific characters in a specific situation, and we don't immediately start thinking about our themes and the reinforcement of those themes through the reinforcement of symbolism.

The writer Ellen Bass once said that she became a better writer when she decided that her readers were smarter than she was. This is generally a good attitude to have when you're writing because you want your story to be offered to the reader with respect just as you'd like your reader to read your work respectfully. Start out by assuming that your readers don't need to be led by the nose to your meanings, whatever you imagine them to be. But there are potential pitfalls here, too. Don't assume that you're too good a writer for your readers and that if they don't understand you, that's their problem. Occasionally, after a writer goes through a critique session with their peers, they will announce in a smug tone that *only* Nora or Adnan or Roshan was smart enough to understand the true meaning of the bent fork in the alley. It's almost invariably one person in class who gets it, often the writer's best friend. Is this a good reason to write stories, to make it into some kind of test for the reader to pass or fail? Perhaps what you think is obvious is actually kind of vague and obtuse. Start out by assuming we're going to "get it," and if we don't, then that might not be because we're hopeless morons. Your work should always be open to revision and recalibration.

When we're writing a story, an image might be repeated, consciously or unconsciously. We might not even notice the repetition until we've finished a draft of the story, but then on rereading our draft, we notice a pattern emerging. *Hey, what are all these mocking skulls doing here?* Maybe we have no idea why we put the image there in the first place, but sometimes these repetitions have everything to do with our characters and the situation they find themselves in. Recognizing these patterns, we might then choose to amplify them in our next draft and see if the pattern we've noticed can be tweaked so that it reflects on our characters in a way that adds to the understanding of the reader. If not, then it's probably best to cut out these stray images as even the smallest details in a story should ultimately contribute to the reader's immersion in the world you are creating. Still, if you write long enough, one of the great joys of writing stories is surprising yourself when you discover that you're a little more deep and meaningful than you thought. This is what we call an *organic symbol*, a symbol that arises naturally from the story rather than being self-consciously infused into it. Stories don't actually need symbols as such. Let's not even refer to them as symbols—it's too loaded a word. Better to use the more innocuous, "central image."

While writing a story shouldn't feel mechanical or formulaic, there's a fairly simple guideline known as *the rule of three* that might be helpful as you write your stories. One big problem with such a story is that often the fork in the alley, or whatever it is, appears only once and so the reader, not being privy to the inner workings of your mind, doesn't recognize that the fork in the alley is anything more than a random fork. At the end of your critique session, it's probably not going to impress anyone when you exclaim, "Fools. Did no one but Adnan glimpse my true meaning?" If you want your bent fork to stand out in the reader's mind, you're going to need to repeat the image. The first time we encounter an image, we tend not to notice it. The second time the bent fork appears, our subconscious mind takes note. The third time we recognize a pattern emerging and we think, *well, that fork must be there for a reason.* And then maybe we exclaim, "Oh, I get it, *fork in the road.* The main character has come to a fork in the road."

But that's pretty heavy-handed, right? Feel free to groan and roll your eyes. Here, the writer is just playing games and we start to feel we're reading an acrostic or some other kind of word game rather than a story that says anything authentic about life.

Even so, we have a confession to make. When that image of the bent fork came to us, it seemed like a random image and we wrote it down. At first, it was a bent fork on the sidewalk, but then, after repeating it a number of times, we remembered the saying, "fork in the road," and we decided to revise the image so it would be close enough to the saying without being obvious. We changed it first to fork in the street. But that seemed too much like road, so we changed it to "fork in the alley." Just to make a point. And, by the way, we're shocked that no one besides Adnan got it.

Happily, the stories we're going to look at now use imagery in a more ambiguous and nuanced fashion than our forks and skulls and crows. Let's look at "Convince Me" first.

1 "Convince Me"

by Jiang Yitan (China)

Translated from Chinese (Mandarin) by Philip Hand

Jiang Yitan is a poet and short story writer, and founder of Dutotime Publishing Company. His books include *Lu Xun's Mustache, The Statue of Clint Eastwood, Hepburn, Oh Hepburn,* and *Forgive You and Forgive Myself (Love Poems).*

There were three of us in the lab, and our goal was to extend the life of white mice. To be more precise, we were researching the flaws in the DNA of each mouse, and finding ways to repair them. Ultimately, we hoped to find the secret to giving *mus musculus* a longer lifespan. We would selectively breed them, observe them over the reproductive cycle, their behavior and their growth, and test whether the next generation came out a little more healthy.

Mice are universally recognized as the best experimental model for human physiology. If this study could take us a significant step toward lengthening the lives of China's people, then the mice which died along the way could rest easy. If I give you a one-line description of our work, it will probably sound like some kind of inspirational motto, but this really was what we were doing: making every generation of mice live longer than the last!

Helping each generation of Chinese people live longer than the last!

After we were selected for the lab, the three of us (the project director named Peng, Chen Jin, and I) all signed a very strict non-disclosure agreement prepared by the HR department. This experiment was a state secret. All calculations, drafts, and laboratory data were the property of the state, and must never be taken out of the laboratory or disclosed to anyone outside of our team. We read through the restrictions, and the consequences if we were to breach them, and each of us solemnly signed our names. Following the Chinese custom, we also inked our fingers, and imprinted the thick contracts with our fingerprints.

Looking at my bright red thumbprint, I thought of my grandfather. He lived to the age of eighty-nine, making him the longest-lived member of my family. In life sciences terms, his 89 years was the best lifespan outcome among the members of our lineage. At the end, he rang his own calling bell, in the most extreme way possible: by refusing to eat. "Even Chairman Mao . . . passed away . . . I have lived long enough . . . I want to go now. . ."

These were my grandfather's last words. The way he chose to die left a mark on me. Even today something unnameable jolts through me when I think of it.

I didn't much like our director, Peng. He was vain. He enjoyed firing obscure biology questions at students and young researchers, and a sickly grin would slowly contort his face as they struggled to answer. Chen Jin didn't speak much. She had just returned from doing a doctorate in the UK. On the day we signed our contracts, she seemed to be arguing with her boyfriend on the phone. I happened to be passing, and I heard her hissing, "I'm not saying I want to split up. I just don't know about going back to Chengdu. Can you just let me think about it. . ." The next time I saw her, she looked very unhappy.

It was the third day of our project. In the lab, Jin was working with her back to me, and seemed to be wiping away tears. The mice closest to her had shrunk into the opposite corner of their cages, and were blinking their pink little eyes.

"No crying in front of the mice, please, Miss Chen." It was Peng. "You'll affect their mood. You know that moods can be contagious. If the mice are upset, they won't eat or sleep properly, and it will throw the calibration of the experiment." His eyebrows arched so fiercely that they looked like little fishhooks.

"I'm not crying. I haven't cried for years..." Jin left the room. I was starting to become interested in my new co-worker.

That afternoon, Peng called us together for a meeting. Chen Jin leaned against a work surface, her finger poking in through the side of a cage for one of the mice to nibble. I murmured to her, "It's good to be working with you."

She glanced at me, and said, "You too."

"We should go and get something to eat sometime," I said. She smiled without immediately replying.

A hundred or more white plastic cages were ranged on the lab benches. One white mouse would live in each. (Though the word "live" was a pathetic joke.) We first numbered every cage: the odd numbered cages housed male mice; the even numbers held the females. We named the mice after their cage numbers for ease of reference: Male One, Female Two, Male Three, Female Four...

We checked the sex of every mouse, and paired them off into Mr & Mrs Mouse couples, whichever ones we felt would get on well together. Director Peng, who loved inspecting the reproductive organs of the mice, called Chen Jin over to stand next to him and take detailed notes. It made me feel sick.

Observing the mice was a major part of our work. Over the last few years I had dissected several hundred mice, at a conservative estimate. Now, alone in the lab, I stood staring intently at one of our specimens. Every second I stared at that mouse, its lifespan ticked one second shorter. Of course, mine did, too. But that second didn't matter to me. The mouse and I had lost the same physical time, but the biological time was very different for each of us. In one minute, the mouse's heart beat 650 times, and it breathed 160 breaths. At three months, the mouse was mature and could parent its first litter, it could be a grandparent at six months, and at two years—well, two years was all the life a mouse had. But it didn't know that. When it wasn't sleeping, a white mouse would spend almost all of its time scurrying frantically around (they love those little wheels), burning through its energy and its cells, scampering towards death. Whereas I could think. I knew that I would eventually die of illness or old age, knew that I would turn into a pile of bones, or a pot of white ash. But in the face of death, there was not much difference between me and the mouse.

No, no, there was. I could dissect the mouse. I could watch it struggle, see its paws twitch, its eyes bulge, feel its breathing gently cease. But I felt no guilt.

It was our lunchtime break. Peng was sitting outside reading his newspaper. "A bristlecone pine named the 'Methuselah' tree is now 4,781 years old," he exclaimed. "It is still living, still producing cones, and still just as green and leafy as ever. 4,781 years! My goodness! Will human beings ever live that long? I would love to see that tree. I am sure people will live to 5,000 years."

I repressed a laugh, and glanced over at Jin. Her mind was elsewhere, her eyes blank.

"Do you two know how long a sea urchin can live?" His voice floated in through the window once more. "Do you know?" I muttered to Jin.

"150 years," she replied evenly.

The director did not hear our answer. He chattered on, more to himself than anyone. "I suppose I should eat more sea urchin, then . . . Sea urchins, a century and a half, extraordinary. Must be a superfood of some kind."

"You free tonight?" Jin asked me. I nodded, and walked out to make a call.

I chose a real Sichuanese restaurant, in honor of her roots in Chengdu. We didn't want Peng making anything of it, so I arranged with Jin that we'd leave work separately and meet at the restaurant. Jin came in her white lab coat. She had gone to her locker to change, she explained, and the key had broken off in the lock. We both laughed at the same moment.

Jin liked the restaurant. It was in a Beijing courtyard, with a big red door set in the middle of a long grey wall, and a string of irregularly shaped windows on either side. The paint on the door was peeling, and it was lit by paper lanterns. Above the lintel, in large print, was the restaurant's slightly alarming comic challenge: Spicy Enough to Burn Beijing.

A server in a cheongsam stood shivering in the cool autumn air. Her eyes widened in shock at the sight of Jin and she timidly asked, "Are you Environment & Health inspectors?" I waved a hand to reassure her, and the professional smile returned to her lips. "Welcome!" she said, in the traditional Sichuan dialect.

As we entered the restaurant, we came face to face with a carved, wooden frieze of the Eight Immortals. Each of the eight was picked out in great detail, but in place of their traditional talismans, all of them were brandishing red chilli peppers. Below the frieze was a long stone trough, with lily pads floating in the water. Red and white koi swam lazily among the stems. Stepping around the tableau, we found ourselves in a courtyard with covered walkways along the three sides. She ordered, and we settled to talking.

I was curious what had brought her back to China. She said, "It's the worst recession in fifty years in Europe. A lot of people are out of work. It's no time to be looking for a job."

I said I wished her all the best for her new life back in Beijing. She turned to look out at the dusky courtyard, and said, "There's not much life here, either."

"You'll get used to it after a while."

"If someone could just convince me, I would quit and go back to Chengdu, where my family is. I'd go and live a different life with him."

"What do you mean?"

Her expression was calm as she turned her eyes back to give me a searching look. "Can you? Convince me?" "I'm not sure anyone can convince anyone of anything, these days."

She said nothing.

"How—how long have you been together?" I asked, breaking the silence.

"Eight years." She laid her chopsticks on the table in the shape of a Chinese character eight.

"When are you getting married?"

"He wants to do it right away."

I smiled. "And you?"

"I want to . . . and I don't want to . . ." She sighed. "Women really are a mass of contradictions. It's no wonder my professors in England said that it's much harder and more time consuming to dissect a woman than it is a man."

"Chengdu's a nice place to live, I heard," I said with a smile.

"It feels alien to me now."

Alien. The word caught something in me. Beijing started to seem alien even as I sat there, eating.

"Tell me about your life," she said, idly. "If you want to."

"My life . . ." I shook my head. "I did a bachelor's, did a master's degree, worked for a couple of years, then came back to do another degree to see if I could get a better job. When I finished the PhD, I just stayed at the Institute. The time goes fast. Five or six years, already, just gone in a flash. These days I only go to about three places: home, lab, book shop, round and round and round. I got divorced three years ago. She took the kid. I'm single now."

At this point, it was starting to sound too much like we were on a date fixed up by a marriage agency, so I stopped and smiled, and she smiled too.

"Don't get me wrong, I like being single. Sometimes, when you get used to living a certain way, you change . . ."

"Are you trying to use your failed marriage to convince me to leave Beijing?"

I didn't know what to say to that. "Marriage is a gamble."

I was not exactly experienced at persuading women on matters of marriage. But that night, in that restaurant, for reasons I can't explain, another me stood in front of me and repeated over and over: You have to convince this young colleague to leave Beijing. The city wears women down so fast. Just look at the women around you: marriage, having a child, raising it. Up early in the morning for the school run, dutifully leaving early for the afternoon repeat. Always kowtowing to the boss to make sure the job stays safe. They get old so very fast.

"Did you do biology because you liked it when you were a kid, or because your family made you?" she asked. I told her that my father was a surgeon, my mother an anaesthesiologist, and that I was their only son. At home, my dad cut his ham with a scalpel. I grew up sharpening my pencils and trimming my exercise books with them. When I was seven, my father showed me how to do my first live vivisections, of a frog and a pigeon.

"I started young, too," she said, excitement flashing in her eyes. "I dissected a frog when I was five, a live one."

Inwardly, I applauded her precociousness.

"But I forgot about that dissection. Then when it was time to choose my exam subjects in high school, I heard the frogs croaking in the pond outside my home, and they suddenly awakened this memory of dissection. And that was it. One perfectly-timed intervention. I'll always thank that frog."

Now the talk was starting to flow.

"When I was doing my degrees, I always spent longer in the lab than anyone else. Dissecting the animals, seeing how their organs fit together, and the way the blood flowed. I loved it! Was it the same for you?"

I nodded vigorously.

"I would wash the body after dissection, and air dry it, then sew it up. Make it into a specimen and put it by my bedside. But there were never any good animals to do, nothing outside of the ordinary rats, frogs, pigeons, dogs, cats . . . We never got a chance to do a human body. Was it the same for you?"

"Exactly the same!" I burst out.

"When I was doing my doctorate in England, I finally learned what real dissection is! I got to open up a gorilla, and a crocodile!"

"I've never done a gorilla or a crocodile," I hastily chimed in.

"You have to dissect a crocodile, to see just what an incredible animal it is. They crawl, but they also leap. The joints in their tails are unbelievable. They have a spring structure, all these spherical vertebrae fitting cleverly together. The tail is like a pole vaulter's pole. Do you know how fast crocodiles can move when they strike?"

I shook my head.

"Forty miles per hour! Faster than a zebra can run!" She quickly took a gulp of beer. "It's such a buzz, cutting open this ancient animal that's been around for 200 million years."

Her language and her emotion pulled me into a different level of awareness. Subconsciously, I had always thought that marrying a man who loved dissecting dead bodies must have been like marrying a cold corpse. That was how it turned out for my ex-wife. Marrying a woman who loved dissection would be the same: a cold corpse. I thought of her boyfriend, that unfortunate man. At the same time, my ex's form seemed to flash through my mind. Had I ever truly loved her body? No . . . . I suddenly felt hurt by the realization, but I also knew with absolute clarity that my senses were on some level numb to the bodies of women.

Her voice interrupted my thoughts. "The woman I roomed with was a fan of vampire movies. She invited me back to her home one time, this really big, really old house. It must have been as old as her whole clan. After dinner one time, she suddenly asked me if I wanted to see the vampire gallery upstairs. She hadn't said anything about it all the way to her house. Perhaps she thought I'd be shocked. But that night I was too nervous to go and see it. I had never seen those films in China. I was scared of vampires . . . Do you like them?"

I watched her, expressionless.

"Later she showed me a lot of vampire films, in our room and at the cinema. It suddenly struck me how much of a gap there was between my experience and how these students in the west learned. I liked biology, and I liked dissecting animals, but it never came anywhere near this level, where it bleeds into your fantasies and your culture. I mean, I was always a bit functional about it. I did the job for material satisfaction, not metaphysical satisfaction. What I learned from vampire films is that all of these dissection techniques I had learned were just techniques. I needed to take them and turn them into a craft. I needed to make the scalpel not a scalpel anymore, but a finger on my hand, living and moving. Those fountains of blood were the symbol for another kind of life. Later, I found I'd changed . . ." Her excited eyes were clouding over with disappointment, but my interest in her had multiplied.

"I had to come back to China because I needed a job. Now I'm here, I think about those memories nearly every day. I don't think I could bear going back to Chengdu. I want to leave him. I know what our future would be like. He loves me, but he loves the me from before. And I love him. I don't want him to get hurt . . ."

"Have you tried?"

"I don't feel anything when he touches me. He says I'm always scratching him with my fingernails. I can't get excited any more. I can't control it . . ."

She poured out her secrets. I empathized with every one of them. In some ways, the people who open up their deepest secrets are the ones who feel the most pain. I raised my drink to her. We touched glasses and tossed the beer back.

>We were the last people to leave the restaurant that night. As we came out, a light breeze swayed the red lanterns hanging by the door. We walked in silence up the quiet alley, both waiting for the other to speak.
>
>"Two of us who love scalpels," I muttered.
>
>She let out a long breath into the darkness.
>
>We came to the end of the alley, and in silent accord, turned towards the lab.
>
>Cars whipped by us, urban streamers of light. Tonight they had an unearthly beauty, a familiar beauty which we had not seen for too long. The pop music that blared from the roadside shops sounded sweeter.
>
>We stood at a zebra crossing, waiting for the traffic light. Shoulder to shoulder we stood, neither of us speaking. The wind was up, and it blew her hair onto my shoulder. My right hand was just inches from her left hand. Our fingers began to move at the same moment, drew near, guiltily near, till a spark shocked them apart. Then they were snapped together by a spark of wild attraction. Finally they gripped tight to each other. At the exact instant the walk signal was preparing to flash, we strode out together onto the crossing, holding on tightly to each other's fingers, sharp as a mouse's claws.

It's rare to experience a happy ending in a short story, so take a moment to enjoy this one. As short stories deal in conflict most of the time, it should be no surprise that happy endings are rare, not that everything is tragic. Still, you'll find that couples holding hands in the end are not the norm in the short story.

Obviously, the central images here are the lab mice. But what do they mean? We're not entirely sure. They might just be . . . mice. You could likely make a case for the mice reflecting some kind of social statement, perhaps a sly commentary on the Communist Party of China and its control over individuals, the mice being the common people and the lab technicians the heartless state. Possibly, but a bit of a stretch. Now you're thinking more like a critic and less like a writer. As a writer, you should be more focused on what the mice say about the characters in the story because we connect to the narrative by connecting with the characters. You certainly can't escape the ubiquity of the mice—they play a role throughout the story, even in the last line. They're also the creatures that bring the couple together, in a way. We're going to make a bold assumption here: enjoyment of the dissection of mice is probably not a point in common of many couples who find themselves attracted to one another. But in our view, that's in part what makes the story so oddly charming.

For a completely different look at attraction, let's look at the story "No Toes." But before you read the story, a couple of cautions. Understand that in the case of fiction, the author and the narrator shouldn't be confused. Michael Mohammed Ahmed is obviously not the high school narrator of the story. A quick glance at his biography reveals that he attended the same Punchbowl High School that's referred to in the story and his name strongly suggests Arab heritage, but to confuse Ahmed with the narrator of "No Toes" would be like confusing an actor with a role they play. There are plenty of actors who play horrible, murderous, villainous people who don't have any of the personality traits of their characters, and the same is true of literature, which is full of unlikeable characters. In fact, unlikeable characters are often more fun and more interesting than characters who are morally and ethically upstanding. How boring is that? You don't have to like a character in order to find them intriguing, illuminating, and/or entertaining. When we talk about having sympathy for a character, we don't mean that you must like that character—the job of the writer is not to make the character likeable, but sympathetic. By sympathy, we mean that we understand in some fundamental way, the motivations of the character, no matter how unlikeable, and that we see what makes them vulnerable. That's an essential part of understanding a character, catching a glimpse of their vulnerabilities. The author James Joyce wrote a story, "Counterpoints," about a man who is berated and humiliated by his boss at work. At the end of the day, he goes home and beats his child. Horrible, yes, but we understand his vulnerabilities. We understand to some degree what motivates him. The challenge for a writer writing about an unlikeable character is to discover those vulnerabilities and to lay them out before the reader in a way that is not too heavy-handed. The thumbnail sketch of the story "Counterpoints" makes it sound a bit too obvious, but it's not. Somehow, Joyce surprises us so that we don't anticipate the protagonist going from victim to monster and when it happens, the turnabout is sobering and shocking.

In the case of "No Toes," we're presented with a character who will likely make you cringe for any number of reasons. He's sexist, ablest, racist, and so superficial in his values that it's a safe bet that you probably wouldn't want to spend an evening with him. Then why would you want to read about him? Good question, but in our case, we find this portrait of this Australian boy from a Lebanese immigrant family, smart and clever in its evocation of a world most readers have probably not experienced. It's also a very good example of a first-person story told by a *fallible narrator*. The fallible narrator is a staple of fiction, a character who reveals more about his shortcomings than anyone else's through the nature of his observations. Such stories tend to drip with irony and wry humor, as does this piece. Go ahead and read the story now. But before you do, if you're unfamiliar with any of the terms, search for them online. "Bogan," for instance, is the Australian equivalent of the term "redneck." You're on your own for the rest of them.

2 "No Toes"

by Michael Mohammed Ahmad (Australia)

Michael Mohammed Ahmad is an Arab-Australian writer, editor, and community arts worker. Mohammed's debut novel, *The Tribe*, won the 2015 *Sydney Morning Herald* Best Young Novelists of the Year Award. His second novel, *The Lebs*, received the NSW Premier's Multicultural Literary Award and was shortlisted for the Miles Franklin Award.

> There's a slut in the water, cuz. That's what the Lebs say as soon as we land on Bondi Beach. Then they take their singlets off and lie down on the sand, a line of bulging noses and chest hair and big biceps. I leave them behind and sway through the waves towards the freckled girl who stands alone and off-balance about three metres from the shore. She is the same height as me, but her hair is bright blonde under the Australian sun and mine is an afro of black, and her skin has pinked like a piglet and mine is browning like a true sand nigger. She wears blue board shorts and a blue bikini, even though she doesn't look like she needs any upper body support because her chest is a pancake. My chest is a pancake too. Like every Lebo, I had one workout routine throughout all of winter, which I performed with a 20-kilo dumbbell in my bedroom in front of a poster of Arnold Schwarzenegger. Monday: biceps. Tuesday: biceps. Wednesday: biceps. Thursday:

biceps. Friday: biceps. Saturday: biceps. Sunday: have a wank. Every day, scream out: "big biceps for summer!"

"Ay give us your number," I say to the girl in the water as I approach her. I don't know why Lebs always say "us" when we mean "me." Maybe it's because we don't like to admit we're alone, we have the Bedouin tribe mentality.

"No," she responds, and then before I turn away from her to look for another chick she adds, "I hate the beach." She sounds like a typical Marrickville gang-banga, her voice husky and chaffing.

"Why?" I ask. I do a fake stretch, curling and tensing my arms above my head so that my biceps bulge before her like brown potatoes.

"It's personal," the girl whispers. Her green eyes suddenly fix on me as though she's in a burka and only has her glare to signal for help. I break eye contact from her in that moment and look down into the water, which is turning red against the setting sun, and just while the waves are being sucked back into the ocean I catch a glimpse of her feet. She has her big toes, which seem to be providing her with balance, but the other eight little toes are all missing. Straight away I snap my gaze back up at her and smile gently. This must be the reason she hates going to the beach—she can't hide her retarded feet here. "I never give out my number," she says. "But tell me yours."

I'm surprised she makes this offer. Maybe she doesn't realise I saw her feet. Do I really want to give a girl with no toes my number? What if she asks me for a foot massage one day? Then again, I have a fat crooked nose like Saudi King Faisal. I guess if No Toes is open-minded enough to date Big Broken Nose then I should be open-minded enough to date her. "If I give you my number how will you remember it?" I ask.

"What, do you think I'm a dumb bitch because I'm blonde?" she spits back.

I tell her the ten digits and she repeats them to me as though they are her own. Perhaps having no toes amplifies your memory, like the way blind people have amplified hearing and smell and taste. Then No Toes gives me a smug little grin, and pointing her finger in the direction from which I came, back to where my eight Lebo mates from Punchbowl Boys High School have started a brawl with two bogan lifeguards, she says, "Now turn around and walk away and don't look back at me or I won't call you."

The following night, No Toes sends me a text message that says, "want 2 hook up at auburn maccas?" I'm in my bedroom doing curls with my dumbbell and Arnie is staring back at me from the black-and-white poster on my wall. He's standing on a beach, sand and rocks and water behind him as he performs the front double biceps pose in his underwear like a hairless god. By the time I reach ten curls, my parents start shouting in the corridor, but they're not angry, they're just Arab. My father says, "She'll get AIDS from his foreskin," and my mum says, "They'll bury her in a box beside the pooftas." They must be talking about my cousin Houda, who recently married a Sudanese Christian. I pump the dumbbell to 19 curls on my left arm, and just as I coil towards 20, I scream out, "Big biceps for summer!" Then I let go of the dumbbell and it clanks against the hardwood floor of my bedroom. I can feel the blood oozing through my arms—the veins along my forearms chiseled like Van Damme's and the muscles along my upper arms bulging like Stallone's. No Toes is gonna love it. I text back, "c u in 20."

I find her waiting for me in front of the McDonald's counter. This time she is wearing brown canvas sneakers, which hide her secret completely, and a pair of skinny jeans and a tight white singlet. I'm wearing sneakers, jeans and a singlet too. Now that the pump from my workout has started to deplete, there is a vein appearing straight down my left bicep and it catches No Toes' sight before she makes eye contact with me and says, "Oi."

We each order a large McChicken meal from the brown-skinned hijabi at the counter. I pay for both meals but No Toes doesn't say thanks. Then we walk side by side, holding the trays in our hands, to the outside seating where Krispy Kreme and the Golden Arches illuminate Parramatta Road. We're surrounded by a hundred wogs who are spread out across the car park, standing in groups around their WRXs and RX7s and Skylines and Celicas eating cheeseburgers and Quarter Pounders. Everywhere I look there are Leb boys with big noses and undercut haircuts in Adidas button-up trousers and black Everlast singlets, and Leb girls with big noses and long mascara-filled eyelashes in high heels and tight black pants and tight pink shirts. No Toes finds an empty table just outside the car park. As soon as we are seated and are staring up at each other, I say to her, "I know you have no toes." Her blonde eyebrows spring up at me and twitch, like she is embarrassed and scared and annoyed all at the same time. I say, "Sorry, I saw them in the water yesterday but I came out with you anyway because I don't care."

She keeps her eyes on me, but slowly her eyebrows come down and she mumbles, "I'm not a ganga." Then she unpacks her McChicken and begins to rip through it, taking large caveman bites like she's never seen food before and chewing quickly with her mouth open, and taking another bite before she has even swallowed the previous mouthful. "Ganga" is short for "gangbanger," and I think she means that she's not desperate and easy just because she's a freak.

"Do you have a boyfriend?" I ask her, slowly unpacking my own McChicken and taking it in both hands and flexing and tensing my arms as I raise it towards my mouth—even eating can be a bi-workout.

"The boys that are interested in me, I'm not interested in them," No Toes answers while she continues to chew on the last pieces of McChicken in her mouth, white meat and white mayonnaise and yellow bun and yellow chicken crumbs swirling between her teeth. I pause just before taking the first bite of mine. I can't believe this girl's confidence. She has no toes for God's sake, she should be grateful that any boy is interested in her. Across the car park, in front of the entry to Krispy Kreme, a tall Leb with a long mullet is shouting out to his mates as they drive off in a yellow Rexy, "Give me that hoe's number, ay listen, don't be a dog cunt, bro." That's Lebs for ya, no shame.

"What happened to your last boyfriend?" I ask No Toes, finally taking a bite from my McChicken. It tastes like a mouthful of salt and sugar and wood—McDonald's hasn't been the same since that white gronk made Super Size Me.

"His parents broke us up because I wasn't Muslim," she says. This may very well be true but most of my Lebo mates from Punchbowl Boys use that line to get out of a relationship with an Aussie once she puts out. Just last night after we decked those lifeguards and fled the beach, my mate Osama sent his head-jobbing girlfriend a text message that read, "I luv u but my mum will never accept u," and then he offered me her number in exchange for a Blue Slurpee from 7-Eleven.

I don't tell this story to No Toes—she seems to be convinced that her ex had good intentions and there's nothing for me to gain from telling her the truth, it'll only damage my own chances with her. Instead I say, "Yeah, Muslim parents are pretty strict about that shit." Then I take another bite from my McChicken and chew casually, like a bimbo.

"Is it the same for you?" No Toes asks. Suddenly I can hear my father's coarse voice inside my head. "You can drink alcohol, you can gamble, you don't need to pray, you don't need to fast, you don't need to give to the poor, just don't ever marry that white devil," he said the first time I ever came home stoned. It was six months ago and all the Punchbowl Boys went out to celebrate because we'd finished our final HSC exam. I wasn't even choofing, I was just sitting in the back of Osama's WRX while the rest of the boys choofed, breathing in their smoke until suddenly I was thirsty as fuck and couldn't stop laughing. I'm about to ask No Toes if she's ever smoked pot when suddenly she blurts out, "I used to steal cars."

"W-what?" I respond.

"For fun, bro, I used to steal them and crash them into trees."

Why is she telling me this? Is she joking? Maybe she's acting like a hard bitch to impress me. Maybe she's intimidated by my big biceps. This might be a good time to do a fake yawn and flex my arms again, but first let me try to think of something to say, shit, nothing is coming out of my mouth, shit, it's too late to do the flex, damn it, I'm just staring at her now. Her fair and freckled face is wincing and her thin eyebrows are concaving and she is staring straight back at me, waiting for me to do something until finally, she sticks her head down over her Macca's cup and begins sucking on the straw.

I can hear her slurping the base of her large Coke by the time I've drunk about a quarter of my own. "Do you have any cigarettes?" she says, looking up at me. Then she puts her mouth over the straw again and begins to rattle through the ice as she searches like an anteater for the last drops of syrup.

"There might be a packet in my car," I tell her. Last year I was taking a piss in the bushes at Greenacre Park, holding a cigarette in one hand and my dick in the other, when I spotted a pus-filled pimple just above my pubes. I quit smoking for good after that but I still had the last three cigarettes from that final pack in my glove compartment.

"Give me your keys," says No Toes, her eyes rolling from her cup up towards me.

"I'll come with you," I say.

Automatically she springs from her seat and onto her feet—good reflexes for a toeless chick. "I'm not gonna steal your car!" she snaps.

I chase after her as she waddles through the car park. "Look, I don't even know you," I plead, "and you just told me you steal cars." Then I stop beside my '89 Celica, which is red and has pop-up headlights like the eyelids of an octopus.

No Toes sits inside my car with the passenger seat tilted right back and her canvas-covered feet hanging out the window. "So listen," she says as she blows cigarette smoke up into the car ceiling. "I texted you because I needed a ride home, you're not one of those horny Lebos who will only do me a favour if I give you a head job, are you?"

The McChicken churns in my guts. What a shifty bitch. Now if I don't give her a lift home, she'll say it's because she rejected me, and not because she's a racist dick-knob. I think of leaving her here at Auburn Macca's, stranded on the corner of St Hillier's and Parramatta roads like a spasticated hooker, but I know that this is not what the Prophet Mohammed would want. I was 11 when I first learned the tale of the deformed midget named Julaybib. After Julaybib had sacrificed his life defending Islam against an army of polytheists, Mohammed stood over his corpse and announced to his followers, "This one is of me and I am of him."

"I'll give you a lift home," I say to No Toes. "You are of me and I am of you." Cigarette smoke leaks through her lips. She sighs at me in confusion. As though I am the retard.

Between Macca's and Berala train station, No Toes says nothing to me except "left" and "right" in a blunt and nasal tone, her head stunted on the road out in front of her. I've accepted she doesn't like me very much, but can she at least make up some bullshit talk just to pass the time until I get her home? I'm not even sure she likes my biceps any more—I've been tensing my grip around the steering wheel since I first reversed out of the Macca's, so that my arm muscles and triceps and veins run from my fingers to my shoulders like a road map, but I haven't caught her checking them out, not even once.

At one minute past nine o'clock while I'm caught at the lights between Park Road and Vaughan Street, I turn on the radio, which is pre-set to 106.5 FM. *Love Song Dedications* with Richard Mercer has just started. For the next three hours, boyfriends and girlfriends and fiancés and husbands and wives across Sydney will be calling Richard to dedicate songs to their loved ones. Last week I was listening and this guy straight outta Bankstown called, telling Richard his name was "Zeb," which means cock in Arabic, and that the love of his life was "Kes," which means pussy in Arabic, and that he wanted to dedicate "Endless Love" by Mariah Carey to her.

"Left," No Toes mumbles as Richard takes a call from a girl named Michaela. "I want to dedicate a song to my ex, Hassan," Michaela says, her cotton-candy voice no older than 16. "We broke up last week."

"Oooooh," Richard responds. "I'm sorry to hear that. I'm sure Hassan is missing you." I am always comforted by Richard Mercer—he sympathizes with everyone, doesn't matter if they're wogs, skips, nips, curries, fags, hoes, junkies, frigids. "His parents don't accept me," Michaela whispers. I quickly turn to look at No Toes, to see if the dedication resonates with her. She is still staring straight ahead, unflinching, her canvas-wrapped feet now up on my dashboard. I keep my gaze on her until she exhales loudly and flicks her cigarette butt out the car window. It swirls and disappears into the night-time air like a tiny meteor.

"And what song do you want to dedicate to Hassan?" Richard asks.

"'End of the Road', do you know it, Richard, it's Boyz II Men," says Michaela.

Then as her call fades out, an R & B tune eases in and a soothing black male voice sings gently, "We belong together, and you know that I'm right, why do you play with my heart, why do you play with my mind?"

"Pull up at number 58," says No Toes, throwing her thin legs off the dash. I straddle the empty street kerb down Campbell Street, driving past Berala train station and a Woolworths and a charcoal chicken shop and then a long row of old housing commission units until I reach building number 58, which is made of red bricks. Then I turn to look at No Toes, who is breathing so heavily now that I can hear her nostrils whistling beneath the music, and Boyz II Men are singing, "Pain in my head, oh, I'd rather be dead." I wonder if No Toes will give me a goodbye kiss on the lips, just to trick me into thinking I have a chance with her to make her escape easier, or maybe she will give me a peck on the cheek, a way of making it clear that we are just friends. Instead she doesn't even look at me, doesn't even say good-bye, just keeps her head facing the window while she unlocks the car door and slips out. I watch her skinny little bum cheeks convulse unevenly as she walks on incomplete feet towards the entrance of her building.

I speed along Rickard Road, where the Bankstown train line dips towards Punchbowl on the left and Jasmine's Lebanese Restaurant erupts into the Bankstown skyline on the right. "Yeah my name's Mark. I wonna dedicate 'Endless Love' to the love of my life, Janie," a young skip with a tight nasal voice says to Richard Mercer. At least twice a night someone dedicates "Endless Love." "Oh Mark, she sounds very special, this girl," replies Richard, deep, smooth voice like a pimp.

"Yeeep," says Mark. "I'm that fool for her, Richard."

Next door to Jasmine's is Hadla, a Lebanese ice-cream shop where hundreds of Arab boys stand outside co-licking lemon-flavoured ice-cream with their fiancées. These guys only ever marry imports from Lebanon who are desperate for visas or Muslim girls from Parramatta who are only allowed out with a chaperone. Mariah Carey is singing, "My first love, you're every breath that I take, you're every step I make," and all the way back to Lakemba I sing along with her. I drive at five kilometers an hour down my street, past a duplex that my twin cousins built together and now live in with their new wives, who are also twins; and past my auntie's McMansion where she lives with her import husband and five sons and only daughter; and past my uncle's McMansion where he lives with his import wife and eight daughters and only son; and past my grandparents' cottage, where they have lived since they fled Lebanon in 1974, one year before the civil war broke out. This is what Lebos do—we crash onto a street and turn it into a village.

I slip out of my car and run through the front gates of my house, which is guarded by two stone lions; the front yard, which has been completely concreted; up the front stairs, which have "Lebz Rule" written on each of them in liquid paper; and straight through the front door, which has been left wide open. The corridor is decorated with a canvas of the Ninety-Nine Names of Allah on the left-hand side and a clock that is shaped like a mosque and belches the Call to Prayer every hour on the right-hand side. Tonight, the corridor smells like mincemeat and fried garlic and onion and the whole house glows because every light, in the corridor, the five bedrooms and the two bathrooms, in the kitchen and the living room, is switched on. I can hear Vin Diesel and car engines screaming out of the television in the living room, which is down the end of the house and runs 24 hours a day, and I can hear the murmurs of my parents and my older brother and my four sisters, who sit around watching *The Fast and the Furious* and eat kefta and rice every night.

From the corridor I turn left into my bedroom and pause before Arnie, standing in his undies and shaped like a perfect vagina from waist to shoulders. I pick up my dumbbell and say out loud "big biceps for summer" and I go into my first curl. Suddenly I am struck with a vision of No Toes standing before me with her smug grin and her green eyes and she takes a blow at my nuts, stabbing into my groin with that big lonely toe. The dumbbell slips from my palm and falls onto my foot and I scream out like a stunned mullet. "Ooaar!" My parents and my brother and my four sisters all tumble into my bedroom, their Semitic noses protruding like spears, and they're all looking around and screaming at the same time, "*shu saur, shu saur?*" which means "what happened, what happened?" I throw myself onto my bed and pull off my left shoe and left sock in one motion. I hold my foot up into the air with both hands. My sole is cracking between my fingers, my dorsal is swelling like a bloated tomato, my veins are twitching like a beating heart, and my toes, my five hairy toes, are throbbing.

Here's a case of attraction that's definitely not mutual, and it's not hard to see why. Even when the protagonist tries to be decent, he winds up sounding ignorant and foolish, such as this bit of dialogue he utters: "I say to her, 'I know you have no toes.' Her blonde eyebrows spring up at me and twitch, like she is embarrassed and scared and annoyed all at the same time. I say, 'Sorry, I saw them in the water yesterday but I came out with you anyway because I don't care.'" Personally, this is our favorite bit of awful dialogue in the story. Actually, the dialogue isn't awful at all—it's perfect because it completely characterizes him and it reinforces the fact that he's fallible, *and* it creates tension in the reader, or it should. Despite the fact that he thinks he's doing her a favor, he's obviously insecure and out of his depth. Throughout the story, he completely objectifies her, oddly fixated on her lack of toes, and he doesn't even seem to have asked her name. He just calls her "No Toes." Perhaps he knows her name, perhaps he's relating the encounter to us as he might relate it to his fellow Punchbowl High companions. But is there anything that makes him vulnerable? Anything that shows a crack in his armor and doesn't simply make him a flat character? We think there are a couple of things at least, but we don't want to simply tell you what we think they are. Instead, go back to the story and identify those moments where his vulnerability shows through.

Let's also take a look at what's repeated in the story. As writers, we don't only repeat images to create symbols—organic, deep, or otherwise. We also repeat dialogue, actions, and even thoughts in order to reinforce them. Take, for example, the protagonist's motto, "Big biceps for summer." We think perhaps that it's a bit ridiculous and funny, but you can bet that the narrator doesn't think so. You certainly noticed the phrase, didn't you? Guess how many times the narrator says this phrase. We don't mean to sound smug (we say, brushing our fingernails against our chest) but yes, three times. It's highly unlikely that the author thought to himself as he was writing the story, *I must make my main character repeat "Big biceps for summer" three times.* Almost certainly, this was an almost intuitive choice, but it's worth noting. When you write something three times you've created a pattern and humans find meaning in patterns.

Barbells are repeated, too, which makes sense because he's obsessed with improving his physique. The barbells function as a kind of prop in the story and serve as outward expressions of his inner desires. This is exactly how we want to use objects in a story—they show us a lot about his inner sense of himself without us getting bogged down in exposition and/or his thoughts. And ultimately they become, what else, organic symbols in that they change their function at the end of the story, and in some ways, pass the final judgment on this character. Like the rule of three, we doubt that Michael Mohammed Ahmed had this in mind when he began the story, but he instead allowed the image to track throughout the story so that it never lost its significance in terms of the protagonist's character. And then when the time was right, they crashed down on the narrator's toes. What are we supposed to make of that? That is part of the enjoyment for the reader, figuring out what has just happened and why.

The most repeated phrase in the story is the title, "No Toes." The repetition clearly shows the protagonist's obsession with the fact that the young woman he's attracted to has no toes. When he says he noticed that she had no toes and that it didn't matter to him, he was clearly lying, perhaps even to himself. He can think of nothing else. Here's a character who is obsessed with physicality, his own and everyone else's. He thinks that having big biceps for summer will turn him into some kind of god, but it's the young woman who has all the confidence while he has almost none, though he talks tough. She rattles him though he never says as much. We're left to infer that through the repetition of his name for her, the barbells, his slogan, and finally, what happens with the barbells in the end. All of these elements are perfectly orchestrated so that the character's shortcomings and vulnerabilities are highlighted. But it's important to remember that this is a polished story that has likely been through a number of drafts. What you should take away from all this is to keep an eye on your images and repetitions of dialogue, action, and description in the way in which they relate to your main characters and what they want.

In discussion of these stories and the others in the book, you might also want to examine what you think the stories say about the cultures in which they're set: both the micro culture and the larger culture. Obviously, you want to avoid generalizations, such as, *Well, obviously, all Chinese people or Lebanese Australians think like this. . . .* That would be rather unfortunate. But undeniably, these stories offer glimpses into places and people you might otherwise never encounter. You might consider what cultural norms expressed in the stories seem different or similar to your own cultural norms and values. You might also consider how your own stories express the cultural norms of your society. What do your characters reveal about certain aspects of your culture, in particular how you treat attraction, that might not be shared universally? It's worth a look, whether you're able to come to any conclusions or not.

Exercises

1. Flip the premise of this story and write from the point of view of someone who must avoid or rebuff the interest of someone else, while still wanting something from that other person.

2. Center a story of attraction around a place where people show off their bodies or try to improve them: a gym, a hairdresser, a locker room, a public pool, or a beach. Try to make the details as authentic as possible so that the reader thinks you know this place well. Again, where is the tension?

3. One character is obsessed with another, but he/she is even more obsessed with an object or an action.

4. Write from a point of view of someone you don't admire but know well. It might not be a particular person but a composite character, a type of person from where you grew up. Again, he/she is attracted or not to someone else. Think about how you might show this person's vulnerabilities.

5. Write a story of attraction or lack of from two people who work together in an environment that is decidedly unromantic. Again, this should be an environment you know or have studied and the characters should be based in this case on people you know well (including yourself) or have observed.

CHAPTER 3
ROUTINES

So far, we've seen how different Asian stories handle conflicts and looked at the problem of creating meaning in our stories without resorting to clichés. And we've discussed some aspect of content, in terms of what it is we choose to write about. In this chapter, we turn to what may seem like the more quotidian subject of Routines in these two stories about the work lives of two very different groups of people, one in Korea and the other in the United Arab Emirates, or the UAE. Both stories feature an ensemble cast, a group of people in undesirable and oppressive work conditions, but the narrative points of view (POV) chosen by each author differs significantly. "We That Summer" by the Korean writer Han Yujoo and "Birds" by Deepak Unnikrishnan, a writer from the United Arab Emirates, are concerned with very dark subject matter—the attraction of suicide in the former and a fate worse than death for migrant workers in the Gulf.

Both stories employ *satire* and pose what are in effect rhetorical questions, ones to which no answer is expected. Satire is sometimes mistaken as simply irony or humor or exaggeration, all techniques which are used. But the real reason to write satire is to critique or expose immoral or foolish behavior, often as a form of social or political commentary. These two stories are a kind of "protest fiction" where the POV sets the tone and affects the way we read these narratives about the seemingly mundane routines of life.

Many beginners assume that the first-person POV, the "I," is the easiest one to use. While it might give us more control, first person is inherently unreliable because it's limited to a single perspective. Unless we are certain we can trust the speaker or narrator, we cannot be certain if the situation and events described are entirely accurate. We cannot be sure what any other character in the story might actually believe or think about the story being told as we never enter their POV. A first-person narrator also cannot really speak for others. However in "We That Summer" the writer takes on a collective *plural* first person which, at first glance, *appears* to be representative of the ensemble cast. But as the story unfolds, the "I" edges out the "we" so that we increasingly question what is in fact the real story.

Read Han Yujoo's darkly comic tale about this group of discontented colleagues in the same shared workspace who all, we are told quite early in the story, "wanted to die."

1 "We That Summer"

by Han Yujoo (Korea)

Translated from Korean by Janet Hong

Han Yujoo, born in Seoul in 1982, is the author of the novel *The Impossible Fairy Tale* as well as three short story collections. She won the Hankook Ilbo Literary Award in 2009 and is a translator, an active member of the experimental group Rue, and publisher of experimental fiction.

> We met often that summer. There were still five more years to go until 2020. Each having spent 1999 somewhere else, we didn't think we would be together to greet 2020, the moment Space Wonder Kiddy would take over the world. Not that we actually thought Space Wonder Kiddy would show up that year. The reason we didn't say 2099 or 2100 was because we weren't sure we would still be around then. Children born in 2000 could probably live past a hundred, but in 2000 we were already in our teens. But there was a good chance we would still be here in 2020.
> We were unhappy, each for a different reason, and so, wanted to die. Even if we were happy, each for a different reason, we still would have wanted to die. We were different in age, but all in our twenties. We had never attempted suicide, but each knew someone who had succeeded. It's not that we actually considered killing ourselves that summer. Still we talked about it once a day, like some ritual. Should we commit suicide? We should commit suicide. These words weren't a request, suggestion, question, or even an answer. When we talked about it over and over like a habit, the word "suicide" no longer meant anything. They say words have a way of coming true, but we didn't take these words seriously. Or it seemed that way at least. I say "we," but I'm by no means our representative or delegate. I don't claim to know the others' thoughts. Even if I happened to be our representative or delegate, there's no way I could ever know.
> Yet that summer I believed I somehow understood what we were all thinking. And if there were things I didn't understand, I didn't try to find out. We somehow managed to get along because we had faith in each other, as little as there was. Faith that we would not reveal the bedrock of who we were, that we would not witness one another at rock bottom. We didn't know exactly what "bedrock" or "rock bottom" referred to. Though we met nearly every day, we dared not ask any questions that weren't superficial. To be honest, we had no idea what kind of questions weren't superficial.
> We began to spend time together the previous winter, but even well into the summer of a new year, we hardly knew one another. We shared the same workspace. One published books. One worked at an office. One made candles. And I read and wrote books. The kind the publisher put out and the kind I read did not overlap. This I learned by glancing at his desk. He probably glanced at mine as well. What we saw filled us with relief.
> Placed on each of our desks was a candle made by the candle maker. They were scented candles. Each was a different scent, but because it was rare that all four candles were lit at the same time, there was never a time when the scents mixed and became overpowering. When asked the name of each scent, the candle maker said something or other, but there was no way to guess the scent from the name. When asked if it was like the artificial lemon fragrance that's added to lemon-flavoured candy, she said maybe, maybe not. Anyhow the candles didn't smell like real lemon. Once when I smelled real lemon while using lemon-scented dish soap, I felt strange. Every time I saw the candle flame wavering in the draft of the air conditioner, I felt strange. My desk was placed right below the air-conditioning vents, so I sometimes felt cold. It was an extravagant thing to feel cold in the summer. I sometimes wondered if this was the only extravagance I would

be allowed. I sometimes wondered if the other three felt this way, but I didn't ask. It was rare I asked anything, because I felt nothing would change even if I knew the answer. Although I never voiced this thought, it seemed the others felt the same, because it was also rare they asked anything. But having said that, we were by no means reserved. We talked non-stop. We talked the most when we peeled the wrapper off a chocolate we had bought, thinking it contained four pieces, when it actually contained three. It was the publisher who had bought the chocolate. You can't make it look like there's four and put in just three, he said. You can't make books that way, he said. I believed this was just one way he took pride in his work. But there are times you need to make books that way, he said. We then concentrated on dividing the three pieces equally amongst us. If we divided each of the three pieces into four and then ate three pieces each, we would eat exactly the same amount. It was the office worker who came up with this calculation.

That summer we ate a staggering amount of chocolate. We were still in our twenties. One was turning thirty the following year. One's age was like a failed joke. The person turning thirty had done his mandatory military service for two years, which equaled 20 percent of twenty years. It was shitty, he said. That was all he said. Another person, who had intended to do his military service for two years, which equaled 20 percent of twenty years, but been discharged after a year due to an unforeseen accident, nodded along, as though "it was shitty" were enough to describe the whole experience, as though any other response weren't possible. Our conversation about the military ended there. Our conversations always started and ended this way. We never talked about something for more than five minutes. Still one conversation led to another, somehow. Even conversations were like failed jokes.

One day in spring, someone told a joke. Even before the punch line, one of us burst into laughter. Nobody else laughed. When the person who'd told the joke asked what was so funny, the person who'd laughed said she'd been thinking of something else. Until the conversation ended, I didn't realize the person who'd told the joke had told a joke.

That spring, no one suggested that we go look at the cherry blossoms. The office worker was the only one to see them. Because his company was located in Yeouido, he had no choice but to see them on his way to and from work. He returned from work, drained by the crowds that had descended on Yeouido to see the cherry blossoms. Stuck to his forehead was a pale flower petal. When someone pointed it out, he swiped the back of his hand across his forehead and the petal smeared like a mosquito. But we didn't read our fates in that flower petal. But who knows if one of us wished, even for a second, to end up the same way? Or maybe we thought it had already happened. Still in our own way, we tried to contribute to society. That's what we believed. We each paid our taxes, health insurance, fines, bills, and the rent, but our biggest contribution to society was buying a lottery ticket once a week. I don't remember who first came up with that idea. The only thing I remember is that we had all agreed. So every week, we took turns buying 5,000 won worth. The person responsible for buying the ticket that week checked the numbers on Saturday. We never won. We had our own reasons for needing money. Though we published books, worked at an office, made candles, and wrote for a living, we needed a lot more money. In fact, we needed money more than we needed things. We placed the lottery ticket we had bought on the table, and each thought about the things we needed to do come Monday. One talked about traveling to an island. One talked about buying a new desk. One talked about getting dental implants. One talked about paying off overdue health insurance bills. For these reasons, we needed a lot of money. Even after we'd had supper together, exchanged a few words that weren't banter or conversation, gone to our own desks to concentrate on our work until early morning, we still needed a great deal of money. The only way we could earn that much was by winning the lottery. Buying a lottery ticket, as opposed to not buying one, raised our chances of winning. A million-to-one chance was still bigger than a million-to-zero chance. And so during the six months it took for winter to become summer, we never missed a single week in buying lottery tickets. Sometimes we ended up winning 5,000 won. Maybe twice in all. We put those winnings toward the lottery ticket. And every Saturday evening when we checked the numbers, we drank beer. If we were hungry, we heated something in the microwave or peeled the cling wrap from the delivered food, and believed we were enduring this life together. Someone would then bring out a deck of cards. After shuffling and dealing dozens of cards, we played a game of attack and defense and tried to get the highest score. Whenever we weren't hungry, whenever we became bored with our work, whenever we didn't want to think about anything, we had an unspoken agreement to play cards. We sometimes made small wagers. The person who got the lowest score went out to buy cigarettes or beer. When we smoked and drank beer, we felt as though we'd become the most useless beings on earth. It didn't feel bad. No. It felt bad.

A low shelf we'd rigged up with bricks and wooden planks ran along the wall below the window. The office worker, who had been a philosophy major, had placed all sorts of philosophy books there, but these books gradually became overtaken by stacks of board games. Thick cigarette smoke climbed into the air until it tormented even us who were smokers. We turned on the air purifier left behind by the strangers who had rented the place before we came, but it was no use. When we went to the convenience store, the owner or the employee on shift took out a pack of cigarettes without bothering to ask what we wanted. This may be the last smoking room on earth, someone said, with self-deprecation and bravado, but we actually believed this might be the case. Even our smoking is contributing to society, this person added. We actually believed this. Then I guess our drinking beer is contributing to society too? someone else said. We believed this too. By paying tax on these things, we were contributing indirectly to society. We didn't ask: Was this all? The books on the shelf couldn't even be used as bricks. Neither could they be used as pot stands for instant noodle, since we only had a microwave to cook with.

Even still, we were cheerful overall, roughly, generally, perhaps a little more than average. As we smoked, we each talked about the first time our parents had caught us smoking, and then someone asked if we knew how to blow smoke rings, and we each proceeded to try. Then one said he would attempt a large ring, and took several deep drags. He blew out all the smoke at once, drawing a circle in the air by turning his head. We burst into laughter. The ring formed in an instant, but soon scattered, because he had turned his head too quickly. The ring vanished like smoke. The smoke vanished like smoke. We laughed until we grew awkward and went back to our desks and hid our faces behind our computer screens. Should we commit suicide, should we commit suicide tomorrow? Should we commit suicide, should we have committed suicide yesterday? We posed questions that were out of the question. When we posed question after question—questions that were out of the question—we didn't want anything to happen. We wanted to grow old this way. It was 2015. We wanted to grow old this way and die this way. When we came together and talked only of absurd things, it felt as though time had stopped. Then someone looked at the clock and said we've wasted the day away. But it was our hearts, our lungs, our lives, our stomachs, our skin, our heads that were wasting away. It was impossible to grow old without wasting away. No one asked, Why don't we ever go somewhere? No one asked, Why don't we ever go, even when we go somewhere?

During the time we didn't spend on cigarettes, beer, games, and lottery tickets, we each concentrated on our work at each of our desks. In our own way, we poured our heart and soul into our work, but our results were not much different from a pot stand for instant noodle. This filled us with relief. All we needed to do was grow old this way. If we weren't able to grow old this way, we could simply commit suicide. Not one became angry, and every month we each paid the rent out of our individual earnings. Anyhow there was a good chance we would still be here in 2020. The talk about Space Wonder Kiddy was a joke. It was the summer of 2015, but not even an *Evangelion* Angel showed up.[1] In all the books we read or cartoons we watched as children, the end of the world was always near. It was always ten or twenty years later. Although we were still in our twenties, we knew that ten years were nothing, and once we entered our thirties, we knew twenty years would be nothing as well. Or at least we believed we knew. We didn't make fun of anything. We couldn't. All we did for fun was joke around and play games. We were courteous to the people who worked at the auto repair shop on the first floor, and we cast a friendly eye on the dogs we encountered on the street. We said hello and goodbye every time we went in and out of the convenience store, and we dropped our gaze and bowed whenever we ran into the landlord. Still we tossed out the garbage in one bag, without separating food waste from regular garbage, and we wasted paper cups, electricity, and Kleenex. Though we didn't toss our cigarette butts just anywhere, there were still times we smoked in the alley, and our lungs were no different from an ashtray. We wasted away, instead of growing old.

Someone bought tomatoes and apricots from the market and left them in the refrigerator. Mold grew on the few remaining tomatoes. We debated whether the tomatoes were rotten or not. Is something rotten even if only a small part the size of a fingernail is rotten? If you can still eat it after removing the rotten part, doesn't that mean it isn't rotten? But how can you pretend not to see the rotten part when you do see it? If we're rotting away, does that mean we're already rotten? How is it that we're not tomatoes? How is it that we couldn't remove our rotten parts?

But still we did not spit out our phlegm. We took turns cleaning the bathroom. We wiped the keyboard and mouse with cotton swabs dipped in alcohol. Yet we didn't feel any sense of accomplishment. Every day dust piled up on the floor, and even if we'd never

---

[1] *Neon Genesis Evangelion* is an apocalyptic anime that first aired in Japan in 1995. Set in 2015 in a futuristic Tokyo fifteen years after a global cataclysm, humans pilot giant bio-machines called Evangelion to battle monstrous beings known as Angels that are attempting to annihilate humanity.

smoked, our lungs were already no different from an ashtray. The motorcycle sped by every night, and the ambulance went by occasionally.

The last time we heard the ambulance siren from the office, we were playing a game called Dungeonquest. It featured numerous cards, a key, four dice, tiles used to create rooms and corridors, and a dragon. You took turns drawing cards to complete the quest. You used the tiles to create a path that led to the lair where the dragon slept atop the treasure. When you finally reached the lair after encountering all sorts of obstacles, you checked the status of the dragon. If the dragon lay sleeping, you gained a Treasure card. But if the dragon woke, you died on the spot.

We got the biggest thrill when we were playing Dungeonquest. A week into the game, no one was able to enter the dragon's lair. One after another the cards presented: bottomless pit, spider web, portcullis, or catacomb. Or they made you combat skeletons, demons, or dark wizards. Diligently we rolled the dice and drew cards and engaged in combat. You needed about fifteen tiles from the starting point to reach the chamber where the dragon slumbered. But we usually died before we could even draw the fifteenth tile. There were times we died as soon as we began. The first step is half the journey, someone said, and we burst into laughter. Even if we managed somehow to plunder the treasure from the dragon's lair, we still needed to go back into the corridors where all kinds of dangers lurked in order to escape the dungeon. Sour grapes, someone said. A vine you couldn't reach, grapes you couldn't eat. We each held a hero card, but our heroes didn't return. Then someone asked suddenly, How long do you think we'll be doing this? We'll probably be doing this tomorrow. Probably a year or even five years from now. With these words, she rolled the dice. Her hero failed the armor test and died on the spot. There were loot cards in her hands, but the loot couldn't save her hero.

It was the same story every night. We each came to the office at different times, but we were usually together late at night. We roughly finished our work, sat around the round table in the center of the office, and left on a quest. To say that we left on a quest might sound romantic, but the reality couldn't be further from the truth. But that didn't mean it was sad or pathetic.

In 1999, we were too young to feel the anxieties that surrounded the end of the millennium. But before 1999, there was 1997, the year of the Asian financial crisis. Though we were younger in 1997, the anxieties we felt then were a kind we experienced firsthand, different from the peculiar anxieties of 1999 that were mixed with optimism for the start of the new century.

Out of the dozen families who lived in our apartment building, three went bankrupt and two vanished, someone said. I was in elementary school then. So grownups assumed I knew nothing, but I knew everything I needed to know. Obviously there were things I didn't know, but any peace or safety, health or happiness, passion or hope I ever knew vanished completely and what was left in their place was the word "fate." But nothing happened to us. My father somehow held onto his position at his company and so I figured it was the same for the other families. But when three went bankrupt and two vanished, I felt something was strange, that something was very wrong. At school, one kid stopped talking and another kid stopped attending. Even in the midst of everything, there were kids who were as rude as ever, but I've never seen such same gloom and despair. Do you think we'll see it again? Do you think we internalized the gloom and despair of 1997 and just got used to it? Do you think we've been stuck in the same time since then?

I was in elementary school then too, someone said, while opening the dungeon door. Weren't we all in elementary school then?

Though a little different in age, we would have all been in elementary school in 1997.

We're lucky we weren't in middle school. We could pretend we didn't understand what was going on. We could pretend we were still immature. My father fried chicken and my mother burned herself while draining the blood from the chicken. I took the food to the customers and tried to steal the wallets they left carelessly on the table, but it was too hard. So I took money from my father's wallet instead. It was easier than taking it from my mother's. I stopped after two or three times. Because there seemed nothing left to take. Imagine that, running out of money because an elementary school kid stole a couple of bills a few times. But at least we were able to fry chicken. I realized then just how much Koreans love chicken.

So do they still fry chicken for a living? someone asked.

No. When the bird flu hit, my parents quit for good. I was my parents' wasted dreams and I grew up wastefully. When I said I wanted to go to art school, they slapped me and chopped off my hair, and even though I was the one who was angry, it was their anger, more than mine, that was to be feared. I grew up in the country and waited my whole life to go away to Seoul for college. If I managed to get in, that is.

Come to think of it, we all held our breath when we entered middle school, and we pretended to stop breathing altogether when we entered high school. At school we were always running away, we were always getting caught, we were always beaten. We were beaten at home and at school, we were beaten by our teachers and friends, and one of us was even bitten by a dog on the street. We all agreed that getting struck on the thighs hurt the most and getting struck on the soles of your feet didn't hurt as much, surprisingly. Have you ever gotten your eyelashes plucked out? one asked. Have you ever gotten your armpit hair plucked out? another asked.

We talked about these kinds of things while we got locked up and released, repeatedly, from the dungeon portcullis. Damn it, is there even a dragon? someone asked, and as a sign of our agreement, we all said, What the fuck, damn it.

All the heroes were Caucasian and possessed German-sounding names. None of us were Caucasian and we all possessed Korean-sounding names. Were there ever dungeons in Korea? one asked, and another replied, There were underground tunnels. It would be nice to commit suicide in an underground tunnel, someone said, and no one thought the comment was pathetic.

When I was in college, there was a senior who liked music. His major was Third World music. I guess you could call him an expert because he was regularly a guest on the radio and wrote articles for magazines. He got hired at a company that imported and distributed music from Third World countries, but maybe he wasn't happy there, because he quit after a few months and set up his own label. He put out a few records and ended up closing. We lost touch soon after, but I heard he was frying chicken somewhere, far away from the school. I wondered often, Why chicken? Because Koreans love their chicken? Because Koreans didn't like Third World music and he wanted to do something they liked? I hardly eat chicken anymore, especially fried chicken, because to me it's like dough soup, something people ate when food was scarce, but there are times I think about the correlation between chicken, Koreans, and private businesses. If there hadn't been any chicken, what would my parents and seniors have fried? Would they have fried something else? You know the saying "If you can't get a pheasant, get a chicken"? But there's no saying that goes, "If you can't get a chicken, get a pheasant."

We shuffled the cards in silence. I have to go to work tomorrow, someone said with a long sigh. No one said anything, but in that instant, we thought about suicide. We were all suffering wounds from a swinging blade, portcullis, club, and arrow. When we drew two or three tiles, our chances of dying were 99.9 percent. That remaining 0.1 percent represented completeness, rather than deficiency. Our chances of dying a hundred years later were also 99.9 percent. In 2015 we were already in our twenties, and unless our bodies were cryogenically preserved, it seemed certain we would not experience the end of another century. That instant I had the thought that we'd thought only about the time and place of our suicide and that we hadn't thought about the actual method. Just as the word "thought" was repeated three times, we thought a lot. We sometimes took initiative, but we were mostly passive. We looked at one another. The lamp that dangled above the round table thrust our faces in both light and shadow. Our murky gazes became snarled above the dungeon. I can't remember exactly what day it was, but we didn't win the lottery that week. The reason I can remember that fact is because we never won.

Greece went bankrupt, same-sex marriages became legalized in America, and stock prices plummeted in China. We thought hard about the countries that didn't appear in the pages of the newspaper, but never mind countries, we didn't appear in the pages of the newspaper and neither would we in the future. We would die nameless, and even if we were to commit suicide, it seemed certain we would die nameless and soon be forgotten, unless we carried out a suicide bomb attack in the heart of Gwanghwamun Gate. It's not that we particularly wanted to leave our names behind, but we couldn't understand why we were upset about the problem in Greece, and we grew angry for some reason when we thought about another country's countless nameless people, and we wondered why concrete individuals had to suffer when an abstract nation like Greece went bankrupt. Where are the individuals when America and China are pitting their strength against one another? We were Koreans, and as concrete individuals, we simply wanted to commit suicide. A win or suicide? We delayed our suicide indefinitely until the moment we would win the lottery. Each week we didn't win, so we extended our lives by a week, week by week. What will you do if you hit the jackpot? we asked one another in a mocking voice, as though conducting an interview, and one person said, I'll commit suicide, and the remaining three said nothing.

Nothing much happened in our everyday. Because nothing ever happened, we felt at peace. There were some useful old sayings, and one of them was "No news is good news." We hoped nothing would happen. When something happened, someone usually died or got sick or went into debt or got her car seized because of unpaid fines or was mugged at home or got raped in the elevator or clogged her toilet, or her home became infested with cockroaches or she got into a car accident and was rushed to the ER or her father or mother died or her aunt took out a payday loan or her dog died or she got slapped in the stairwell, lost her footing, and broke her leg or she went missing or she became a victim of voice phishing.

I almost became a victim of voice phishing once. He claimed to be calling from the Seoul District Prosecutor's Office. I asked him what the problem was and the person said my bank account was being used in fraud. I said, "You asshole, you want to fucking die?" and he said, "How hard does it have to be to make a goddamn living?" and hung up. I was so angry that I called the number that had shown up on my cellular phone and got an automated voicemail message. I waited for the beep and left a message filled with curses.

When I told this story, one person said she had received a similar call, but had given out her bank account number and password right away. She hadn't been able to help herself. It was because the caller had cited her friend's name and said this friend had died. He had then asked for her account balance. When she mentioned the amount, he let out a sigh and hung up. Only then did she realize she had fallen prey to voice phishing. That hurt my pride, she said. Getting a con artist to pity you, now that's something you can take pride in, someone said. What's there to take pride in if you're going to commit suicide anyway? another asked. Suicide is the one thing you can take pride in, said someone else who had remained silent all along.

Did we actually want to die then? I'm not sure. I truly wanted to die, and I actually didn't want to die. Only one of us had earnestly attempted suicide.

When I was little, I read a story by Bang Jeonghwan about a girl who killed herself by falling asleep in a sealed-up room filled with lilies. I stole money from my mother's purse, bought two bouquets of lilies, put them by my head, and fell asleep. The next morning, I woke up alive. The stolen money was discovered and I was beaten until sap flowed from the trampled lilies like pus and I got a fractured rib. I thought I was going to be beaten to death. But everything turned out great for my mother. People were told I fell down an embankment and the insurance company gave us enough to cover all the hospital fees, plus a bit more for consolatory payment. The consolatory payment gave me no consolation. Even if I had ended up dying, it wouldn't have turned out like a fairy tale. With these words, this person picked up a card, and then died instantly from a swinging blade. The hero had 40 won worth of loot. The actual currency of the game was gold, not won, but we tended to downgrade the value of loot, calling it 40 won, 50 won, or such. A proper burial could not be given to this hero that had died a heroic death, clutching 40 won. The dungeon became his grave. His prison cell was his ancestral tablet and the cobwebbed urn was his coffin.

I want to grow old this way, and when I die, I want to be buried here, someone said, glancing around the office. Should we turn this place into a mausoleum? If we get rid of all the books and games from the shelves, get some dividers, and put the burial urns there, isn't that a mausoleum? What if we performed the ancestral rites for people with no family or offered up prayers for those who don't have any visitors? We all fell into deep thought. We were going to die without reproducing, and though everything in the world was uncertain, it was certain we would not produce any offspring and that we would die one day, and so it was also certain there would be no heir to offer ancestral rites or prayers when we died. Though I never wanted to receive ancestral rites, but still, but maybe. What if we perform the rites whenever one of us dies? someone suggested. Then how about the last person to stay alive? another person said. Should we let in a new person each time someone dies? the third person said. I'll die last then, I said. I don't care if I don't get ancestral rites. Every year, I'll fry pancakes and grill skewers and pour drinks, but if you're going to die, could you do it on the same day? That way, I'd only have to perform the rites once a year. None of us held any religious beliefs. Now there's an idea, someone said. Should we die today then? said the one who had died by swinging blade. The dragon seemed to be asleep. If there actually was a dragon. We exchanged another look. Then how should we do it? said the person locked up in a portcullis. We wanted to die in the most passive way possible. Should we hold our breath? We immediately blocked our mouths and noses, but ended up gasping and panting even before a minute passed. What if we all die and end up winning the lottery next week? someone said. When's next week? another said. Next week is next week, stupid, I said. Our heroes were a long way from the chamber where the dragon lay sleeping. Even if we were to make it there, it seemed the dragon would wake up and torch us with flames as soon as we entered its chamber. We didn't have to go there to know this. It was a feeling. We lived according to our feelings, and sometimes our feelings were right and sometimes they were wrong, but we had no choice but to live according to them. I'll keep the winnings then, I said. I'll set up a trust fund and perform your ancestral rites for a long, long time. Do you even know what a trust fund is? someone asked. I know what stocks are, I said. I'll buy some stocks with the winnings and even if I end up losing everything, I'll offer your rites for a long, long time. Oh, don't I feel better, someone said.

There's no way to know if we truly wanted to commit suicide that summer. I wanted to commit suicide. I half genuinely did. Since I couldn't peer into the others' heads, I didn't know if they genuinely wanted to commit suicide, but my guess was that they, too, half genuinely wanted to commit suicide. Useless sentences scatter.

I went to a Christian college where I was required to attend chapel for four years. It was a useless time in every way. The explanation of the Bible was worth listening to, but when a Christian celebrity climbed up on the pulpit and said, "God loves you, because God loves you," I stuck the earphones in my ears and listened to music for the rest of the service. But it was then that I realized what had seemed to me like nonsense—the repetition of the same words—was actually meaningful. We wanted to commit suicide. The reason was because we wanted to commit suicide. Just the way some deaths happen for no good reason, there was no good reason for suicide. We simply wanted to commit suicide. Even if our minds were analyzed or it became possible to read our thoughts through the advancement of technology, all that a person would find, if he peered into our heads, would be the words "I want to commit suicide, I want to commit suicide." That's why we said we wanted to commit suicide over and over like a habit. It was the most violence we could inflict on ourselves. We wanted to inflict greater violence on ourselves than the violence we'd experienced at the hands of others. It was our own form of revenge. On others and on ourselves. Looking back now, the chapel time wasn't entirely useless. I've never thought much about Christianity and what I knew was virtually nonexistent, but I'd heard of "original sin." In other words, it was a sin that we were born. With this thinking, every problem was easily solved. Since it's a sin to be born, let's commit suicide. We didn't think about the fact that most religions considered committing suicide as sin. With death before us, we became atheists. Since there was nothing beyond death, there would be no sin. That's what we genuinely thought. That's what we needed to believe. I say "we," but I'm by no means our representative or delegate. I don't know what the other three are doing now. One would have actually committed suicide and one would have attempted suicide but failed.

    Until the end of that summer, no one made it out of the dungeon. No one got even far enough to experience a fiery death for waking the dragon. All we did was suffer one attack after another near the starting point by a swinging blade or skeleton. We possessed 40 won or 100 won in loot. It was a dreary number. Day after day, the muggy weather continued. Our clothes gave off a sour smell. We sat under the air conditioner and smelled one another's sweat and sourness that the lemon-scented candles couldn't take away and felt a sad kinship. But we didn't hope the summer would end. When summer ended, autumn would come, and when autumn ended, winter would come. A new year would start and one of us would enter his thirties, feeling like shit. Without having committed suicide. When we closed and opened our eyes, we hoped we would be old. When we closed and opened our old eyes, we hoped we would be dead. We didn't ask or wonder or interrogate someone or pick a fight with anyone to find out why we buried ourselves in only these thoughts. We wanted to disappear like this, and that went for me too. So one day that summer, we decided to go through with it—one by one, we decided to commit suicide. We did rock-paper-scissors and I was the first to lose. We would roll the die in the order of who had first lost. One by one, we would toss the die onto the impenetrable dungeon. And the person who rolled the lowest number would be the first to commit suicide. What do you want on your ceremonial table? I asked all of a sudden. Fuck it, who cares? I picked up the die. No one looked at me. No one looked at the die. No one looked at the dungeon. I tossed the die. I got 4. I passed it to my left. The die was tossed. That die was rolling. That die kept rolling. That summer we waited for the die to stop moving. It was 2015. That summer the die kept rolling. That die kept rolling.

You're forgiven if, after reading this story, you wonder, *what just happened?* We've taught this story a number of times, and sometimes students come away a bit frustrated initially. But we've gone on to have good discussions about the story and also think about the somewhat subversive techniques Han Yanjoo uses to create a group of malcontents with too much time on their hands to drink, smoke, and play games, and who test our patience with their collective wishy-washiness. But like most satires, a lot rests on the tone of the narration, and like most satires, the story is meant to be funny (though not so much in a laugh-aloud way) and dead serious in its societal critique

    So, yes, who are these people and what is it they really want out of life? Their brief resumes are presented thus: "One published books. One worked at an office. One made candles. And I read and wrote books." They're a reasonably well-educated and privileged group of four who "dared not ask any questions that weren't superficial" and who, in their shared workspace, appear to be able to work as much or as little as they want and spend time talking about nothing in particular.

    To crack open what this story is really about, look at how the collective POV constructs the story. This is about one short but intense time as the opening line indicates: "We met often that summer" and it's 2015. Yet we're immediately told that all of them were apart in 1999 but collectively did not think they "would be together to greet 2020," even though they would all only be in their thirties by then. By the second paragraph, we discover why there is such a lot of uncertainty expressed about their existence, because the narrator declares "We were unhappy, each for a different reason, and so, wanted to die" and that summer, it appears they talk a great deal about suicide, in between their other frivolous activities. We eventually learn that money is important to them and that every week, each takes a turn to buy 5,000 won of lottery tickets, and we discover what each wants that money for—travel, a new desk, dental implants, to pay off overdue insurance bills. They also get bored at work and indulge in card games, drinking beer, and smoking cigarettes, which seems to trouble them because "we felt as though we'd become the most useless beings on earth."

This sense of uselessness morphs into the central question the story poses:

> Should we commit suicide, should we commit suicide tomorrow? Should we commit suicide, should we have committed suicide yesterday? We posed questions that were out of the question. When we posed question after question—questions that were out of the question—we didn't want anything to happen. We wanted to grow old this way. It was 2015. We wanted to grow old this way and die this way.

Not much happens in this story. There is no conflict among the characters, nothing changes, life and existential questions of death and suicide go on. The most thrilling event that summer is their playing Dungeonquest, a board game where each player is a hero who gets a limited number of turns by rolls of the die to amass more wealth and fortune than the other three. The game allows the group to commit a form of suicide because each one dies in turn.

So what is the story really saying? Dig deeper and it's clear that Han uses the repetitiveness of routine to achieve both effect and meaning. For one thing, the sameness of their lives speaks to the underlying anxieties they all feel about their own society and the world beyond that compels their attention. Even though it is the "same story every night," except for the quests in their game, they know their reality is neither "romantic" nor meaningful. "But that doesn't mean it was sad or pathetic," the narrator says, which immediately makes us feel the opposite that, yes, indeed, these characters are sad and pathetic. But what's made them sad and pathetic?

> In 1999, we were too young to feel the anxieties that surrounded the end of the millennium. But before 1999, there was 1997, the year of the Asian financial crisis. Though we were younger in 1997, the anxieties we felt then were a kind we experienced firsthand, different from the peculiar anxieties of 1999 that were mixed with optimism for the start of the new century.

The turning point happens after this paragraph when the POV shifts notably from "we" to "I." This allows the narrator to acknowledge the true problems in their world, through personal stories, despite all attempts to maintain a false optimism. The narrator recounts bankruptcies in her or his neighborhood, and the others chime in about troubling experiences when they were in elementary and middle school which center around emotional and even physical abuse. One apparently has had their eyelashes pulled out, another their armpit hair. One is beaten for wanting to go to art school. Their seeming privileged life begins to lose its luster. There is also the disconnect of Caucasian figures in their nightly game when they are all Korean. It is difficult for them to understand why world events cause them such anxiety, but how could it not, when the world has inflicted such violence on them? They have become so disassociated from their own pain that they can ponder more over why Koreans love fried chicken more than they wonder why their parents and classmates inflicted such pain on them. The stories they each tell from their past—of lives out of control, both personally and on a global scale—leads to the narrator's understanding that what they really want is to inflict violence on themselves, to make sense of their aspirations and desires in light of the hopelessness they feel. By the end of the story, we begin to see that the disconnection in their lives is tied both to their secret emotions and present posturing, as well as to the global connectedness they cannot escape from, the lives ahead they feel fated to lead, and that suicide provides no answer. The die will simply keep rolling as they die and are reborn in Dungeonquest.

This game, by the way, is what we would consider a *motif*. A motif is something that is repeated, in music, in literature, in art and forms a recognizable pattern. In literature, a motif takes on a symbolic significance, though not necessarily in an easily articulated fashion. Dungeonquest forms a funny (in a very dry sense) counterpoint to the character's half-hearted suicidal ideations. While they can't quite muster the energy to actually kill themselves, and are as ineffectual at that as they are at everything else, in Dungeonquest, none of them can manage to stay alive. None of them seem to see the irony in this—like everything else, their failures at both endeavors, staying alive and killing themselves, form a kind of ironic game of ping pong that only the reader sees entirely.

Consider in your own fiction using a repetitive action, such as a game, as a kind of barometer of the characters' feelings and desires. When you have such a motif in your story, just make sure to keep track of it. Don't introduce it, mention it a couple of times, and then drop it. If you do, then you're letting down the reader by making us think something about it was important. Such dropped clues are called *red herrings*. Of course, you can't necessarily know from the beginning if the patterns you introduce in your stories will pan out. If they don't, no harm done. Just take them out. On the other hand, if your character starts playing Dungeonquest and you're not sure why, let them play a bit and see where they lead. It might be somewhere unexpected.

By contrast, the world of "Birds" is peopled by those who also wish to die, but can only do so only when they venture beyond the construction site that is their workplace. This story is satire in the form of a fable that presents a fantastical, speculative reality. Read Deepak Unnikrishnan's gothic and horrifying tale of migrant workers in Abu Dhabi, who are drawn there by the high pay despite the dehumanizing conditions of their lives.

2 "Birds"

by Deepak Unnikrishnan (UAE)

Deepak Unnikrishnan is a writer from Abu Dhabi. His book *Temporary People* was the inaugural recipient of the Restless Books Prize for New Immigrant Writing. It was longlisted for the Center for Fiction's First Novel Prize and won the 2017 Hindu Prize.

> Anna Varghese worked in Abu Dhabi. She taped people. Specifically, she taped construction workers who fell from incomplete buildings.
> Anna, working the night shift, found these injured men, then put them back together with duct tape or some good glue, or if stitches were required, patched them up with a

needle and horse hair, before sending them on their way. The work, rarely advertised, was nocturnal.

Anna belonged to a crew of ten, led by Khalid, a burly man from Nablus. Khalid's team covered Hamdan Street, Electra, Salaam, and Khalifa. They used bicycles; they biked quickly.

Anna had been doing this for a long time, thirty years, and many of her peers had retired—replaced, according to Khalid, by a less dependable crew. Seniority counted, and so Khalid allowed her to pick her route.

Anna knew Hamdan as intimately as her body. In the seventies, when she first arrived, the buildings were smaller. Nevertheless, she would, could, and did glue plus tape scores of men a day, correcting and reattaching limbs, putting back organs or eyeballs and sometimes, if the case was hopeless, praying until the man breathed his last. But deaths were rare. Few workers died at work sites; it was as though labor could not die there. As a lark, some veterans began calling building sites death-proof. At lunchtime, to prove their point, some of them hurled themselves off the top floor in full view of new arrivals. The jumps didn't kill. But if the jumpers weren't athletic and didn't know how to fall, their bodies cracked, which meant the jumpers lay there until nighttime, waiting for the men and women who would bicycle past, looking for the fallen in order to fix, shape, and glue the damaged parts back into place, like perfect cake makers repiping smudged frosting.

When Anna interviewed for the position, Khalid asked if she possessed reasonable handyman skills. "No," she admitted. No problem, he assured her, she could learn those skills on the job.

"What about blood, make you faint?" She pondered the question, then said no again.

"OK, start tomorrow," said Khalid. Doing what, she wondered, by now irritated with Cousin Thracy for talking her into seeking her fortune in a foreign place, for signing up for a job with an Arab at the helm, and one who clearly didn't care whether she knew anything or not. "Taping," Khalid replied. "The men call us Stick People, Stickers for short. It's a terrible name, but that's OK—they've accepted us."

Construction was young back then. Oil had just begun to dictate terms. And Anna was young, too. Back in her hometown, she assumed if she ever went to the Gulf she would be responsible for someone's child or would put her nursing skills to use at the hospital, but the middlemen pimping work visas wanted money—money she didn't have, but borrowed. Cousin Thracy pawned her gold earrings. "I expect gains from this investment," she told Anna at the airport. Anna arrived, flying Air India, Khalid was waiting. "Is it a big hospital?" she asked him as he drove his beat-up pickup.

"Hospital?" he repeated. Over lunch, he gently broke it to her that she had been lied to.

"No job?" she wept. There is a job, Khalid assured her, but he urged her to eat first. Then he needed to ask her a few questions.

"Insha'Allah," he told her, "the job's yours, if you want it."

Anna built a reputation among the working class; hers was a name they grew to trust.

When workers fell, severing limbs, the pain was acute, but borne. Yet what truly stung was the loneliness and anxiety of falling that weighed on their minds.

Pedestrians mostly ignored those who fell outside the construction site, walking around them, some pointing or staring.

The affluent rushed home, returning with cameras and film. Drivers of heavy-duty vehicles or family sedans took care to avoid running over them. But it didn't matter where labor fell. The public remained indifferent. In the city center, what unnerved most witnesses was that when the men fell, they not only lost their limbs, or had cracks that looked like fissures, but they lost their voices too. They would just look at you, frantically moving what could still move. But most of the time, especially in areas just being developed, the fallen simply waited. Sometimes, the men fell onto things or under things where few people cared to look. Or they weren't reported missing. These were the two ways, Anna would share with anyone who asked, that laborers could die on-site.

Then there were those who would never be found. A combination of factors contributed to this: bad luck, ineptitude, a heavy workload. A fallen worker might last a week without being discovered, but after a week, deterioration set in. Eventually, death.

Anna had a superb track record for finding fallen men. The woman must have been part-bloodhound. She found every sign of them including teeth, bits of skin. She roamed her territory with tenacity, pointing her flashlight in places the devil did not know or construction lights could not brighten. Before her shift ended in the morning, she returned to the sites, checking with the supervisor or the men disembarking Ashok Leyland buses to be certain no one was still missing, and that the men she had fixed, then ordered to wait at the gates for inspection, included everybody on the supervisor's roster. The men were grateful to be fussed over like this.

Anna wasn't beautiful, but in a city where women were scarce, she was prized. She also possessed other skills. The fallen shared that when Anna reattached body parts, she spoke to them in her tongue, sometimes stroking their hair or chin. She would wax and wane about her life, saying that she missed her kids or the fish near her river, or would instead ask about their lives, what they left, what they dreamt at night, even though they couldn't answer. If she made a connection with the man or if she simply liked him, she flirted. "You *must* be married," she liked to tease.

If she didn't speak his language, she sang, poorly, but from the heart. But even Anna lost people.

"Sometimes a man will die no matter what you do," Khalid told her. "Only Allah knows why."

Once, for four hours Anna sat with a man who held in place with his right arm his head, which had almost torn itself loose from the fall. A week prior, Anna had a similar case and patched the man up in under two hours. But in this case, probably her last before retirement, nothing worked. Sutures did not hold. Glue refused to bind. Stranger still was that the man could speak. In her many years of doing this, none of the fallen had been able to say a word. "Not working?" he asked. Anna pursed her lips and just held him. There was no point calling an ambulance. No point finding a doctor.

"Remove the fallen from the work site," Khalid had warned her, "and they die." It was simply something everyone knew. Outside work sites, men couldn't survive these kinds of falls. If the men couldn't be fixed at the sites, they didn't stand a chance anywhere else.

The dying man's name was Iqbal. He was probably in his mid-thirties and would become the first man to die under her watch in over five years. In her long career, she had lost thirty-seven people, an exceptional record. She asked about his home. "Home's shit," he said. His village suffocated its young. "So small you could squeeze all of its people and farmland inside a plump cow." The only major enterprise was a factory that made coir doormats. "Know when a village turns bitter? If the young are bored—." Iqbal trailed off.

He'd left because he wanted to see a bit of the world. Besides, everyone he knew yearned to be a Gulf boy. Recruiters turned up every six months in loud shirts and trousers and a hired taxi, and they hired anyone. "When I went, they told me the only requirement was to be able to withstand heat," Iqbal said. Then there was the money, which had seduced Anna, too. "Tax-free!" he bellowed. They told him if he played his cards right, he could line his pockets with gold.

Before making up his mind, Iqbal had visited the resident fortune-teller—a man whose parrot picked out a card that confirmed the Gulf would transform Iqbal's life. He packed that night, visited Good-Time Philomena, the neighborhood hooker, for a fuck that lasted so long "a she-wolf knocked on the door and begged us to stop." Then he sneaked back into his house and stole his old man's savings to pay for the visa and the trip.

"Uppa was paralyzed—a factory incident. Basically watched me take his cash," Iqbal said. Anna frowned. "I wouldn't worry," Iqbal reassured her. "My brother took good care of him."

"And how is he now?" Anna inquired.

"Died in my brother's lap," he replied. "I couldn't go see him." As Anna continued to hold Iqbal's head, he told her he expected to have made his fortune in ten years. By then, he'd have handpicked his wife, had those kids, built that house. His father, if he'd lived, would've forgiven him. Former teachers who scorned him by calling him Farm Boy or Day Dreamer would invite him to dine at their place. But then he fell, didn't he? Slipped like a bungling monkey. He was doing something else—what, he seemed embarrassed to share.

"What were you up to?" Anna urged. "Go on, I won't tell a soul."

Iqbal smiled. "I was masturbating on the roof. The edge," he confessed. He had done this many times before. "It's super fun," he giggled. "But then a pigeon landed on my pecker . . ." The bird startled him. He lost his balance.

"You didn't!" Anna laughed.

"Try it, there's nothing like it. It's like impregnating the sky." Or, he added, "in your case, welcoming it."

"Behave," Anna said. "I could easily be your mother's age. Or older sister's."

"The heat," he said softly. "The heat felled me."

"Not the bird?"

Iqbal broke into a grin. "I came on a bird once. It acted like I'd shot it."

Like Anna, Iqbal had known heat ever since he was a child. He knew how to handle it, even when the steam in the air had the potential to boil a man's mind. But the Gulf's heat baked a man differently. First it cooked a man's shirt and then the man's skin. On-site, Iqbal trusted his instincts. Water, sometimes buttermilk, was always on hand, but frequent breaks meant a reduced output, and Iqbal knew his progress was being monitored. He had trained as a tailor, as his Uppa was a tailor; he knew learning a new trade took time. So he followed one rule: when his skin felt like parchment paper, he stopped working and quenched his thirst, sometimes drinking water so quickly it hurt. The sun never conquered him. His body was strong. But what he couldn't control, he told

Anna, were the reactions of people he passed in the street, especially if he volunteered to go to one of those little kadas to buy water or cold drinks for his mates in the afternoon.

"How so?" Anna wondered.

"In the summer," Iqbal continued, "you burn, the clothes burn. You smell like an old stove." Then he asked her, "Don't you burn?"

"Everyone burns here," she replied quietly. "But you fell today? What was different?"

"It seemed like the perfect day," Iqbal said dryly. "What do the others tell you?"

"The others?"

"Those who fall," Iqbal didn't wait for an answer. "Outside, whether you believe it or not, heat's easier to handle. For me, anyway." On building tops, he insisted, most men shrivel into raisins. "Men don't burn up there; they decay."

"But it's cooler up there, no?" Anna asked.

"Fully clothed, in hard hats? No," said Iqbal. "I once saw a man shrink to the size of a child. At lunchtime, he drank a tub of water and grew back to his original size." Still, the open air allowed the body to breathe. "You have wind." Indoors, in the camps, in closed quarters, packed into bunk beds, not enough ACs, bodies baked, sweat burned eyes, salt escaped, fever and dehydration built. Bodies reeled from simply that. Anna nodded. There was a time Anna patched up a man with skin so dry, she needed to rub the man's entire body with olive oil after she pieced him together.

Even though they were all immune to death by free fall, there was nothing they could do about the heat. At lunch break, getting to the shade under tractor beds and crane rumps became more important than food. With shirts as pillows and newspapers as blankets, the men rested.

Iqbal asked Anna if she would mind scratching his hair.

"You're new," he teased. "You look new, like a bride."

Anna smiled. "I have grandkids now." She dug her nails into his scalp.

"They told you to fear the sun, didn't they?" said Iqbal.

"Who?"

"Recruiters," said Iqbal.

"No," she replied.

"Well, no one mentions the nighttime," Iqbal sighed. "They should." At night, heat attacked differently, became wet. "I knew a man," Iqbal continued, "who collected sweat. He would go door to door with a trolley full of buckets. After a week's worth, this man—Badran was his name—dug a pit near the buildings we lived in. It would take him a long time to pour the buckets of sweat into that pit. The first couple of times, I watched. Then I began to help. Soon we had a pool—a salty pool. It was good fun. We floated for hours."

"Didn't Badran get into trouble?" Anna asked.

"Badran was a smart fellow," said Iqbal. "He resold some of that pool water to this shady driver of a water tanker. The driver would get to the camp at around three a.m., take as much water as truck could carry. Everyone knew. The important people all got a cut."

"Where did he take the water?"

"I asked Badran many times," said Iqbal. "He never said."

"Badran must be doing well for himself," said Anna.

"He was, I suppose," said Iqbal. "He died a few months ago."

"How?"

"Accident," replied Iqbal. "Was his time."

"Where?"

"We were returning home in a pickup. Near Mussafah the driver hit something. Badran fell . . . the wheel . . ." Iqbal paused.

Anna didn't push him. She knew what he meant. Every night, Anna told Iqbal, she had dinner at this little cafeteria owned by a man from her town who served her leftovers that weren't on the menu. She ate for free while Abdu, the cafeteria owner, gossiped. Abdu made a good living. Where his place was, every night, trucks and buses ferrying labor would stop. Badran and Iqbal may have stopped, too, sitting by the windows, worn out.

"Maybe," said Iqbal. "Once I sat next to a man who was so hot he evaporated before my eyes. I took his pants; someone took his shoes; his shirt was ugly, so no one wanted that."

Anna laughed. Iqbal's speech was slowing. She continued massaging his scalp.

"I once knew a man who wanted to die," said Iqbal. "He'd realized pretty early it was hard to die in the workplace or in the camps. He wasn't unhappy. He just wanted to die."

"So, did he?" asked Anna.

Iqbal grinned. "You see, that's how this story gets complicated. Charley knew what he wanted, but he was also fair. He had a wife and kids back home he wanted to make sure were provided for. He'd figured the best way to do that would be to die performing some work-related task. That way they would be compensated."

"Did he succeed?"

Iqbal thought about the question. "I am not sure," he finally said.

"What happened?"

"Well, he asked me to help. I liked him, you know. I said yes. He said it would take some time, a year or two, but it could work. So Charley tells me that every couple of months he would give himself an accident. He'd start with small ones. Fall off the first floor, lose a few toes. Then he would build up: third floor, sixth floor. Thing is, he'd tell me beforehand. A note, some secret code indicating when he planned to do this, and where. So I'd wait for the deed, and before anyone found out I'd go to him, remove one piece of him—don't know, a finger or something—then throw that into the trash bin. Stick People would fix him up at night, but there would be a part missing. He promised himself four accidents a year. If he played his cards right, in three years, he'd be properly broken, just not fixable, and the company would be bound to inform his family. So that's what we did for a while."

"His family wouldn't have gotten a cent," Anna confided.

"Let me finish," said Iqbal. "We'd done enough for me to administer the hammer blow in a few months; it had taken longer than we had anticipated—six years. One night, Charley sought me out. "I want to live; he said. I didn't know what to say. I had removed a few fingers, toes, a kidney, his penis. His legs were half the size they'd been when he arrived, and now he wanted to live."

"What did you do?" Anna asked.

"He's very happy now," smiled Iqbal. "Sometimes he asks me if he can watch me jack off since he can't anymore."

"Was he there today?"

"No, not today," Iqbal's breath grew increasingly labored. "Soon," is what he said. Anna nodded, gently touching his face. Iqbal turned towards her. "Do you know the prayer for the dead?" She shook her head.

"There's this dream I've been having . . ." Iqbal began.

"Listening," said Anna.

"A man I knew, Nandan, kept a bird, a pigeon in a cage, that he brought to work every day." As Nandan worked Iqbal shared, he never let this bird out of his sight.

"Never?"

"Not for a second," Iqbal confirmed. "The bird could fly, but he weighted it down with an iron lock around its neck. It weighed enough to make the bird stoop all the time." Iqbal felt bad for the bird, trapped in that cage, so he made up his mind to set it free when Nandan wasn't looking. "I almost succeeded," he said. He was on the roof, picking the lock, about to set the bird free, when Nandan cornered him. Someone had seen Iqbal headed for the roof with the birdcage. Nandan demanded Iqbal give back his bird. "I wouldn't, of course," said Iqbal. In a fit of rage, Nandan lunged for the bird. Iqbal slipped, losing his grip on the bird; it fell to the ground a few feet away from both men, not far from the edge of the roof, eighteen stories up. The bird, in a panic, or perhaps, hope, began hopping toward the edge and jumped. "But I hadn't had time to remove the lock," said Iqbal.

"That's terrible," said Anna.

"In a way," said Iqbal. "After the incident, I began having these dreams."

"Dreams?"

"Promise not to laugh," said Iqbal.

"I promise," said Anna. Weeks after the pigeon fell to its death, Iqbal began having dreams in which he stood atop the roof of some building he helped construct. "My family's with me; we all have wings. The sun's cold. You following me? Cold! We fly." And as they fly, he shared, he notices that their feet possess talons, with which they can grip the top of the building, and they pull, and they fly, and they pull, and they fly, or try to fly, until they rip the building off its foundations, taking it with them, towards the gelid sun. It was Iqbal's final tale. Before dawn, he was gone.

Anna stayed with him for a few minutes, wondering if she ought to wait until morning, but she decided against it, filling out a note she attached to his chest. Deceased, it said, listing Khalid's company's name and address and a point of contact. Then she got back on her cycle.

*   *   *

Hamdan, Anna's haunt, her hood, was growing, from a tiny city center to a mutating worm that refused to tire. The streets grew streets, parked next to slabs of steel and glass towering over trees planted to grow in exactly the same way. Roads were widened and swept regularly to keep them spotless and black. Imported planners erected tall, stringy American-style street lights. If you paid attention, you could hear mercenary architects barking instructions to create the perfect city: *Move. This. There. That.* They never slept, shouting orders into the night, into the wee hours of the morning, never resting. The city was a board game and labor its pieces, there to make buildings bigger, streets longer, the economy richer. Then to leave. After.

Hamdan had once been little, with a runt-like city center, unsure and uncertain, but was now coached in ambition to exact maximum mileage from death-proof labor as they constructed its buildings. Anna had trouble keeping up with the pace. More workers than ever were falling.

Once, after Iqbal, a man she helped patch up, Kuriakose, sought her out, stood outside her door, begged her to come with him to his boss to demand unpaid wages. He just wanted to return home. She could fix this, he was sure. She went along. The boss had called the cops. Before arresting her, an officer asked her what she did. When he heard she worked for Khalid, he let her go with a warning. Khalid had been furious. "There's a system in place here; we obey," he said.

"What happened to him?" she wanted to know. Kuriakose was sent home. His roommates collected some money for him, but he had to go.

"The lies are there to see," Khalid liked to say. "It falls like slime. It falls off people like slime." The man had a point. There were no lies at the gates as ships docked, people pinned like barnacles, as planes landed spitting out new arrivals, as smugglers chucked live cargo miles away from port or land. Everyone came to secure their futures.

The city flirted with these people, making all give and give up. The air was spiked; everyone wanted a taste. Anna, too, she admitted. She had thought about bringing her family over, but she didn't want her children turning into in-betweens. Children she saw everywhere, those with cultivated accents, kids fattened by cable and imported chocolate, coddled by Japanese electronics and American telly. No, her kids would respect her land; they would know it. "Know the land, not the mother," Khalid had warned her. They'd been walking near the corniche.

"You see that," Anna said, pointing at a dark man fixing the sprinklers, as dark as the tiny nanny pushing a baby stroller past them, less dark than the men in the buildings nearby, nutting and bolting, even falling quietly when they slipped, falling quickly. "I've been lucky; my kids don't understand."

"Tell them," Khalid replied, "before they stop caring." Then he held her hand. But Khalid had been right. Her husband, then her children faded from her life. "What to say?" she asked Khalid. He said nothing. He couldn't understand; he had sent for his wife as soon as she was pregnant with their first child. With little to say, the two of them watched the barricaded sea. There was some tide, spittle, chewing-gum wrappers, fizz cans, little fishes licking ice-cream cups, and matches floating like little rafts, hitting the stone walls, where algae clung. Not far away, a thin man roasted peanuts in a wok of salt. The night was damp and the sky was flecked with gray.

Anna cycled slowly. "It's like impregnating the sky," she said out loud. Iqbal's words. I ought to try it at least once, she thought, deciding to take a shortcut by the corniche, which was now under construction. Months ago, on her morning walk, she had noticed Caterpillar scoopers and tractors parked near the date palms. She heard dredgers in the water. There was smoke everywhere. The sea was being kicked farther out. More fountains were being built. Anna didn't understand why, but she sat on a bench and wept. The construction was part of a larger plan. Anything with an old soul was being taken apart. It was what they did with the old souk, with its markets: tore it down, moving the merchants to a more modern building.

"They put us in a room!" Kareem Ikka, her grocer, scoffed, offering Anna piping-hot chai. The toy sellers were put in rooms, too. Her son and daughter had visited twice. The first time, she took them to the souk on a Friday, where they had to make their way past wayward tanks, robot monkeys, rotating princesses, woofing dogs. They bumped into people, she made them smell attar. She bought them cotton candy and a falooda each. The only mall she'd taken them to was in Hamdan Center. If they visited now, she wouldn't know where to take them. She didn't know the new malls as well. Or her children. But those thoughts would need to wait. She had arrived at her destination.

Watchman Babu greeted her with a smile. They were old friends. "Best job in the world," he told her once. The man who owned the empty building, a big shot named Majid, refused to sell. He was biding his time, waiting for its property value to soar. When he died unexpectedly, his son Rashid, who had been very close to his father, couldn't part with the building, and kept it, even though his brothers wanted him to sell. There was now an on-going property dispute. The case was being heard in the courts. Babu had been there from the beginning. He lived on the first floor, where he hosted parties for his bachelor friends. One such party, many years ago, led him to the roof. It wasn't a tall building, only six floors, but when his friends found his crumpled body, they had no hope, until Anna happened to cycle past. She saved his life, but he lost use of his right leg and an eye. Over time, they became firm friends, and sometimes Babu allowed Anna to sleep on the roof, which she did when she wanted to think. Tonight, she wanted to think. She fell asleep on the cot Babu laid out for her. She was soon dreaming.

She was standing on the roof of a very tall building, near the edge. Below, the city looked like drops of paint. The wind was strong. Iqbal was there; he gave her a friendly nod. There were many other faces she didn't recognize, men and women. There were hundreds of them. It was a hot day. The sun was brutal. It was then that she noticed that she had on the most magnificent wax wings—perfectly detailed. The others did, too, testing them by flapping them up and down to see if they worked. Anna wanted to try her new wings immediately, but sensed everyone was waiting for a signal. Then she heard the door to the roof open. She turned around and watched as hundreds of red-eyed pigeons, the size of schoolchildren, with their wings clipped, bells on their feet, iron lockets on their necks, walked towards them, extremely disciplined. Each bird stood behind a wax-winged man or woman. The one behind her stood so close Anna could smell its scent, hear it cooing. Anna's legs trembled. Before she had a chance to ask what now, the bird gave her a firm push. As she fell, she recalled asking Iqbal what the birdman Nandan had named his pigeon. As she tried flapping her giant wings, doing it all wrong, having trouble catching drift, she remembered Iqbal laughing. "Take a guess," he had said. She was falling with her back to the ground, peering upwards. The glint of the sun made it difficult to see. She sensed people falling past her, falling with her, dropping like rocks, trying to steady themselves, putting those wings to work. As she flapped harder, she thought she faintly caught sight of many bird heads peering down at her. Their beaks were moving. "Fly," they seemed to be mouthing. "Fly!"

To fully appreciate this story, it's helpful to understand that migrant workers from all over Asia are contracted to work for the wealthy Gulf states, as for example in the United Arab Emirates or UAE, of which the city of Abu Dhabi is the capital. Workers leave behind families in their home countries, as the protagonist Anna does. Although they are well paid compared to what they can make back home, they effectively become second-class citizens, generally with no rights to citizenship no matter how long they live in their countries of employment. As depicted in "Birds," work at constructions sites is dangerous and difficult, and living conditions are cramped and uncomfortable.

The POV in "Birds" is a third-person narrative that closes in on that of the protagonist Anna Varghese. She is one of the "Stick People, Stickers for short," an ironic name Unnikrishnan uses for her job of patching up construction workers who fall from high-rise, incomplete buildings. Although this story, like Han's, also focuses on work routines, and ultimately, very little changes for the protagonist, the tone and narrative energy is markedly different. For one thing, the story opens with a reliable fabulist voice that describes an entirely absurd situation, of Anna fixing up injured men "with duct tape or some good glue, or if stitches were required, patched them up with a needle and horse hair." A *fabulist* is a storyteller who is unapologetically making things up that are normally considered impossible in our everyday world. Unnikrishnan constructs an absurd and impossible world from the outset in a confident and matter-of-fact manner, which immediately allows the reader to suspend disbelief.

To successfully create an alternate universe, it's important to establish the rules of the world early in the story. This is the case in "Birds": the construction sites are "death-proof" because no matter how often workers fall, they do not die; Anna, we learn, has done this job for thirty years, and now has seniority and great expertise; to prove the veracity of this job, there is a brief flashback to when she first interviewed and is asked about her "handyman skills" and whether or not blood makes her faint.

Yet it soon becomes apparent that what lies behind the satire is a *moral tale*, a parallel to the actual plight faced by migrant workers. In the same flashback, we learn the following:

> Construction was young back then. Oil had just begun to dictate terms. And Anna was young, too. Back in her hometown, she assumed if she ever went to the Gulf she would be responsible for someone's child or would put her nursing skills to use at the hospital, but the middlemen pimping work visas wanted money—money she didn't have, but borrowed.

Anna is lied to by these work visa pimps and only when she arrives in Abu Dhabi does she discover that her job is not what she was promised. Nonetheless she remains and in time becomes the Stick Person everyone relies on.

Once these and other rules about the world are established, the story unfolds in an episodic fashion, as stories about some of the men Anna saves are recounted. Many of the construction workers long for death because the loneliness, brutal working conditions, and dry desert heat become intolerable. Abu Dhabi becomes a hell where people burn up and shrivel from the heat. A technique Unnikrishnan employs is to tell a story within a story as we learn about one man who does die, Iqbal, and who tells Anna his own experiences and life while also narrating stories about several other men: Badran, Charley, and Nandan. This is comparable to Han's approach in "We That Summer" as the other characters take turns recounting their memories. However, the third-person POV in "Birds" broadens out to use more storytelling techniques such as dialogue and dramatic scenes than in Han's story, and each character we meet is much more fully developed, while those in "We That Summer" remain relatively anonymous.

There is also another narrative voice at work in "Birds," which provides a critique, through a combination of language use and metaphor, about the socioeconomic conditions of this fictional-real world of Abu Dhabi. For example, most pedestrians ignore the fallen workers, who like fallen angels lie on the streets until Anna or another Stick Person comes to their rescue. The voice becomes a sharply critical one as it describes what happens:

> The affluent rushed home, returning with cameras and film. Drivers of heavy-duty vehicles or family sedans took care to avoid running over them. But it didn't matter where labor fell. The public remained indifferent.

Likewise, the story also chronicles the relentless pace of progress that leads to the inhumane working conditions. The city is cast as an entity that has a will of its own, helped along by a global, capitalistic will:

> Hamdan, Anna's haunt, her hood, was growing, from a tiny city center to a mutating worm that refused to tire. The streets grew streets, parked next to slabs of steel and glass towering over trees planted to grow in exactly the same way. . . . If you paid attention, you hear mercenary architects barking instructions to create the perfect city: Move. This. There. That . . . . The city was a board game and labor its pieces, there to make buildings bigger, streets longer, the economy richer. . . . Anna had trouble keeping up with the pace. More workers than ever were falling.

Both stories are critical of the worlds their characters live in for the existential despair caused by the demands of a globalized economy. But it's important to note that they don't criticize these worlds explicitly—they do so implicitly, allowing readers to discern for themselves what's wrong with this picture. The protagonists in both stories do achieve some kind of understanding, if not peace, about their respective situations. For the unnamed narrator in "We That Summer," it is an acceptance of who they are within the rules and demands of their Korean world. For Anna, we witness one moment where she meets Iqbal again in a dream and, instead of jumping or falling, attempts to fly. Everyone on the rooftop, including her, has wings, and she is surrounded by real giant pigeons with clipped wings. Iqbal pushes her off and she flaps her own wings, "doing it all wrong." The metaphor is unmistakable—life for these migrant workers will always be about "clipped" freedom, just as suicide remains an intriguing, but unattainable, option for the young office workers in Korea.

We should note that it's unusual for a published story to end with a dream, in part likely because change happens so effortlessly and randomly in dreams, and sometimes dream symbolism can seem heavy-handed. What do you think in this case? What is the justification for ending "Birds" with a dream sequence? How might you justify a dream sequence in a story such as this and not in, say, Han's "We That Summer"? We'd suggest it has something to do with the internal logic of the story. By that, we mean that every story sets its ground rules in terms of what is permissible and what isn't. In a story that is essentially recreating a realistic world, a dream sequence might seem like dodge formulated to escape the necessity of dealing believably with a character's conflict. But what about a fabulist story in which the ground rules have created an already dream-like world? We'll leave you with that thought to mull over as you consider the ground rules of your own stories.

Exercises

1. Reverse the POV in these two stories and write two new openings: "We That Summer" from a third-person narrative with one main protagonist and "Birds" from a collective first-person plural voice.

2. Write a story that repeats a certain action or incident. How can you use that repetition to create meaning that is larger than what is actually occurring in the story?

3. Think about a socioeconomic problem where you live that seems wrong or unfair to you. How can you critique or satirize that problem by narrating a story that unfolds through the voice of its fictional characters?

4. Focus on a routine that you fell into for a certain period of time. Describe that routine and then create a set of characters who follow the same or a comparable routine in a story and see where that takes you.

5. Write down a dream and start a story from it. Now, remove the dream and end the story with the dream you previously led with, or an entirely different dream. How necessary are the dreams as catalyst or resolution? Can you cut them out completely and have an even more satisfying story? What's gained or lost by the inclusion of the dream?

CHAPTER 4
LITTLE FISH

When we first began writing, we tended to want to push toward an outcome or message, and explained in a heavy-handed way why things turned out as they did in our stories, for example: *Lily was a poor and uneducated young woman of superior intelligence, but because of harsh reality she ended up in jail for shoplifting food because she was starving. She might have been the single tear shed on society's cheek if cruel society cared enough to cry!* While this might very well be the situation of your protagonist, for Lily's story to work, it cannot just be about why she's a victim of society. A magazine editor once told us about such stories of the Callousness of Society, "I might agree with your politics but your story is still terrible."

This is why your choice of the point of view (POV) from which you will tell the story is so important. One traditional POV is "omniscience," referring to a godlike state of knowledge, which, if employed subtly, can be a useful technique when we try to write stories about the inequities of life. We mortals don't have much practice with omniscience, and in our amateur hands, it can feel heavy-handed. If used well, the omniscient POV can inject meaning into your fiction beyond what individual characters in the story know to be true. Omniscience is used variously, but successfully, in two of the three stories we'll examine in this chapter (and in the third story, an argument can be made that the author demonstrates a quite subtle form of omniscience—but more on that later). In each of the stories presented here, the narrator or storyteller knows more than the characters do about their situations and directs the narrative, to a greater or lesser degree. A nineteenth-century literary classic that famously employed omniscience is Henry James's *What Maisie Knew*, about a sensitive child of divorced, dissolute parents, who grows up discovering a great deal about all her adult guardians, but remains perpetually in a peculiar state of half-knowledge. The omniscient POV is one that fell somewhat out of favor for the Anglo-American short story over the last century, but is used more readily in stories from Asia.

The stories in this chapter dramatize the lives of the faceless anonymous in society, but to write beyond a collective plight we have to make individual lives real. As James Joyce famously noted, "it's through the particular that we illustrate the universal." In following that dictum, these stories illustrate a great deal about social and economic inequity, the suffering caused by political unrest, the inhumanity of work that offers little more than a subsistence living in some of the wealthiest nations in the world. But a common aspect of all three is that the characters presented here are realistically drawn, as if directly from life, as opposed to using satire or speculative/science fiction as in the stories of Chapter 3. What the omniscient POV does is to dramatize what such individuals are *unlikely* to know about their situation, either because they lack the experience to know, or are denied such knowledge, or, perhaps, may not actually want to know too much more about the world beyond their own lives. It can also show us the *reality* of their emotional lives, despite what they are forced to say or do by virtue of being a "Little Fish."

Additionally, the stories in this chapter share a common characteristic—all three use extremely local references, whether cultural, geographical, or linguistic. How to do this *without* being too heavy-handed about adding "local color" or alienating the reader is the other craft technique we'll explore in these contrasting stories from India, Singapore, and the Philippines.

But how do we write about "Little Fish" without falling into the trap of sounding preachy or pompous, or worse, presumptuous about such lives? The fact that you know everything about your characters' lives doesn't mean that you should provide a running commentary about their lives. Are you that movie theater companion who yaks incessantly throughout the movie, warning the characters to not to open that door, telling your seat mate your opinions of the way the characters dress, behave, or the personal lives of the actors? If so, you might have a difficult time keeping your reader from putting down your story. No one wants to be told how to feel, whether in the movie theater or on the page. Paradoxically, the more you know about your character, the less you want your manipulation of the reader's emotions to be apparent. You're still and always manipulating the reader—art does that. But you want the reader to feel as though they are experiencing these emotions on their own, in concert with your characters. As a result, sometimes readers think that the tone of a particularly harrowing story is "matter-of-fact" or "bloodless," but that's merely the author allowing you, the reader, to experience the story as the characters do. Sometimes this bloodless tone actually amplifies the horror of the situation as in this *day-in-the-life-story* by Dilip Kumar, "A Clerk's Story."

Mehboob Khan, the protagonist of "A Clerk's Story," narrates in copious detail in diary form each moment of an otherwise ordinary day, exploded by the political, religious, and racial violence that is the reality of India's recent history. Kumar uses the second-person POV as the omniscience that guides the story. He also includes a vast amount of local geographical and cultural references, as well as the names and backgrounds of people in Khan's life. It is important to know that the original story is in Tamil, one of the many languages of India and an official one in Kovai, a major city in the state of Tamil Nadu. Dilip Kumar is a leading writer in the Tamil language of short fiction, and "A Clerk's Story" was adapted into an award-winning film titled *Nasir* by Arun Karthick in 2020. This is a highly political story about an apolitical man, Mehboob Khan, a somewhat romantic Muslim sales clerk who adores his wife (she is away visiting her mother), recites and reads poetry, listens to Hindi film love songs, looks after his polio-stricken, orphaned nephew, and leads a highly ordered life where each day is an obsession over obtaining enough money and food for his household. Read this story and consider the complexity of information delivered through this unusual tale, set in the Indian state of Tamil Nadu.

1 "A Clerk's Story"

by Dilip Kumar (India)

Translated from Tamil by Padma Narayanan

Dilip Kumar is an award-winning Tamil writer, editor and literary translator who is considered a pioneer of Tamil short stories. His books include *Cat in the Agraharam and Other Stories* and two other story collections, and he is also editor of two anthologies of Tamil fiction.

The clock shows 06.03. Your name is Mehboob Khan; you are, as yet, sleeping.

Kovai is steeped in the peace of early morning. A dilapidated building on Variety Hall Road; if you open the small front door placed between two huge thinnais—raised platforms—you see a narrow passage. On both sides of this passage are six small rooms, the habitat of three Muslim families. Your family occupies two rooms, one on the left and the other on the right side of the passage, just opposite each other. Your family—very much like your habitation—is small. Your mother Fathima is known as Ammijan. Your wife, Taj Begum. (She has now gone to her mother's place in Kozhunjivadi. You have been married for 20 years now; you have no children.) Your nephew, Iqbal.

You are now 42 years old. You are short, complexion fair. You have a protruding tooth, a long nose, large eyes—but tiny irises. You always wear a knee-length Liberty cut, a cream-colored shirt and loose pants folded at the ankles. Your education: eighth class. You are employed as a sales clerk at an apparel shop, Fashion Palace, on Raja Street at a salary of 1,800 rupees per month. Your working hours are from nine in the morning to nine at night. You get a break from one to three in the afternoon. Sunday mornings you iron clothes at TipTop Drycleaners at piece rate to augment your income. You know a smattering of Urdu, Hindi, Tamil and Malayalam. You are a hard worker, and one who can speak humorously and make others laugh. You smoke ten Mangalore Beedis a day and drink four cups of tea. (Three at the shop, one at home.) You go for your midday prayers when you find time for them.

Moreover, you are also endowed with a half-baked philosophical attitude. So you like poetry. On Sundays you compose poems along the lines of Hindi film songs of the fifties and sixties. All your songs inevitably include some of these words: zindagi (life), jaam (wine goblet), Rab (God), ishq (love), vakth (time), dil (mind, heart), pyaar (love), javani (youth), tanhayi (loneliness) and mauth (death). The fans who appreciate your poems are Leeladhar, Nandu, Arjun Das and Veeru, your co-workers at the shop. They are all Sindhis with some knowledge of Hindi and Urdu. Just like you they are school drop-outs. You launch your compositions in front of them during lunch time when the manager of the shop Tikam Das is not around. When you recite your poems, you start with your right hand placed on your chest and with wave-like motions nearly brush the noses of your listeners. The ones in front of you will encourage you with their pronouncements of "Vah, janab," or "Masha Allah, kya baath hai." You bow your head and put your palm to your forehead three times, doing salaams, acknowledging their praise.

You are now lying down curled up like a question mark. Your front teeth peep out of your darkened lips. Your face displays supreme peace. In deep slumber, you look like an innocent, helpless being, a sight that induces and seeks great love from any beholder.

06.33. You open your eyes. Your movements wake Fathima up. She has been doing this, unfailingly, for the past 42 years. She gets up and switches on the light. The two-foot tubelight shows Iqbal lying on his chest, clearly revealing his stump legs. (Seven years ago, the bus that was driving from Kovai to Tarapuram and a lorry coming from Tarapuram to Kovai had a head-on crash, resulting in the instantaneous death of 20 of its passengers. Among those victims were your sister Khathija and her husband Saiyad. The polio-stricken Iqbal had stayed back in Kovai and so is alive today.) You let out a sigh, "Yah Allah!" You go to the backyard, ease yourself, brush your teeth, wash your face and come back. Like any other day, you wear your shirt, pick up the brass mug, set out for

Mubarak Tea Stall on Nawab Hakim Road to buy "parcel" tea. (You can bring it home and do not have to drink it on the spot.) Karim Thatha is wriggling on the thinnai, half awake. He asks you the same question that he asks every day, "Kidhar? Chai lakkane?" Where are you off to? To fetch tea?

Nawab Hakim Road is enveloped in a dreamy sort of calm, covered as it is in fog. An old Hindi film song wafts down from the speaker placed in a corner of the Mubarak Tea Stall. You walk looking up at the sky. Your heart brims with strange emotions. The pale moon and the emerging clouds spit out a melancholy beauty.

07.15. You listen to Bhoole Bisre Geet on the radio. Suraiya, Begum Akhtar and Talat Muhammad are making your heart melt. Today, you get to hear two of Begum Akhtar's ghazals, one after the other. She torments you with her "Ey mohabbat tere anjaam pe rona aaya/ Zindagi kuch bhi nahin phir bhi jeeye jaatey hain."

You have seen Begum Akhtar's photo. Her broad forehead and deep-set eyes flit before your mind. She is no mortal. Allah seems to have turned all the sorrows of the world into nerves and placed them in her throat, you feel.

07.30. Iqbal goes crawling to the backyard and then calls out to you, "Mamu! Mamu!" You wash his bottom and put his shorts on him. Iqbal's lifeless legs feel cold to the hands, like dead lumps. You remember Ammijan telling you that there was no wheat in the house. You have to borrow 50 rupees from Dhasthagir next door, who works as a mechanic.

07.45. You peep into Dhasthagir's house and see him brushing his teeth, his mouth frothing with toothpaste. He sees you and, with just the lift of his eyebrows, asks, "What do you want?" You hesitate for a minute; your eyes fall on the newspaper Daily Thanthi on the table.

You manage to drawl, "Kuch nahin . . . akhbaar." Dhastagir bends down, picks up the newspaper and stretches it out towards you. You come back to the thinnai with the Daily. You read on . . . Has the popular actress got married secretly? . . . A lorry knocked against a bullock cart . . . Daring daylight robbery . . . Piteous death of the bride . . . Andiyar's musings . . . Kerosene prices go up from tomorrow . . . Kannitheevu . . . People's Forum . . . A letter complaining about the smelly glasses at the tea shops, because they have not been washed properly . . . Karthik clashes with Rambha . . . You decide that now you have to borrow the 50 rupees from Leeladhar, Nandu or Arjun Das at the shop.

08.15. You go to have your bath at the common bathroom in the backyard. You have a good wash after a vigorous rub of Lifebuoy soap. You like everything to be clean, spic and span. You always have your nails all clipped and shining. "It might not be possible to keep one's mind free of dirt; so at least let the body be clean," is your motto. For days after your nikah—your marriage—you bathed using only Rexona soap. Taj Begum loved Rexona soap. The entire house smelled of it when she came out of her bath. That was how much soap she used. But she had a tendency to sweat a lot. She was always covered in sweat. Those days, she bathed once at night as well. The smell of her sweat mixed with the aroma of Rexona soap made you go nuts. You pushed your nose between her breasts that looked like two large pears, inhaled the scent and laughed. Taj Begum enjoyed your adoration of her, but would pout in pretence, pat your cheek fondly and say, "Yeh kya badhthaameezi?" But now everything has changed. I will write a letter to Taj Begum today, you decide.

08.45. You are walking along Oppanakkara Street on your way to the shop. Buses are blaring out movie songs and two- and four-wheeled vehicles have begun to race helter-skelter across the road. As the day advances, the smoke and sound will increase. The road seems to have shrunk from what it was before. You say salaam to all the familiar faces you come across and continue towards your destination. From his perch at the till, Ganashyam, the proprietor of Hotel Kailash, calls out, "Kya pehelwan, sab khairiyath tho hai na?" and continues with his counting of money.

Nandu crosses the road to join you just as you reach the shop. The manager, Tikam Das, is expected only at 10 o'clock. Nandu is the one to open the shop. Nandu does not have any shoulder problem, yet he always walks with his right shoulder raised a little, as if he had a catch there.

Nandu has a prominent nose on his broad face. So, behind his back, people refer to him as Garuda, the holy vulture. When you bend down along with him to raise the shutters of the shop, the stench of the Charminar cigarette that he has just smoked assails you.

09.15. The shop boy Shanmugam is done with his job of sweeping the shop. Nandu waves lighted camphor in front of the pictures of Lakshmi, Guru Nanak and Siva, gets done with the job of propitiating them for the day. Nandu, Arjun Das, Veeru are all at their respective counters. Now the boxes have to be taken off the racks one by one, dusted and kept ready for inspection by the buyers. You are in charge of the "Ladies and Children" section. All the lower-middle class customers and those who come from the nearby villages get sent down to you. Your simple appearance will put them at ease and make them talk to you without any inhibitions. They are certain to fall for your engaging talk and buy some gown or underskirt. Leeladhar, Arjun Das or Veeru will be attending to the upper-class, urbanised, fashionable customers. Your manager Tikam Das thinks you have neither the ability nor appearance to handle such high-end customers.

Today is the day when the showcase decorations have to be changed and a new arrangement set up. You are assigned to that job. Shanmugam will assist you. This will take up three to four hours of your time. One by one, you remove the dresses displayed last week and empty the showcase. Shanmugam enters the showcase-cubicle and begins to rub the glass doors—after first sprinkling water on them—with scraps of Malai Murasu newspaper. You instruct him, insisting that he should remove all the insect droppings that make tiny dots all across the glass. Even as he is busy getting the showcase clean, you neatly fold the clothes you have taken out. Then you enter the showcase again and give Shanmugam a packet of sacred ash, Kanda Vilas vibhoothi. You tell him to make a paste of the vibhoothi, rub it all over the glass, leave it on for some minutes and then wipe the glass clean. You choose the dresses that are to be put out on display this week.

After Shanmugam finishes his work and makes his exit, you set up the background with some dupattas that are part of salwar-kameez suits and blouse pieces. You then quickly go about hanging different kinds of baba-suits and other men's clothes everywhere. The black mannequin who adorns the centre of the showcase was dressed in a salwar-kameez last week. So this week you choose a nightdress made of translucent material. The pale pink nightie you drape on that doll with nipple-less breasts and a void between her thighs fits her perfectly. You playfully pinch her hole-less marble nose.

By the time you step out of the showcase, clothes are spread out on all the counters. A good many customers must have visited the shop.

It is 13.00 hours. You hasten to the mosque. Though the heat is not severe, you are not able to walk as fast as you used to. You had hydrocele before your marriage; like two huge palm fruits your testicles would toss and make walking difficult for you. Yet you could walk faster than now.

13.45. Iqbal is drawing pictures on an old notebook with a sketch pen. Iqbal can draw very well. Today he has drawn a cottage with a wicker fence, surrounded by a vast expanse of grassland in which there roams a young deer under clouds in the sky, a few birds and in a corner, the sun. Everything looks nice except that the deer's face looks like a dog's.

"What price have you set on this villa, janab?"

"We don't sell this for anything less than a thousand rupees. Since you are my Mamu, I shall give it to you for one rupee."

"Does that include the price of the little deer as well?"

"NO. The little one is not for sale."

"Why so, janab? Is there any ban on selling it?"

"We are not allowed to sell the little deer."

"What do we do then? From whom should we get the permission to buy it?"

"We have to take the little one's mother's permission."

"That can be done; but where is the mother?"

"I have yet to make her."

"Shall I come back tomorrow?"

"No, come next Friday."

You gather Iqbal in your arms. Both of you burst out laughing.

After you have changed, Ammijan serves both of you food. You eat whatever there is of the rice to which she had added some seasoning and a boiled egg. Your hunger is not appeased. You drink some water and lie down on the mat.

15.05. Tikam Das has gone away to have his lunch. Nandu stands near the counter, one shoulder raised a little. Leeladhar, Arjun Das and Veeru sit in a corner on wooden stools, listening to some folk songs on the radio. They perk up on seeing you.

Leeladhar, "Have you eaten, Mehboob?"

Mehboob, "Don't we eat every day?"

Arjun Das, "Don't be so forlorn. Is your wife still away at her mother's place?"

Mehboob, "I am not sad or anything."

Leeladhar, "When is she coming back?"

Mehboob, "Next week."

Leeladhar, "How does your Begum get through her nights without you?"

Mehboob, "Chee! What kind of talk is this?"

Leeladhar, "What 'chee chee'? You don't know them! These vixens might act as if they have no desires at all. You have to be smart and get the job done properly. You have to make them moan, 'Enough! Enough!' As soon as your joru comes back this should be your priority. I have gone through it all, so listen to me."

Leeladhar was fond of going to the late-night movies. He would go to a second show at least four days in a week. Somehow Leeladhar's wife got involved with an auto driver. That man "who knew all the routes" would arrive the minute Leeladhar left the house. One day Leeladhar came home early because he could not get a ticket to watch the movie and the wife and auto driver were caught red-handed. The issue became serious and led to the threshold of divorce. Everything got sorted out only after Leeladhar's father-in-law begged him to forgive his daughter and forget the incident. Leeladhar's wife, Sheelu, was short and very fair complexioned. If you saw her you would think that this cat would never even want to taste a little milk. Her face was deceptively innocent.

The conversation takes different directions and veers all round. Suddenly, Arjun Das says, "Let all that be. You recite some poem, Mehboob."

Mehboob, "What fancy poetry do I know? Everything I know is old, nothing new."

Arjun Das, "That's alright, old means old, so be it. Recite any one of them."

Mehboob, "Naa Baba! I have to write a letter."

Arjun Das, "To whom?"

Leeladhar, "Who else would it be but his wife?"

Veeru, "Stop making all this fuss. Recite one poem and then go write your letter."

You give it some thought and get ready with some preliminary actions necessary to recite a poem.

No hold have I on life
Neither any grievance
I am not a simpleton to hate it
But today
At the evening of my youth
I stand on one bank of silence.
Merciless time flows in spate
To rest in centuries
On the other bank loneliness comes down in rain
My dear friend, Mehboob asks, what
else is life if not loneliness and silence?

Even as you are reciting the last line, those around you begin to cry out, "Wah! Wah!"

16.00. "Bhen chod" Bhagavan Das arrives asking, "Has Tikam Das come yet?" The Hindi phrase "bhen chod" means "sister fucker." But Bhagavan Das is not the kind to do anything like that; moreover he is 75 years old. It is just that he is in the habit of using the term, "bhen chod" on an average of once every ten seconds, so it has become the prefix to his name. The man, who lives in Ainthmukku, has a readymade garments factory in Uppara Street. On his way to the factory he registers his presence at this shop day after day. He is very close to our proprietor Kishan Chand and the manager Tikam Das. He comes and sits for awhile, keeps up a monologue unmindful of whether anyone listens to him or not.

Today his topic is a certain sales tax officer.

"Bhen chod! Tax you must, who can refute it? You specify the amount and I pay it. But do you have to be flinging the accounts ledgers all around? You want some bribe? I agree to give it. Bhen chod! Ministers, MPs, MLAs . . . all have their share of the loot. So you want some of it as well. Bhen chod, that is fair. But don't dare say that my accounts are cooked up. I fled from Pakistan in just my torn pajamas. In 1948, I sold pepper pappads in Colaba, bhen chod, to climb my way up. If I'm lying, bhen chod, God will not forgive me."

With one shoulder raised, Nandu is listening to him with a smile. After a while, Bhagavan Das calls out to Shanmugam, "Boy! Get me a glass of water. Bhen chod, this heat . . ." and gets up from his chair.

16.30. You begin to write a letter with your head bent over a white sheet of paper at the "Socks and Ties" counter.

To my dearer than life Taj, endowed with the softness of a thousand roses and the charm of a thousand moons, here is your slave Mehboob penning this missive. We are well here. May Allah keep you and your people well there.

The house seems empty without you. But in a way, it is good that you are not here now. The condition in our house is nothing to boast about. I have not had my ironing job for the past couple of weeks.

Rice, dal and wheat have all been used up. Yesterday Ammijan had gone to Kottaimedu to visit Noor Chithi. She sent us some two dozen eggs and some fish. Other than that we have been just about managing, borrowing five or ten rupees from Karim Thatha. Today I have borrowed 50 rupees from Leeladhar. Only after we have been paid our salary the day after tomorrow will we get some breathing space.

Iqbal is well. He assists Ammijan in so many little ways, crawling as he has to, all around the place. Yesterday, heedless of Ammijan's remonstrations, he ironed my pants and shirt. He has drawn a picture of Abbajan, with a photo to guide him. It is Iqbal who misses you the most, even more than I do. He keeps constantly moaning with a sorrowful face asking, "When will Mamijan come?" Though he did not come out of your womb, he is very much your son. Every time I see his legs, my heart trembles, lamenting, "Should Allah's darbar mete out such justice?"

It is very clear that Ammijan is not able to cope with all she has to do. But she stoically manages to carry on. Last week I had taken her to the "Big Hospital" for a check-up. They made her take many tests because they suspect she may have cancer of the uterus. The test results will be given to us only on Monday. Whatever they are, the doctors say that it is better to remove her uterus. If you return soon, we can begin to make arrangements for the surgery. Unable to bear the pain in her lower abdomen, she curls up on the floor ever so often. It is heart-rending to see her lying all bundled like a baby. She will be 65 next month.

How is your Abbajan's health condition? I hope he has his sugar levels under control. I also hope that your brothers are all doing well.

My salaams to your Abbajan and my love to all others.

Your

Mehboob Khan

16.45. It is time for the manager to return. Nandu lights a clump of incense sticks and takes them around the shop waving it in front of all the pictures of gods, the till, all the counters and racks. The customers trickle in.

19.30. Having sold some 16 vests with sleeves, 7 underskirts, 6 panties, a dozen handkerchiefs, 2 baba-suits and 5 frocks to different customers, you go out to have a tea. After a cup of tea at Nambiar's teashop, you light up a beedi. Puffing at it, you go into the big bazaar, past the wholesale sellers of potatoes and onions right up to the end where the grocery shops are. You walk back, tossing a smile to Mahendran Chettiar standing at the entrance of Rajeswari Hall.

20.00. Not many customers are around at the shop; it is all very quiet. You go to the shirt counter to help Leeladhar fold the shirts that have been unfolded for customers' inspection. As on all other days, the proprietor Kishan Chand—followed by his wife in a white nylon sari and a white sleeveless blouse—comes into the shop carrying a bag full of vegetables.

Tikam Das gets up from his seat. After they both sit opposite each other at the payment counter, Shanmugam, as usual, brings them glasses of water. Kishan Chand lights up a beedi even as he turns the pages of the accounts book.

20.30. Crushing the butt of his third beedi into the ashtray, Kishan Chand gets up from his seat. A few minutes later, the shop-lights are switched off. Nandu begins to enter the figures of the bill book into the adding machine at the cash counter.

You send Shanmugam to the KK block to get a masala vadai for the mouse trap. There are some three or four rats in your shop. Thieves and traitors all!

20.45. The day's sales have fetched 18,437 rupees. Not worth any mention. Kishan Chand always says that the daily sales should be 0.75 percent of the total value of stocks in the shop. You turn off the showcase lights and begin to take down the sample garments hung high up facing the entrance.

Suddenly, you see Bhagavan Das standing inside the shop. He tells the manager, "Did you hear the news, Tikam? Some serious riot in Ukkadam. Seems someone stabbed someone else. Close the shop quickly, before some trouble flares up. This country will never come up, bhen chod, only a military regime will set things right."

21.10. The shop is closed. You are on your way home. You notice a sudden spurt of uneasiness on the street. The doors of the shops are being shut one by one in quick succession. The streets suddenly look deserted. Shanmugam and you begin walking faster. Shanmugam lives in Perur. He has to go up to the B1 police station and take a bus from the stop there. Oppanaikkara Street looks deserted. You use the fifty rupees borrowed from Leeladhar to buy a full-sized bread and some dry chops. Variety Hall Road seems comparatively less affected. Karim Thatha, who is sitting on the thinnai, says, "I heard there was trouble at Ukkadam."

"Nothing seems to be the matter on our side. Yet the shops have all been closed."

21.45. As always, Iqbal is waiting to have his dinner with you. Ammijan has made some chapattis and potato kurma. Together with the chops that you brought home, the three of you finish your dinner. You give the forty rupees that is left in your pocket to Ammijan and come out to the thinnai to have a smoke.

22.30. You close the front door and come in. Iqbal is asleep. You go lie down by his side. After a couple of minutes you hug him close.

The next day.

08.45. You sit outside on the thinnai browsing over Dhastaghir's newspaper. Iqbal sits by your side watching the happenings on the street. Dhastaghir has gone off to his mechanic's shop. His parents are expected to return from their village this afternoon. Ammijan is inside the house. Karim Thatha is having his bath. You wonder if at least today you will get to iron clothes at Tip Top dry cleaners. Since it is a Sunday, there is not much activity on the road. Everything is so peaceful.

09.15. Some loud noises are heard from the western side. You hear sounds as if people are hitting at and breaking down the shutters of all the closed shops. You also hear frenzied voices. You hurry to the street climbing down from the thinnai. You see a huge mass of people entering your street from the Oppanakkarai street junction.

Raising fearsome slogans the crowd walks slowly onto your street. Each one in that crowd is carrying something in his hand—sticks, rollers, kerosene cans. You are bewildered.

Seeing you standing in the middle of the street, the crowd runs in your direction, shouting all kinds of foul words and abuses.

What has happened? Who are these people? Why are they in such frenzy here? You stand there totally confused. All you realise is that you are in some danger. You run to pick up Iqbal. You think that you can escape the mob if you run to Nawab Hakim Road. But before you can do that, the crowd is all around you. Iqbal is clutching your neck tightly.

Many in that crowd have come all bathed and clean shaven. They are in sleeved vests and khaki half pants. They hoist their sticks and rods up above their heads and shout slogans. A young, fair-complexioned man with broad shoulders and a thin moustache, frowning with his forehead and brows wrinkled, gnashing his teeth, is running towards you with his baton raised in his hand.

The first blow descends on the nape of your neck. You break out into a cry, "Amma!" Your breath comes faster. Your senses are sharpened. You lose your balance and slide forward. The next blow is on the centre of your head. Blood gushes forth from your head. Somebody snatches Iqbal and flings him away. Screaming, he falls somewhere in the distance. You raise your head. Your forehead is all covered in blood. Your eyes roll; another blow is aimed at your neck and left cheek. Your left cheek is torn and the flesh is hanging out; blood is bubbling out of here as well. Unable to bear the pain you fall down raising a scream. Even before your body touches the ground, more hard blows are showered on you. You have been completely knocked down now. Many legs stamp on you. Many more attack you with their rods and boards. You have fainted.

You realize you are very close to death. No other thought is in you in that moment when you are in the presence of death.

Have they killed Iqbal?

What is going to happen to Ammijan, cooking in her kitchen?

Will they burn Karim Thatha alive even while he bathes? Will they smash up Dhastaghir's house?

How is Taj Begum?

You just die, without any thought for the young deer that Iqbal had drawn, Fashion Palace, Shanmugam, Veeru, Nandu, Arjun Das, Leeladhar, Tikam Das, Kishan Chand, Bhagavan Das, Tip Top Dry Cleaners, Mubarak Tea Stall, Mangalore Ganesh Beedi, Begum Akthar, Suraiyya, your as yet unwritten poems . . . You die without any of this coming up in your consciousness.

You are dead.

The chronological minute-by-minute diary narrative Kumar uses reflects that ordered existence of this one significant day, the day of Mehboob's death at the hand of rioters. Yet the details of the riots and racial and religious conflicts are spare, unlike the copious details of what Mehboob does that day. The last line, "You are dead" is all the more chilling for the matter-of-fact manner in which it's delivered. There's an effective dissonance created in the knowledge that the "you" being addressed, Mehboob, has lost the ability to process knowledge such as his own death, and only the "you" who is the reader can understand and be horrified by it.

Many writers want to address, in our fiction, the larger conflicts we witness in the world around us. At the time of writing, the Covid-19 crisis is a worldwide phenomenon that has upended many lives. Right now, many are busily writing stories about plagues, deadly viruses, apocalyptic scenarios of thousands of people dying from uncontrolled infections. The same happens in the face of political and social unrest when suddenly, everyone tries to write a story about heroes and victims caught up in whatever turmoil rages, replete with details about the turmoil. But will these make the most memorable fiction, especially when thousands of journalists are already telling us what is actually happening, in real time, with interviews of real heroes and victims, as well as analysis by experts and political observers?

Instead, as fiction writers we do better by writing the stories that resonate *regardless* of the specific historical, political, social, environmental, or medical calamity. This is the brilliance of Kumar's story. By immersing us in the minutiae of this one day in an ordinary man's life, the insanity of his death, by complete strangers who attack him viciously, is deepened. For example, early in the morning before he awakens, we see him in a perfect moment, rendered all the more tragic by the fate that awaits him:

> You are now lying down curled up like a question mark. Your front teeth peep out of your darkened lips. Your face displays supreme peace. In deep slumber, you look like an innocent, helpless being, a sight that induces and seeks great love from any beholder.

Kumar's use of the second-person POV simultaneously establishes both a distance and an intimacy. On the one hand this narrative omniscience presages Mehboob's fate with a continual foreboding commentary of which the protagonist is not entirely cognizant: the sky offers "a melancholy beauty"; when he looks at the photo of a beautiful actress and singer, we learn that "Allah seems to have turned all the sorrows of the world into nerves and placed them in her throat, you feel"; he is short of money so food is scarce and "you eat whatever there is of the rice to which she (the housekeeper) had added some seasoning and a boiled egg. Your hunger is not appeased." At the same time, we become embroiled in his most intimate moments: when he awakens "your movements wake Fahtima up. She has been doing this, unfailingly, for the past 42 years"; his nephew crawls out to the yard and calls out, "Mamu! Mamu! You wash his bottom and put his shorts on him. Iqbal's lifeless legs feel cold to the hands, like dead lumps"; he recalls his wife after they first got married and how much she loved to use Rexona soap and "the smell of her sweat mixed with Rexona soap made you go nuts. You pushed your nose between her breasts that looked like two large pears, inhaled the scent and laughed." As his day unfurls, we see him surrounded by the frenetic energy of the city, and learn the many duties he must fulfill. By the time he is surrounded by his killers, and "you realise you are very close to death," his only thoughts are about the people he cares about, and none of the obsessive details of his daily work and life.

While we may not know the history of the racial and religious conflicts in India, the story showcases this quiet clerk, making him memorable. And the bonus is that we can learn all the details of culture, language, and geography Kumar inserts because of the specificity of his references that evoke this one day and place and time through the death of this man.

* * *

We are often tempted to use special occasions as the setting for a story. Family celebrations such as births, weddings, graduations, and public or religious holidays such as New Year's Day, Eid al-Fitr, Easter, Yom Kippur, Vesak are all occasions that lend themselves to stories. But a mistake writers sometimes make is to simply describe the festivities or customs the characters engage in, which, however interesting, would be better suited to a feature story about the holiday. Instead, the real reason to use such celebratory or commemorative occasions is the possibility they offer for conflict (especially in family occasions), the unexpected emotions such times arouse and the meaning that can be gleaned about the very nature of the occasion or holiday.

In Jeremy Tiang's story, "National Day," a group of construction workers go for a visit to St. John's Island on the evening before Singapore's national day. These men are a subgroup, virtually invisible to this first world country's residents—because they come from poorer Asian nations, speak marginal English (the official language in Singapore), and are drawn together as construction workers and their shared alienation from mainstream society. As in "The Clerk's Story," the events occur on one specific day but the omniscient POV here is the plural first person and thus initially appears to be the group's storyteller. But the *voice* is entirely that of a narrator who speaks in a different key, even while retaining the emotional tenor of the "Little Fish" group who are confronted by the failure of hope on this day. This is an important aspect of truly omniscient stories. Flannery O'Connor once remarked that an omniscient narrator is like another unnamed character with their own voice and diction. One of our favorite examples of this is John Cheever's short story, "The Wrysons," about an unbearably straight-laced and bourgeois couple living in Westchester County in the early 1960s. The omniscient narrator is so disdainful of his characters that he spends the entire long first paragraph of the story lambasting them and telling us how utterly boring they are. His choice of words for them, however, are anything but boring, and he proceeds to tell us a hilarious story about one night when they inadvertently reveal their true selves to one another.

In Tiang's story, the construction workers are journeying to St. John's off the coast of Singapore to get a good view of the air show and fireworks. We follow the group as they line up, board the boat, arrive at the island, find a space to perch to witness the country's annual celebration. As a *journey narrative*, the protagonist, in this case the collective "we," must encounter an obstacle or challenge to be overcome at each step of the journey, which happens in "National Day." Journeys in classic literature, such as *The Odyssey* or Monkey's *Journey to the West* or James Joyce *Ulysses*, all follow this pattern and can be thought of as a series of episodes that lead to the journey's end.

The beauty of this story is that at every step of the journey, the very concept of a national day and public holiday, which should be celebratory with time off, is subverted. From the start, we know that this is not much time off for them, because "tomorrow is a public holiday, so we will start work later than usual, not for our sakes but because the residents complain if construction starts too early while they are asleep." Right away, there is the tension of "us," these migrant construction workers, and "them," the Singaporeans. To board the ferry, they pass "the Formica counters with their bored, resentful clerks, punished for one infraction or another with a holiday shift," and we recognize that these men understand exactly what life is like for the other "Little Fish" they encounter. They also decide to board without buying a ticket as Arul says they only check on the way back, and they listen to Neelish who wants to take the risk because "always we end up listening to him."

Now let's read Jeremy Tiang's story "National Day" from his award-winning collection *It Never Rains on National Day*. This story can be read as a running commentary on the inequities between the condition of life for these "Little Fish" men and the country that employs them.

But what also emerges alongside this critique is their homesickness, their alienation, their hope for something better from this work they do.

2 "National Day"

by Jeremy Tiang (Singapore)

Jeremy Tiang is a novelist, playwright, and translator from Chinese. His books include the short story collection, *It Never Rains on National Day*, as well as the novel, *State of Emergency*, which won the Singapore Literature Prize in 2019. He is a member of the translation collective Cedilla & Co.

> So we take a boat to St John's Island because where else can we go, every other place will be crowded and just for one night we want to leave the dormitories, the noise and stink of eight bodies pressed into each small room, just for a few hours we want to escape. Tomorrow is a public holiday so we will start work later than usual, not for our sakes but because the residents complain if construction starts too early while they are still asleep, and the foreman will not say anything if we are back at the site before ten.
>
> Even the ferry terminal is packed, this country is so small that people slosh around and are pushed into each corner. We gather near the bus stop, most of us arriving together from the site but some also from other errands. Antony's girlfriend Veronica has come to see him off, to snatch a few extra minutes with him, and we pretend to look away but still hoot when they kiss. She is embarrassed but smiles gamely, a friendly girl. He waves her onto the bus and strides over to us, a heavy plastic bag tugging at one arm, and we are complete.
>
> We walk past the Formica counters with their bored, resentful clerks, punished for one infraction or another with a holiday shift. Arul has been before with one of the young things he carts around, and he says they only check tickets on the way back, sometimes you can talk your way out of it, say you lost the stub. We are unsure if this will work for so many of us but Neelish says *Come on, let's take the risk,* and as always we end up listening to him.
>
> There are a few piers with boats going in different directions, some to Indonesia, some closer by, and we follow the lines down, looking for our berth. Most of the passengers are local and Neelish says, *Look, at them running away from their own birthday party, what kind of people are they, that would never happen back at home.* We try to shush him but he chatters on. Few heads turn to look at us, no one cares what we have to say.
>
> The boat is smaller than we expected, even smaller than a bus, but somehow it contains all of us effortlessly. To the front are young men with plastic fishing boxes and sheaves of gear, and the rest of the space is occupied by teenagers in identical red T-shirts, maybe twenty or thirty of them. We sit on a bench facing back towards the mainland, clearing a space for Jairam's crutches, leaning across each other to talk in our mixture of languages, fractured English and Tamil and Bengali, reaching for whatever words we can find to make ourselves understood. Around us the sailors coil ropes and pull gates shut.

Something slackens and then we are moving, slowly at first and then juddering faster. A cool spray rises as we move past the other boats, then leaving the concrete embrace of the harbor behind for the relief of open water. The sun is not setting yet but the shadows are long, and the tall buildings of the city are at their most attractive, glittering as brightly as the water. They look like beautiful toys, like we could reach out and pluck them from where they stand, the great wheel of the Flyer, the three reaching fingers of the casino, the hard-angled glass and steel of the CBD.

We gape and take pictures if we have cameras on our phones. Mohan points at the lotus flower museum and shouts, *Look, I built that*. Ah, we laugh at him, *but have you ever been inside*, knowing he hasn't because who could afford that admission fee and just to look at old porcelain or some foreign painting? Still, we cannot resist doing it too, calling out what we've made, office buildings, skyscraping banks, the Gardens by the Bay with their giant metal trees. *That's mine, I built that*. Despite ourselves, we feel a flicker of something at being a part of this machine, and having operated the cranes and laid the bricks that brought the great city into being.

The boat pulls past Sentosa Cove but it takes us a moment to recognize it, knowing that the houses there cost fifty million dollars at least, as expensive as the moon. From this side they look merely grubby, washed-out pastels behind a scrubby screen of trees, not the palaces we imagined, but then nothing human-made could look well against the blue-green sea, its neat triangular waves in parallel lines as regular as a child's drawing.

Our conversation sputters and we fall into a lull, hypnotized as the mainland slips away and there is space, as if someone has drawn a circle a mile across and placed us alone in its center. The trip takes less than an hour, and soon we are passing the giant oil drums of Pulau Bukum, the twin green hillocks of the Sisters Islands, and then St John's, its name inscribed in white letters on the slope approaching us, slightly overgrown with grass.

The fishermen are ready to disembark first, leaping onto the jetty before the boat has quite docked, juggling heavy bait boxes and carbon rods, then the teenagers form an orderly line and troop ashore, breaking off in clusters for a photograph under the welcome arch. We are the last to disembark but that is fine, we are not in a hurry and it is easier to maneuver Jairam on shore without other people in the way. The crew stand with one foot on the step and the other on land, either side of us, holding the boat in place.

We stand for a moment, telling ourselves this is still Singapore, and yet it is not, this is more like home, so many trees, such silence. A tidy path leads away from the dock and we obediently follow it. There is nothing to the island, it can barely be half a mile in each direction. There is a small hill at one end with a campsite at its peak, where we can see the teenagers shucking their rucksacks, standing in a circle and holding hands. From a safe distance as we amble, a couple of scrawny cats eye us and we wonder what it must be like to come here maybe on a boat, only to find there is nothing, no food, no way back. Mohan, soft-hearted, throws them the remains of a banana from his pocket, but they wait till we are far away before darting up to it.

There are signboards all along the path, green and white and yellow, and Feroz snorts, *These people don't know what to do unless there are black and white words to instruct them, they don't dare wipe their own backsides without government approval*. We stare at the different-sized rectangles, making out the words do not pluck flowers no fishing beyond this point warning no lifeguard on duty.

Looping back to the beach as the sun rests off the top of the tallest buildings on the horizon, we find a place to settle. A floating rope twenty meters from land cordons off the safe swimming area but we wouldn't want to go in anyway, the water here is oil-slicked and gritty, and even the beach is fouled from the ships passing by and the refinery. We sit on towels and sarongs, anything we thought to bring.

Antony pulls from his plastic bag biscuits and fruit and other things that Veronica gets from her ma'am, she says they are given but maybe she just takes them, we don't ask, although the bread is hard and the apples starting to brown and soften, they would just go to waste otherwise. We are grateful because the canteen is closed on holiday evenings and we haven't had dinner yet.

What time do they start? says Feroz, it is his first National Day here and he is as excited as a child. *Soon soon,* we tell him, *eat some fruit, uncle.* We call him that because he is older than us, probably too old to be on a construction site but he lied to the recruiting agent who didn't care as long as he got his cut. What else can he do? It's the last chance for him, scraping together three lakh rupees to cover all the fees, hoping he can stay here long enough to earn that back and make a little more, not much, enough to retire on, hoping he is one of the lucky ones, not like Jairam, not like the ones who come back still in debt, the hollowed-out men every village has.

A wave breaks unexpectedly high and Jairam flinches. We tell him not to worry, we are above the high water mark, and Neelish says, *Yes, but if you're not nice to us we'll roll you down the beach, see if you can swim with one leg.* Neelish has been taking steady nips from a small bottle containing we don't want to ask what, but from the heat rising off him it must be samsu or toddy, something strong. Eat some bread, we tell him, something to soak up the alcohol, but he barely puts any in his mouth, rolling the rest into little pellets that he flicks into the waves.

What if it rains? says Arul, but it won't, it never rains on National Day. We have heard that they seed the clouds a week before to dry them out. The sky is a clean blue bowl, the thin moon just visible. Even with wind blowing off the sea, the air is blood-warm and heavy around us. *Look,* says Feroz, who has not taken his eyes off the skyline, and he is right, something has started, a hum of thirty thousand people's excitement that we can feel even from here, and then fighter jets buzzing low over the city, apparently just missing half a dozen buildings and disgorging crimson parachutists billowing plumes of colored smoke behind them. *Showing off,* sniffs Neelish, but even he is unable to take his eyes off the tiny falling figures.

Gouts of music come to us, distorted by the wind, something jaunty with a thumping beat as if we are in a nightclub, and then some kind of military band. *That's the army marching in,* says Sundram, who watched the whole thing on a coffeeshop TV last year. The rest of us have only seen moments, repeats in the news and pictures in the papers the next day. Guns are fired in quick sequence, pop pop pop pop, and there is more cheering. It is getting dark now. We pile up driftwood and palm leaves and newspapers from the bins, and Antony manages to get the fire going with his lighter, looking a bit shifty as he pulls it out because Veronica's always asking him to quit, he should, cigarettes are so expensive in this city. We don't really have any food to heat up although Arul makes a half-hearted attempt to toast some bread on a stick. The temperature will drop quickly now the sun is gone, and it's comforting to huddle around the glow and warmth.

I recognize this tune, says Feroz, brow furrowed, and we laugh, *Of course you do, uncle, it's that one. The theme song of this year,* it's been played everywhere, on radio and at train stations, something something island sunshine home, syrupy and bland even in these choppy bursts. *Did you know the whole thing costs them seventeen million dollars every year?* says Neelish, who spends his money at Internet cafés looking up facts like these. *Imagine it, so much money for such bad music.* What would we be doing, on an ordinary night? Sitting on our beds, ignoring the others around us loud on their disposable phones, or lying with heads under our pillows waiting for sleep to take us into another day, a step closer to return. Our few hours here feel stolen, an escape from normality rather than a return to it, as if our other lives have been utterly erased, as if there is nothing left but the scaffolding that we climb up and down all day, our feet never on solid ground.

From up the hill behind us comes the sound of teenagers singing at the camp: *Christ is the Lord of all.* They have just one guitar, equally tuneless, their dirge as deadening as what drifts to us across the water, now back to the band music, pink and green floodlights shooting up into the darkening sky and swaying in time to the beat. Mohan the clown howls like a dog, his impression so unexpectedly accurate that we laugh all over again.

A branch in the fire releases a burst of sparks and we jump. Even with the neon lines of the city back the way we came, there is something primal in the air, as if the noises on the mainland are the crashes and screams of war and we are the only ones who made it out, refugees crouched around our campfire as dark shadows approach. Many-limbed banyan trees stoop above the beach, their tendrils trembling even when the breeze dies down.

What next? says Feroz, but we do not know. Is this one of the years when they bring in the tanks, or will there just be more children dancing? Maybe the tanks are only for when one of the neighboring countries needs frightening. Not us, our countries are too poor to attack this island, however small it may be, and how could our governments drop bombs on this city when so many of their own citizens are working here?

We stare out to sea as if we can actually follow the show, even though all we can see from here are the leftovers, lasers flicking across neighboring buildings, helicopters hovering, speedboats churning by close to shore after finishing their turns by the floating platform. Celebrations in our own countries are not so choreographed, so tightly managed. How much fun can they be having? Yet we hear the clapping and stamping from across the water.

Jairam quietly rubs lotion into the stump of his knee, which must be giving him pain, though we have never heard him complain. Antony waves his mobile phone around until he finds reception and has a whispered conversation with Veronica, asking what she's doing and whether she misses him, and the rest of us think of women, girls we left behind in our villages who may or may not be waiting for us, maids or masseuses we encountered here now gone back or departed for countries even further away from their own. We feel not loneliness exactly, but a hollowness in the vicinity of the chest, a helplessness heightened by the wide ocean and starless infinity of the sky above us.

The fishermen are giving up now, walking past with a few tiny specimens dangling from strings. They flung their rods from the causeway over to Lazarus Island, but now are moving back inland. Some seem to live in the kampong huts by the foot of the hill—caretakers? we wonder—and others are at the holiday bungalows, local boys who probably wear G2000 shirts and ties all week and are using the break to flee for a day, to fish and lie in the sun while they can, before responsibility and time thicken their waists and weigh them down. Some look in our direction as they pass but no one speaks to us.

We are getting a little bored, though no one will admit this, but even boredom is a luxury, to be so still that we wish to move again. Some of us look at our phones, others build small sandcastles with plastic cups. The parade doesn't hold much interest for us, at the moment it will be more dancing that we can't see, hundreds of children or civil servants or volunteers running across the stage in neoprene costumes, telling some version of a story that doesn't include us.

Sandaled feet crunch decisively across the sand and then a handful of the teenagers are standing a safe distance away, looking ready to run. A slightly older man, maybe twenty, wearing the same red T-shirt as his charges steps towards us, his voice whiny but trenchant as he says, *What are you doing?*

We are uncertain how to answer, it seems too obvious, so we say nothing, and stare at our feet or at him, and he continues, *You're not allowed to camp here, and you shouldn't light a fire, can't you read the signs?*

You're camping here too, points out Antony, but the man pretends not to hear. He says, *It could be dangerous, I have a whole group of teenagers here, we shouldn't have to put up with this after paying for the use of our campsite, all your illegal activity.*

We say, several of us at once, *We're next to the water, how can it be dangerous, we know what we're doing, do you really think the fire will rush up the hill and burn you?* Not all of us speak English but we try our best to make ourselves understood, waving and pointing to show what we mean. The man's face clenches around the edges and he says, *Okay, I'm asking you guys nicely, please get off this island now.*

This isn't your island, mutters Jairam from the ground, the only one who hasn't stood up, and Arul says, *How, how, you tell me, the last boat for the day has left, you expect us to swim back to land, is it?*

The teenagers have been whispering amongst themselves, and now one of them comes over to the leader, a narrow-faced girl with a wispy fringe and pink plastic glasses, maybe fourteen, her skinny legs awkwardly connecting gym shorts and white ankle socks. The man curves his arm protectively without actually touching her, as if some kind of barrier was needed between us. *Do you need help, Wilson?* she says.

Give me your phone, he says, and when she hands it over he brandishes it in our direction, gripping it so tightly the veins in his forearm stand out. He says, *I can call the police, is that what you want, just one phone call and the police will come and catch you, and you can kiss your work permit goodbye.*

Go ahead and call, says Neelish, walking forward in a manner that is not exactly threatening but certainly not friendly. *Call your police, do you think we're scared, you think they'll come out specially to catch us, everyone's busy at the parade and all, even the coast guard boats are over there, but you can try, I don't think we're so important that they'll come out here just for us, and you're not so important either.*

The girl flinches as if he has smacked her, and the grouped teenagers rustle like they want to say something but do not dare. *You people*, says the man, *you people coming here, we let you into our country and you just take advantage, shouting and making noise and leaving your rubbish anywhere. When will you learn that we have laws here? If you don't like to obey our rules you can just go back home, go away.*

You think you're so clean, we're the ones who clean up after you, sneers Neelish, and we all nod because it is true, we have seen how dirty the streets are each day, how the troops of sweepers clean them just before dawn. We see this and think we are lucky to at least be doing our work, making something that will last, not vanishing unremarked with the sunlight.

We are all motionless now, we have faced people like this before, whenever we try to rest in a park or under a block of flats they come and tell us to leave, not to make the place untidy, not to sit so close to their children. But now there truly is nowhere for us to go, and we wait to see what this man will say. He is a child himself, really, and we pity him as his powerlessness dawns on him and he almost weeps to look so helpless in front of his group. *I warned you,* he says, but the energy has gone out of his voice. He kicks hard at the fire, scattering it, and then almost runs away, his sneakers soot-smeared and his charges flocking after him. Their red T-shirts all have a sturdy cross and the name of a church on the back, marked out in tartrazine yellow.

He's the same age as my son, says Feroz, *I don't think he'd dare to talk to his own father like that.* Neelish drops to his knees and says with an unexpectedly soft voice, *Thambi, are you all right?* And we see Jairam brushing the embers off his stump and saying, *Yes, don't worry.* He wasn't able to get out of the way, of course. He is bleeding a little, the skin on his wound is so fragile still, but fortunately the fire doesn't seem to have touched him.

We use any cloth we can find to clean him up, but not the sea water, it's too dirty. *Those people,* says Mohan as the hymns start again up the hill, but we shush him because there is no point being angry, no point saying anything nor wondering if they will actually call, if the police will be waiting at the docks when we go back. No one rebuilds the fire and it dies out, and then there is only amber light from the lampposts by the path, and the glimmer of the moon on us.

I'm fine, says Jairam again, and Neelish says, *You'd better be, we don't have any way to get you off this island, you'd better be fine.* Jairam is pale from having been in the dormitory for the last four months, on only one-third sick pay and our employer arguing about every step of the medical compensation, and we know that he is a long way from fine, but it serves no purpose to talk about it.

There is a streak of stark white light over the city that turns into a starburst of magenta, and then one of green and yellow. *It's started,* says Feroz without enthusiasm. We sit and watch the fireworks as they spiral and dance in the sky, the reason Neelish persuaded us to come to this island, and the view is as impressive as he promised, but they are not for us, and we see now that we were mistaken in thinking we would be able to enjoy them, they are as foreign and untouchable as the gleaming buildings across the bay, as the teenagers now securely behind the fence of their campsite.

The display goes on for about ten minutes, zigzags and circles and arcs. When the last spray has fizzled away, they play more music. At the parade, people will already be starting to leave in order to beat the crowds and on TV the hosts will be screaming, *Happy birthday, Singapore!* We stay where we are, still sitting, looking at the sky where afterimages linger.

After a long time, Jairam speaks. *In the village I come from,* he says, *every year twenty thirty forty men come to Singapore, they pay so many lakh taka to the agents and disappear, sometimes we never see them again, or they come back and still have debts, but one or two of them will send money home and reappear after many years, so rich, gold teeth and all, the only concrete houses we have belong to people like that, and I thought I could be one of them, someone has to be lucky so why not me, why not take the chance, and now.*

He stops there. Neelish looks at him, Neelish who was beside him when the high-tension steel cable snapped and swung free, whipping through Jairam's leg. We know he still wonders whether he could possibly have moved a little faster, pushed his friend out of the way, maybe flung himself into its path. Nothing more for anyone to say.

And so we remain where we are, one by one lying down on the sand, allowing our eyes to shut. Across the water the celebrations trickle to an end, and even though the lights of the city are as bright as before, something else ends, some energy, as Singaporeans remove themselves and return to their flats, happy to have experienced something positive together and ready for a day of rest, a pause in their busy schedules.

And then we are all sleep, except Neelish, who stands and looks at the sea. Feroz snores raspily and Jairam's bad leg twitches, but they do not wake, and Neelish takes careful steps towards the water, leaving his slippers neatly on a rock before he steps into it, still warm even this late at night. He feels coarse sand and pebbles beneath his feet and the greasy sheen of dirty water against his skin but continues, his trousers wet and then his shirt, kicking his legs when they no longer reach the bottom.

When Neelish reaches the floating barrier he ducks under it and then is in the open sea, slight currents pulling him this way and that, the rolling black surface just visible. From this angle, the city buildings seem even higher, even further, but he continues striking out towards them, not looking back, his face tight and angry as if the water has offended him. Now he thrashes his arms and legs in an inexpert way, his energy pouring into the ocean, propelling him forward a few inches at a time. The waves swell and tumble, but he keeps his head above them. It is just under a mile to the mainland. Perhaps he makes it.

There is an almost relentless telling that occurs in this story through the narrative POV. There is no mistaking the attitude the narrator embraces—that these "Little Fish" are marginalized, workers who identify with the similarly invisible street cleaners, who won't admit that this grand celebratory moment they have hyped up to witness has begun to bore them because "even boredom is a luxury, to be so still that we wish to move again" because their lives in Singapore are about working constantly, under difficult conditions, to save enough to go home. All around them, they see the affluence that is out of reach. Yet we are often told that in fiction, we need to "show don't tell." So how is it that Tiang's constant *tell, tell, tell* works for this story?

In part this is due to the specificity of his local references, which provides the reader a close look at these men's lives. Note, for instance, Arul's words: *How, how, you tell me, the last boat for the day has left, you expect us to swim back to land, is it?* The syntax and cadence of that sentence is very "Singlish," the Singaporean English that the locals speak. But even though the "we" is supposedly a collective voice of the group, the *language* is that of a more fluent and knowledgeable voice. Notably, unlike in the Korean story "We That Summer," there is no clearly identifiable "I" of this "we," but the first-person plural achieves some of the same distance and intimacy that occurs in "A Clerk's Story."

The power of this omniscience is the control exercised over each scene in the details selected. For example, the defiantly critical attitude of the group towards Singaporean culture is noted: "Celebrations in our own countries are not so choreographed, so tightly managed. How much fun can they be having? Yet we hear the clapping and stamping from across the water." By juxtaposing what the group believes against the reality of the events, there is no real answer to whether or not their idea of celebratory joy is believable. However, the story is not about believability, but about the divisions in this society that perhaps will never be bridged. It is a bleak hope we are presented with, this wish that coming to Singapore to work as these men do is at best, a belief that "someone has to be lucky so why not me, why not take the chance, and now." It is a provocatively chilling slice of life with "nothing more for anyone to say."

Angelo Lacuesta's story, "An Errand," is about another Little Fish, Moroy, the driver of a businessman referred to only as "Sir." Moroy has delivered Sir and Sir's mistress to the Baguio Country Club, only to be sent back to Manila because Sir has ostensibly forgotten something, a tee-shirt with the image of Mona Lisa on it. He also asks Moroy to bring back Sir's medicine pouch, but almost as an afterthought.

In order to understand how unreasonable this request is, you have to know a little about Manila, Baguio, and the sometimes almost feudal society of the Philippines. Metro Manila is a megalopolis of nearly 25 million people, and the traffic is famously snarled. Baguio is a mountain town, about a three and a half hour drive from Manila if there were no traffic. Known as the Summer Capitol because of its cool climate, it is famous for flowers, strawberries, the homes of the well-heeled, and the Baguio Country Club, built originally during the American colonial period of the country. Here, on its patio, you can observe the wealthy teeing off at the golf course, families enjoying a buffet breakfast, and maybe a general or a senator dining with his mistress. Sometimes, the wealthy send their drivers to the club from Manila just to pick up some loaves of their famous raisin bread. As there are few days in Manila that are absent of traffic, a trip between Manila and Baguio is likely to take six or seven hours, sometimes longer. So, when Sir tells Moroy to go back and fetch a tee-shirt and medicine pouch, it's no small task.

Now that we're sufficiently prepared to embark on this journey, let's ride along with Moroy and Sir.

3 "An Errand"

by Angelo Lacuesta (Philippines)

Angelo R. Lacuesta (a.k.a. Sarge Lacuesta) is a writer and editor in the Philippines and winner of many awards for his short stories, including the Philippine Graphic Award, the Palanca Memorial Award, and the NVM Gonzalez Awards. His most recent book is the graphic story collection, *Stay: 21 Comic Stories*.

> A low, insistent drone came to him first, rising and dipping like the waves he grew up with on Samal Island. Skimming above the waves was a girl's voice, saying *ser, ser, ser*.
>
> Moroy swung his arm up and opened his eyes to look at his watch: 3 a.m. It was his way of checking that it hadn't been stolen. Behind the luminous hands and the starry black dial wasn't a girl but a boy who looked like he was still in high school. *Pebrero* read

the patch on his security guard's uniform. He lightly rapped his knuckles on Moroy's arm, like a timid night janitor knocking on the door to the ladies' CR.

There were seven other men in the room, drivers and minders, a couple of them he knew by face and name. The sound of the sea was the sound of their snoring, their breaths coming hard and stale through all that fat in their throats. He was not on Samal Island. He felt an ache in his own throat and knew he must have been snoring, too.

Whoever put this Pebrero on the night shift must be pulling an inside job, Moroy thought, as he put on his shirt-jack. What could Sir possibly want at this hour? He inhaled audibly as he walked past the boy who was texting. The only staff at the drivers' dormitory, the boy's only real job, it seemed, besides answering the rare landline call and turning away late check-ins, was to switch on the low-watt evening light at the entrance and switch off everything else, the TV and aircon in the lobby. He couldn't possibly keep the drunks and girls away.

Outside, the air had dipped further into the cold of pre-dawn. Moroy put a hand in his pants and squeezed the button on the car key. He pressed another button and the engine started, making a sound softer than the faint sound of snoring that still hung in the air.

The hotel was a five-minute drive from the drivers' dormitories. His windshield was wet. His headlights probed the fog. His wipers were on full. When he drove up to the entrance, Sir was already there, shuffling on the top step, the lobby guard by his arm. He was still dressed in the golf t-shirt and shorts he had worn that morning when they drove up from Manila.

Moroy pressed the window switch. Sir spoke into the gap as soon as it appeared.

"Kunin mo yung t-shirt kong Givenchy, yung may Mona Lisa na design sa harap," he began. He asked if Moroy knew the Mona Lisa, the painting in the Louvre in Paris, the one with the girl, smiling. He showed his teeth when he said *smile*. "I mean, you don't know if she's smiling or not. Get the t-shirt. Bring it here."

"Sa kotse ba sir?" *Is it in the car?*

No, at home came the reply.

"Sa bahay—sa Maynila, sir?"

"Oo. Sa Maynila."

"Yes sir." Moroy blinked as he said it, perhaps a little bit longer than he should have.

"Great!" Sir said, adding, "By the way, bring along my medicine pouch, the small one in the bedside table. My side, not Norma's."

"Yessir." It was time-consuming, expensive, and it all seemed completely unnecessary.

Moroy knew that shirt. He also knew it meant Brenda, the girl who gave Sir that shirt. The girl Sir often personally took home from his office, speaking to her loudly so the security guards and the other drivers could hear that her place was conveniently on the way to theirs. Which was a complete lie. Brenda lived with her mother and her grandmother on Tenth Street in Cubao, which was, on any given hour of the day, a good two or three hours away from Legaspi Village. If they were lucky. Sometimes there was dinner, or a few drinks, on the way to dropping her off, but Moroy never really thought anything of these occasions.

Brenda was easily the prettiest one in the office. She had a little fat on her, but Moroy was OK with a little bit of fat. He liked some on them sometimes. He found it sexy that a girl would allow herself to let go a little bit. She would not be a thin woman on the way to being fat, or even vice versa; she would be a woman who didn't care, or acted like she didn't.

Brenda had something like that. From behind he saw a little valley and a lump, low on her hips, right where she wore the waistline of her pants and her skirts, like she was made of soft, flesh-colored clay and someone took another lump of clay, rolled it into his hands, and slapped it around her little body, massaging it half-heartedly until it only partly melted into her flesh. It made her look a little clumsy, a little careless. But it was more than just fuck-what-the-boys-think fat. This was teen fat. Growing-up fat. She had just graduated from college and this was her first job. Moroy figured she was too young to know why she took it in the first place, but was also at just the right age to trust her instincts.

He held Sir's gaze as the car window closed. He was wide awake, had never slept. She was probably in his room, playing in the bathtub, making shapes out of the bubbles, brushing them off with her breath when they threatened to grow larger.

Baguio was still very dark, and the glare of the hotel's lighting in the mirror made everything else even darker. The fog had grown thicker. If he was going to make it fast he had to take Kennon Road, which was full of twists and banks, but it was going to be a real thrill. The hotel lights disappeared and there was nothing but fog ahead of him and behind him. Moroy had never really been able to tell what Brenda looked like from the driver's seat. She had ridden along dozens of times, even alone, those times she needed to go somewhere for work and didn't feel like taking a cab. But she always sat behind him. The passenger's seat was always Sir's place. He couldn't even smell her perfume, the way he smelled the other staff whenever they rode with Sir to a meeting. Brenda was too young for perfume. Her gift of the t-shirt was especially touching. He kind of knew how much it must have cost. He'd made it a habit to sneak a look at the receipts stapled to the shopping bags Sir and Ma'am left in the car. Those Givenchy shirts—he couldn't even pronounce it—most probably cost more than a thousand pesos.

Brenda was a college graduate, sure, and had a B.S. in business, but she didn't graduate from Ateneo, or La Salle, or UP, or abroad, like Sir's friends did. She had graduated from the rival school of Moroy's own college. A school with something like 70,000 students. He himself had never graduated, and the reasons had softened and blended into each other over the years until what remained was his own self-resentment. There surely must have been a pretty good reason for it, and money was really the only reason he could think of.

She obviously didn't make very much; he was sure even he made more money than she did, but her family could obviously afford for her to graduate. Although her credentials and her transcript were enough to get her hired by someone like Sir, from here on, it would be her looks that would take care of the rest. "Ang kagandahan ay puhunan," they would say at the office. *Beauty is capital.*

That didn't subtract from her strong points, though, or from Sir's. He was a businessman. Though Moroy couldn't really put a finger on what Sir did for a living, he figured that he was pretty good at what he did, and well respected in his field. That accounted for his money and his powerful connections. But it was mostly luck that Moroy could count on to explain the fact that this fine looking chick would allow Sir to get near her.

Moroy was on Kennon now, barreling through the zigzag like he was riding a motorcycle instead of a Land Cruiser. The bulletproof cladding made it heavier and faster. If this was a test, he was going to pass it.

"Sinusubukan niyo ba ako?" Moroy had picked up his trademark line from President Erap back in the day. He recalled the time Sir had left 77,800 in cash in a tightly rubber-banded envelope in the glove compartment. When he returned it to him the next morning he used that line on his employer, in half-jest: "Sir, are you putting me to a test?" Sir laughed, but Moroy thought he had laughed a little too hard. There was something else there, unhealthy, as if Sir was beginning to worry about his speed and his strength, but maybe it gave him a kind of stability, like a spinning top.

He thought about the money now on the stretch between Kennon to Pangasinan, right before the roads gave way to the new expressway that skipped the slog of small towns, with their churches and municipal halls, their student crossings and tricycles. That new expressway certainly cost a lot of money, too. He thought about Mona Lisa and the medicine box, and the money inside it, and before he knew it he had chewed up the entirety of EDSA and was in front of the house, buoyed by the euphoria that came with missed sleep. Moroy barked at the mayor doma to get the t-shirt from the laundry. He didn't need to ask about Ma'am. He knew she was out at the Eleuterios for mahjongg. He went up the stairs, feeling his weight and his breath with every step. He entered Sir's room and took a moment to appreciate it, the bright light, the vast space, the rich, woody smell, the sudden quiet. The floor was freshly polished and the bed made. His steps felt too loud as he walked over to the night stand and opened the drawer: envelopes, USB sticks, a 9mm pistol in its holster. He reached into the space and found the medicine box, a tin can repurposed from its previous life as a candy container, smaller than he had expected it to be. Before he could open it, the mayor doma entered the room, holding up the t-shirt on a hanger: that Mona Lisa, smiling without smiling, her arms folded as though she were waiting impatiently.

The first real bottleneck between Makati and Balintawak was the last left turn on EDSA, where the entire avenue changed course by the SM City Mall. In the lull Moroy suddenly felt his missed sleep, and his hunger.

There was a Pancake House just across the entrance to Congressional Village. A boy tapped on the flank of the SUV until he settled into the parking space. He felt the pit of his stomach burn as he waited for his meal. Must be hunger, must be old age. It must be genetic. He heard Sir and Ma'am talk about "genetic" all the time. It was the reason for many things: cancer, idiocy, political appointments.

How old was Sir? Even though he looked so youthful, Moroy assumed he was much older. Genetic. Or plastic surgery. Sinusubukan mo ba ako? He remembered Sir's face, the thing that flashed when he said it. Fear, or guilt, or nothing, really. He was overthinking again.

"Thinking it over? Or overthinking?" Brenda had said to Sir once, her little voice carrying from the back seat. She had a clever little voice, and she used it as effectively in person and on the phone when speaking to Sir. They had been on the way to a meeting in Valenzuela, Bulacan. What was an hour's drive had stretched into three. She said it after they'd been sitting silent for a long time. Overthinking. He knew what thinking it over meant, but it was the first time he had heard that word, overthinking.

"Overthinking?" Sir said, the top of his head suddenly flitting to the side in his rearview. "What does that mean?" He repeated: "Overthinking?" Sir obviously knew what it meant.

Brenda used the very same friendly, accommodating tone she used on their most difficult clients. "You know, when you worry too much about something it becomes something else already. Like distrust. Or fear."

"Fear?" Sir said, as though he suddenly didn't know what that meant, too. Nothing was said after that. Finally, they arrived at their client's sardine canning factory.

Brenda—he had never really seen her face because it had been so ingrained in him to avert his eyes, but he was so sure now that she looked special, beyond just being pale-skinned, well-scrubbed, and well-dressed like the rest of them. She had "right manners and good conduct." She paid the right compliments, never intruded on privacy, and pretended to be amused, even delighted, when Sir told something about his family life. Ma'am was an interior decorator who had her own set of difficult clients, and their child went to Ateneo Grade School. Brenda was English-speaking like the rest of them, but whenever she spoke, Moroy knew she wasn't quite in the league of Sir and his close circle of old friends. He couldn't really put a finger on it, but he knew that was how Sir exactly wanted it.

A billboard advertising a family-owned resort straddled a boundary dike between two ricefields burned pale by the sun. The amenities were in bullet points: world-class swimming pool and water park, luxurious rooms and suites, family restaurant.

The radio had been tuned to DZBB "sais treynta." He'd been following the senate hearings on the latest budget scam. He knew exactly what some of those people looked like, he knew their voices from the way they spoke to their drivers and their minders. They all knew what they were up to even before the senate hearings. He turned the radio down and brought the SUV to a stop on the shoulder. Cars blasted their horns as they drove past. He thought about taking the detour. Although it wasn't even midmorning he felt hungry again.

He saw the shirt hanging in the rear and remembered his errand. The canister had cradled itself in a crevice in the passenger seat. He took the lid off and saw no cash inside—an ATM card would have fit pretty nicely. Instead there was a little pool of blue pills, a dozen or so, that had settled gently on the bottom, edge to edge. He knew what they were from stories told by other folks like him—drivers, minders, bodyguards, handlers. A blue-colored mixture of pity and a feeling of great responsibility washed over him.

This was not just an errand. This was another test. Sir had laid on his shoulders an uncommon trust and responsibility. He remembered Sir once asking Brenda who she was texting with so much on her phone. "A friend," she finally said, after she had let some time pass as if she hadn't heard the question. He spoke to her in the low tone he used when he didn't want Moroy to hear, and she answered with a laugh, like a high exhale, a laugh she barely suppressed, a laugh at the game SIR? SIR was trying so hard to play. He felt an irrational hatred come over him: like he wanted to screw her.

Moroy dropped his window as he passed the country club guardhouse, making sure the window opened just enough to see the lady guard through his mirrored shades, and that she could see the crocodile patch on his chest. Sir had given him that shirt at their staff

Christmas party, all wrapped in a big stiff paper bag that announced "Lacoste." Its gartered cuffs lightly, but precisely, embraced his upper arms, its brazen, multicolored vertical stripes going against every other shirt he owned. He brought his hand up and perched it on the top of the steering wheel to make sure she saw his Submariner. It was fake, of course, but it was a real class-A knockoff Sir had bought for him on one of his trips to Bangkok. He had never told anyone, not that the people around him knew what a Rolex was, though more than once or twice he had been surprised. His regular massage therapist at his favorite chop-chop joint, for example, had exclaimed "Uy! Rolex!" when she saw it sitting on the sidetable. "That's fake," he said, firmly and with finality, but the girl was on to him, did a double take and exclaimed "Weh! Hindi nga?" What made her think he was kidding?

The lady guard didn't look up from her cellphone. If she only knew who he really was, how close he was to the very top. He was listened to. He had some bearing on things. He was one of the good guys.

He didn't know how long he had been away. Sir had texted him twice already, at around 7 a.m. and right as he entered Kennon. And then nothing. He remembered the way he shifted and sighed in the backseat after they'd brought Brenda home on one of those nights she agreed to come out with him. He'd be pretending he was worried about work, about home, about money. He would tell him to hurry home, hurry home, take this road, take that turn, as if he needed to be told, as if he didn't know the way.

Moroy fixed the hotel valet with a stare through his sunglasses as he stepped out of the SUV, leaving the door open as he walked into the lobby. It was 11 a.m.

He went up the elevator and knocked on his door, "Sir, sir, sir," remembering to tighten the I's. It opened a crack and a hand reached out, fingers stretched upward like a cup, ready to receive the delivery. Moroy put on a poker face and deposited the canister into Sir's hand, its insides making a clicking sound. The hand withdrew, and came out again, frozen upward in a signal to wait.

Moroy tried to see into the room but it was dark inside. He strained to hear Brenda's voice but heard nothing. The hand darted out, holding up one of the blue pills in the middle of an OK sign. Moroy felt like he had been found out. He had made a mental note to himself to filch one but had forgotten. He cupped his hand under his master's to receive the parting tip.

When the valet brought the SUV up the driveway Moroy could see, even through the double-tinted windows, the Mona Lisa swinging on its hanger from the back handrail, and he gave her the same knowing, close-lipped smile.

In terms of technique, the POV of this story differs somewhat from the other two in that it's largely told from Moroy's perspective, a close third-person perspective or *third person, limited*. Except for some of the action and description of the Philippines landscape, what unfolds in the story is seen through his eyes, as are his judgments about "Sir" and Brenda, "the girl Sir often personally took home from the office." Take for example, the initial conversation with Sir about the errand.

"Yes sir." Moroy blinked as he said it, perhaps a little bit longer than he should have.

"Great!" Sir said, adding, "By the way, bring along my medicine pouch, the small one in the bedside table. My side, not Norma's."

"Yessir." It was time-consuming, expensive, and it all seemed completely unnecessary.

In describing the blink as "perhaps a little bit longer than he should have," we have to wonder who is making this judgment. The key word is "should"—despite Moroy's "yessir," the signal to the reader is that Moroy can't entirely conceal his disbelief, and perhaps annoyance, at the inconvenience and time wasted by such a request, even though, being Sir's driver, he would only think but never say that. If Moroy had said, "Are you crazy?" he probably would have regretted it immediately, but that blink suggests something much subtler that the author is doing, not exactly breaking character but physicalizing Moroy's dismay at the request and then letting us know that as the man's employee, he really can't register any such dismay without tearing at the power dynamic between them. Yes, it's Moroy, but would Moroy articulate this idea on a conscious level? That's not to suggest that he lacks intelligence, but that it's the kind of observation that likely wouldn't be made *in the moment* by this character. To write the truth about this "Little Fish," both the conscious and unconscious must be shown, and a dash of omniscience helps.

Through Moroy's POV, we understand Sir to be a foolish, married older man who lusts after Brenda, a young employee. Their story unfolds through a discourse about fear—a flashback to a ride when Moroy recalls Brenda and Sir talk about worrying too much—as well as Moroy's flash of "irrational hatred" for Brenda when he thinks she's laughing at Sir, plus his desire to have filched one of the blue tablets which he forgets to do before handing the bag to his employer. Sir rewards Moroy with one of the blue pills—almost certainly Viagra—and despite this unreasonable errand he is probably no better or worse than any other employer. We can see, by the way, that this Viagra was the real reason for the errand and not the Mona Lisa tee-shirt, which we see in the end unclaimed and unneeded. Why do you think Sir has resorted to the ploy of the tee-shirt and not simply said, "Fetch my Viagra?"

Even though Moroy maintains a "poker face" and nothing outwardly changes, this innocuous errand affects him emotionally. What do we know about Sir? His Land Rover has bulletproof cladding, he deals in large sums of cash, and his bedside drawer has a 9-mm pistol in its holster, all suggesting involvement in questionable, illegal, or dangerous enterprises. Towards the end of the story, when Moroy finally arrives at Sir's location, tired and hungry, he adopts his employer's stance, making sure the lady guard at the country club guardhouse sees the Lacoste crocodile logo on his shirt. He has, in effect, become like Sir, trying to impress Brenda by sending Moroy on a ridiculous errand to fetch the Mona Lisa shirt, and finally, wanting to feel he is elevated beyond his "Little Fish" life through his connection to Sir, *a butterfly on the back of a carabao* (water buffalo) as the saying goes. These details, subtly inserted, show us Moroy beyond his own limited POV. He will continue doing other pointless errands for Sir, regardless, because that is his job, but for one moment, we see him fully through his imagination based on what he *does* know, against the backdrop of what he will never fully be able to know, or experience, about Sir, Brenda, or himself.

On a related note, if we want to tell the story of a non-mainstream or specific culture, using the language of that world can add color and meaning to your story. We all belong to many different large groups such as a religion or nation or ethnicity, as well as to various subgroups, for example, players or fans of a sport, and each has its own language. For example, if you want to write a story about a tennis match, you would use the scores "love" or "deuce" even though this is meaningless to a reader who doesn't know tennis. But just as it's important not to alienate the reader, it's equally as important not to over-explain or over-translate, but instead to guide the reader's understanding of what is implied as in this extract from "An Errand":

> "Sinusubukan niyo ba ako?" Moroy had picked up his trademark line from President Erap back in the day. He recalled the time Sir had left 77,800 in cash in a tightly rubber-banded envelope in the glove compartment. When he returned it to him the next morning he used that line on his employer, in half-jest: "Sir, are you putting me to a test?" Sir laughed, but Moroy thought he had laughed a little too hard.

Here Lacuesta allows the Tagalog question to stand on its own at the beginning of the paragraph, but switches to English when Moroy actually says the line to Sir. The line is described as a "trademark line from President Erap back in the day" which characterizes Moroy as someone who pays attention to current affairs, as well as canny enough to try to put his employer off guard by using it "in half-jest." Incidentally, "Sir" is what employers in the Philippines are called, especially by domestics, drivers, and others of the serving class, but this becomes apparent through usage in the story, without explanation. These are ways to lighten the heavy-handedness inherent in both techniques of an omniscient POV and in the use of "local color."

Stories aren't the real world of course, but approximations of the world, or translations. Character dialogue, for instance, is not exactly the way people speak, but is *stylized* to seem like real dialogue. The same is true of the ways in which we portray certain characters, particularly their thoughts. Some Modernist Western writers such as James Joyce, William Faulkner, and Virginia Woolf attempted in their fiction to mimic the disorderliness of our rush of thoughts through a technique known as *stream of consciousness*, a term that's widely misused in creative writing classes to mean, "I don't understand what the writer is saying." Another widely misunderstood form of writing is *surrealism*, which is often interpreted in creative writing classes as, "Not only can't I understand this, but it's really weird." Like stream of consciousness, the Surrealists, a largely but not exclusive movement of French writers and philosophers, were trying in their writings and films to rely on their characters' subconscious minds more than their conscious ways of perceiving the world. Of course, both of these explanations are inadequate thumbnail descriptions, and we encourage you to further investigate these literary techniques/movements, but our point is that no matter how we represent our realities, we are presenting a stylized view, an interpretation. Even in *realist* stories, if you write a story from the POV of a child, it's not likely to sound the way children really do, but hopefully close enough, an approximation that carries us through the story.

We can venture to say that the authors of these stories are not themselves drivers, migrant construction workers, or clerks killed by mob violence. While there have been plenty of working-class writers and readers, historically, the writing of literature has been an endeavor of the middle classes and before that, the aristocracy. It's unfortunate when writers from middle-class backgrounds write about working-class characters in ways that patronize, sentimentalize, or exoticize them, but that's not the case with any of these writers. Who knows where they found the germs of the ideas for these stories? A newspaper story? An anecdote someone told? The observations of a group of laborers on St. John Island or a drive from Manila to Baguio in a friend's car? Or none of these. In writing such stories, the details must seem authentic as must the characters. For the former, one can employ research, observation, interviews. For the latter, a sympathetic imagination is crucial, as well as an ability to resist delivering political or moralistic bromides to the reader. Fiction and nonfiction are different in terms of representation, though this subject can be a divisive one. A nonfiction writer who writes a fake memoir of his time as a migrant construction laborer in Singapore is either delusional or unethical. There are those who would say that fiction writers should stay in their lanes, too, and while the reasons for these feelings are myriad, complex, and not easily dismissed, we believe that straying from one's lane is not in and of itself irresponsible or unethical. Fiction derives from the Latin *fingere, to contrive*, and it shares its root with *figment* and *feign*. The characters of these stories are figments. They are contrived. And at best, we feign to have entered the consciousness of anyone but ourselves.

Exercises

1. Select a "Little Fish" profession and write a story about an individual who does that work and have her or him perform the job around one specific day or incident. Use "An Errand" as a model.
2. Write a diary narrative of a short time frame, for example, one hour or one day, about the life of an ordinary person with as much detail as possible. Use a background situation that is from a real conflict or emergency but make the details of the person's life the central story.
3. Choose a celebratory occasion as a setting for a story and create a set of characters who will be involved in this occasion. What happens to them? Why?
4. Make a list of "Little Fish" jobs. For each one, identify who the "Big Fish" is as contrast for a story.
5. Interview someone who does a "Little Fish" job that you're interested in. Next, use the interview as the basis for a short story about the person you've interviewed. What conflict(s) can you identify, either through the interview or through your imagination?

CHAPTER 5
SHEDDING SKINS

In college we were told that we should never confuse the author of a short story and its main character or narrator. In general, that's a principle we still adhere to. You might recall we mentioned this issue in relation to the story, "No Toes," with its rather clueless first-person narrator. While we have never met the author, it's a safe bet that he does not share the same narrow worldview as his narrator. We can tell this in part by the narrator's very cluelessness. It's one thing for a narrator to portray himself unwittingly as a numbskull, but it would be quite a disaster for the author to be just as clueless as his narrator. Unfortunately, a few times in our careers a writer naively wrote something for a workshop that we *thought* was meant to be satirical, but wasn't. When we started critiquing the story, it slowly dawned on us that there was no daylight between the author's views and the protagonist's views. This is the premise of the classic film, *The Producers*, in which a couple of con artists decide to produce a play that is guaranteed to be a flop so they can bilk their investors. Instead, the terrible musical, *Springtime for Hitler*, written earnestly by a neo-Nazi, winds up being a smash hit.

Author/Educator Brent Spencer once shared with us the best/worst such instance of a naïve author. When he was teaching an introductory creative writing course at Stanford, a student wrote the worst opening in the history of creative writing courses, as far as we can tell. The story takes place one morning at Auschwitz with the main character, David, depressed and not feeling so hungry because his parents were gassed last night. Walking across the "courtyard" of Auschwitz, David hears the commandant yelling after him: "David, David, you can't skip breakfast. Don't you know it's the most important meal of the day?" Everyone in the workshop treated the story as if it were another *Springtime for Hitler* until Brent noticed the fallen face of the young man who had written these immortal words. While the author and his protagonist were definitely not one and the same (he obviously had no idea of the realities of the Holocaust), the ignorance expressed in the story was the author's own ignorance and not merely his protagonist's, as is the case in "No Toes." In part, we can tell by the *tone* of "No Toes" that it's meant satirically. Tone is sometimes difficult for beginning writers to pick up on, and they don't always sense the irony of a story or essay—the assumption in most writing we come across is that if the author has written something down, then they believe it's true. But that's not the case always in literature. Many a freshman has been horrified by Jonathan Swift's darkly satirical essay, "A Modest Proposal," written in 1729, in which the narrator suggests that the way to solve the problem of poverty in Ireland is to eat the babies of the poor. We can tell by the dissonance between the matter-of-fact tone and the monstrous proposition being made that the author is satirizing the callousness of the rich toward the poor. Similarly, in "No Toes," the narrator's war cries of "Big biceps for Summer" and his obsession with the young woman's toes are so exaggerated as to make us suspect the author is having a little fun at the expense of his protagonist. That's also why Brent Spencer's workshop assumed that the story of David skipping breakfast at Auschwitz had to be a parody.

While you should never simply assume that an author and their protagonist are one and the same, authors do write about themselves all the time, sometimes overtly and sometimes covertly, sometimes so covertly that *they* don't even recognize all the biographical details in their work.

There are several different modes of life writing:

Biography

Autobiography

Memoir

Autobiographical Fiction

Autofiction

Autobiografiction

The first two are meant to be largely accurate and verifiable accounts of a life, another person's life in the case of biography and one's own life in autobiography. An autobiography differs from a memoir in that the former typically takes up the entire span of the life lived thus far while a memoir often deals with a portion of someone's life. The memoir form, while autobiographical (unless it's a faked), is largely meant to be as accurate as possible, but such books deal with the vagaries of memory and the great majority of memoirists fill in the details they don't remember (dialogue, descriptions, gestures) by reimagining the scene in question. Memoirists feel differently about how much embellishing is okay, but memoir is largely understood to be a re-creation (with the emphasis on creation) and not the same as reportage.

Autobiographical fiction is the most uncomplicated of the latter half of this list. As the name suggests, this is fiction that is heavily influenced by the events of the author's life, but purports only to be based on it, not tethered to it as a memoir is supposed to be.

The last two odd words on this list might seem a bit odd at first, but they're useful to know about and consider. The term "autofiction" was first coined by French novelist Serge Doubrovsky in 1977, describing his book *Fils*. Until relatively recently the term was largely used by French authors to describe their work. Over the years, attempts to define exactly what encompassed autofiction were debated among French writers and academics. While space allows for only a brief and overly simplistic discussion of the form, the critic Vince Colonna divided the term into two types: *autofiction biografique* (biographical autofiction) and *autofiction fantastique* (fantastical autofiction). Doubrovsky, when he originally formulated the idea, saw autofiction as a recognition of "the fictive component in every attempt at writing a self," but the autofictionist Catherine Cusset insists that "the only fiction in autofiction is the work on language. The facts are real, and the project is to reach a certain truth." While she sees autofiction as distinct from contemporary memoir, we would beg to differ and suggest that it sounds an awful lot like the way many American writers approach writing their own memoirs. On the other hand, *autofiction fantastique* suggests a much more flexible approach—here, the facts might not be real, or greatly exaggerated, but on some level there's still a sense of autobiography happening, at least at an emotional and/or intellectual level. In the English-speaking world, "autofiction" as a mode of writing has become trendy, but it often means something quite different from the original use of the term by Doubrovsky. In many cases, it's less akin to memoir and closer to the highly self-conscious form of writing that evolved in the 1960s and 1970s: *metafiction*. This type of fiction involves fiction about the process of writing fiction. The idea was that *realism* was as artificial as any other way of portraying the world in print, and writers of autofiction often playfully wanted to subvert standard notions of authenticity in realist fiction. Writers such as John Barth, Kurt Vonnegut, and Ronald Sukenick often named their protagonists after themselves and "engaged in ironic self-portrayal" in the words of Marjorie Worthington. American autofiction largely grows out of this tradition, and American autofictionists tend to use their real names and write hybrid works that might or might not have a relation to the realities of their lives. But don't ask them how much is "true." They're not saying.

The final term on our list (there *will* be a quiz) is "autobiografiction." Doesn't that just roll off the tongue effortlessly? We have author Stephen Reynolds to blame for this awkward term, who, in 1906, wrote a brief essay in which he mused on the possibility of writing fictional works that presented nonetheless accurate interior emotional/spiritual maps of the author's life. The term lay dormant for a century until it appeared as the title of a Comparative Literature Conference in 2010 at Goldsmith's College, London, and was subsequently the subject of critic Max Saunders's comprehensive literary study, *Self-Impressions*. Awkward as the term might seem, it captures some of the hybridized nature of writing that falls in between the cracks of invention and autobiography.

There are yet more terms for such hybrid types because critics love to invent terms, but we feel we've covered the spectrum with the ones mentioned previously. Besides, for practitioners, terms are only useful inasmuch as they help us understand the traditions within which we're writing. They likewise sometimes give us permission to write the strange things that seem otherwise to defy categorization. One day we read about *autobiografiction*, and we say, "Oh, right, I guess I've been writing autobiografiction all along. Hey Ma, I'm an Autobiografictionist."

Let's read Xu Xi's "All About Skin" and return to our discussion of these issues of autobiography and imagination afterwards.

1 "All About Skin"

by Xu Xi (USA)

for my muse Jenny Wai

Xu Xi was born and raised in Hong Kong of the 1950s and 1960s, and has split most of her life between the city and New York. An Indonesian-Chinese author of fourteen books of fiction and nonfiction, she is considered one of Hong Kong's leading writers in English.

> I went to Derma the week before Christmas to buy an *american* skin. I was apprehensive because Derma's expensive and doesn't allow trade-ins. But their salesman gave me credit on pretty generous terms, and let me take it away the same day, which made me feel good.
>
> This was not an impulse purchase, you understand. I've been pricing *americans* for donkeys' years. My last topskin, which I got fourteen years ago at Epiderm International, was an *immigranta*. It was okay, but only really fit if teamed with the right accessories. That got to be a pain. Going *american*, though, is a big step. After Derma, there's no place else to go but down, at least as long as they're number one.

You see, my history with skins is spotty. I stay with one a long time, sometimes too long, because change makes me itch. The thing about an old skin is that even if it's worn or stained, it hangs comfortably because you know where it needs a bit of a stretch or a quick fold and tuck. Before *immagranta*, I wore *cosmopol* for seven years. The latter was always a wee bit shiny between the legs, although I knew enough to deflect glare with *corpus-ceiling glass*, my preferred underskin, from SubCutis.

But I'm getting ahead of myself. A chronology of my history with skins will keep names and dates straight. It's sort of like skinning a lion. First, you have to shoot the beast.

Like most folks on our globe, I got my first topskin from my parents on my eighth birthday. Now I know there are some who start off at six or even as young as five, like the wearers of *nipponicas* and *americans*. We were a conservative family, though, and when I slipped into *china cutis*, the only product line People's PiFu sold back then, I was the proudest little creature strutting around Hong Kong. This was in the 1960s. My idea of skin began and ended with *china cutis*, basic model.

Mind you, there's nothing wrong with basics. This one gave me room to breathe and plenty of growing space. During the teenage-diet thing, it adapted nicely enough, although Ma worried about premature tummy sags. You know what mothers are like. If there isn't a real problem to worry about, they'll find one.

For years, I simply didn't think about skin. Passing exams was all that mattered so that I too could be a face-valued citizen. I practiced tending to wounds and cuts, bruises and scars, sores and boils. What fascinated me were bites—a plethora of bug nibbles bursting out on the back of my thighs; fang prints snakes sank into my ankles; crab kisses slashing my fingers; teeth marks dogs lodged in my shoulder. Papa was pallid the day I came home from the beach, my back and arms covered with huge red splotches. They looked awful but didn't itch, which was merciful, and disappeared the next day. Sand crabs, Ma said. Durable, my old *china cutis*. There are days I miss it.

My problem began round about age nineteen. Being ambitious types, my parents packed me off to schools abroad. I salivated at Derma's store windows in New York, desperate for an *american*. They were all the rage, and outrageously expensive. "You can buy that yourself when you're earning your own money," Papa declared. "I can't afford it." I stormed and pouted, scratching my face and legs till they bled, giving Ma something to really cry about. He wouldn't relent. It wasn't just the money. He and Ma had worn their *china cutises* since they were eight and couldn't see why I wouldn't do likewise. From their perspective, I was acting like a spoiled brat. They were right, I suppose, but you find me a nineteen-year-old who isn't stuffed full of the fashion of her times.

So I passed the exams, got my face-valued citizen parchment, and by my mid-twenties had this great job in advertising. Paris three times a year! Imagine. It was a pretty exciting life, I must say, despite my skin.

In the spring of '79, I dared to visit Integume of Paris.

If you think Derma's hot, you've never shopped at Integume. From the moment you enter their store—no, store's too pedestrian—their boutique, you're engulfed by the unimaginable possibilities of skin. Moisturizer wafts through the atmosphere. Never, never, it whispers, will even the tiniest blemish dare to mar this surface. *Jamais!* You wander around this cutaneous paradise where an array of products tempts you with seductive promise: *euro trash tannis, decadence glorious, romance du monde ancien, french chic* . . . skins! Meters upon meters of skins, both natural and quality synthetic, draped fetchingly, lovingly, placed with the kind of care that plunges skin-deep.

The saleslady offered to take my old *china cutis* in trade, saying it was in big demand and commanded good resale value. Secondhands were rare because few wearers upgraded abroad back then. I really didn't care one way or another because I was sick to death of *china cutis*. I mean, it couldn't tan or wrinkle, and even a little makeup made me feel all Suzie Wong. The only reason I stuck it out so long was, well, family is family after all. But enough is enough. It was time to go *cosmopol*.

The beauty of *cosmopol* is its flexibility. I could slip in and out of it into something more comfortable whenever I wanted. China cutis stuck to me like a fragile layer of dried rice glue. It flaked periodically—showers of scarf skin—and had to be treated with such respect. That was the worst part, the respect. Four thousand years of R&D had gone into its design. Personally, I thought the design had already run its course, but then, I've always been "one step too many beyond," as Ma says. When Mao, the primo *china cutis* wearer of the last century created a big to-do by jumping into the Yellow River, thus proving its durability, it was downright asinine.

But the truth of the matter is my *china cutis* had gotten loose and sloppy. Fashion-wise, the look was making a comeback by then, but not in any real way. Mine sagged. I wallowed in free space. Ma had suggested I return it for a newer model, but those weren't a marked improvement. People's PiFu hadn't modernized their product line for global consumption yet. It was just an ill-destined style.

So I traded it in. My father would've killed me had he known. He didn't, though, thanks to *cosmopol*.

I owe a lot to that Integume saleslady. She showed me how to enhance my *cosmopol* skin with separates and coordinates. Stuck with *china cutis*, I didn't know about all the accessory lines. I confess I was pretty extravagant for a while there. From Integume, I went to SubCutis where I bought three underskins—a *sub-four seas, lady don juan* and *corporate rung*. They were expensive, but worth it. Like the saleslady said, you make the big one-time investment and add extras as you go. Besides, Integume allowed layaway, and SubCutis was running a special promotion for customers of Integume. A year later, I added *underwired g-strung* and *corpus-ceiling glass* to my skinrobe. All in all, I made out okay.

Being able to slip any one of these over or under cosmopol was such a liberation. If I were feeling particularly daring, I could combine accessories by themselves. None of them worked that well solo, probably because they were all synthetic. *Underwired g-strung* slid off at the slightest provocation. *Corporate rung* was generally a tight fit, although the crotch was absurdly loose. The designer hadn't quite gotten the hang of that one, especially in female petite.

The real test, though, was passing muster with Papa. By wearing *cosmopol* with *sub-four seas* underneath, I could fool him into thinking I had on my china cutis. Things were looking good. But none of this explains why, after a good seven years, I decided to give up *cosmopol* for an *immigranta*.

To tell you properly, I have to go back to Derma and their *american* line. You have to understand that I never lost my yen for *american*. I'm a sucker for advertising, and

Derma could really launch a marketing campaign. Even though they'd only been around a couple of centuries, everyone thought they were the real thing. It was a question of focus. Their entire strategy depended on narrowing everything down to one product. Derma equaled *american*. The same idea worked for People's PiFu a few centuries earlier. Their problem was different—times had changed and they hadn't. Renaming their company and sticking on a new logo back in the late 1940s was not sufficient to create the fundamental transformation they desperately needed.

But during the years I ran around in *cosmopol*, Derma had been steadily losing market share to All Nippon Cutis.

Let me digress a moment. All Nippon Cutis were smart. They invested in R&D for some ten years to produce a top quality *american*-like skin. I read about them in *Forbes*. Their chairman sent fifty of their top designers and executives to Paris for two years to check out Integume's styles. After that, those same folks went to New York for another two years to study Derma's market leadership. By the time they actually started designing in Tokyo, they had the marketplace all figured out.

The world, they decided, wanted Derma's strength with Integume's flair. Somehow, the frivolous fun inherent in SubCutis needed to be integrated. The smartest thing All Nippon Cutis did was to compete in Derma's primary marketplace, which was an easier target than Integume's international market dominance.

You know the rest. At the beginning, the very rich would fly to Tokyo to buy an *america dreama*. By the mid-eighties, All Nippon Cutis had opened branches all over the U.S. You remember their commercials—Lincoln's head superimposed on the Statue of Liberty crying "Cutify!" Market forces being what they are, within a year, you could get an *america dreama* out in Jersey for half the price of Derma's *american*.

Their *america dreama* impressed me. They couldn't call it *american*, of course, because of trademark infringement. I had moved to New York by then, but Ma told me that the product was a big hit even in Hong Kong. In Tokyo, it became very fashionable as a second skin to *nipponica*.

At that time, I wouldn't have dreamed of buying from Derma. Not only was my *cosmopol* still serviceable, but Derma's prices were quite unjustified. Oh I know they were all natural, while All Nippon Cutis used blends, but big deal, my old *china cutis* was all natural too. Even when the hoopla about *america dreama* turning yellow after repeated sun exposure made the news, no one cared, not really, because, first of all, the scientists who claimed that were working for Derma, and most people had begun to believe that skins should be replaced after even as little as three to five years. I find that a little wasteful myself, but All Nippon Cutis made a good point by offering to recycle old skins.

As impressive as it was, I wasn't quite sold on what amounted to only a make-believe *american*. Which meant my alternative was Epiderm International, makers of *immigranta*, *asia personals*, and *ec*, among others.

My problem was that *cosmopol* wasn't fitting quite right.

Life in New York was expensive enough without keeping up my *cosmopol* skin. It was flexible, but only if pampered a lot. You needed the best face creams and lotions, and could only be seen in the most fashionable places. Worst of all, it radiated this worldly air, while hinting at a sexual undertow, but avoiding any engagements that would ravage its surface charms. Debt did not aid its sustenance, as I was still paying off my balance at Integume.

At least *cosmopol* could be cashed in. Unlike *china cutis*, which had great trade-in value but generated no cash, New Yorkers would kill for secondhand *cosmopols*. I actually made a profit, because naturally, with the original trade-in, I hadn't paid full price, although the interest alone was staggering.

For almost six months, I went around without a main skin. Luckily, I had all those secondary ones. Depending on my mood, I usually wore either *corporate rung* or *corpus-ceiling glass*, with *sub-four seas* underneath. It was an uncomfortable time. I was sometimes tempted to slip on *lady don juan* with *underwired g-strung* to get back that cosmopol feeling, but was just too embarrassed. I hated admitting I didn't have a main skin, but I needed to pay down debt, even if not completely, before my next investment.

The day I purchased my *immigranta*, I dreamt about flying back to Hong Kong to see my parents. This was the real reason to lose *cosmopol*. Lying to them was fine when I was younger, but now, it made me feel like a hypocrite. It wasn't their fault I didn't like *china cutis*. They couldn't have foreseen my life.

Even then, it was another six years before I finally made it home. I had retired *lady don juan* and *underwired g-strung* to my back closet, because the market for those secondary styles had pretty much gone bust. You remember the beginning of the dual skin craze. Anyone who was anyone wouldn't dream of being without a second skin. SubCutis hung on, but just barely. Word flew on the street that they were going to file Chapter 11. I won that bet when they succumbed to a buyout by All Nippon Cutis. You have to figure there's a niche market somewhere for their questionable lines. Besides, the rest of their products did have mainstream appeal.

It was a big bet, which was good, because the money paid for my trip home. I had left advertising and was working on the fringes of Wall Street, a bad place to be post Black Monday. With my debt on *immigranta*, I lived paycheck to paycheck. Maybe I was sticking my neck out unnecessarily with that bet. But the great thing about my *immigranta* skin was that it absorbed immunity to risk.

I suppose that's why I kept it so long. I didn't have to lie to my parents because it was the one other acceptable skin in their eyes. Call them old-fashioned, but they like the chameleon complexion of *immigranta*, especially because on me, it looked enough like *china cutis*. What they didn't know was that I had slipped *golden peril* on underneath. I'd picked that one up cheap at a SubCutis fire sale before going to see them. I'm awfully thankful for fickle fashion trends; products in a downturn sometimes prove extremely attractive, given the right circumstances.

So why *american* now? You might say I got caught up in the wave of market forces, because I'm past much of that fashion stuff. Derma went through some pretty shaky years, losing considerable market share to All Nippon Cutis, who took their range way out there with *ho-ho hollywoodo*. Tacky, I think, but who could predict its huge appeal, from Los Angeles to Beijing? Even Epiderm International horned in on Derma's territory with their Epiderm US subsidiary, whose *emigrantis* and *global villager* became ludicrously popular. All Nippon Cutis retaliated quickly enough with *worldo warrior*. For awhile there, I almost shed *immigranta* for one of these newer models.

Derma had it all wrong. Their feeble attempt to launch *heritage hides* was laughable. Imagine thinking Mr. Ed singing "Got to Know about History" would make any impact? I think it was voted the worst commercial of 1988. Price was another factor. Some say they priced themselves out of their own marketplace.

Derma refused to entertain the idea of growth even though revenues were down 30% and profits almost non-existent. In the meantime, All Nippon Cutis merged with the largest hairbank in Frankfurt, while Epiderm was borrowing heavily both in London and New York to finance their expansion. *The Wall Street Journal* suggested that Epiderm's reliance on junk bonds would be their undoing, but you couldn't be too critical of junk in those days. Even Integume dived right in, expanding and grabbing share in markets like Moscow, Shanghai, and Prague, as well as in places like Cincinnati, Seattle, and Minneapolis, where *cosmopol* became more popular than *american*. By now, Derma was a distant number four behind those three global leaders, at least in sales and profits. If you count market size, People's PiFu is right up there, but of course, prices aren't comparable, given their rock bottom manufacturing costs.

In the end, everything turned on principle, plus a little Chinese intrigue.

You've heard the conspiracy theories, about how the CIA negotiated with Soong & Dong to flood the global market with synthetic epidermatis. There are even whispers that it had to do with WTO membership for the motherland. I don't believe those rumors myself, but you must admit the sudden availability of top-quality synthetic raw material, at a third of the prevailing price per kilo, was unprecedented. Ever since the worldwide skin crisis of the seventies, the industry's been wary of shortages. Survival has depended on reducing costs, which meant going synthetic.

Price wars raged. Folks started buying five, ten, even as many as twenty topskins, never mind the multiples in underskins. Even my parents each bought a second, although Ma complained that synthetic just didn't feel as good. Suddenly, skin took on a whole new dimension. The markets for other bodyparts went into shock, unable to compete against this surge in demand for skin and only skin. Meanwhile, futures in natural epidermatis were priced 25% up even in the nearest months, which battered Derma. Rumor had it they were buying supplies from People's PiFu, who of course didn't suffer an iota, given their government-regulated market.

And then, in the middle of 1997, the worldwide skin market crashed.

It was bound to happen. Folks were carrying debt over their heads in skins. Even with cheaper prices, an average one still comprises a hefty percentage of most incomes. Besides, as Papa declared, how many skins can a person wear anyway? Used, recycled, and even slightly defective new skins flooded the stores. Now, everyone's fancy skins were worth less than a mound of toenails.

Things looked bleak.

Folks are funny. They self-correct pretty quickly in the face of disaster. Everyone laid low on skins for awhile. Television pundits compare the past few years to the Great Eyelash Famine as well as the New Deal in Teeth. I don't pay much attention to pundits myself. They invent connections where there are none.

Derma's comeback was quite the media circus. Among the larger companies, they had the upper hand now because they hadn't invested in growth, and consequently, weren't sitting on useless inventory or excessive debt. There's nothing quite like cash, is there? But I have to admire their new CEO for some pretty quick moves. First, there was the hostile takeover of Epiderm International, instantly transforming Derma into the largest in the industry. That caught Integume and All Nippon Cutis completely off guard. By the time they proposed buying SubCutis, that company's parent, All Nippon Cutis, was too broke not to capitulate.

Ultimately, however, it was brilliant marketing that invigorated them. "Why pretend? Slide into a genuine *american*. One is all you'll ever need." Sales picked up, thanks to their clever offer of low-interest, long-term loans. If you bought a top-of-the line, they threw in an Epiderm topskin or SubCutis accessory on layaway at a discount. They didn't have to lower prices or redesign their main line. Timing was all. Folks were sick to death of hype.

Well, I wasn't going to be left behind over something as important as skin. Skin-buying is something you do once in a purple sun, or at least, that's the way it used to be in my father's day, as he loves to remind me. Derma refinanced my debt with SubCutis and Epiderm. It made my millennium celebration.

I'd like to stay with *american* for awhile. You know, give myself time to get used to it. It fits well, neither too tight nor too loose. I still have faith in this classic model.

But the skin industry's so unpredictable these days.

Epiderm US launched two niche lines in time for Christmas, *indigo jazz* and *latin hues*, and sales were bigger than anyone predicted. Maybe they're not so niche. And how about that rash of IPOs of small companies in the middle of last year? Who would have thought the stock prices of Kimchee Kasings, Hide-the-Curry, and TagalogitPelts could triple by year-end? Some analysts think these upstarts could give Derma a run for their money. Nothing's what it seems anymore.

Also, People's PiFu has been making noises recently about going public here, saying they'll list on the New York Stock Exchange. Now that's earth shattering news in my books. They hired this youngish CEO a few years back—quite a change for them—and just launched a brand new product line, *sinokapitalist*. I like it. It's got a kind of postmodern pizzaz, something I can't quite define, that seems right for this century. Papa thinks it's ridiculous, although he grudgingly admits now that *china* cutis has run its course.

Let's just say I've learned from my fashion mistakes. Besides, for all we know, the next trend will be in chins, or something else equally unexpected. I'll wait a bit, to see how this new model fares, before I even think about exchanging my *american* skin.

Putting aside issues of autobiography for a moment, let's look at how this piece of fiction follows and departs from traditional short story structure. Does the story have a conflict, crisis, and resolution as some of the more realist stories we've read so far possess? If we placed it side-by-side with Angelo Lacuesta's story, "The Errand," we'd likely conclude that Lacuesta follows the form of the short story in a more traditional manner ("traditional" shouldn't be confused, by the way, with "boring") than Xu Xi's story. "The Errand" is a journey story with beginning, middle, and end while "All About Skin" follows more on the line of a report or a history. Stories take many forms, and in some cases, appropriate other forms, such as reports, letters, and even such unlikely candidates as recipes and tests. One of our favorite authors, Franz Kafka, famously wrote "A Report to an Academy," in which an ape named "Red Peter," who has learned human ways, recounts to a scientific conference his conflicts and reasons for his transformation since being captured in the jungle.

All three stories that we've just mentioned have this in common: they're about identity—in Lacuesta's case, it's the conflict of the reality of Moroy's life as a driver, low on the societal ladder, and his aspirations to be more like his boss. In the case of the Kafka's story, it's at least in part about the conflict between the seemingly noble institutions of society and the sometimes cruel results of an individual's ability to control their own destiny. In the case of Xu Xi, it's quite literally and metaphorically about the skins we wear and how we shed identities as we grow and move through society.

The next question then is how autobiographical is this story really?

We don't necessarily have to know anything about Xu Xi's life to enjoy this wry look at the ways in which people pick up and shed identities in their lives, but it would be a major oversight to overlook the specifically Asian context of this story. Xu Xi was born in Hong Kong, then a British overseas colony, to parents of mixed Chinese and Indonesian heritage. Growing up in Hong Kong, she was not British but she was not fully Chinese either, not to herself or her classmates. She spoke Cantonese and British-English, but her sights, and those of her family, were always on America. She attended college as an undergraduate in upstate New York while a number of her siblings attended the University of Iowa (Go Hawkeyes!). She received her MFA in Writing from U Mass-Amherst. She spent many years in the corporate world, shuttling back and forth between Asia, Europe, and the United States, became a naturalized American citizen, took care of her aging mother in Hong Kong, while living a global life, constantly crisscrossing borders. Now she's studying Bahasa Indonesia to connect more with her Indonesian roots. Certainly, this biographical note, perfunctory as it is, should echo in the reader's mind as they read her story. In these ways, we might see "All About Skin," despite its almost cavalier tone, as autobiographical as it explores the multiple mutations of identity Xu Xi has experienced in her lifetime. That's not to say that the traditional parents portrayed in the story are anything like her own real parents, but that the interior emotional map from which she was writing was in some measure autobiographical. The correlations aren't one-to-one, but they're present nonetheless. If this is the case, then how would you categorize this story: as autofiction or autobiografiction?

The story "Dragon Menu" is likewise about identity, but in this case, we know very little about the author's life, so instead, let's return to the idea of metafiction and the notion of the *alter ego*. This concept of an "other" self is one that most of us should be pretty familiar with. Our protagonists are not *necessarily* our alter egos, but in some cases, they certainly are such, and the concept has long fascinated fiction writers. Two of the most famous fictional accounts of alter egos are Robert Louis Stevenson's *Strange Case of Dr. Jekyll and Mr. Hyde* and James Thurber's *The Secret Life of Walter Mitty*. The transformation to the alter ego in the Stevenson novella comes about as the result of a serum Dr. Jekyll drinks, and in the case of the Thurber story, the alter egos of Walter Mitty are simply daydreams. In the case of "Dragon Menu," the nameless narrator of the story simply declares matter-of-factly that they are not sure when thirteen-year-old Zhaishao "took up residence in my brain." Zhaishao is a gamer and lives in a dazzling animated world that the narrator likes to view when they are "feeling low." So read this story that is about an "other" self in this fantastical story by Chinese author Zhang Xinxin.

2 "Dragon Menu"

by Zhang Xinxin (China)

Translated from Chinese (Mandarin) by Helen Wang

Zhang Xinxin's acclaimed oral history *Chinese Lives* is co-authored with the journalist Sang Ye. She is author of many novels, novellas, short stories, essays as well as several screenplays. A Beijing native, after Tiananmen she was stranded in the United States, where she continues to write and also directs series for television.

1

Thirteen year old Zhaishao, whose soft cheeks have yet to witness their first spot, and who has yet to develop a life he can call his own, keeps all his assets on his hard drive: pirated movies, music downloads, computer games. I'm not sure when he took up residence in my brain, but when I'm feeling low I look at the world through his eyes, and all the problems of the real world dissolve into dazzling animation. Through his eyes I see his life, in a Post-Peking-Man town in the Dragon Bone Mountains. It used to be a small place surrounded by fields, but that was before the farmers downed tools and moved into the city. Later on, as outsiders arrived looking for work, the old residents became micro-landlords, and earned their living renting out the tiniest of spaces. The main industry in the town is construction . . . well, it was, until the day the dragons came. Exactly when they arrived, Zhaishao does not know. He finds it difficult to distinguish between life on-screen and off-screen. The only thing he knows for certain is that these dragons are not alien invaders.

2

Standing on the street, Zhaishao watches as a dragon flies past a window, its silver scales catching the sun like crystals. Perhaps it has escaped from the digital world on screen? Then it is gone, and grey sky fills the window again. He catches a glimpse of another dragon's front leg. The purple scales are not computer-generated, it is not plastic, and there is an iron chain clamped on the leg. His eyes follow the chain. It leads to a hand, to a group of his classmates walking along, each one with a dragon on a lead. A chill creeps over his shoulder as he feels the sudden shame of falling behind. He looks down at the street and there is a little dragon perching on his shadow's shoulder, like a bird. It looks like the dragon he saw before, the little silver one. He holds out a piece of dark chocolate. The dragon leaves the chocolate but snaps viciously at his palm, leaving two tiny rows of teethmarks.

As they come to the footbridge, his classmate whips a small hammer out of his trouser pocket, chips a piece of concrete off the pillar and pops it into the dragon's mouth. The dragon chomps with relish, spraying crumbs as it eats. The other dragons rush to snatch the crumbs from the ground, heads down, tails up, dust flying.

Dragons eating concrete? Is this a dream, wonders Zhaishao. He watches in amazement as the dragons gnaw on the pillars. A skirmish breaks out. Zhaishao beckons to the little silver dragon on his shadow. "Come up!" Actually, he just wants to show it off to the girl who lives in the apartment block by the footbridge. She looks at him from her window like a solitary star in the sky. She's a classmate—was a classmate, until her face went pale and she stopped coming to school. He's heard she won't last the summer. From her window high up, he's just another little figure down below, but if he jumps about with a silver dragon on his shoulder she will see its scales glint. But this dragon does not want to play: it will not come up, it will not eat concrete, and when Zhaishao tries to catch it, it flies off. He notices some color on its front leg. It seems so familiar.

The dragons are eating away at the footbridge. As the concrete disappears, all that is left are the steel sinews weaving in and out, up and down, a dense interlocking spiral structure, like a tower of prehistoric fish bones on the beach. A dragon leaps up and bangs its head against it, sending a chunk of concrete crashing down and knocking over a cart full of sand and lime that had been left underneath. The youngsters scramble away as best they can, but the dragons keep their heads down and concentrate on the morsels of concrete. All except Zhaishao's little dragon which grabs hold of his T-shirt, and hauls him out of the sand. He notices a set of colored bands on its front leg, the same ones he has seen on the girl's wrist! Zhaishao races home and as he runs inside he sees the little silver dragon vanish into the tall block by the footbridge and a dragon shadow appear in the window high up.

3

The conversation at the dinner table is steeped in science. The phenomenon of people turning into dragons can be attributed to the environment, pollution, global warming and the ozone layer, intones the television in the background. A mere re-awakening of non-human DNA that has lain dormant for millions of years, says Zhaishao, repeating the word "mutation" from a Hollywood movie. Toxic food, say his parents, without looking up from their chopsticks. They are more concerned about the roof over their heads and the floor beneath their feet, about property values, re-financing, the new lease, the price per square meter, . . . after each mouthful of rice they start talking about property again, and Zhaishao hears the painful cry of a wounded dragon. His thoughts turn to the little dragon girl, and as usual, he puts down his rice-bowl and chopsticks and returns to his room, to his own little world.

High up above the footbridge, her window stands out in the dark of night. It seems even brighter than before. Is it her silver body shining? He looks at the palm of his hand. If humans are bitten by dragons do they go mad? Like getting rabies? The two rows of dragon-teeth marks on his hand make a wonderful pattern. They are bleeding slightly. He smiles to himself. No one else in the world has a pattern like this on their hand.

Across the road a group of dragons is eating a building, drawn by the tantalizing smell of concrete released by the cracks in the walls. At least the block has already been condemned as dangerous—the residents are calculating the compensation! But young Zhaishao looks serious: concrete is being eaten, the dragons are invading. By the roadside people are selling weapons to deal with the dragons. Some have bought steel halters to try and catch them, but the concrete-eaters have run off in all directions. The youngsters have bought swords to go chasing after dragons. Zhaishao will join them, he will be a Dragonslayer too. (It's a disaster movie! A coming of age movie! But he is the softie of the group. To put it simply, he will never be able to destroy the little dragon girl he loves.)

4

On his way out to join the Dragonslayers, Zhaishao sees a pair of dragons sitting on the living room sofa. When did his parents become dragons? They had only finished their rice, but now they are moaning with hunger and pawing pitifully at their bellies: they can't bring themselves to eat their own home. Zhaishao locks the door as he leaves, and, dragging a small trolley behind him, heads off to look for some concrete.

Zhaishao looks up at the apartment blocks on either side of the road. He is shocked by what he sees. It has taken the dragons no time at all to strip the concrete from these buildings. The walls are just frames, the floors are just girders. Each building is like a 3D maze, or an iridescent Rubik's Cube. The shattered shards of fallen glass glister and mirror the transparent maze, and the random movement of people and dragons in their own little worlds creates a world of never-ending fractal animation. The reflected world on the ground is more vivid, more profound, more infinite than the life in the buildings. Then, one by one, the metal grilles at the windows appear so prominent, so dominant. Ubiquitous. Ridiculous. With the new openwork walls, can these metal bars seriously keep anyone—or anything—out?

The entire city feels like a zoo. People walk about in their metal cages, they shower, make love, watch TV, eat food, slipping seamlessly through the metal frames from one room to another. The dragons walk about in their metal cages too, doing exactly the same things. Except they eat differently: their bodies are so long that they can stand in their own place and eat the concrete in the next-door apartment. With a stretch of the neck and a twist of the body, they can scoff the concrete upstairs and downstairs too. There are so many dragons it is becoming a dragon town.

Zhaishao looks at the teeth marks on his palm. They are bleeding more than before. Why have his parents turned into dragons, but he has not? He does not understand. Had he been about to turn into a dragon when the dragon girl bit him? Is that why he hasn't changed? OMG! SHE'S SOOO AWESOME!

The old streets of the old town re-appear through the tumbledown walls of the apartment blocks: the black rooftiles, the red lattice walls, the grey bricklaid floors. It is still a small town after all, thinks Zhaishao. The most genuine thing in it is probably his own place. As long as his hard-drive is still there, his life will be fine. Oh, and he'd need his mobile phone. But he doesn't care about the rest, just as he has stopped caring about fairytales, and seeing white horses in the clouds.

5

Her window is immediately over the top of his computer screen. He sits in front of it all day and all night. His window is only a frame, since the dragons have eaten the rest, but hers is still intact. A lone guard watching over her window, Zhaishao drops off to sleep.

Maybe, after moving house for the first time, when he came back to look for his Toy Story Cowboy, she had also come back to look for her rag-doll. Maybe in the dark, his hand had touched hers, or by some stroke of magic, her lips had touched his, so so softly. Maybe the meeting of their souls was written in the spatial motion of the planets. I don't know, and neither does my little Zhaishao. All I know, and all he knows, is that whenever he thinks of her, his heart skips a beat, and that beyond the three-dimensional world of his computer screen there is a fourth dimension. It doesn't matter where they first met, or that she has turned into a dragon. None of that matters.

When Zhaishao wakes up, something has changed. There are dragons eating the steel structures! A second generation of dragons that eats concrete and steel! The people inside the metal structures have turned into dragons, and they are eating too. They are all eating at the same time, and as they eat the buildings diminish. The steel structure of the entire town is gradually disappearing. It is like a movie playing backwards: the buildings grow back into the ground, the mish-mash of roads re-appears, the cars crawling in traffic come to a standstill.

The wheels and bolts have been eaten. The engines have been eaten . . .

Zhaishao starts to drift amid the dereliction, the urban landscape morphing into a metaphysical metropolis. As apartment blocks disappear, computer screens and TVs begin to proliferate, and mobile phones twinkle like stars in the sky, except they are twinkling on earth, flickering, glimmering, buzzing, humming. The people still on two legs go in and out of their temporary shells, the rich in their tall wooden towers, the ordinary folk in straw huts and the migrant workers under plastic sheeting. Some climb into the broken shells of cars, with black rubber tires, rows of seats, a steering wheel, a board here and there, just like the make-believe games they played as children . . .

Outside, the world has gone quiet, except for the sound of rushing water. It is the sound of fountains, of sand sliding down dunes. The dragons have digested the concrete and excreted sand. The tall concrete buildings have been replaced by dunes of white sand. The greenery is still there, although there have never been many trees in this small town. There are little gardens in the streets, pots of flowers on balconies, seductive little oases in the desert—no need for a mirage.

As the human population diminishes, the number of dragons increases. But the first generation dragons are now dying of hunger. The wind whittles away at their bodies till their bones fall higgledy-piggledy to the ground, the larger bones stacking up like giant bricks making a white dragon bone wall.

6

Zhaishao watches as two new humans-turned-dragons emerge, one from a wooden building and one from a straw hut, look back at their shells and eat them. He understands immediately: a third generation of dragons is appearing.

The third-generation dragons can eat everything: plastic, glass, wood, rubbish. The town is covered in the stuff, but before long everything has been cleaned up, even the last bits of greenery.

The Dragonslayers have vowed to trace the dragons back to their source—the first human-turned-dragon, the Mutant Dragon. The final act will be an execution, elimination of the mutation. In Zhaishao's palm the bite marks ooze blood. His stigmata. His call of duty.

7

Zhaishao has his suspicions. All the buildings in town have been eaten. The building opposite has also been pulverised, yet that window is still there, floating in the air. It is like an illusion, yet so real, and from time to time she appears there. The humans-turned-dragons must share his suspicion for a crowd has gathered beneath the window. There is yelling and shouting. Without stopping to get dressed, Zhaishao leaps into action. He must go to her rescue.

Yes, she is the Mutant Dragon, but how did she become the first one? I am trying to work this out. Perhaps she really was sick, with an incurable disease, and had been lying in bed by the window. Turning her head on the pillow, she could see the back of his computer through the window. At night-time, when all the lights in the building had gone out, she could see this single dark square with colored lights shimmering around the edges, like a rectangular eclipse. The girl stared and wondered how she could go to see what it was. Her father was into bionics, and used the flat as a workshop in which to seek for the elixir of immortality, that lost ancestral art. The girl simply wanted to know what was behind the lights. She dreamed of putting her feet on the ground, of getting out of bed, walking into the sunshine, and across the footbridge. She drank the potion her father had made, turned into a dragon, and floated in the air by her window. Damn the legend of Chang Er drinking the elixir of immortality and flying to the moon! How did I get caught up in this stuff? Do I really have to explain how the girl became the first dragon? Does it matter if she was the first? Does it matter what she dreams? What matters is that she is at the heart of his troubled mind.

Zhaishao has already endured the full range of impossibilities: through burning flames, across sheets of ice, past bolts of thunder, but he still has to get through the crowd of dragons. They come up to him and bite at his body, ripping and tearing at his skin with their sharp teeth. They eat his T-shirt, his pants, his slippers. He runs naked towards the little dragon girl's window. When he sees her, he reaches up to her. She stretches out her leg with the colored bands. Their fingertips touch. As the dragon claw turns into a hand, a wild outbreak of laughter explodes behind him. He looks round and sees the Dragonslayers brandishing their swords at the dragon girl.

"She's the one!"

Zhaishao moves to protect her. "Don't kill her! She's my girl!"

"Wake up!" they shout, thrusting their swords towards him. "She's not real! She's an illusion! She's living in your head, you've got to get rid of her, root out this madness, then everything can go back to how it was!"

Swords slice through the air. The little dragon girl leaps into the air. There is nowhere to land. As the swords slash, my Zhaishao's heart begins to pound. He leaps up to block the swords. He sees them slice at my shoulder, my leg, my waist. And at that moment the Dragonslayers change. They roar furiously as they turn into dragons. Their swords fall from their claws. They look up in amazement, mouths gaping, as though drinking in the air in which the dragon girl is floating. His friends have become the fourth generation of dragons.

8

If the third generation dragons are indiscriminate omnivores of all material things, I wonder what the fourth generation dragons will eat?

Perhaps they will feed on the nonmaterial assets of the twenty-first century: on visual images, and intangible things that are conceived in the brain. This is something I had never imagined. Yes, I am tired of being surrounded by material things. Yes, I find the overconsumption in this world ridiculous. I think of myself as a materialist turned minimalist. So why shouldn't it be the same with conceptual stuff? Why, when there is so much of it around, do people still feed the need to go on producing more and more? Each brain is a hive buzzing with activity: there is an astronomical number of synapses, a Big Bang every nano-second. In the infinitely interlinking universe of my mind, I have had the craziest of thoughts. I have tried to banish them, to throw them out, to refuse any space to mental waste. How many times have I had to pluck from the wastebasket something spectacular that I could not be bothered with before? I CANNOT—I WILL NOT—make the conscious decision to eliminate creativity, because I have to live. Keeping the creative juices flowing in my brain is fundamental to my quality of life.

If the fourth generation dragons can survive on things that exist in cloud storage and 3G, I can live with that. But I will not let them take my Zhaishao, or his little dragon girl. He faces this crisis with eyes wide open, his heart beating wildly, his body constricted by something he cannot name. Then, all of a sudden, she flaps her dragon wings and flies up to the window. She looks back. I leap up, grab hold, and off we fly. I float in the lightness of air, and roll like a cloud over town. The mad wind pulls at every hair on my head, its cold breath stinging my scalp, ringing in my ears. I cling on for my life, and peer down at what is left of the town below. The earth is vast and the sky is huge. We have taken so much from the earth, but the dragons have devoured all the material things we humans have made. There is nothing left for them to eat.

Three generations of dragons are dying. The harsh wind dries their bones, piling them up into dragon-bone walls. I see the Dragonslayers tie themselves together, like a dragon-plane, running together to take off, to escape. But the sand is too deep and their dragon-plane sinks. They try again, and sink again. They cannot survive for much longer. Eventually, they will perish too, and their bones will join those of Zhaishao's parents. They're just another brick in the wall.

I feel myself falling. My dragon girl's wings are shrinking. We crash into the walls of the dragon corpse maze. The dragon bones are sharp and densely packed. They stab me like knives and arrows. My dragon girl flaps her ever-diminishing wings as she struggles to fly. But it is no good. Tears roll down my face, and drops of rain—her tears—fall on my head. She grows smaller and smaller, until she is a shadow over my head.

My foot lands on a sharp cone, which jabs into the sole of my foot. I walk along the long dragon-bone wall, a white meandering wall in the surging black waves of the sea. Like a sand-dune, the wall shifts as the black waves crash against it. The sun shines fiercely on the sand, the myriad dots of light like a fixed-frame sea spray.

Dazed, I search for yesterday, the long blur of yesterday. There, on the hard, white dragon bone islands stands my Zhaishao. The black waves surge around him. Eyes wide open, a solitary boy, a naked exile in a desolate world.

In the same way that the narrator doesn't know how Zhaishao took up residence in their (the gender of the narrator isn't specified so we're using ungendered pronouns for this reason) brain, we simply have to accept it as a matter of course. This is a smart strategy when writing about something fantastical—instead of going to great lengths to explain and justify an unusual aspect of the world you're creating, write it as though that detail or occurrence is simply an unremarkable and everyday thing. This is a way to claim a kind of *authority* in your narration. If you act sure of yourself, your reader will likely accept what you throw their way—to a certain extent. Simply claiming authority doesn't exactly mean you've earned it—the right tone is a start, but it's only a start. The *internal logic* of your story needs to be consistent and your details need to be rich enough that we don't doubt what you've written.

We learn, too, that Zhaishao has difficulty distinguishing the "screen from reality," which strikes us as a pretty intriguing clue, these concentric circles of reality and fantasy intertwined. Here we have an author who has created a narrator who has a thirteen-year-old boy living in their brain who can't tell the difference between the screen and reality, whose world is being invaded by dragons, which might or might not be animations. One thing is for certain is that they're not aliens. That last bit is especially intriguing. If they're not aliens then that must mean they are either from a different dimension or already exist on earth. Either way, people are transforming into these dragons and the world Zhaishao knows is being dismantled by their appetites. We can read this on a literal level, if we wish, but then what we come away with seems a bit unsatisfying. What are we supposed to take away from the story literally? Like Xu Xi's story, this can be read as a story of identity perhaps—it's ambiguous enough that different readers in different places will interpret the story in various ways, and as long as the interpretations are too far removed from the clues in the story, who is to say who is correct? The author? Well, you don't likely have the author standing over your shoulder directing you how to read their story and even if you did, as we've pointed out previously, the author doesn't always see everything in their own story. We might also consider whether a reader in Shanghai or Guangzhou might read this story allegorically. While dragons aren't exclusive to China, they are certainly associated with the country and culture. To another reader, the story is simply about isolation. Or conformity. Eugene Ionesco's famous play, *Rhinoceros*, written in 1959, features a small French town in which everyone, except for one person, transforms into rhinos. Transformation stories, such as "Dragon Menu," "Rhinoceros," and Franz Kafka's classic "Metamorphosis," are almost always on some level about identity, the individual, and society. It's hard to imagine them about anything else.

The story might be about all of these possibilities, and it's not the author's job to tell us which is the right one. When you're writing such a story, it's not your job to leave signposts that are so obvious we will have no choice but to read it in the way you want it read. Free your characters and free us. Most importantly, free yourself to explore unfettered by concerns about being misinterpreted, your alter egos and multiple identities.

Exercises

1. Write a story in which a character or characters transform into something impossible. Don't worry about how absurd it is—you could write a perfectly wicked story about someone who turns into a vending machine, for instance, or a cell phone. Try not to pick ones that are too close to ones that you know have already been used. Part of the fun in this is how clever you can be in choosing an object that carries some kind of inherent cultural currency, like the dragon in "Dragon Menu." Of course, you don't want to be too heavy-handed, so if you're American, you might want to take a pass on everyone turning into a bald eagle. On the other hand, who are we to say? Maybe the next great American novel will simply be titled, *Eagle*. *Note: please remember we gave you the idea and a finder's fee would be greatly appreciated.*

2. Write a version of your life as if your identity were a commodity. Perhaps write an autobiography in cars or hair styles or songs or shows you've watched.

3. Take something you can't change about yourself, as in Xu Xi's "All about Skin," and write a pseudo-autobiography in which you can change it. Imagine a world in which you had to earn enough money to purchase various facial expressions, for instance.

4. Write a story in which the main character has your name and is identifiably you, except that most of what happens in the story didn't actually happen.

5. Write something that is based quite closely on your real life, but call it fiction. Give the main character a different name and write the story in the third person or second person, but not in the first person. Do you feel more freedom to write "truthfully" under the guise of fiction or does the disguise tend to make you invent more? The answer to that question might help determine what kind of writer you are on the continuum of autobiography and invention.

CHAPTER 6
INVADERS

As is already evident, the clash of cultures is a prevalent theme in many of the stories we've selected for this book. One reason we find such stories compelling is because they do reflect the conflicted state of our globalized, transnational world; the migration of people worldwide has diversified population in many countries, which does contribute to conflict. In Asia, there's also the history of colonialism by European powers as well as what we might term the "American invasion." In this chapter, we'll look at the "invader" in two stories that showcase an American presence in Asia. "Farangs," by Rattawut Lapcharoensap, is contemporary, set in a Thai beach resort whose economy depends on foreign tourists where the clash is racial, sexual, and economic. The second story, "Boondocks," by Robin Hemley, is a historical short story set during the Second World War in the Philippines. Notably, both stories employ humor delivered partly through a linguistic comedy that divides the American and the local characters. Both are also remarkable in the way the writers are able to appropriate and represent a culture that is not entirely their own by the effective use of *archetypes*. These are nuanced, layered, and also offer the element of surprise.

When we want to write a story of a cultural clash, it's often too easy to fall into the trap of taking sides of one of the groups. Here's that terrible *gweilo*, *gaijin*, *bule*—all pejoratives used in different Asian countries for the outsider—usually a white man who plunders and rapes, or gets a local woman pregnant and then abandons her. One of the more famous examples of this is Puccini's 1904 opera *Madame Butterfly*, in which Pinkerton, a white American naval officer, marries Cho Cho San, a geisha, gets her pregnant but abandons her for his white American wife. Butterfly eventually accepts her fate, gives up her son to the Pinkertons, and commits ritual suicide. This tragic love story forces our sympathies for Butterfly and Pinkerton comes off as insensitive and clueless. In fact, the opera is based on an 1898 short story of the same name by an American writer, John Luther Long. In that version, Pinkerton is portrayed as less naïve and Butterfly has quite a mischievous personality. The cultural divide between Pinkerton and Butterfly is evident, especially in terms of language, with some (admittedly dated) attempt at humor. The plot is similar to that of the opera. However at the end, Butterfly begins the ritual suicide but the sight of her baby boy stops her. She takes her child and disappears so that when the Pinkertons arrive at her house, it's empty.

Which version do you like better? We find the original short story far more intriguing because the Japanese geisha defies the passive Asian female stereotypical image of one who gives in to her fate, in this case caused by an insensitive white lover. It may not be as dramatic as the opera, but both Butterfly and Pinkerton are fully fleshed characters. Although the story is dated, especially in its worldview and the rendering of Butterfly's English as a kind of faux pidgin, it provides a historical perspective for Lapcharoensap's "Farangs," the pejorative in Thai for foreigners. Here is another white-Asian romance gone wrong, but in this contemporary version, language is both the connection and the divide. Go ahead and read the story now.

The Art and Craft of Asian Stories

1 "Farangs"

by Rattawut Lapcharoensap (USA)

Rattawut Lapcharoensap is Thai American and a "5 under 35" writer honored by the National Book Foundation in 2006. Born in Chicago, he grew up in Bangkok and is best known for his story collection *Sightseeing*. In 2010 he received a Whiting Award in fiction.

> This is how we count the days. June: the Germans come to the Island—football cleats, big T-shirts, thick tongues—speaking like spitting. July: the Italians, the French, the British, the Americans. The Italians like pad thai, its affinity with spaghetti. They like light fabrics, sunglasses, leather sandals. The French like plump girls, rambutans, disco music, baring their breasts. The British are here to work on their pasty complexions, their penchant for hashish. Americans are the fattest, the stingiest of the bunch. They may pretend to like pad thai or grilled prawns or the occasional curry, but twice a week they need their culinary comforts, their hamburgers and their pizzas. They're also the worst drunks. Never get too close to a drunk American. August brings the Japanese. Stay close to them. Never underestimate the power of the yen. Everything's cheap with imperial monies in hand and they're too polite to bargain. By the end of August, when the monsoon starts to blow, they're all consorting, slapping each other's backs, slipping each other drugs, sleeping with each other, sipping their liquor under the pink lights of the Island's bars. By September they've all deserted, leaving the Island to the Aussies and the Chinese, who are so omnipresent one need not mention them at all.
>
> Ma says, "Pussy and elephants. That's all these people want." She always says this in August, at the season's peak, when she's tired of farangs running all over the Island, tired of finding used condoms in the motel's rooms, tired of guests complaining to her in five languages. She turns to me and says, "You give them history, temples, pagodas, traditional dance, floating markets, seafood curry, tapioca desserts, silk-weaving cooperatives, but all they really want is to ride some hulking grey beast like a bunch of wild men and to pant over girls and to lie there half-dead getting skin cancer on the beach during the time in between."
>
> We're having a late lunch, watching television in the motel office. The Island Network is showing Rambo: First Blood Part II again. Sylvester Stallone, dubbed in Thai, mows down an entire regiment of VC with a bow and arrow. I tell Ma I've just met a girl. "It might be love," I say. "It might be real love, Ma. Like Romeo and Juliet love."
>
> Ma turns off the television just as John Rambo is about to fly a chopper to safety.
>
> She tells me it's just my hormones. She sighs and says, "Oh no, not again. Don't be so naive," she says. "I didn't raise you to be stupid. Are you bonking one of the guests? You better not be bonking one of the guests. Because if you are, if you're bonking one of the guests, we're going to have to bleed the pig. Remember, luk, we have an agreement."
>
> I tell her she's being xenophobic. I tell her things are different this time. But Ma just licks her lips and says once more that if I'm bonking one of the guests, I can look forward to eating Clint Eastwood curry in the near future. Ma's always talking about killing my pig. And though I know she's just teasing, she says it with such zeal and a peculiar glint in her eyes that I run out to the pen to check on the swine.

I knew it was love when Clint Eastwood sniffed her crotch earlier that morning and the girl didn't scream or jump out of the sand or swat the pig like some of the other girls do. She merely lay there, snout in crotch, smiling that angelic smile, like it was the most natural thing in the world, running a hand over the fuzz of Clint Eastwood's head like he was some pink and docile dog, and said, giggling, "Why hello, oh my, what a nice surprise, you're quite a beast, aren't you?"

I'd been combing the motel beachfront for trash when I looked up from my morning chore and noticed Clint Eastwood sniffing his new friend. An American: her Budweiser bikini told me so. I apologized from a distance, called the pig over, but the girl said it was okay, it was fine, the pig could stay as long as he liked. She called me over and said I could do the same.

I told her the pig's name.

"That's adorable," she laughed.

"He's the best," I said. "*Dirty Harry. Fistful of Dollars. The Good, The Bad and The Ugly.*"

"He's a very good actor."

"Yes. Mister Eastwood is a first-class thespian."

Clint Eastwood trotted into the ocean for his morning bath then, leaving us alone, side by side in the sand. I looked to make sure Ma wasn't watching me from the office window. I explained how Clint Eastwood loves the ocean at low tide, the wet sand like a three-kilometer trough of mud. The girl sat up on her elbows, watched the pig, a waterlogged copy of *The Portrait of a Lady* at her side. She'd just gone for a swim and the beads of water on her navel seemed so close that for a moment I thought I might faint if I did not look away.

"I'm Elizabeth. Lizzie."

"Nice to meet you, Miss Elizabeth," I said. "I like your bikini."

She threw back her head and laughed. I admired the shine of her tiny, perfectly even rows of teeth, the gleam of that soft, rose-colored tongue quivering between them like the meat of some magnificent mussel.

"Oh my," she said, closing that mouth, gesturing with her chin. "I think your pig is drowning."

Clint Eastwood was rolling around where the ocean meets the sand, chasing receding waves, running away from oncoming ones. It's a game he plays every morning, scampering back and forth across the water's edge, and he snorted happily every time the waves licked over him, knocked him into the foam.

"He's not drowning," I said. "He's a very good swimmer, actually."

"I didn't know pigs could swim."

"Clint Eastwood can."

She smiled, a close-mouthed grin, admiring my pig at play, and I would've given anything in the world to see her tongue again, to reach out and sink my fingers into the hollows of her collarbone, to stare at that damp, beautiful navel all day long.

"I have an idea, Miss Elizabeth," I said, getting up, brushing the sand from the seat of my shorts. "This may seem rather presumptuous, but would you like to go for an elephant ride with me today?"

Ma doesn't want me bonking a farang because once, long ago, she had bonked a farang herself, against the wishes of her own parents, and all she got for her trouble was a broken heart and me in return. This was when English was still my first and only language, and the farang was a man known to me only as Sergeant Marshall Henderson. I remember the Sergeant well, if only because he insisted I call him by his military rank.

"Not Daddy," I remember him saying on many occasions. "Sergeant. Sergeant Henderson. Sergeant Marshall. Remember you're a soldier now, boy. A spy for Uncle Sam's army."

And for the first three years of my remembered life—before he went back to America, promising to send for us—the Sergeant and I would go on imaginary missions together, navigating our way through the thicket of tourists lazing on the beach.

"Private," he'd yell after me. "I don't have a good feeling about this, Private. This place gives me the creeps. We should radio for reinforcements. It could be an ambush."

"Let 'em come, Sergeant! We can take 'em!" I would squeal, crawling through the sand with a large stick in my hand, eyes trained on the enemy. "Those gooks'll be sorry they ever showed their ugly faces."

One day, the three of us went to the fresh market by the pier. I saw a litter of pigs there, six of them squeezed tightly into a small cardboard box amidst the loud thudding of butchers' knives. I remember thinking of the little piglets I'd seen skewered and roasting over an open fire outside many of the Island's fancier restaurants.

I began to cry.

"What's wrong, Private?"

"I don't know."

"A soldier," the Sergeant grunted, "never cries."

"They just piggies," Ma laughed in her stilted English, bending down to pat me on the back. Because of our plans to move to California, Ma was learning English at the time. She hasn't spoken a word of English to me since. "What piggies say, luk? What they say? Piggies say oink-oink. Don't cry, luk. Don't cry. Oink-oink is yummy."

A few days later, the Sergeant walked into my bedroom with something wriggling beneath his T-shirt. He sat down on the bed beside me. I remember the mattress sinking with his weight, the chirping of some desperate bird struggling in his belly.

"Congratulations, Private," the Sergeant whispered through the dark, holding out a young and frightened Clint Eastwood in one of his large hands. "You're a CO now. A commanding officer. From now on, you'll be responsible for the welfare of this recruit."

I stared at him dumbfounded, took the pig into my arms.

"Happy birthday, kiddo."

And shortly before the Sergeant left us, before Ma took over the motel from her parents, before she ever forbade me from speaking the Sergeant's language except to assist the motel's guests, before I knew what bastard or mongrel or slut or whore meant in any language, there was an evening when I walked into the ocean with Clint Eastwood—I was teaching him how to swim—and when I looked back to shore I saw my mother sitting between the Sergeant's legs in the sand, the sun a bright red orb on the crest of the mountains behind them. They spoke without looking at each other, my mother reaching back to hook an arm around his neck, while my piglet thrashed in the sea foam. "Ma," I asked a few years later, "you think the Sergeant will ever send for us?"

"It's best, luk," Ma said in Thai, "if you never mention his name again. It gives me a headache."

After I finished combing the beach for trash, put Clint Eastwood back in his pen, Lizzie and I went up the mountain on my motorcycle to Surachai's house, where his uncle Mongkhon ran an elephant-trekking business—mr mongkhon's jungle safari, a painted sign declared in their driveway. come experience the natural beauty of forest with the amazing view of ocean and splendid horizon from elephant's back! I'd informed Uncle Mongkhon once that his sign was grammatically incorrect and that I'd lend him my expertise for a small fee, but he just laughed and said farangs preferred it just the way it was, thank you very much, they thought it was charming, and did I really think I was the only huakhuai who knew English on this godforsaken Island? During the war in Vietnam, before he started the business, Uncle Mongkhon had worked at an airbase on the mainland dishing out lunch to American soldiers.

From where Lizzie and I stood, we could see the grey backs of two bulls peeking over the roof of their one-story house. Uncle Mongkhon used to have a full chuak of elephants, before the people at Monopolated Elephant Tours came to the Island and started underpricing the competition, monopolizing mountain-pass tariffs and staking their claim upon farangs at hotels three stars and up—doing, in short, what they had done on so many other islands like ours. Business began to sag after the arrival of MET and, in the end, Uncle Mongkhon was forced to sell his elephants to logging companies on the mainland. Where there had once been eight elephants roaming the wide corral, now there were only two—Yai and Noi—ageing bulls with ulcered bellies, trunks hung limply between their crusty forelegs.

"Oh, wow," Lizzie said. "Are those actual elephants?"

I nodded.

"They're so huge."

She clapped a few times, laughing.

"Huge!" she said again, jumping up and down. She turned to me and smiled.

Surachai was lifting weights in the yard, a barbell in each hand. Uncle Mongkhon sat on the porch bare-chested, smoking a cigarette. When Surachai saw Lizzie standing there in her bikini next to me, his arms went limp. For a second I was afraid he might drop the weights on his feet.

"Where'd you find this one?" he said in Thai, smirking, walking towards us.

"Boy," Uncle Mongkhon yelled from the porch, also in Thai. "You irritate me sometimes. Tell that girl to put on some clothes. You know damn well I don't let bikinis ride. This is a respectable establishment. We have rules."

"What are they saying?" Lizzie asked. Farangs get nervous when you carry on a conversation they can't understand.

"They just want to know if we need one elephant or two."

"Let's just get one," Lizzie smiled, reaching out to take one of my hands. "Let's ride one together." I held my breath. Her hand shot bright, surprising comets of heat up my arm. I wanted to yank my hand away even as I longed to stand there forever with our sweaty palms folded together like soft roti bread. I heard the voice of Surachai's mother coming from inside the house, the light sizzle of a frying pan.

"It's nothing, Maew," Uncle Mongkhon yelled back to his sister inside. "Though I wouldn't come out here unless you like nudie shows. The mongrel's here with another member of his international harem."

"These are my friends," I said to Lizzie. "This is Surachai."

"How do you do," Surachai said in English, briskly shaking her hand, looking at me all the while.

"I'm fine, thank you," Lizzie chuckled. "Nice to meet you."

"Yes yes yes," Surachai said, grinning like a fool. "Honor to meet you, Madame. It will make me very gratified to let you ride my elephants. Very gratified. Because he"—Surachai patted me on the back now—"he my handsome soulmate. My best man."

Surachai beamed proudly at me. I'd taught him that word: "soulmate".

"How long have you been married?" Lizzie asked. Surachai laughed hysterically, uncomprehendingly, widening his eyes at me for help.

"He's not," I said. "He meant to say 'best friend.'"

"Yes yes," Surachai said, nodding. "Best friend."

"You listening to me, boy?" Uncle Mongkhon got up from the porch and walked towards us. "Bikinis don't ride. It scares the animals."

"*Sawatdee*, Uncle," I said, greeting him with a wai, bending my head extra low for effect; but he slapped me on the head with a forehand when I came up.

"Tell the girl to put on some clothes," Uncle Mongkhon growled. "It's unholy."

"Aw, Uncle," I pleaded. "We didn't bring any with us."

"Need I remind you, boy, that the elephant is our National Symbol? Sometimes I think your stubborn farang half keeps you from understanding this. You should be ashamed of yourself. I'd tell your mother if I knew it wouldn't break her heart."

"What if I went to her country and rode a bald eagle in my underwear, huh?" he continued, pointing at Lizzie. "How would she like it? Ask her, will you?"

"What's he saying?" Lizzie whispered in my ear.

"Ha ha ha," Surachai interjected, gesticulating wildly. "Everything okay, Madame. Don't worry, be happy. My uncle, he just say elephants very terrified of your breasts."

"You should've told me to put on some clothes." Lizzie turned to me, frowning, letting go of my hand.

"It's really not a problem," I laughed.

"No," Uncle Mongkhon said to Lizzie in English. "Not a big problem, Madame. Just a small one."

In the end, to placate Uncle Mongkhon, I took off my T-shirt and gave it to Lizzie. As we made our way towards the corral, I caught her grinning at the sight of my bare torso. Though I had been spending time at the new public gym by the pier, I still felt some of that old adolescent embarrassment returning again. I casually flexed my muscles in the postures I'd practiced before my bedroom mirror so Lizzie could see my body not as the soft, skinny thing that it was, but as a pillar of strength and stamina.

When we came upon the gates of the elephant corral, Lizzie took my hand again. I turned to smile at her and she seemed, at that moment, some ethereal angel come from heaven to save me, an angel whose breasts left round, dark, damp spots on my T-shirt. And when we mounted the elephant Yai, the beast rising quickly to his feet, Lizzie squealed and wrapped her arms so tightly around my bare waist that I would've gladly forfeited breathing for the rest of my life.

Under that jungle canopy, climbing up the mountainside on Yai's back, I told her about Sergeant Henderson, the motel, Ma, Clint Eastwood. She told me about her Ohio childhood, the New York City skyline, NASCAR, T. J. Maxx, the drinking habits of American teenagers. I told her about Pamela, my last American girlfriend, and how she promised me her heart but never answered any of my letters. Lizzie nodded sympathetically and told me about her bastard boyfriend Hunter, whom she'd left last night at their hotel on the other side of the island after finding him in the arms of a young prostitute. "That fucker," she said. "That whore." I told Lizzie she should forget about him, she deserved better, and besides Hunter was a stupid name anyway, and we both shook our heads and laughed at how poorly our lovers had behaved.

We came upon a scenic overlook. The sea rippled before us like a giant blue bedspread. I decided to give Yai a rest. He sat down gratefully on his haunches. For a minute Lizzie and I just sat there on the elephant's back looking out at the ocean, the wind blowing through the trees behind us. Yai was winded from the climb and we rose and fell with his heavy breaths. I told Lizzie about how the Sergeant and my mother used to stand on the beach, point east, and tell me that if I looked hard enough I might be able to catch a glimpse of the California coast rising out of the Pacific horizon. I pointed to Ma's motel below, the twelve bungalows like tiny insects resting on the golden shoreline. It's amazing, I told Lizzie, how small my life looks from such a height.

Lizzie hummed contentedly. Then she stood up on Yai's back. "Here's your shirt," she laughed, tossing it at me.

With a quick sweeping motion, Lizzie took off her bikini top. Then she peeled off her bikini bottom. And then there she was—my American angel—naked on the back of Uncle Mongkhon's ageing elephant.

"Your country is so hot," she said, smiling, crawling towards me on all fours. Yai made a low moan and shifted beneath us.

"Yes, it is," I said, pretending to study the horizon, rubbing Yai's parched, grey back.

After *Rambo*, lunch with my mother and a brief afternoon nap, I walk out the door to meet Lizzie at the restaurant when Ma asks me what I'm all dressed up for.

"What do you mean?" I ask innocently, and Ma says, "What do I mean? What do I mean? Am I your mother? Are you my son? Are those black pants? Is that a button-down shirt? Is that the nice silk tie I bought you for your birthday?"

She sniffs my head.

"And is that my nice mousse in your hair? And why," she asks, "do you smell like an elephant?"

I just stand there blinking at her questions.

"Don't think I don't know," she says finally. "I saw you, luk. I saw you on your motorcycle with that farang slut in her bikini."

I laugh and tell her I have hair mousse of my own. But Ma's still yelling at me when I go to the pen to fetch Clint Eastwood.

"Remember whose son you are," she says through the day's dying light, standing in the office doorway with her arms akimbo. "Remember who raised you all these years."

"What are you talking about, Ma?"

"Why do you insist, luk, on chasing after these farangs?"

"You're being silly, Ma. It's just love. You make it sound like I'm a criminal."

"I don't think," Ma says, "that I'm the silly one here, luk. I'm not the one taking my pet pig out to dinner just because some foreign girl thinks it's cute."

I make my way down the beach with Clint Eastwood towards the lights of the restaurant. It's an outdoor establishment with low candlelit tables set in the sand and a large pit that the bare-chested chefs use to grill the day's catch. The restaurant's quite popular with farangs on the Island. Wind at their backs, sand at their feet, night sky above, eating by the light of the moon and the stars. It's romantic, I suppose. Although I'm hesitant to spend so much money on what Ma calls second-rate seafood in a third-rate atmosphere, Lizzie suggested we meet there for dinner tonight, so who am I to argue with love's demands?

When we get to the restaurant, Lizzie's seated at one of the tables, candlelight flickering on her face. Clint Eastwood races ahead and nuzzles his snout in her lap, but Lizzie's face doesn't light up the way it did earlier this morning. The other customers turn around in their seats to look at Clint Eastwood, and Lizzie seems embarrassed to be the object of his affections.

"Hi," she says when I get to the table, lighting a cigarette.

I kiss one of her hands, sit down beside her. I tell Clint Eastwood to stay. He lies down on his belly in the sand, head resting between his stubby feet. The sun is setting behind us, rays flickering across the plane of the sea, and I think I'm starting to understand why farangs come such a long way to get to the Island, why they travel so far to come to my home.

"Beautiful evening," I say. Lizzie nods absent-mindedly.

"Is there something wrong?" I finally ask, after the waiter takes our order in English. "Have I done anything to offend you?"

Lizzie sighs, stubs out her cigarette in the bamboo ashtray. "Nothing's wrong," she says. "Nothing at all."

But when our food arrives, Lizzie barely touches it. She keeps passing Clint Eastwood pieces of her sautéed prawns. Clint Eastwood gobbles them up gratefully. At least he's enjoying the meal, I think. On weekend nights, I often bring Clint Eastwood to this restaurant, after the tables have been stowed away, and he usually has to fight with the strays that descend on the beach for leftovers farangs leave in their wake: crab shells, fish bones, prawn husks.

"Something's wrong," I say. "You're not happy."

She lights another cigarette, blows a cloud of smoke.

"Hunter's here," she says finally, looking out at the darkening ocean.

"Your ex-boyfriend?"

"No," she says. "My boyfriend. He's here."

"Here?"

"Don't turn around. He's sitting right behind us with his friends."

At that moment, a large farang whom I can only assume is Hunter swoops into the seat across the table from us. He's dressed in a white undershirt and a pair of surfer's shorts. His nose is caked with sunscreen. His chest is pink from too much sun.

There's a Buddha dangling from his neck. He looks like a deranged clown.

He reaches over the table and grabs a piece of squid from my plate.

"Who's the joker?" he asks Lizzie, gnawing on the squid. "Friend of yours?"

"Hunter," Lizzie says. "Don't do this."

"Hey," he says, looking at me, taking another piece of squid from my entrée, "What's with the tie? And what's with the pig, man?"

I smile, put a hand on Clint Eastwood's head.

"Hey you," he says. "I'm talking to you. Speak English? Talk American?"

He tears off a piece of squid with his front teeth. I can't stop staring at his powdered nose, the bulge of his hairy, sunburned chest. I'm hoping he chokes.

"You've really outdone yourself this time, baby," he says to Lizzie now. "But that's what I love about you. Your unpredictability. Your wicked sense of humor. Didn't know you went for mute tards with pet pigs."

"Hunter."

"Oh, Lizzie," he says, reaching out to take one of her hands, feigning tenderness. "I've missed you so much. I hate it when you just leave me like that. I've been worried sick about you. I'm sorry about last night, okay baby? Okay? I'm really sorry. But it was just a misunderstanding, you know? Jerry and Billyboy over there can testify to my innocence. You know how those Thai girls get when we're around."

"We can talk about this later, Hunter."

"Yes," I interject. "I think you should talk to her later."

He just stares at me with that stupid white nose jutting out between his eyes. For a second, I think Hunter's going to throw the squid at me. But then he just pops the rest of it into his mouth, turns to Lizzie, and says with his mouth full:

"You fucked this joker, didn't you?"

"Please, Hunter."

I look over at Lizzie. She's staring at the table, tapping her fingers lightly against the wood. It seems she's about to cry. I stand up, throw a few hundred bahts on the table. Clint Eastwood follows my lead, rises clumsily to his feet.

"It was a pleasure meeting you, Miss Elizabeth," I say, smiling. I want to take her hand and run back to the motel so we can curl up together on the beach, watch the constellations. But Lizzie just keeps on staring at the top of that table.

I walk with Clint Eastwood back to the motel. It seems like we're the only people on that beach. Night is upon us now. In the distance, I can see squidding boats perched on the horizon, fluorescent searchlights luring their catch to the surface. Clint Eastwood races ahead of me, foraging for food in the sand, and I'm thinking with what I suppose is grief about all the American girls I've ever loved. Girls with names like Pamela, Angela, Stephanie, Joy. And now Lizzie.

One of the girls sent me a postcard of Miami once. A row of palm trees and a pink condo. "Hi Sweetie," it said. "I just wanted to say hi and to thank you for showing me a good time when I was over there. I'm in South Beach now, it's Spring Break, and let me tell you it's not half as beautiful as it is over there. If you ever make it out to the U S of A, look me up okay?" which was nice of her, but she never told me where to look her up and there was no return address on the postcard. I'd taken that girl to see phosphorescence in one of the Island's bays and when she told me it was the most miraculous thing she'd ever seen, I told her I loved her—but the girl just giggled and ran into the sea, that phosphorescent blue streaking like a comet's tail behind her.

Every time they do that, I swear I'll never love another, and I'm thinking about Lizzie and Hunter sitting at the restaurant now, and how this is really the last time I'll let myself love one of her kind.

Halfway down the beach, I find Surachai sitting in a mango tree. He's hidden behind a thicket of leaves, straddling one of the branches, leaning back against the trunk.

When we were kids, Surachai and I used to run around the beach advertising ourselves as the Island's Miraculous Monkey Boys.

We made loincloths out of Uncle Mongkhon's straw heap and an old T-shirt Ma used as a rag. For a small fee, we'd climb up trees and fetch coconuts for farangs, who would ooh and aah at how nimble we were. A product of our Island environment, they'd say, as if it was due to something in the water and not the fact that we'd spent hours practicing in Surachai's backyard. For added effect, we'd make monkey noises when we climbed, which always made them laugh. They would often be impressed, too, by my facility with the English language. In one version of the speech I gave before every performance, I played the part of an American boy shipwrecked on the Island as an infant. With both parents dead, I was raised in the jungle by a family of gibbons.

Though we've long outgrown what Ma calls "that idiot stunt," Surachai still comes down from the mountain occasionally to climb a tree on the beach. He'll just sit there staring out into the ocean for hours. It's meditative, he told me once. And the view is one-of-a-kind.

"You look terrible," he says now. "Something happen with that farang girl?"

I call Clint Eastwood over. I tell the pig to stay. I take off my leather shoes, my knitted socks, and—because I don't want to ruin them—the button-down shirt and the silk tie, leaving them all at the bottom of the trunk before joining Surachai on one of the adjacent branches. As I climb, the night air warm against my skin, I'm reminded of how pleasurable this used to be—hoisting myself up by my bare feet and fingertips—and I'm surprised by how easy it still is.

When I settle myself into the tree, I start to tell Surachai everything, including the episode on the elephant earlier that afternoon. As I talk, Surachai snakes his way out on to one of the branches and drops a mango for Clint Eastwood down below.

"At least you're having sex," Surachai says. "At least you're doing it. Some of us just get to sit in a mango tree and think about it."

I laugh.

"I don't suppose," Surachai says, "you loved this girl?" I shrug.

"You're a mystery to me, phuan," Surachai says, climbing higher now into the branches. "I've known you all these years, and that's the one thing I'll never be able to understand—why you keep falling for these farang girls. It's like you're crazy for heartache. Plenty of nice Thai girls around. Girls without plane tickets."

"I know. I don't think they like me, though. Something about the way I look. I don't think my nose is flat enough."

"That may be true. But they don't like me either, okay? And I've got the flattest nose on the Island."

We sit silently for a while, perched in that mango tree like a couple of sloths, listening to the leaves rustling around us. I climb up to where Surachai is sitting. Through the thicket, I see Clint Eastwood jogging out to meet a group of farangs making their way down the beach. I call out to him, tell him to stay, but my pig's not listening to me.

It's Hunter and his friends, laughing, slapping each other's backs, tackling each other to the sand. Lizzie's walking with them silently, head down, trying to ignore their antics. When she sees Clint Eastwood racing up to meet her, she looks to see if I'm around. But she can't see us from where she's standing. She can't see us at all.

"It's that fucking pig again!" Hunter yells.

They all laugh, make rude little pig noises, jab him with their feet. Clint Eastwood panics. He squeals. He starts to run. The American boys give chase, try to tackle him to the ground. Lizzie tells them to leave the pig alone, but the boys aren't listening. Clint Eastwood is fast. He's making a fool of them, running in circles one way then the other, zigzagging back and forth through the sand. The more they give chase, the more Clint Eastwood eludes them, the more frustrated the boys become, and what began as jovial tomfoolery has now turned into some kind of bizarre mission for Hunter and his friends. Their chase becomes more orchestrated. The movements of their shadows turn strategic. They try to corner the pig, run him into a trap, but Clint Eastwood keeps on moving between them, slipping through their fingers like he's greased.

I can tell that Clint Eastwood's beginning to tire though. He can't keep it up much longer. He's an old pig. I start to climb down from the mango tree, but Surachai grabs me by the wrist.

"Wait," he says.

Surachai climbs out on to one of the branches. He reaches up for a mango and with a quick sweeping motion throws the fruit out on to the beach. It hits one of the boys squarely on the shoulder.

"What the fuck!" I hear the boy yell, looking in the direction of the tree, though he continues to pursue Clint Eastwood nonetheless.

They have him surrounded now, encircled. There's no way out for my pig.

I follow Surachai's lead, grab as many mangoes as I can. Our mangoes sail through the night air. Some of them miss, but some meet their targets squarely in the face, on the head, in the abdomen. Some of the mangoes hit Lizzie by accident, but I don't really care anymore, I'm not really aiming. I'm climbing through that tree like a gibbon, swinging gracefully between the branches, grabbing any piece of fruit—ripe or unripe—that I can get my hands on. Surachai starts to whoop like a monkey and I join him in the chorus. They all turn in our direction then, the four farangs, trying to dodge the mangoes as they come.

It's then that I see Clint Eastwood slip away unnoticed. I see my pig running into the ocean, his pink snout inching across the sea's dark surface, phosphorescence glittering around his head like a crown of blue stars, and as I'm throwing each mango with all the strength I have, I'm thinking: Swim, Clint, swim.

Who wins and who loses in this thwarted romance? Is it Lizzie or the *protagonist-narrator*? If your answer is neither, then you've recognized the complexity of each character. On the face of things, Lizzie is a coward, abandoning her Thai lover for Hunter, the boorish boyfriend who is described by the narrator as looking "like a deranged clown." In fact, there is something quite deranged about the entire situation of this tourist paradise, which the author signals in that long, lyrical opening paragraph that lists every national *stereotype* imaginable about the farangs that invade each summer. Note, too, the use of *bathos*, or an anticlimactic shift, at the end of that opening paragraph:

Ma says, "Pussy and elephants. That's all these people want." She always says this in August, at the season's peak, when she's tired of farangs running all over the Island, tired of finding used condoms in the motel's rooms, tired of guests complaining to her in five languages.

Lapcharoensap uses bathos in the cultural clash of language as well, often to good comic effect in the dialogue. For example, when the protagonist takes Lizzie to see Uncle Mongkhon to rent an elephant for a ride, he deliberately mis-translates what everyone around him is saying in Thai so that Lizzie has no idea how insultingly rude they are. Incidentally, this is an extremely effective way to render a non-English-language scene entirely in English, without using any non-English words or translations. It shows the cultural *attitude* of the Thais who must humor these foreign tourists, yet the comedy of the linguistic divide remains intact.

One important technique Lapcharoensap uses is not trying to explain Thai culture (as Long tediously does in "Madame Butterfly"), but shows it instead through dialogue, action, and the perspective of all the Thais around the narrator and Lizzie. He flips this around completely in the restaurant scene when Hunter comes to "claim" his girlfriend and humiliate the narrator. For example, before Hunter comes over Lizzie says that Hunter is there, and the narrator refers to him as her "ex-boyfriend," to which she emphatically responds *no*, and calls him *my boyfriend*. Later, when Hunter joins them and rudely eats their food, he demonstrates his sexist "ownership" of Lizzie as well as his open disdain for her Thai friend, who remains silent during Hunter's rant.

> "You've really outdone yourself this time, baby," he says to Lizzie now. "But that's what I love about you. Your unpredictability. Your wicked sense of humor. Didn't know you went for mute tards (retards) with pet pigs."

As obviously rude as Hunter is, the fact that Lizzie is unable to intervene or say much shows us just how wide a divide there is from her first encounter with the narrator compared to this one. She's had her romantic moment with him, and despite everything she's told him, it's almost a foregone conclusion that she is now prepared to return to her abusive boyfriend. The rudeness depicted of the Thais when the narrator first brings Lizzie to them collides with this rude behavior, and all the protagonist can do is throw money on the table and walk away. Study this scene, because it's a very effective and dramatic moment in the story, one that is full of pathos, but which never descends into sentimentality.

One final word on Clint Eastwood, the pet pig that provides the surprising climax to the story. The pig provides comic relief, but is also important as an extension of the narrator, a mixed-race bastard whose father has abandoned him but has turned him into a kind of freak, fluent in American culture and language, but trapped by circumstance to fall hopelessly in love with one white girl after another, none of who will remain with him. The ironically named pig Clint Eastwood is lovable but also easily overlooked, like him, the "monkey boy." But by the end of the story both become the center of their universe over which they do exert control. Re-read the sections involving the pig and look at how Lapcharoensap transforms the comedy of the pig into a cathartic outcome in the story.

By contrast, "Boondocks" is a much darker story, despite its humor. It also offers a trenchant commentary on American military invasions of Asia. Unlike "Farangs," where the military presence is part of the back story, Hemley's story is rooted clearly in that presence. Read it now and think about the significance of language and perspective in this story of a tragically horrifying cultural miscommunication.

2 "Boondocks"

by Robin Hemley (USA)

for Lawrence Reid

Robin Hemley has published fourteen books, most recently, *Borderline Citizen*. His awards include three Pushcart Prizes and a Guggenheim Fellowship. He has lived and taught widely in Asia and currently lives in Brooklyn, where he is director of the George Polk School of Communications at Long Island University.

>The word for mountain in Pakoran's language was "bundok," but Taylor and his friend, Jerry, couldn't pronounce it right. There were a lot of things they didn't know and it didn't end with words. They didn't know the right clothes to wear and they didn't know how to talk to someone older than them. They didn't know how to talk to someone younger than them. They didn't know how to throw a rock at the annual rock throwing festival when you threw a rock at the men from the next village lined up together and they threw rocks at you and the size of the bruise showed how big your kamote crop would be. They didn't know the right hot springs to bathe in and they didn't know the wrong ones not to bathe in. They didn't know the words to the songs accompanying the sacrifice of a pig and they didn't know how to take a head or how to tattoo their chests when they took a head. There wasn't really much they knew. They knew how to drink and they knew how to be with women. They knew how to shoot Japanese soldiers when they came nearby the village. Even so, they were friendly and everyone in the village liked them. They were like children that everyone looks after because their parents have died.
>
>Pakoran was the special friend of Jerry, Taylor's best friend. Jerry liked to take long hikes in the "boondocks" and he often invited Pakoran along with him. On these hikes, Pakoran taught Jerry some things he didn't know, like how to catch a snake before it bites you and how to spot the place where a snake is almost certainly hiding before you get close enough for it to bite you and the special song to sing if it bites you and you are going to die. He taught Jerry how to know if you are not alone in the forest and what is out there and how far away it is from you and if it's a man, a woman, a pig, a dog or a creature like, a manananggal, and which trees are the ones where kapre's sit smoking and waiting for their victims. He taught him how to make a cup from a leaf and what plants you could eat and which ones you couldn't. Really, Jerry knew almost nothing, but he taught Pakoran some English in return, When you wanted to ask someone to do a kindness for you, you called them a "crazy asshole." And when you offered someone food, you said, "This will make you crap like crazy."
>
>"Not creep," he said. "Crap."
>
>"Creep."
>
>"Crap. Come on, you little booger, get it right."
>
>And so Pakoran practiced until he could say crap like an American and he even started to say boondock instead of "bundok."
>
>The best thing Taylor and Jerry knew how to do was to drink tapuy. They drank it every night and it made them sing songs late into the morning. Everyone knew they were

their special tapuy singing songs, and Taylor even taught Pakoran one. And when two lovers woo, they still say I love you.

Taylor and Jerry drank so much tapuy that the village ran out one evening, but Taylor said that that was a lie and he broke into the village rice stores, convinced they had hidden the tapuy there. He had such strange ideas. Tapuy was made of rice but no one would think of hiding it in the rice. It might spill and ruin the rice the village depended on. No one would have kept tapuy from Taylor. He was a guest in their village ever since he and Jerry had appeared one day and told them about the Japanese invasion and how they were their common enemy and how they would protect the village if the village protected them. Now, Taylor stood at the door of the rice stores, bellowing and throwing the rice in great handfuls onto the path. He even toppled the rice god that stood in front of the store room and when the villagers approached to ask him to stop throwing away their rice, he threw rocks at them instead and one rock hit Pakoran. It raised a bruise, but this was not the time of the rock throwing festival and the pain he felt meant nothing. He ran home to his father crying, but Pakoran's father had already heard and Pakoran met his father on the path with some other men, all carrying head axes.

That night, they played the gongs in the village to ease Taylor into the afterlife. Jerry had fallen asleep and slept through everything, even the gongs. Only in the morning did he discover what had happened to his friend. He started yelling then, screaming some of the words of special favor to the villagers. "Crazy assholes," he yelled. They all agreed that he missed his friend and wanted to join him. This was the favor he was asking of them.

A couple of days later, when the next batch of tapuy was ready, Pakoran offered some to Jerry and Taylor with the words "This will make you crap like crazy." He hoped they were still friends. At least Pakoran had made Jerry smarter than Taylor before he died, and now in the afterlife Jerry would know some useful things that other people outside of the boondocks didn't.

Think about someone very different from you whom you've encountered. What misconceptions do they have about you? What do you not understand about the way they talk or behave? As fiction writers, should we attempt to write about someone whose experiences and background are completely unlike our own? We believe that fiction is about imagination, and that writers should be able to cross borders of culture, language, gender, religion, and so forth if they wish, but that it's important to do so *responsibly*.

In Chapter 5, we discussed the problem of confusing the character in fiction with the author. A related aspect of that is to assume only someone who is from a particular culture or country has the "right" to write about it. The award-winning Asian-American writer Brian Leung once told us about a MFA class that he taught at Purdue where a student of color told a white American student he was "not allowed" to write stories set in China from a Chinese person's POV, *because he was not Chinese*. Brian, who is mixed-race Chinese-Caucasian, pointed out that he himself doesn't speak a word of Chinese (he was born and raised in the United States), while the student in question was fluent in Chinese, had read Chinese literature, and had lived in China for many years. But according to the first student's logic, Brian would be "allowed" to write about China, even though he knows far less than the white American student. So you can see the illogic that sometimes enters into the thinking of what we can or cannot write.

An important aspect of writing about the "other" in a culture or environment that is not our own is to find a way to "own" it. In "Boondocks," the author, Robin Hemley, tells us very little about exactly where they are, but the language clue is "bundok" in the first sentence, which is Tagalog for mountain and from which the American expression "boondocks," meaning a rural or remote area, derives (and yes you can find all this easily enough by a little research online). Even if you did not know that Hemley is an American who has lived in the Philippines and other parts of Asia, is married to a Filipino and also speaks Tagalog, we can be pretty sure he is likely not someone like Pakoran. But you recognize from the way he uses language in the story, and from what he tells us about the culture of this remote village, that he has more than a passing knowledge than can be gleaned from, say, just googling a tourist guide of the Philippines. *How* he acquires this knowledge is less important than the fact that he *has* somehow acquired it for this story (Hemley actually was told about a real incident that is similar to what occurs in the story, which was the inspiration for the fiction). In the case of Lapcharoensap, we know he is a Thai writer in English who has spent many years in the United States. Whether or not he, like the narrator of "Farangs," is the mixed-race son of an American military officer who has abandoned him and his mother, or has worked in a Thai beach resort, is completely immaterial. What he uses is his knowledge of both Thai and American cultures to *dramatize* this clash of cultures, the way Hemley does in "Boondocks." When we read both these stories, we intuitively sense the *authority of the writer* in the details of culture and place they inject into the narrative. If you're interested enough in any kind of "other" to write about it, then it's incumbent upon you to do your homework.

Beyond doing our homework, a good technique to use to enter into the other's experience is to show it from a POV that clearly does *not* understand or only half understands the other's experience. We saw an example of this in "National Day" in Chapter 4, where the migrant workers comment on the Singaporean life and culture that they can only see from the outside. In "Boondocks," we see Taylor and Jerry, two American soldiers, making fun of the villagers they claim to be protecting from the Japanese and getting drunk every night on the village's tapuy. But the POV is that of Pakoran, who shows us these two men from his understanding of what life is supposed to be like, that is, that of the remote village he comes from. In a similar bathetic way as we saw the bathos employed in "Farangs," the boorish behavior of the two "invaders" is defused, because, as Pakoran explains "there wasn't really much they knew" and that despite their ignorance and limited abilities (shooting Japanese soldiers and being with women), Pakoran recognizes them as "friendly" and considers them "like children that everyone looks after because their parents have died."

We said earlier that both "Farangs" and "Boondocks" deal with archetypes as opposed to stereotypes. An archetype is a sort of perfect example of a particular type. The Lizzie we first meet in "Farangs" who has no inhibitions becomes a very different girl when she's with her "ex-not ex" boyfriend. She is of two extremes—the foreign woman who falls in love with a foreign culture and foreign man and opens herself completely to him but quickly reverts to the passive American girlfriend of an emotionally abusive and controlling boyfriend. Likewise, Jerry in "Boondocks" is the perfect clown or wiseguy, deliberately teaching Pakoran ridiculous English to be funny. However, both these images are subverted when we see Lizzie from the POV of the Thais and Jerry from the POV of Pakoran and the other villagers.

Such archetypes can be useful to contrast the central character who is more fully fleshed out, like the unnamed protagonist of "Farangs."

It is very important that writers exercise their right to imagine and try on the skin of the "other" in their stories. However, it's also equally important to do your homework and search for empathy for even the less sympathetic "other" if you wish to write good fiction that illuminates the human condition, instead of merely presenting stereotypes and exotica.

Exercises

1. Think of someone whom you know but find either completely impossible to understand or quite annoying. Write a story from that person's POV about you doing something they disapprove of. Your story doesn't have to be about anything unusual or melodramatic. In fact the more ordinary an incident, for example, how you sit at the table at a meal or the way you talk to your parents on the phone, and so forth, the more you can give yourself permission to *imagine* what goes on in the other's mind when they observe you.

2. Use a place you've only visited once (or seldom) as the setting of a scene. Create two characters—one who lives or is from there and the other who is the visitor—and have them get into an argument. Write the scene twice, once from each character's POV.

3. Write a story where two characters (or two groups of characters) speak different languages and only have minimal or limited ability to speak the other's language (e.g., they could both have English as a common language that neither one is entirely fluent in, or one could speak English and the other a language you know). Have a *significant* misunderstanding occur—as in both stories in this chapter—about what an action one does that insults the culture of the other. Write this with minimal (or no) use of any words in the non-English language(s) used for the story.

4. Retell a story from your own experience that you found very funny. This could be something told to you or something you or someone you know did that kept you laughing for a long time. Turn it into fiction. Are you able to retain the humor? What worked in the transformation? What did not?

5. Pick one of the following: a country, culture, or religion, one that you consider the most foreign to your own and about which you have very little knowledge or experience. Do some research and find one detail that intrigues you—this could be a word from the language, a plant or flower, a practice—and use it as the image for the starting point of a story. The story does not need to be about or in that country, culture, or religion. You just need to allow your imagination to take what you learn from your research to create fiction.

CHAPTER 7
DIASPORAS

Several years ago, we visited Ho Chi Minh City during one of the milestone anniversaries of the reunification of Vietnam, and one night we ventured out for a beer at a small outdoor eatery at one of the city's main intersections, an enormous traffic circle bustling with motorcycles and pedestrians. Sitting on a plastic stool, watching the Vietnamese world go by, our attention drifted to two massive advertisements plastered on billboards across from one another: one depicted a tank, a dove, and a young man and woman looking hopeful and proud. The year of reunification, the end of what the Vietnamese call the American War, 1975, appeared prominently, as well as the current year. We had grown up in the United States during this turbulent era, and had known it as "The Vietnam War." Although we were quite young at the time, the reason for the war never made much sense. The US rationale for the war was to stop the spread of communism in Southeast Asia, the so-called Domino Effect. Why we cared so much how other countries wanted to govern themselves baffled us, even at our tender age. Previously, the Vietnamese, led by Ho Chi Minh, had fought and defeated the colonial French. Into the breach, America marched to make the world safe for capitalism, if not democracy. Across from the billboard's reminder of the country's costly victory (millions of Vietnamese civilians and soldiers died) stood an equally enormously symbolic billboard . . . for Starbucks. Taking in that juxtaposition for a bit, we poured a little more beer in our glass, took a sip, and pondered (a little cynically, we admit) the irony that capitalism had prevailed after all over communism. Not through bombs but through baristas. What, we wondered, would Ho Ch Minh, himself, think of such a sight?

The suffering of the Vietnamese people did not stop with the end of the war. Like nearly all wars, the endgame created a refugee crisis, in this case a diaspora of Vietnamese all around the world. Not all diasporas result from war and not all displacements and migrations come about as the result of trauma. The two stories we will examine in this chapter both deal with tragic separations, but only Nam Le's story, "The Boat," deals with the aftermath of war. The other, Noelle Q. de Jesus's "Dreams in English," concerns what might have been, in different circumstances, an unremarkable story of emigration and newfound love. Both stories push their protagonists to the extremes of love, loss, and displacement. What we'd like to focus on is how each author brings the reader so convincingly and compellingly into worlds that have been turned upside down for their characters.

In order to care about what's happening to a character, we have to know who they are, and that means we have to know something about their personal histories to a greater or lesser degree. Not every story demands we know more than the bare essentials, but stories that deal with great traumas are usually going to require that you create a character whose history we know intimately. One common mistake of the novice writer is to frontload all of the character's history before moving the story forward. Exposition, as a rule, slows down the momentum of a story considerably and rarely draws a reader into a story, especially at the beginning. Consider, for instance, the first paragraph of Nam Le's "The Boat":

The storm came on quickly. The crosswind surged in, filtering through the apertures in the rotten wood, sounding like a chorus of low moans. The boat began to rock. Hugging a beam at the top of the hatch, Mai looked out and her breath stopped: the boat had heeled so steeply that all she saw was an enormous wall of black-green water bearing down; she shut her eyes, opened them again—now the gunwale had crested the water—the ocean completely vanished—and it was as though they were soaring through the air, the sky around them dark and inky and shifting.

What do we know about Mai by the end of that paragraph? We know that Mai is a woman, but we don't know Mai's age or where she's from. She could be French, Japanese, Vietnamese, or perhaps an American whose parents read the name on a website of baby names. She could be on her parents' yacht circumnavigating the globe or maybe she's using her chip implant in VR mode and she's safe (relatively) in her stilt house in the Greater Brooklyn Marsh in the year 2155.

If you read only this paragraph and we asked you to continue it, to imagine who Mai is and what the circumstances are, how she wound up in this situation, what would your reaction be? If we hadn't already read the story a number of times, our reaction would likely be panic. That's because we know very little about ships at sea in distress, though we once drifted out onto Long Island Sound in our uncle's sailboat when he forgot to tie it to the dock and it took us fifteen minutes to start the engine with him yelling at us the whole time as if it was our fault. Stressful, yes, but nothing like what Mai is apparently going through. And, well, frankly, we know the author Nam Le a little bit, having spent a delightful evening with him at a night market in Darwin, Australia, after attending a literary festival there. As we learned in Chapter 6, we're just going to embarrass ourselves if we try to write a story about a culture we know little to nothing about, so thanks, but we're going to take a pass on that exercise.

But we'd like to make a different point about this opening paragraph. The way that Nam Le begins his story is known as in medias res, or "the middle of things." The idea is to start off the story not at the beginning, but far along into the conflict, backfilling crucial information as you go. Not all stories begin in this way, but why don't you take a look now at the opening paragraphs of the stories in this book and see how many take this approach? The advantage of this strategy is that it dumps the reader into a scene, and makes them feel as though they are experiencing in the moment what the character feels. Yes, that makes the reader feel off-balance, but in a short story it's a good thing for a reader to feel off-balance, at least initially.

With every sentence you write, you should be divulging information about the character and reinforcing what we already know. The information shouldn't *seem* like information, but simply a part of the ongoing unfolding of events—before you know it, you will have delivered enough clues to the reader so that they are able to form a picture of your characters, their histories, and how they feel about the situation in which they find themselves. Part of the tension of a story derives from the steady drip of clues the writer gives us, and of our desire to satisfy our curiosity about who the characters are.

Now consider this opening sentence: *I was on the back porch washing greens when Harold drove around the side of the house in a pickup with a stolen canoe on top and a bushel of oysters in back.*

Go ahead and see what you come up with by continuing from this opening. Consider the clues about character and situation that the sentence suggests. After you've written for fifteen minutes or so, take a break. Next, read "The Boat" and then we'll return to our discussion of in medias res.

1 "The Boat"

by Nam Le (Australia)

Nam Le was born in Vietnam, and arrived in Australia with his parents as a very young child. His acclaimed short story collection *The Boat* is the recipient of many prestigious awards, including the International Dylan Thomas Prize, the PEN/Malamud Award, and the Prime Minister's Literary Award for Fiction.

The storm came in quickly. The crosswind surged in, filtering through the apertures in the rotten wood, sounding like a chorus of low moans. The boat began to rock. Hugging a beam at the top of the hatch, Mai looked out and her breath stopped: the boat had heeled so steeply that all she saw was an enormous wall of black-green water bearing down; she shut her eyes, opened them again—now the gunwale had crested the water—the ocean completely vanished—and it was as though they were soaring through the air, the sky around them dark and inky and shifting.

A body collided into hers, slammed her against the side of the hatch door. The boat righted and she slipped again, skidding in jets of water down the companionway. The hatch banged shut. Other bodies—she was on top of them—thighs and ribs and arms and heads—jammed this way and that with each groaning tilt, writhing toward space as though impelling the boat to heave to, back into the wind. The rocking got worse. Light was failing fast now and inside the hold it had become uncannily dim.

Inches away from Mai's face, a cross-legged man tipped forward, coughed—once into his hands, then keeled back onto his elbows. His face was expressionless. When the smell arrived she realized he had vomited. In the swaying half dark, people pitched forward and back, one by one, adding to the slosh of saltwater and urine in the bilge. People threw up in plastic bags, which they then passed on, hand to hand, until the parcel reached someone next to a scupper.

"Here."

Mai pinched the bag, tried to squeeze it out through the draining slit, but her fingers lost their hold as the boat bucked. The thin yellow juice sprayed into her lap.

On the steps below her, an infant started crying: short choking bursts.

Instantly she looked for Truong—there he was, knees drawn up to his chin, face as smooth and impassive as that of a ceramic toy soldier. Their eyes met. Nothing she could do. He was wedged between an older couple at the bottom of the steps. Where was Quyen? She shook off the automatic anxiety.

Finally the storm arrived in force. The remaining light drained out of the hold. Wind screamed through the cracks. She felt the panicked limbs, people clawing for direction, sudden slaps of ice-cold water, the banging and shapeless shouts from the deck above. The whole world reeled. Everywhere the stink of vomit. Her stomach forced up, squashed through her throat.

So this was what it was like, she thought, the moment before death. She closed her eyes, swallowed compulsively; tried to close out the crawling blackness, the howl of the wind. She tried to recall her father's stories—storms at sea, waves ten, fifteen metres high—but they rang shallow against what she'd just seen: those dense roaring slabs of water, sky churning overhead like a puddle being mucked with a stick. She was crammed in by a boatload of human bodies, thinking of her father and becoming overwhelmed, slowly, with loneliness. As much loneliness as fear. Concentrate, she told herself. And she did—forcing herself to concentrate, if not—if she was unable to—on the thought of her family, then on the contact of flesh pressed against her on every side, the human warmth, feeling every square inch of skin against her body and through it the shared consciousness of—what? Death? Fear? Surrender? She stayed in that human cocoon, heaving and rolling, concentrating, until it was over.

She opened her eyes. A procession of people stepping over her, measuredly, as though hypnotized, up the companionway and onto the deck. She got up and followed them.

The night sky was starless. Only moonlight illuminated everything, emanating from a moon low and yellow and pocked, larger than she had ever seen it before. Its surface appeared to her as clear and as close as the ridges of a mountain from a valley. Pearly light bathed the stunned and salt-specked faces of the hundred people on deck, all of whom had expected to die but were instead granted this eerie reprieve.

Nobody talked. Night, empty of sound, held every soul in thrall—the retching, the complaint of babies, the nervous breathings, now all muted. The world seemed alien, somehow beyond the reach of Mai's mind—to be beneath the giant moon, and have nothing but space, and silence, all around.

A fog rolled over the water.

Mai looked sternward and saw Quyen slumped, arms out—stretched, collapsed to one knee. Her head lolled against her left shoulder. Her forearms were bleeding from rope burn—she must have been stranded on deck when the storm came in; someone had strapped her, spread-eagled, to a low horizontal spar, and saved her life.

Mai searched for Truong.

From below deck there now came a humming of prayer. Then someone gasped—Mai swung to find a face, then several, turning pale, hands to mouths beneath stupefied eyes.

"Do you hear?"

"What is it?"

"Be quiet! Be quiet!" an urgent voice commanded. "Listen."

But when the noise on the boat ceased, there still came from every direction the sound of people whispering, hundreds of people, thousands, the musical fall and rise of their native tongue. Barely intelligible. Sometimes right next to Mai's ear and she would whip around—but there would be nothing except the close, gray fog.

In a whisper, "It's nothing—the wind, that's all."

"Who's there?" someone demanded loudly, unsteadily, from the prow.

No answer, just the lapping of low murmurs.

On the foredeck, a man turned to his companion.

"Here?"

The second man nodded. Beneath the moonlight Mai recognized him. It was Anh Phuoc, the leader of the boat. He was, Quyen had told her, one of those mythic figures who'd already made his escape and yet returned, again and again, to help others.

He nodded and looked out into the haze.

And now she realized where they were—where they must be. Everyone had heard about these places. They had ventured into the fields of the dead, those plots of ocean where thousands had capsized with their scows and drowned. They stared into the fog. All drawn into a shared imagination, each in some space of unthinking as though they had leapt overboard, some madness possessing them puncturing the glassy surface of the water and then plunged into black syrup, coming up into breath but panicked, disoriented, flailing in a viscid space without reference or light or sound.

"Try to sleep."

It was Quyen; she had untangled herself from her station and crawled forward. Mai turned to her, then looked away. There was a sort of death in her face.

"I saw Truong, down—" Mai began, then saw that he had appeared silently behind his mother. He stood close by Quyen without touching her. For a moment Mai was seized with a desire to take the boy up and press him hard against her chest, to keep him—his stillness, self-containment, whatever it was about him—close to her. But she, too, was contained, and didn't move. She began to smell incense from the hold. People praying to their ancestors. It lightened her head. A dim thought struggled, stabilized, in her mind—maybe the voices on the water were those of their ancestors. Maybe, she thought, they were answering their prayers. What did they know? What were they so desperate to communicate?

"It's over now."

She let herself pretend Quyen was speaking to her and not to Truong.

"The storm's over, Child. Try to sleep."

Mai submitted, and when she closed her eyes, knowing they were both beside her, she found the hum of the phantom voices almost lulling-almost like the wash, when she dozed off, of a monsoon starting, or a wedding, dim-sounding on distant mid-day streets. A sea wind bearing men's voices up from the wharf. At times she thought she almost recognized a voice. When her eyes opened a second later it was morning: the moon had disappeared and the cloud streaks were already blue-bruised against a sky the color of skin.

The first five days they'd traveled on flat seas. It had been hot, and Mai had faced the choice of being on deck and burnt by the sun or being below in the oven-heated hold. In the beginning people swam in the ocean, trailing ropes off the slow-moving junk, but afterward the salt on their bodies cooked their skin like crispy pork.

She spent as much time as she could bear out of the hold which simmered the excrement of a hundred people. Their boat was especially crowded, Quyen had explained, because it carried two human loads: another boat organized by the same guide had at the last minute been confiscated by the Communists.

Each family kept mostly to itself. Mai was alone. She stayed close to Quyen and Quyen's six-year-old son, Truong. He was a skinny child with an unusually bony frame and a head too big for his body. His eyes, black and preternaturally calm, were too big for his head. He spoke in a watery voice—rarely—and, as far as Mai could tell, never smiled. He was like an old man crushed into the rude shape of a boy. It was strange, she thought, that such a child could have issued from Quyen—warm and mischievous Quyen.

When Mai first met him they'd been gliding—silently, under cover of night—through a port full of enemies. Even then his demeanor had been improbably blank. The war had that to answer for too, she'd thought—the stone-hard face of a child barely six years old. Only when the boat shifted and his body leaned into hers had she felt, astonishingly, his heartbeat through his trunk—an electric flurry racing through the concavities of his back, stomach and chest. His body furious with life. He was engaged in some inward working out, she realized, and in that instant she'd grasped that nothing—nothing—was more important than her trying to see whatever it was he was seeing behind his dark, flat eyes.

Two nights later, as Mai had been trying to sleep on deck, the song began. The faint voice drifted out of the hold with a familiar undertow. It was an old Vietnamese folk song:

I never thought to be a soldier's wife,
You were not born to foreign lands preside;
Why do the streams and hills our love divide?
Why are we destined for this faithless life?

In the shade of the hibiscus hedge her mother had once sung the same words to her during the years her father was away at war. The hibiscus flowers outside their kitchen in Phu Vinh, which bloomed only for a single day. And though dusk came, her mother would keep singing the soldier's wife's lament, her long black hair falling over Mai's face soft as a mosquito net, and Mai would trace the darkening red of the flowers through that curtain of hair.

Mai followed the song into the hold. She stopped at the bottom of the companionway steps; in the darkness she could just make out Quyen's form, lying on her side in front of Truong as though shielding him. Her voice was thin, attenuated in some way, stripped of vibrato. It didn't slide up to notes the way traditional singers' did. Mai stood on the dark steps and listened:

The path of wind and rain is yours to take,
While mine does mourn an empty room and bed;
We reach to touch each other, but instead . . .

Her mother, who had waited each time her husband went to sea, again when he left to fight the Communists, and then—five years later—when he left once more, to report for reeducation camp. That was supposed to have been the last time. He was supposed to have been gone for ten days—the prescribed sentence for low-ranked soldiers. Mai remembered: on the eleventh day the streets were swept, washed, festooned with lanterns—women in their best and brightest outfits. The war had been lost, their husbands and fathers were coming home. Mai and Loe wore clothes their mother had borrowed. All through the afternoon they'd waited, through the night, too, the lanterns growing more and more dazzling, the congee and suckling pig cold, congealed. The next morning Mai's mother sent for word but received none. What could she—could any of them—do?

Overcome with feeling, Mai wanted to ask Quyen to stop singing—not to stop singing. Never to stop. How could she explain it all? Afterward, she had seen her mother caught on that cruel grade of time, growing old, aging more in months than she had in years—and yet she had given no comfort to her. She had been a daughter selfish with her own loss. From that day on, she never again heard her mother sing.

Squatting down, Mai dried her eyes with her sleeves. The song continued. With a shock, Mai realized Quyen's mouth was not moving. She was asleep. The singing cut off as Truong lifted, turned his head, staring at Mai with large obsidian eyes. Stunned, she said nothing. She looked back at his pale face, the slight, girlish curve beneath his nose to his lips. The intentness of his gaze. Then, slowly, she felt whatever turmoil broke and banked inside her becoming still. Watching her the whole time Truong opened his mouth and took a deep breath:

You took my love southeast before I asked
Whereto you went, and when you should return;
Oh warring soul! through bitter years you learned
To treat your sacred life like leaves of grass.

Quyen stirred. Her eyelids still closed, she murmured, "Yes, you miss your father too. Don't you, my prince?"

He stopped singing. Shadows sifted in the darkness.

Here was how it began: her mother brought her through the dim kitchen into the yard. Her father had been released three months prior, from reeducation camp, and immediately admitted into the hospital in Vinh Long. He had gone blind. The doctors were baffled because they could identify no physical abnormality, no root cause. His reeducation had blinded him. Mai, in the meantime, continued trundling every day from corner to corner, selling cut tobacco to supplement their family income. Her father's sickness was not unlike the war: something always happening elsewhere while she was forced on with her daily routine.

That day had been a slow one and she'd come home early.

In the yard, beneath branches of mastic and white storax flowers, next to the deciduated hibiscus hedge, her mother had hooked her fingers under her waistband and handed her a damp bundle of money. The ink faded from the sweat of counting and recounting.

"Child can spend it however Child likes but try to keep, *nha*?" Knowing her mother's usual frugality, Mai struggled to respond but her mother said nothing more, wiping her hands stiffly on her pajama pants and turning back into the house.

Two days later she told Mai to go visit her father at the hospital.

"Child is a good child," he told her after a long silence, his eyes fixed on some invisible locus in the air. He'd barely reacted when she came in and greeted him—it was only her second visit since he'd returned from reeducation camp. What had they done to him there? She remembered him being gaunt three months ago, when he'd first returned, but now his whole face was sunken—as though its foundation had finally disintegrated, leaving his features to their slow inward collapse. His eyes extruded from their deep-set sockets like black stones.

"How is Ba?"

"Ba is unwell," he said, rubbing his stubbled chin. He spoke to her as if to a servant. He didn't even look in her direction.

Mai hesitated. "Can Ba see?"

He didn't seem blind to her. She'd always imagined blindness to be a blacking out—but what if it wasn't? What if he could see—his eyes seemed outwardly unchanged—but had now chosen not to? What if his eyes were already looking elsewhere?

She said, "Ba will get better."

"Child is a big girl now. How old is Child now?"

"Sixteen."

"Heavens," he cried. Then jokingly, "So Child has a boyfriend, *ha*?"

Mai blushed and her father's hand searched for her head, patted it. Instinctively she twisted her cheek up into his rough palm. She'd come with so much to say—so much to ask—but he might as well have been deaf as blind. He laughed humorlessly. "At sixteen, Ba had to look after Ba's whole family."

Mai didn't reply. She felt insolent looking at his face when he didn't look back.

"Look after your mother," he said.

Look at me, she wanted to say. She considered moving into his fixed line of sight but didn't dare. Just once, she thought. Just look at me once, Ba, and I'll do anything you say.

"And obey her, *nha*?"

"Yes, Ba."

He gave a single nod, then smiled, but it was nothing more than a flexing of his lips.

"Obey your mother. Promise, *nha*?"

"Yes, Ba."

"Child." His voice lowered conspiratorially and, her breath quickening, Mai stooped down closer to him. He was going to talk to her. Once, that had been her whole life. He smelt like rusted pipes. "Stop it," he whispered. She held her breath, watching his eyes. They were still locked in midair. "Stop crying, Child."

She held herself still as he patted her head again.

"Good girl," he said.

The next day her mother put her on a bus to Rach Gia. It was a five-hour trip, she was told. Here was a plastic bag for motion sickness. In the market she would be picked up by an uncle she had never met. "Give this to him," her mother said, and pressed a fold of paper, torn from an exercise book, into her confused hands. Just before she got on the bus, her little brother, Loe, tugged at her shirt and asked if she minded if he used her bicycle.

"Use your own bicycle."

She boarded. Watched the two of them through the scuffed, stained window. Then, on the street, her mother raised one hand from her thigh in a hesitant motion, as though halfway hailing a cyclo.

"Ma?"

Mai pushed through the scree of indifferent bodies and rushed out to her mother. She stood there, breathing hard, sensing the larger finality in their parting. Her mother asked if she still had the money. Yes. Remember not to let anybody see it. Yes. Her mother smiled abstractedly, then brought her hand onto Mai's head and eased down, combing hair between her fingers.

"Child," she said softly, "remember, *nha*? Put your hat on when Child gets off."

Mai stammered, "Child hasn't said good-bye to Ba."

Her mother's hand followed the contours of her skull down into the inlet of her neck, a single motion. "Don't worry," she said. "Ma will say. For Child."

As the bus pulled out, a residue of memory surfaced in Mai's mind. Seeing her father off the first time—seven years ago, when he left for the war—her mother had clung fast to his elbow, her body turned completely into his, her face creased as though it were having trouble holding together a coherent emotion. But the second time—five years later, at the end of the war—her face had completely smoothed itself over. It had learned how to be expressionless.

Mai looked out of the back window—searching for her mother's face—but the street, like a wound, had closed over the space where it had been.

After hearing him sing Mai caught herself, time and time again, searching for Truong. She was most at ease sitting in the shade of the hatch door, facing the prow, watching him with the other children. The only structure on the foredeck was the pilothouse and the children played in a small clearing behind it—a concession of territory from the adults teeming all around. Many of the children were twice Truong's age. He played with them laconically, indifferently, often leaving a game halfway through when he was bored, inevitably pulling a small group along—eager for him to dictate a new game.

Unlike the others he didn't constantly look around to find his family. He lived in a space of his own absorption. Quyen, too, seemed content to let him be. Hemmed in always by dozens of other sweaty, salt-gritted bodies, Mai watched him, stealing solace, marveling at how he could be in the sun all day and remain so pale.

It seemed impossible she'd known him only a few days.

According to Quyen, Truong's father—her husband—had already made his escape. She told Mai that he had arrived safely in Pulau Bidong, one of the larger Malaysian refugee camps, eight months ago. He was waiting for them there.

Why hadn't they traveled together?

"We are going to America," Quyen continued, passing over Mai's question. "My husband has already rejected one offer from Canada. He says he has made friends in the Red Crescent."

"Red Crescent?"

"Do you have any family there?"

After a while Quyen, misreading Mai's silence, continued, "You are probably going to Australia, no? Many people are going there now."

"No. I don't know."

"You don't know?" She pursed her lips in mock decision: "Then Mai will come with us."

"*Thoi*," started Mai uncertainly.

"You must come. That one likes you," Quyen said, gesturing at Truong. "He talks about you all the time."

Mai flushed with pleasure, not fully understanding why—as she knew Quyen was lying. "He is very good," she said. "Very patient."

"Yes," Quyen replied. She reflected for a moment. "Like his father."

"And who has ever heard of a young boy who can sing like that? It's a miracle. He will make you rich one day."

"*Thoi*, don't joke."

She looked at her friend, surprised. "I am not joking." Together they turned toward him. He stood skinny and erect, his clothes hanging from his limbs as though from a denuded tree's branches. His hands directing the ragtag crew to throw their sandals into a pile. Mai wondered briefly if it made Quyen proud—seeing all those children scrambling to obey her son. The game was one her brother used to play. Relaxing her mind, Mai could almost fool herself into thinking he was there, little Loe, springing away as the designated dragon swung around to protect his treasure hoard. He was about the same age as Truong. Her thoughts started to drift back to her last meeting with her father, at the hospital, when Quyen interrupted:

"That one was an accident."

Mai immediately blushed, said nothing. "He slid out in the middle of the war."

How could she joke about such a thing? Mai still remembered her father's photo on the altar those five years, the incense and prayer, the hurt daily refreshing in her mother.

"You must miss him," said Mai. "Truong's father."

Quyen nodded.

"When were you married?"

"Nineteen seventy-two," Quyen answered, "in the middle of everything." For a moment her expression emptied out, making her seem younger. "I was your age then."

"Maybe more accidents will happen," Mai said, swallowing quickly through her words, "when you see him again. When we reach land."

Quyen snorted, then started laughing. Her face had recomposed itself now—was again knowing, shrewd, self-aware. She was pretty when she laughed. "Maybe," she said. She prodded Mai. "And what about you?"

But the mention of land—coming even from her own mouth—canceled out any joke for Mai. She had been trying not to think about it. From every quarter everyone now discussed obsessively, their situation: they were on a broken-down junk, stranded in the Eastern Sea—here, or maybe here—an easy target for pirates—everyone knew about the pirates, had heard stories of boats being robbed and then rammed, of women being taken, used, dumped. On top of that they were starving, some of them beginning to get sick. No one, however, gave voice to the main fear: that they might not make it.

Mai pushed the dread down. Desperate to change the subject she said the first thing that came to mind. "Wasn't it dangerous to escape," she asked, "with Truong so young?"

Her laughter subsiding, Quyen settled into a smile. "It was because of him," she said at last, "that I decided to escape." The smile hardened on her mouth.

They both turned toward him again. It had been three days.

Watching him—letting in the thought of another day, and after that, another—Mai realized that Quyen's determination, as much as she tried to take part in it, felt increasingly superficial to her. She studied the boy's face. Above his awkward body it remained as stony and impassive as ever.

In Rach Gia, in the milling market, Mai had been met by a man with a skewed look who talked to a spot behind her shoulder. He called her name by the coriander-selling place. She was waiting for him, her hat on, next to a grease stand, petrols and oils and lubricants spread out like lunch condiments.

"Mai," she heard, "Mai, *ha*?" and, still sick from the lurching bus trip—it had been her first ride in an automobile—she was swept up by this man who hugged her, turning her this way and that.

"Child has the letter?" he grunted into her ear.

She was confused. He said it again, thrust her out at arm's length and glared straight at her for the first time. She tried hard not to cry.

"Heavens," he said, hastily letting go of her and stepping back.

His face spread in an open, unnatural smile before he walked away. All at once Mai remembered her mother's instructions. The folded paper. She ran after him and pressed it into his hand. He read it, furtively, refolded it into a tiny square, and then he was Uncle again.

The first hiding place was behind a house by the river. Uncle told her to climb to the top of a plank bed and stay there, don't go anywhere. She lay with the corrugated aluminum roof just a few thumbs above her head, and in the middle of the day the heat was unbearable. The wooden boards beneath her became darkened and tender with her sweat.

A few days later Uncle came to get her—it was after the worst of the afternoon heat—and made her memorize a name and address in Rach Gia in case anyone asked her questions. She felt light-headed standing up.

"When Child reaches land," he told her, "write to Child's mother. She will say what to do next." She nodded dumbly. It was the first and final confirmation of her life's new plan: she was leaving on a boat. He looked at her and sighed. "She said nothing for Child's own protection." He gave her another abbreviated hug. "Does Child understand?" He wasn't, in all likelihood, her real uncle—she knew that now—but still, when he left, she felt in her stomach a deep-seated fluster. It was the last she saw of him.

The second hiding place was a boat anchored beneath a bridge on the Loe Thang river. Mai stayed down below deck for days and days, with sixty people maybe, among cargo sacks of sweet potatoes. No one talked; every sound in the dark was rat-made. She caught herself whimpering and covered her mouth. Once in a while the owner brought a few kilos of rice and they cooked it with potatoes over low kerosene flames and ate, salting their bit, chewing quietly. People coughed into their sleeves to muffle the sound. Parents fed their babies sleeping pills.

One night the owner appeared with another man who came in and tapped her on the shoulder. He tapped five other people as well. They all followed him out of the boat into the hot dark strange openness. A rower waited nearby and after some hesitation and muted dissent they climbed into his canoe, sitting one behind the other, Mai in the middle. The new man—the guide—instructed the rower to cross the other side of the river. But he didn't, he kept on paddling downstream for what seemed to Mai like hours and hours. At one point she found herself falling asleep. She woke to the sound of wood tapping hollowly against wood. They were pushing into the midst of a dark cluster of houseboats. The rower stopped, secured a lanyard to one of the boats and leapt aboard. He lit a small lantern and began passing large drums reeking of diesel into the canoe. Moments later they moored against the riverbank. The rower crept onshore with a hoe and exhumed something long and gray from beneath a coconut grove.

"Detachable sail," someone whispered.

Mai turned around. The speaker was a young woman. She sounded as though she might have been pointing out bad produce at a market stall.

"It's a detachable sail," the woman repeated.

Mai began asking her what that was when the rower turned, silencing them both with a glare. A moment later Mai felt a cupped hand against her ear.

"My name is Chi Quyen." The woman used the word *Chi*, for "older sister." She reclined, smiling grimly but not unkindly, then leaned forward again, "Chi too is by herself."

Mai nodded. Shyly, she lifted a finger and crossed her lips.

For a long time they glided soundlessly, close to shore, and then they entered a thick bed of reeds. They stopped. The rower turned around, shook his heavy head and made the sign for no talking. It was dark. He struck a match and lit an incense stick and planted it in the front tip of the canoe. After a while Mai became confused. No one else seemed to be praying. When the stick burned down the guide asked the rower, in a low voice, to light another one. At least an hour passed. Occasionally Mai made out the rower's profile, hard and somber. She took the dark smell of sandalwood into her body.

The canoe swayed. "Maybe they're waiting," a new voice whispered gruffly. "Move out of the reeds so they can see the signal."

"Keep your head down!" the rower spat.

At that moment Mai realized the incense stick—its dim glow, its smoke, perhaps—was their signal.

Someone else said "They won't wait."

"Move out of the reeds," the man repeated.

Mai felt a hot breath in her ear: "If they come, follow Chi, *nha*? Jump out and swim into the reeds. You can swim no?"

"If who comes?"

"Fuck your mother, I said keep your head down!"

Someone behind her hissed and the canoe rocked wildly from side to side. The rower whirled around. Then, through the reeds a light like a car beam flashed on and off. Fumbling, the rower lit a new incense stick, planted it at the canoe tip and paddled swiftly and silently, back out. They saw it ahead, barely visible, the weird, weakly thrown light from the banks. An old fishing trawler, smaller than she'd imagined—maybe fifteen meters long—sitting low in the water. It inched forward with a diesel growl. A square pilothouse rose up from the foredeck, a large derrick-crane straddling its back deck, and the boat's mid-section congested with short masts and cable rigs. Two big eyes painted on the bow. The canoe drew alongside and three men leaned over the gunwale above them and pulled them up, wrist by wrist. Everyone was aboard within a minute. Before being ushered down the hatch, Mai looked back and saw the canoe abandoned in the boat's wake, rocking on the dark river.

Inside the hold, the stench was incredible, almost eye-watering. The smell of urine and human waste, sweat and vomit. The black space full of people, bodies upon bodies, eyes and eyes and eyes and if she'd thought the first boat was crowded, here she could hardly breathe, let alone move. Later she counted at least two hundred people, squashed into a space meant for fifteen. No place to sit, nor even put a foot down; she found a crossbeam near the hatchway and hooked her arm over it. Luckily it was next to a scupper where the air came through.

Quyen settled on the step below her, whispering to a young boy. She caught Mai's eye and smiled firmly.

The boat continued its creeping pace. People padded the engines with their clothes to reduce the noise.

"Quiet," an angry voice shushed downward. "We're near the gate."

But no one had been speaking. Through the scupper Mai peered into the night: their boat was gliding into a busy port. Pressed hard beneath her was the body of the boy Quyen had been talking to.

"Natural gate a hundred meters long," she heard suddenly. The water carried the low sound clearly. Then she realized the voice came from above deck, so subdued the person might have been talking to himself. "About ten meters wide. On the rising tide."

Then another voice under the wind, "Viet Cong . . . manned with two M30s—"

"Automatic, no?"

"Machine guns."

"What did Phuoc say about the permit?"

In the darkness, thought Mai, to feel against you the urgent flutter of a child's heart. The hopped-up fragility of it.

A tense sigh, "Even with the permit."

"Leave at night and they shoot. They shoot anything."

The speakers paused for a short while. Then a voice said, "We'll find out soon enough."

She settled forward against the young boy, not wanting to hear any more. Trying to block it all out: the voices, the smell. It was unnerving to think of all those other bodies in the darkness. Black shapes in the blackness, merging like shadows on the surface of oil. She crouched there, in the silence, beneath the hatchway. Spying on the bay through the scupper. Gradually, inevitably, the dark thoughts came. Here, in the dead of night, contorted inside the black underbelly of a junk—she was being drawn out into an endless waste. What did she know about the sea? She was the daughter of a fisherman and yet it terrified her. She watched as Quyen reached back and with a surprisingly practiced gesture pressed her palm against the boy's forehead. From above, watching the set of his grim face, Mai thought of her father. Their last meeting. His blindness. He'd taught her not to blame the war but how could she not?—all the power of his own sight seemed still intent on it.

Through the crack of the scupper the land lights, like mere tricks of her eyes, were extinguished one by one. Someone cut the engines.

She pulled the young boy's body closer to her; it squirmed like a restless animal's.

"Truong," a voice whispered sharply from beneath them. She peered down. It was Quyen.

"Don't be a nuisance, Child." Quyen looked up at Mai, then said ruefully, "This is my little brat. Truong."

"Yours?" Mai frowned. "But—"

From the deepest part of the hold, several voices shushed them. In the silence that followed, even the tidal backwash seemed loud against the hull. Then a grind of something against the boat. Mai had never heard a sound so sudden and hideous.

"What is it?"

"A mine? I heard they put mines—"

The metal shrieked each minute movement of the boat.

"Heavens!"

"But boats pass here, must pass here every day"

Fiercely: "Quiet!"

The sound sheared off leaving behind a deep, capacious silence. Mai stiffening at every creak of the boat, every dash of water against its rotten sidewood. Then, without warning, the call and fade of a faraway voice. She crushed her cheek against the crown of the young boy's head and for the first time felt him respond—both of his small fists clamping her forearm. She shut her eyes and trained herself to his frenzied heartbeat, as though its pulse—its fine-knitting rhythm—carried the only possible thread of their escape. Long minutes passed. The boat glided on, pointed headfirst into the swell. Finally the fierce voice coughed:

"We're safe for now."

Murmurs rose up. The hatch was lifted. Under the sudden starlight Mai could see the whole of the boy's face, arching up to meet the fresh air.

"Child," said Quyen, "greet Chi. Properly."

He looked up at Mai—his eyes black and clear and unblinking. "*Chao* Chi," he said in his reed-thin voice.

All around them people's faces were untensing, bodies and voices stirring in restless relief. But Mai, clutching this strange young boy, found herself shivering in the warm night, relief only a sharp and unexpected condensation in her eyes.

Once the storm passed, six days out, everything changed.

Fishermen on the boat agreed that this storm had come on faster than any they'd ever experienced. It destroyed the caulking and much of the planking on the hull. The inboard was flooded, and soon afterward, both engines cut out completely.

What food had been left was spoiled. Water was short. Anh Phuoc, whose authority was never questioned, took charge of rationing the remaining supply, doling it out first to children, then the infirm, then everyone else. It amounted to a couple of wet mouthfuls a day.

The heat was unbearable. Before long the first body was cast overboard. Already a handful of people had been lost during the storm, but this was the first casualty witnessed by the entire boat. To the terrible drawn-out note of a woman's keening the bundle was tossed, a meek splash, into the water.

Like everyone else, Mai looked away.

After the storm it seemed to Mai that a film had been stripped from the world. Everything became more intense—the sun hotter, the light more vivid, the sea darker, every word a discordant affront to the new silence. The storm had forced people into their privacies: the presence of others now assailed each person's solitude in facing up to the experience of it. Children turned introverted, playing as though conducting conversations with themselves.

Even time took on a false depth: the six days before the storm stretched out, merged with memory, until it seemed as though everything that had ever happened had happened on the boat.

A man burned his clothes to let up smoke. He was quickly set upon, the fire smothered—the longer they drifted the more fearful they became of pirates. That night another bundle was thrown overboard. Minutes later they heard a thrashing in the water. It was too dark to see anything, yet, still, everyone averted their gaze.

Thirst set in. Some people trapped their own urine. Some, desperate for drinkable water, even allowed themselves the quick amnesia and prayed for another storm. It was fantastic to be surrounded by so much water and yet be dehydrated. Mai soon realized she wouldn't make it. The day following the storm she imitated some of the other youth, hauling up a bucket tied to the bowline. Under the noon sun the seawater was the color of amethyst.

She drank it. It was all right at first. It was bliss. Then her throat started scalding and she wanted to claw it out.

"You stupid girl," Quyen reproached her, demonstrating how to use her fingers to induce vomiting. She hugged her fiercely.

"Heavens, you can't wait? We're almost there."

But what did Quyen know? Mai had heard—how could she possibly have not?—that other boats had successfully made the crossing in two days. She tried to sleep, to slide beneath the raw scour of pain in her throat. They'd been out seven days. How much longer? Her father was persistent in her thoughts now—all those weeks, even months, he'd spent on this same sea, in trawlers much like this one. He'd been here before her.

That afternoon, when she awoke, her muscles felt as though they had turned to liquid. She could feel her heart beating slurpily. She followed the weakening palpitations, counterpointing them to the creak and strain of the boat, the occasional luff of the sail. The sun brilliant but without heat. She was even thirstier than before.

"I'm not going to make it," she said. Saying it touched the panic, brought it alive.

"Don't speak," said Quyen. "Go back to sleep."

Mai struggled into a half-upright position. She made out a small group of children next to the bulwark, then pressed her imagination to find him again, little Loe, turning with a snarl as he growled, "Dragon!" She smiled, bit back tears. Behind him, her old school friend Huong was selling beef noodles in front of the damp stink-shaded fish market. Straight through the market she followed her daily route, picking up speed, past fabric stalls and coffee yards, the dusty soccer field where sons of fishermen and truck drivers broke off from the game to buy cigarettes, and then to the wharf, her main place of business, among the taut hard bodies crating boxes, the smell of fish sauce, the rattling talk of men and the gleaming blue backs of silver fish, ice pallets, copper weighing scales bright in the sun, the bustle of docking and undocking, loading and unloading-

A bare-chested man turned around and looked directly at her.

"Ba?"

It filled her with joy to see him like that again: young and strong, his eyes clear and dead straight. He looked like he did in the altar photograph. It was her father before the war, before reeducation, hospitalization. Back when to be seen by him was to be hoisted onto his shoulders, gripped by the ankles. His hands tough, saltish with the smell of wet rope. She moved toward him, she was smiling, but he was stern.

"Child promised," he said.

During his long absences at sea she had lived incompletely, waiting for him to come back so they could tell to each other each moment of their time apart. He spoiled her, her mother said. Her mother was right and yet it changed nothing: still he went away and still, each time, Mai waited.

Her sudden, fervent anger startled her.

"Why send Child away? Child obeyed Ba." Her mind sparked off the words in terrific directions. "Child could have waited for Ba to get better." They had promised each other. He had left for ten days and returned, strange and newly blind, after two years. A thought connected with another: "It was Ba who left Child."

He stood there, tar-faced, empty-eyed, looking straight at her. She lifted her hands to her mouth, unable to believe what she had just said. The words still searing the length of her throat.

"Child is sorry," she whispered. "Ba and Ma sacrificed everything for Child. Child knows. Child is stupid."

He would leap off the boat and swing her into the crook of his arm, up onto his shoulders. Her mother fretting her hands dry on her silken pants, smiling nervously. I can't get it off me, he would say. His hands quivering on either side of Mai's rib cage—It's stuck, I can't get this little beetle off me!

She missed him with an ache that was worse, even, than the thirst had been. All she'd ever known to want was his return. So she would enjoy the gift of his returning, and not be stupid.

"Child is sorry."

He didn't respond.

"Child is sorry, Ba."

"Mai."

He was shaking her. She said again, "Child is sorry," then she felt fingers groping around in her mouth, a polluting smell and then her eyes refocused and she realized it was not her father she saw but Truong, standing gaunt over her.

"Thank heavens," came Quyen's murmur.

Looking at him she finally understood, with a deep internal tremor, what it was that had drawn her to the boy all this time. It was not, as she had first assumed, his age—his awkward build. Nothing at all to do with Loe. It was his face. The expression on his face was the same expression she had seen on her father's face, every day, since he'd returned from reeducation. It was a face dead of surprise.

She gasped as the pain flooded back into her body. She was awake again, cold.

"Mai's fever is gone," Quyen said. She smiled at Mai, a smile of bright industry—such a smile as Mai had never hoped to see again. Unexpectedly she was reminded of her mother, and, to her even greater surprise, she found herself breaking into tears.

"Good," whispered Quyen. "That's good."

Mai wiped her eyes, her mouth, with the hem of her shirt. "I'm thirsty," she said. She looked around for Truong but he seemed to have slipped away.

"You should be. You slept almost two days."

It was evening. She stood up, Quyen helping her. Her legs giving at first. Slowly she climbed up the hatch. On deck she shielded her eyes against the sunset. An incandescent red sky veered into the dark ocean. Rows and rows of the same sun-blotched, peeling faces looked out at nothing.

"Everyone's up here," Quyen whispered, "because down there are all the sick people."

"Sick people?"

Mai checked the deck, then searched it again with growing unease. He'd been standing over her. Keeping her voice even, she asked, "Where is Truong?"

"Truong? I don't know."

"But I saw him—when I woke up."

Quyen considered her carefully. "He was very worried about you, you know."

He wasn't in the clearing with the other children. Mai shuffled into the morass of arms and legs, heading for the pilothouse. Nobody made way for her. At that moment Truong emerged from the companionway. She almost cried out aloud when she saw him—gone was the pale, delicate-faced boy she'd remembered: now his lips were bloated, the skin of his cheeks brown chapped in the pattern of bruised glass. An awful new wateriness in his gaze. He stood there warily as though summoned for punishment. Mai mustered her voice:

"Is Child well?"

"Yes. Are you better?"

"Truong, speak properly!" scolded Quyen.

"How is Chi Mai?"

"Well. Better." She leaned toward him, probing the viscosity of his eyes. His face's swollenness gave it a sleepy aspect.

"Ma said Chi Mai was very sick."

"Chi is better now."

"Tan and An were more sick than Chi," he said. "But Ma says they were lucky."

Mai smiled at Quyen; she hadn't heard him talk so much before. His voice came out scratchy but steady. He stood before them in a waiting stance: legs together, hands by his sides.

"Chi is glad for them."

"They died," he said. When Mai didn't respond he went on: "I saw the shark. All the uncles tried to catch it with that"—he pointed to a cable hanging off the derrick-crane—"but it was too fast."

"Truong!"

His eyes flicked to his mother. Then he said: "Fourteen people died while Chi Mai was sleeping."

"Child!"

He balled up his hands by his sides, then opened them again.

"Chi Mai isn't sick anymore, *ha*?"

"That's right," Mai and Quyen said together.

It was difficult to reconcile him with his frail, wasting body. Seeing him, Mai's own body felt its full exhaustion. "Now . . . let's see . . ." She lifted one hand until it hovered between them, palm down. "Child wants to play slaps?"

His black eyes stared at her with something akin to pity. "Pretend this is the shark," she exclaimed. Quyen glanced up at her. Immediately—horrified, shocked by herself—Mai pulled back her hand. "Chi is just joking."

Later that evening, a young teenage girl with chicken legs wandered over to the gunwale and in a motion like a bow that didn't stop, toppled gracefully over the side.

"Wait!" someone cried.

"Let her be," another person said. "If she wants to, let her be."

"Heavens, someone save her. Someone!" The first man stumbled to his feet, wild-eyed. "You do it. Go on. Jump."

He stood like a scarecrow, frozen. Everyone watched him. He walked to the side and looked down at the shiny, dusk-reflecting water.

"I can't see her," he said.

"She must not have any family," Quyen whispered to Mai.

"She has the right idea," another low voice said. "Is there any better way to go?"

"*Thoi*," Anh Phuoc said, coming over. "*Thoi*, that's enough."

Reeducation camp. For two years those two words had framed the entirety of her imaginative life. Her father, of course, hadn't talked about it when he returned—nor her mother. Now, for the first time, someone talked to her about it. Anh Phuoc had fought in the same regiment as her father—had been sentenced to a camp in the same district. No, he hadn't known him. By the time the Communists took Ban Me Thuot in March 1975, the Americans were long gone and the Southern regiments in tatters—soldiers deserting, taking cover as civilians, fleeing into the jungles. Escape on every man's mind. Soon they all learned there was no escaping the Communists: not in the country they now controlled. They were skilled, he said, at turning north against south, village against village. He fell quiet.

Mai waited. She watched him remembering. Nine days had passed and now she noticed how severely he had aged: his eyes gone saggy, his skin mottled with dark sun spots.

"In the camps," he said, "they do what they do best. They take a man—and then they turn him against things."

From the back deck a middle-aged woman started wading in their direction through the sprawl of bodies. She held the port gunwale with both hands for balance, "Husbands against wives," he went on. "Children against parents. Your only chance is to denounce everyone, and everything, they tell you to."

The woman reached them. She made her complaint in a hoarse voice. She was owed water. She had tendered hers to another child who had collapsed, she said, and pointed aft. Anh Phuoc held Mai's eyes for a second, then followed the woman.

Her father wouldn't have denounced her—she was sure of that. Not in his own heart. But again she understood how necessary it was to stay on the surface of things. Because beneath the surface was either dread or delirium. As more and more bundles were thrown overboard she taught herself not to look, not to think of the bundles as human—she resisted the impulse to identify which families had been depleted. She seized distraction from the immediate things: the weather, the next swallow of water, the ever-forward draw of time.

"Mai!"

It was Anh Phuoc. She stood up, hauled herself on weak legs along the gunwale, toward the rear of the boat. Past the hatch she suddenly saw Truong propped up against the rusty mast of the derrick-crane, his chin drooping onto his chest, arms bony and limp by his sides.

Mai leapt forward, swiping her elbows and knees from side to side to clear space. The surrounding people watched listlessly.

"Water!"

No one reacted. She looked around and spotted an army flask—grabbed it, swiveled the cap open, held it to his mouth. A thin trickle ran over his rubbery lips before the flask was snatched away. She looked up and saw a man's face, twisted in hate the moment he struck her, his knuckles hard as a bottle against her cheek. She fell over and covered Truong's body.

"She stole water."

"I'll pay it back," said Anh Phuoc roughly.

Truong started coughing. Mai sat back, her cheek burning, and mumbled apology in the direction of the man. He was picking the flask up from the ground. People glanced over, disturbed by the waste. There had been a minor outcry the previous evening when a woman—an actress, people said—had used the last of her ration to wash her face.

Truong squinted up at Mai. Everything about him: the dark sore of his face, his disproportioned, skeletal limbs, seemed to be ceding its sense of solidity. She touched his blistered cheek with her fingers–was reminded of the sting on her own cheek from the man's blow.

"Ma," he wheezed.

"It's alright," she said. "Ma is coming. Chi is here."

"Where's Quyen?" asked Anh Phuoc. He stood up quickly and walked off.

Truong said, "Child wanted to count the people."

He coughed again, the air scraping through his throat. Watching him, a helpless feeling welled up within Mai and started to coalesce at the front of her skull. "Child," she whispered. Quyen arrived. She seemed to be moving within a slower state, her face drawn, hair tangled. She saw Truong and bent down to him. "Look," she murmured, "you hurt yourself."

"He fainted," said Mai.

"Why didn't Child stay with Ma?"

"I don't like it down there," he said.

"Oh, Mai," Quyen exclaimed, turning to her. "Are you all right?"

"He shouldn't be in the sun. He needs more water."

"It's too dark to count down there," Truong said. He brought up his arms, dangled them loosely over his knees. An old man's pose. Quyen squatted down and enfolded him, clinching him between her elbows, raking one hand through his hair and cupping his forehead with the other.

"I was so tired," said Quyen. "Thank you."

"He needs more water."

"Does Child know?" She was speaking to Truong. "Does Child know how lucky he is? To have Chi Mai look after him?"

Anh Phuoc leaned down close to both of them. "Come with me," he muttered. They followed him forward to the pilothouse, everyone watching as they passed. Once inside he closed the door. Carefully, he measured out a capful of water from a plastic carton and administered it into Truong's mouth.

The sight—even the smell—of the water roused an appalling ache in Mai's stomach, but she said nothing.

"Good boy," said Anh Phuoc.

Quyen's eyes followed the carton. "Is that all there is?"

Holding the tiller with one hand, he reached down and opened the cupboard beneath it. Three plastic white cartons.

"That's all," he said, "unless it rains."

"How long will it last?"

"Another day. Two at the most."

Her temple still aching, Mai looked out of the pilothouse windows. From up here she could see the full length and breadth of the boat: every inch of it clogged with rags and black-tufted heads and sunburned flesh. Up here would be the best place to count people. She wrenched her eyes away from the water carton and looked out instead at the sky. Not a cloud in sight. But the sky was full of deceit—it looked the same everywhere. She looked at the horizon, long and pale and eye-level all around them. Whatever direction she looked, it fell away into more water.

The tenth day dawned. Engines dead, the boat drifted on. Gray shadows strafing the water behind it. The detachable sail hoisted onto a short mast's yard and men taking turns, croaking directions to each other as they tried to steer the boat, as best they could, to the south.

Mai watched Truong with renewed intensity. Since Mai's recovery Quyen had kept to herself, remaining huddled, during the day as well as night, underneath the companionway stairs where they all slept. That morning Mai had found her sitting in the slatted light, staring vacantly into the dark hold. Squeezed between two old women.

"How is Truong?" Quyen asked her quietly.

Mai said, "I keep telling him to come down."

"He doesn't like it down here."

Mai nodded, not knowing what to say.

Quyen dropped her chin and closed her eyes. Mai looked her over. She didn't look sick.

"Is Chi alright?"

Quyen nodded almost impatiently. One of the women beside her spat into her hands. When Quyen looked up her face was distant, drawn in unsparing lines.

"Look after him, *nha*? Please."

Above deck, each hour stretched out its hot minutes. Mai lay on her back under the derrick-crane, her head against someone's shin, limbs interwoven with her neighbors'. Truong wedged beside her. The crane cast a shadow that inched up their bodies. She threw her sleeve over her face to ward off the sweltering sun. At one point a wind blew in and the boat began to sway, lightly, in the water. She was riding her father's shoulders. Her mother watching them happily. Whenever he was home he brought with him some quality that filled her mother so there was enough left, sometimes, for her to be happy.

Truong started singing. Softly—to himself—so softly she wouldn't have heard him if her ear hadn't been inches from his mouth. She gradually shifted her arm down so she could hear better. He sang the ballad from the third night. She listened, hardly daring to breathe, watching the now-darkening sky knitting together the rigs and cables of the crane above them as though they were the branches of trees.

When he finished, the silence that surged in afterward was unbearable. Mai reached across her body and gently took hold of his arm.

"Who taught Child how to sing like that?"

He didn't answer.

The next morning, back below deck, she woke up to find a puddle of vomit next to his curled-up, sleeping body. It gleamed gray in the early light of dawn.

"The child has the sickness," a voice said without a second thought. It was one of the old women who had camped with them beneath the companionway stairs. The hatch was open and light flowed in like a mist, dimly illumining the three other bodies entangled in their nook. The deeper recess of the hold remained black.

"No, he doesn't," said Mai.

"Poor child. He is not the last. Such a pity."

"Be quiet!" Mai covered her mouth, abashed, but no one reproached her. Several bodies stirred on the other side of the stairs.

Barely awake, Quyen rolled over to her son and propped herself up on an elbow. She brushed his cheek with her knuckles. For a second, in the half-light, Mai thought she saw an expression of horror move across her friend's face.

"Child is sorry," Mai murmured to the old woman.

Truong's eyes were glazed when he opened them. He looked like a burnt ghost. He leaned over, away from his mother, and dry-retched. There was nothing left in him to expel. Another of their neighbors, a man who smelled of stale tobacco, averted his legs casually.

"What it can do to you," the old woman said, her gums stained crimson from chewing betel leaves, "the ocean."

"Does Child's stomach hurt?" asked Mai.

"Yes."

"What it can steal from you and never give back. My husband, both my daughters."

"It's just a stomach-ache," said Quyen, then looked up as though daring the old woman—or anyone—to disagree. A gang of eyes, unmoving, inexpressive, watched them from the shadows. That evening, Anh Phuoc ladled out the last rations of water.

He shuffled wearily through the boat, repeating the same account to anyone who stopped him, intoning his interlocutors' names as though that were the only consolation left him to offer them. Weak moans and thick silences trailed him.

When Mai poured her ration into Tuong's cup, Quyen frowned, and then flinched away. "Thank you," she said at last. For the first time she used the word for "younger sister."

"It's nothing. I already took a sip."

"Poor child," repeated the old woman, shaking her head. Truong took some water in, then coughed some of it out.

People looked over. In the dusk light his face was pallid and shiny.

He opened his mouth. "Ma," he said.

"I'm here," said Quyen.

"Ma."

Quyen bit her lips, wiped the sweat from Truong's brow with a corner of her shirt. Finally his eyes focused and he seemed to look straight at Mai.

"It's so hot," he said.

"*Thoi*," said Quyen, dabbing above his eyes, around his hairline.

"I want to go up."

"Sleep, my beloved. My little prince. Sleep."

Mai wanted desperately to say something to him—something useful, or comforting—but no words came. She got up to close the hatch door.

The old woman took out a betel leaf and inserted it into the slit of her toothless mouth.

His sickness followed the usual course. Muscle soreness and nausea in the early stages. That evening his blisters began to rise, some of them bleeding pus. He became too weak to swallow water.

In the middle of the night, Mai woke to find Truong half draped over her stomach. His weight on her so light as to be almost imperceptible, as though his body were already nothing more than bones and air. "Everything will be fine," she whispered into the darkness, her thoughts, still interlaced with dream, scattered remotely across space and gray sea. Back home she'd slept on the same mat as Loe. Her mother by the opposite wall. She reached down and touched Truong's brow.

He stirred awake. "Is Child alright?"

"I want to go up."

The skin on his face was hot and moist. Mai lifted her eyes and noticed Quyen, mashed in the shadow of the companionway steps, staring at both of them.

"Take him," she said dully.

Mai found a spot for them by the pilothouse, surrounded by sleeping families. When dawn came, Truong's head slid with a slight thud onto the planking. Half asleep, Mai sought his shoulder, shook it. His body gave no response. She sat up and shook him again. His clothes stiff with dried sweat. Nothing.

"Truong," whispered Mai, feeling the worry build within her. She poked his cheek. It was still warm—thank heavens!—it was still warm. She checked his forehead: hotter than it had been last night. He was boiling up. His breath shallow and short. With agonizing effort she cradled his slight, inert body and bore him up the stairs into the pilothouse.

Anh Phuoc was slumped underneath the tiller, sleeping. Three infants were laid out side by side on the floor, swaddled in rags.

He woke up. "What is it?" He saw Truong in her arms.

"Where's Quyen?"

She laid him down. Then she turned to find Quyen.

"Wait." Anh Phuoc got up, surveyed the boat through the windows, then retrieved a flask from behind the bank of gauges. He unscrewed the cap and poured a tiny trickle of water into a cup. "This was for them," he said, gesturing at the motionless babies. "How they've lasted twelve days I don't know." He screwed the flask cap back on and then, with tremendous care, handed her the cup. "But they won't make it either." He paused.

"Let me find Quyen."

Truong wouldn't wake up. Mai dipped one finger into the cup, traced it along the inner line of his lips. Once it dried she dipped her finger again, ran it across his lips again. She did this over and over. One time she thought she saw his throat twitch. His face—the burnt, blistered skin, its spots and scabs—the deeper she looked, the more his features dissociated from one another until what she looked into, as she tended him, was not a face, but a brown and blasted landscape. Like a slow fire it drew the air from her lungs.

Commotion on deck. Someone shouting. She jolted awake. Checked Truong—he was still unconscious, his fever holding: A weird tension suffusing the air. Another death? Mai opened the pilothouse door and asked a nearby woman what was happening.

"They saw whales," the woman said.

"Whales?"

"And then land birds."

It was as though she were sick again, her heart shocked out of its usual rhythm. "Land? They saw land?"

The woman shrugged.

All at once Quyen burst out of the hold, her hair disheveled and her eyes watery and red. She spotted Mai.

"Here!" Mai called out excitedly. "Chi Quyen, here!" She stood on tiptoes and scanned all the horizon she could see. Nothing. She looked again. "Someone said they saw land," she announced aloud. Realizing people were scowling at her, she turned toward Quyen. Too late she caught a new, rough aspect in her eyes. Quyen strode up into Mai's face.

"Where's my son?" She pushed into the pilothouse. Mai stumbled back, tripping over the doorsill.

Inside, Quyen saw Truong and rushed toward him, lowering her head to his. She emitted a throaty cry and twisted around to face Mai.

"Stay away," she declared. "You've done enough!" Her voice was strained, on the verge of shrillness.

"Chi," gasped Mai.

"I've changed my mind," Quyen went on, the pitch of her words wavering. Her expression was wild, now—cunning. "He's my son! Not yours—mine!"

"*Thoi*," a man's voice interjected.

Mai spun and saw Anh Phuoc in the doorway.

"What's the matter?"

Quyen glared at him. He waited for her to speak. Finally, her tone gone sullen, she said, "She took my son."

He sighed. "Mai was looking after him."

Quyen stared at him, incredulous, then started laughing. She clamped both hands over her mouth. Then, as though in embarrassment, she dipped her head, nuzzling Truong's chest like an animal. Mai watched it all. The thick dense knot back behind her temple. Quyen's body shuddered in tight bursts awhile, then, slowly, hitchingly, it began to calm. It seemed for a moment as though Quyen might never look up again. When she did, her face was utterly blanched of expression.

"Mai wouldn't hurt Truong," said Anh Phuoc tiredly. "She loves him."

Quyen threw him a spent smile. "I know." But she didn't look at Mai. Instead, she turned and again bent over the unconscious shape of her son. That was when she began to cry—silently at first, inside her body, but then, breath by breath, letting out her wail until the whole boat could hear.

* * *

He was her shame and yet she loved him. What did that make her? She had conceived him when she was young, and passed him off to her aunt in Da Lat to raise, and then she had gotten married. With the war and all its disturbances, she had never gone back to visit him. Worse, she had never told her husband.

"He would leave me," she told Mai. "He will."

But she couldn't abandon her only son—not to the Communists—not if she could find a way out of the country. Even if he didn't want to leave, and even if he didn't know her. Her aunt had balked, and Quyen had been forced to abduct him. She'd been wrong to have him—she knew that—but she'd been even more wrong to give him away. Surely, she thought, she was right to take him with her. Then, when she saw him weakening—then falling sick—she realized that perhaps he was being punished for her shame. Whether he lived or died—perhaps it wasn't for her to decide.

She begged Mai to forgive her. Mai didn't say anything.

"He doesn't love his own mother," said Quyen.

"That's not true."

Quyen leaned down and unstuck his hair from his forehead and parted it. They'd moved him back down into the hold under the companionway stairs, for shade.

Quyen sniffed. "It's fair. What kind of mother watches that happen to her only son—and does nothing?"

"You were sick."

Quyen turned to her with a strange, shy expression, then lowered her gaze.

"I knew you would take care of him," she said

"Of course."

"No." She looked down at her son's fevered face. "Forgive me. It was more than that. My thoughts were mad." She gave out a noise like a hollow chuckle. "I thought of asking you . . ." she said. "I was going to ask you to take him in—to pretend he was your son." She shook her head in wonderment. "He likes you so much. Yes. I thought—just until I could tell my husband the truth."

Mai remained quiet, her mind turbulent.

Quyen sniffed again. "*Thoi*," she declared. "Enough!" Caressing her forearm—still scored with rope marks from the storm six days ago—she smiled into the air. "It's my fault."

"Chi."

"Whatever happens to him."

Mai stared down, unsteadily, at the marred, exposed field of Truong's face.

"You don't have to answer," Quyen continued in her bright voice. "Whatever happens, I deserve it."

He entered into the worst of it that afternoon, moving fitfully into and out of sleep. His breath short, irregular. Their neighbors kindly made some space for him to lie down. When some children came to visit, Quyen rebuffed them without even looking. Mai sat silently opposite them, next to the old betel-gummed woman, transfixed by her friend's intensity.

Then, at the end of the afternoon—after five long hours—Truong's small body suddenly unclenched and his breath eased. The lines on his forehead cleared. It seemed, unbelievably, that he had prevailed.

"It's over," Mai said joyfully. "Chi, the fever has broken."

Quyen cradled him in her lap, rocking him lightly. "Yes, yes, yes, yes," she sighed, "Sleep, my beloved."

His clothes were soaked with sweat. For a fleeting moment, as Mai saw his face unfastened from its distress, the fantasy crossed her mind that he was dead. She shook it off. Quyen's hair fell over her son's face. They both appeared to her strangely now, as if at an increasing remove, as if she were trying to hold them in view through the stained, swaying window of a bus.

Truong hiccuped, opened his eyes and rasped, "Ma has some water?" With an almost inaudible moan Quyen hunched over and showered his brow with kisses. Outside the evening was falling, the last of the light sallow on his skin. After a while Truong gathered his breath again.

"Ma will sing to Child?"

"Sing for the poor child," said the old woman.

Quyen nodded. She started singing: a Southern lullaby Mai hadn't heard for years, her voice more tender than Mai had imagined it could be.

Truong shook his head weakly. "No-not that one." He made an effort to swallow. "My favorite song."

"Your favorite song," repeated Quyen. She bit her lip, frowning, then swung around mutely, strickenly, to Mai.

Mai reached out to stroke Truong's hair. She said, "But Child must sleep, *nha*?" She waited for him to completely shut his eyes. Quyen found her hand and held it. Mai cleared her throat then surprised to find her voice even lower, hoarser than Quyen's, she started singing:

I am the vigil moon that sheds you light
My soul abides within the Thousand Peaks;
Where drunk with wine and Long-Tuyen sword you seek
And slaughter all the leopards of the night.
And in the steps of Gioi Tu, seize Lau-Lan
And quash the Man-Khe rivers into one.
You wear the scarlet shadow of the sun:
And yet your steed is whiter than my palm . . .

Abruptly her voice broke off, then she swallowed, picked up the thread of melody again, and sang it through, her voice as hard as Quyen's face was tender, her voice resolute and unwavering, sang it through to the very end.

The old woman nodded to herself.

The next morning—the morning of their thirteenth day—a couple of the fishermen sighted land. A swell of excitement, like a weak current, ran through the boat. People looked at one another as though for the first time.

"We made it," someone quietly announced, returning from deck. He paused on the companionway, his head silhouetted against the sunlight. In the glare, Mai couldn't make out his face. He said, "We're safe now." The words deep in his throat.

Quyen and Truong were underneath the stairs. Mai had left them to themselves during the night. Now, with those others strong enough, Mai followed the man above deck. Outside, the dawn sun steeped through her, as though her body were made of paper. Dizziness overwhelmed her when she saw the half-empty deck—had they been so depleted? She thought, with an odd pang, of Truong, his incessant counting. Then she saw the prow, teeming with people, all peering ahead, attitudes stalled in their necks and shoulders. She made her way forward, then spotted, far ahead, the tiny breakers on the reefs, and behind those, the white sand like a bared smile. Birds hanging in midair over the water.

During the night she had come to her decision. Her thoughts starting always with Truong and ending always with her father, upright in his hospital bed, staring at some invisible situation in front of him. A street with its lights turned off. She came into morning feeling a bone-deep ache through her body. The boat would land—they would all land—Mai would write to her family, and wait for them, and then she would look after Truong as if he were her own child. The decision dissolved within her, rose up with the force of joy. She would tell Quyen. She would look after him, completely, unconditionally, and try not to think about the moment when Quyen might ask her to stop.

Nearly weightless in her body, Mai descended the companionway. When she reached the bottom she spun and searched behind the stairs. There they were. The hold awash with low talk.

"Chi Quyen."

She was about to call out again when she sensed something amiss. Quyen's back—folded over Truong's sleeping form—it was too stiff. The posture too awkward.

Mai moved closer. "Chi?" she asked.

Quyen's crouched torso expanded, took in air. Without turning around she said, "What will I do now?" Her voice brute, flat.

Mai squatted down. Her heart tripping faster and faster, up into her throat.

Quyen said, "He didn't."

She said, "All night. He wouldn't wake up."

She was wrong, thought Mai. What did she know, thought Mai. When she'd left last night, Truong had been recovering. He'd been fine. He'd been asking Mai, over and over, to sing to him. What could have happened?

Quyen shifted to one side. He was bundled up in a blanket. The bundle tapered at one end—where his legs must have been. Mai could see no part of him. How could this be the end of it? She wrung the heels of her hands into her eyes, as if the fault lay with them. Then she felt Quyen's face, cool with shock, next to her own, rough and wet and cool against her knuckles, speaking into her ear. At first she recoiled from Quyen's touch. What was she saying? She was asking Mai for help. She was asking Mai to help her carry him. It was time, she said. Time, which had disappeared tended every moment on the boat—until there had seemed to be no shape to it—seemed now to snap violently shut, crushing all things into this one task. They were standing—when had they gotten up?—then they were kneeling, facing each other over the length of him. Quyen circumspect in her movements, as though loath to take up any more space than her son now needed. She seemed not to see anything she looked at. Together, the two of them brought the bundle aft, through the shifting, silent crowd, past the derrick-crane, where a group of the strongest men waited. There, the wind turned a corner of the blanket over and revealed the small head, the ash beauty of his face, the new dark slickness of his skin. With a shudder Quyen fell to it and pressed and rubbed her lips against his cheek.

Anh Phuoc, standing with three other men, waited for Quyen to finish before touching her shoulder.

He said, to no one in particular, "We'll make land soon."

As though this were an order, Mai took Quyen's arm and led her the full span of the boat to the prow. Again, the crowd parted for them. They stood together in silence, the spray moistening their faces as they looked forward, focusing all their sight and thought on that blurry peninsula ahead, that impossible place, so that they would not be forced to behold the men at the back of the boat peeling the blanket off, swinging the small body once, twice, three times before letting go, tossing him as far behind the boat as possible so he would be out of sight when the sharks attacked.

Let's return now to the first sentence about the stolen canoe and the bushel of oysters. What assumptions did you make about the "I" of that sentence? We've used this sentence, the first sentence of Charlie Smith's "Crystal River," many times, and the vast majority of students over the years have assumed that the "I" is a woman. Why? We're not trying to make anyone feel awkward or bad about their choices, but implicit gender bias is likely the cause for thinking the narrator is a woman. Until relatively recently, and still in many cultures, preparing food (washing greens) is seen to be "woman's work." Actually, the "I" is a man and he is the friend and sometime lover of Harold.

What else is implied in this sentence? Do we have any sense of the *setting* of the story? Maybe we don't know exactly where the story is set, but Charlie Smith has given us clues. If you guessed the United States, in some rural area, you're right. What were your clues? Maybe the pickup truck, the back porch, perhaps the canoe? If you guessed the American South, you'd also be correct. What are your clues for this? Likely, the "greens" gave it away if you know anything about the South, where greens (usually collard greens) are as common as grits.

Final question: Where did that first sentence take you narratively? Did you go with the stolen canoe and focus on what a rascal that Harold is? "Harold, how many times I got to tell you, don't involve me in any of your shenanigans?"

That's not where Charlie Smith takes it. He knows he's got your attention with the stolen canoe—that's what's known as a *Macguffin*, a trigger for the plot of the story. The Macguffin's function is to intrigue you. Instead, Smith focuses on the oysters. We might also consider this a classic *Bait and Switch*, setting us up for one thing but delivering something else. About two pages are devoted to the narrator and Harold preparing the oysters to eat. Several pages in, the narrator lets us know that the canoe has "Ft. Benning Rec" stenciled on its bow—it's one that Harold "relocated" from the army, claiming to have lost it on a rough stretch of the Toccoa River. By this time, the reader has been sucked into the narrative and the canoe is simply a reflection of Harold's character.

For us, it's simpler to continue Charlie Smith's first line than Nam Le's, though we are no more from the American South than from the south of Vietnam. The American South and American characters and landscapes are a standard fare of American pop culture, which has been exported to the far reaches of the globe. That's not to say that stereotypes of say, white Southern Americans are fine and dandy to write—stereotypes, by and large, should be avoided. But we're more likely, as long as we have access to big and little screens, to have been exposed to many more versions of American society than of Vietnamese. That, we'd like to gently remind you, is one of the reasons for this book.

What we'd like to turn our attention to now is how Nam Le divulges crucial information about the main characters: Mai, Truong, and Quyen. We learn Mai's history through *flashbacks*, *dreams*, and *exposition*. All of these are worthy ways to provide us with a character's background so that we can better sympathize and understand what led up to the predicament in which they now find themselves. There's no set way to incorporate these devices into your fiction, but a good rule of thumb is that you don't want to rely on them too heavily, otherwise you risk losing or confusing the reader. Don't give us page after page of exposition going into the protagonist's past—decide what's absolutely necessary for the reader to know and when they need to know the information. Consider breaking up long passages of exposition into a patchwork throughout the story so the reader doesn't get bogged down in it. When dealing with dreams and flashbacks, try to avoid sending your character into a flashback or a dream without a real-world trigger, something that instigates the looking away from what's happening in the present of the story.

Let's look at how Nam Le does it. He keeps us in the immediacy of the storm until the ninth paragraph. Here, Mai closes her eyes.

> She tried to recall her father's stories—storms at sea, waves, ten, fifteen meters high!—but they rang shallow against what she'd just seen: those dense roaring slabs of water, sky churning overhead like a puddle being mucked with a stick.

That's barely a toe in the past, and yet it's giving us important hints. Her father had stories of the sea. Was he a fisher, a sailor of some kind? Later we learn more about him, that he was sent to a reeducation camp, that he suffered from a mysterious blindness. This small bit of information though is enough for now—we don't need his entire biography. Not only would that be tedious, but it would interfere with the harrowing present moment and we'd likely forget most of it. You can only expect your reader to take in small bits of information at one time.

The first extended expository passage about how Mai and others came to be in their predicament comes several pages into the story, announcing itself via white space. As a short story writer, white space is your friend. It usually signals a break, a scene shift. Lately, however, we've noticed an odd habit of some students to put white spaces between *every* paragraph as though they're writing a business letter and not a short story. We in our infinite Royal We-Ness think this is rather gauche and declassé and well, unnecessary. It's like everyone suddenly saying "on accident" instead of the correct "by accident," but don't get us started.

* * *

That's another way to signal a shift, those three little asterisks.

Within that first flashback, notice how Nam Le uses the song Truong sings both as a device that leads to her meeting him and his mother, Quyen, but also as a memory trigger. The song is the same one her mother sang when her father was away at war, a plaintive folk song that speaks of loss. Notice how important songs are to this story as fragile sites of culture and tragedy.

Much of this story is told reflectively, in a series of scenes and summaries that add up to the present moment. For the most part, the past is delineated from the present pretty clearly, and reality from dream, but not always. When Mai falls into a fever sleep for two days, the past and present collide. One moment she's struggling into a sitting position, after having told Quyen she doesn't think she'll survive. She sees a small group of children in the hold and she presses "her imagination" to find her brother, left behind in Vietnam, in that group. That word "imagination" is the only clue we need—what she sees next seems to be a mixture of delirium and memory. And then:

A bare-chested man turned around and looked directly at her.

What follows is a moving exchange between Mai and her phantom to whom she first berates and then begs forgiveness. The fever dream ends abruptly without any overt signaling from the author.

"Child is sorry, Ba."

"Mai."

He was shaking her. She said again, "Child is sorry," then she felt fingers groping around in her mouth, a polluting smell and then her eyes refocused and she realized it was not her father she saw but Truong, standing gaunt over her.

"Thank Heavens," came Quyen's murmur.

Throughout the story, Nam Le skillfully weaves the past and present together, while never confusing an astute reader. *Transitions* can often be difficult to follow but as long as you signal to the reader through a subtle (but not too subtle) segue, or white space or asterisks or even hashtags, that you're shifting consciousness, time, and/or place, the narrative will read coherently.

Now let's take a look at another story of diaspora, Noelle Q. de Jesus's "Dreams in English." Here, we have a story told from the point of view of the person left behind, not the person who has left their home country. Another difference is that while Mai has left her country out of desperation, Margie in de Jesus's story has left for educational opportunities. One similarity, however, is the fact that the characters have secrets from one another. In Quyen's case, it's that Truong, while her biological son, is almost a stranger to her and vice-versa because he did not live with her. In Margie's case, the secret her father, Pablo learns forces him to confront the facts that he is a stranger to his daughter, though he thought he knew her better than he did.

We love secrets. We love secrets that characters keep from one another and we love secrets that characters keep from themselves. We sometimes tell ourselves when we're writing a story that all our characters have secrets and we need to discover what they are. That doesn't mean that all the secrets have to be revealed or even be a part of the story (sometimes secrets are good for you, the author, to better understand your characters, and that's justification enough) but they *can* be useful in the way the story builds and what it reveals. We're not suggesting either that the secrets should be sprung on you or your characters. Typically speaking, *I-am-your-father-Luke* moments don't work so well in short stories if they're not set up carefully. You shouldn't aim to throw in a twist at the end just to spice things up. Such gestures tend to feel gimmicky if you don't lay a plausible foundation for them. Consider your own secrets. Imagine what might happen if you told your parents about the night you or your partner about that one time. That same tension you feel at the thought of such a revelation is a powerful driver of short stories, too. In "Dreams in English," note how and when Pablo learns the secret and how this secret threads through the story and influences Pablo's change as a character. Let's read it now:

2 "Dreams in English"

by Noelle Q. de Jesus (Philippines/Singapore)

Noelle Q. de Jesus is a Filipino American writer whose first book, *Blood: Collected Stories*, won the US-based 2016 Next Generation Indie Book Award for the Short Story. A Palanca Award winner and a University of the Philippines' Writers Workshop fellow, her most recent book is *Cursed and Other Stories*.

In the last letter Pablo remembered from Margie, though he could not say when that was exactly, she told her father she had started to dream in English. She was even starting, she confessed in her scratchy script, to think in the language. Pablo thought it was incredible. As a child, Margie could not speak or understand a word of English—she would respond only to words in Tagalog. Her teacher had called the parents over to talk about Margie's "problem."

"Margie is a cheater," the woman said rather harshly, showing them two identical drawings of a hut,

each with a very nicely drawn coconut tree, its green leaves peeking from behind the bamboo thatched roof.

"This is Ana's drawing, Margie's seatmate," the teacher said, pointing to the big scrawling letters in the corner of the paper. Dulce had not been able to suppress an exclamation, so impressed that some of Margie's classmates could actually write their own names, knowing full well Margie couldn't.

"And this is Margie's," the woman said, holding up the exact same drawing and the same scrawling letters spelling out the word, "ANA," a perfect forgery.

"I assure you, Mr. and Mrs. Garcia, the children were instructed to do their own drawings." The teacher shook her head.

When Dulce had confronted the five-year-old Margie, the child just shrugged her small shoulders, already her own person. "I couldn't understand, so I just copied the girl beside me," she said proudly in Tagalog.

And this little girl that had won herself a scholarship to study art and art history in America was now dreaming in English? It was truly amazing. Pablo wondered what Margie's first dream was about, and wished to God that he could ask her, because if she could answer, he knew she would tell him.

He watched his daughter, lying so still in this hospital bed far away from her home. He watched the movement of her chest, the way it rose and fell with every breath. Pablo clung to that movement with hope clenching in his own chest. It was the only sign, after all, that beneath all the tubes and the tape, Margie's heart was beating. Margie was alive.

Pablo tried to recall the dream that he had, his last night in Manila; it seemed like it happened a thousand years ago. It had that same familiarity, more a memory, and certainly, it was the best dream he had in a long time. It carried him afloat on a happy cloud so pleasing that even within it, he became very much aware he was dreaming, aware of Dulce, sleeping warm beside him in their bed, in their house. What had it been about? A happy spell with his wife sailing on magenta and orange technicolor seas on a boat he built with his own hands? Or was it a memory of Cherisse, his once-upon-a-time mistress for three years, now friend, the wife of a colleague? Was it an imaginary basketball game with only four players and a bubble-like basketball that never burst?

He regretted it wasn't Margie herself that he dreamed of. It might have been of her, as the chubby cherub she once was, leaping into his arms, showering him with kisses as she embraced him, all the while grabbing fistfuls of his hair. The sensation of her solid little body, warmly damp from perspiration, the soles of her feet chalky black with dust. That was a million years ago. Pablo felt he betrayed her. There was his little Margie, fallen ill all by herself in this cold country, and Pablo had lain there asleep, dreaming his own silly, selfish dream.

That was when the telephone rang, shrill and persistent as the American voice that continued to ring in his ear, even after he had replaced the receiver. The voice said Margie was in the hospital, in a coma. She was ill. A virus, they said, had infiltrated her nervous system. Pablo could barely understand the words in English.

In a different world, Pablo thought as he sat in the gleaming white-walled room with this quiet man, waiting to find out whether his 22-year-old daughter would live or die—that would be the nightmare, and Pablo, sleeping at home beside his wife, dreaming about his mistress—that would be the reality.

He glanced at Brian. Brian Jacobs. Pablo didn't much like the look of him. If it were true that little girls grew up to fall in love with men just like their fathers, then he felt mildly insulted. The controlled American man took charge the minute Pablo arrived, called his daughter "Marge" and spoke to the doctors and hospital staff as though he were the one, in fact, the only one who mattered? This man, just his daughter's . . . well, what would he be? Did people nowadays still use the word "boyfriend"? Pablo steeled his heart against the thought the same way he had steeled himself against everything. He could not accept this, not till he heard from Margie herself who this man was.

Pablo tried to recall her letters. No mention of this tall man with light brown hair, the color of the *panocha* with which he sweetened his coffee. No, she wrote she had a great schedule, she liked all her classes and the professors. She was happy winter was over, she loved the spring, and she had begun to dream in English. No man named Brian had figured on the pink stationery.

"Do you remember Margie ever mentioning Brian? In a letter or maybe during a telephone call?" Pablo had asked Dulce last night.

"No, but why does that matter? Why is that so important to you?" Dulce cried, her voice edged with hysteria and piercing reproach.

He heard Brian snore. The man was tall but not bulky or barrel chested. He was stretched out like a ladder against a wall in stiff, exhausted sleep. At least he can sleep, Pablo thought and felt foolishly proud that he could not. The hospital staff probably didn't know what to make of them—such an odd couple they made. He, an old man, emotional and foreign, given to silent, endless weeping, and then Brian—brusque and blunt, his distress apparent but muted as though preserved beneath glass of his cold expression.

Pablo stood up. He had to leave that spic-and-span waiting lounge. He wanted to see his daughter that very minute, even while he dreaded the sight. Pablo walked the halls towards the ICU, trying to be purposeful, but inside, bit by bit, his stomach turned to ice with apprehension. It was the same as it had been this morning, just as it had been the day before. There was the bed that dwarfed his daughter. There was the tray of untouched food that came in the morning and was taken away at noon. How angry the American had been when the staff moved Margie to the ICU, but forgot to bring along the flowers he brought her daily. Lilies and some other kind Pablo could not name. Marge's favorites, Brian said.

"They have to be where Margie can see them when she wakes," the man told them. It was brave and sentimental, but it embarrassed Pablo, even while he admired it. The monitor continued to beep regular dashes of green signalling Margie's heart, brain and life. Nothing changed.

As for Pablo, he could only think: this was not his daughter. His skin turned to prickly gooseflesh seeing hers: white as onion skin paper marked with splotches of squeamish bruised blue. Margie's skin had always been taut, tawny resembling fruit you couldn't even buy in Manila—peaches or nectarines. Pablo felt faint with aching. He said her name, half expecting her eyes to flutter open. But the lids were swollen, translucent, barely closing over the white slivers of her eyes. This was not Margie. This stranger in the bed was as alien as the man who led Pablo to her.

For the first time in his life, Pablo felt ice-cold fear; it contrasted with his involuntary, scalding tears. He blinked them away, not wanting Brian to see. This man who held Margie's hand, kissed her cheek and stayed by her bed, even while he, her own father, remained standing at a stoic distance. Pablo felt foolish, too fearful to display emotion before a stranger. Instead, he just stood there, blinking away his tears.

"Come back, Marge," Brian whispered. "Come back, baby." The man then squeezed his daughter's hand and kissed it, right there for him to see. Pablo had a memory flash of the boys that had come to call on his daughter. Back then Pablo was strict, unfriendly, detesting the thought of them, constantly quelling the urge to prohibit such visits altogether. These gangly, awkward and acne-faced, they stood to greet him. "Good afternoon, sir," their voices cracked with a breakthrough manly pitch, instantly laughable. Pablo's disgust became amusement, sometimes even pity—they were so unsettled by his presence. Sometimes he was even moved to sit and chat. After they left, Margie always asked, "What do you think?" Pablo would only laugh; no boy was ever going to be good enough.

But this Brian was a man. He indulged himself in a bizarre notion: how wonderful Margie did not grasp Brian's large hand in her small one with a reciprocal squeeze. The gesture was then solely the American's, and perhaps under normal circumstances, Margie would have nothing to do with it, except be its embarrassed recipient, too innocent to know how to refuse. And yet, Pablo thought, bringing his heart to breaking point, had Margie's hand moved, it would mean she was awake.

It was the fourth day. The doctor had said they would need to try another course; Margie's organs were showing stress. She was concerned about the kidneys. But today, she had nothing new or especially helpful to say.

"We keep doing what we're doing, and we observe."

One of the nurses was a Filipina named Gloria who came to take the tray.

"Sir, why don't you have a bite—maybe get some fresh air?"

Pablo said no, he would wait for Dr. Goldberg's afternoon rounds. He knew Gloria was from home the minute he heard her speak. Her drawling American accent did not hide this truth. Rather than feel comforted, Pablo was irritated by her. She was too friendly. Her lapses into Tagalog to him were overly familiar and inappropriate. Pablo disliked her presumption even though that was unfair, too. No matter what she had seen, she could not know what he was feeling. He hated that Brian had even made it a point of introducing them.

"Good to meet you, *po*. Don't worry. We are taking good care of Marge." Gloria nodded to Brian encouragingly as though they were on the same team. Pablo felt instantly offended on Margie's behalf. He couldn't say a word, just nodded his head, knowing he was being rude. But it was a shock to be in this formidable hospital with its long white corridors. Hospital? The café and waiting lounge in the lobby looked more to him like a shopping center or a five-star hotel. It didn't even smell like a hospital, not like one in Manila anyway. And Dr. Goldberg was unlike any doctor Pablo had ever known. She seemed to him more like a doctor in the movies—crisp, business-like and altogether terrifying. Tall, thin and blonde, the doctor's expression was as inscrutable as her glasses perched high on the bridge of her nose. She made no effort to comfort him the way doctors at home did. Back home, doctors were always relatives or friends of the family, connected in ways more than medical. But Pablo forced himself to ask only one question.

"Please, tell me. How did this happen?"

"I know this is difficult, Mr . . ." Like Gloria, the nurse, Dr. Goldberg glanced briefly at Brian. ". . . Garcia . . ." She went on to explain the disease, using terrifying words: seizure, sedation, coma.

"I really can't tell you how this happened. But it seems to be viral . . . similar to meningitis. That much we do know. We are hoping your daughter remains stable and her internal organs hold out. Unfortunately, the seizures cause terrible damage . . . to the organs."

"But meningitis . . . there are treatments for meningitis . . . aren't there?" Pablo sputtered.

"Yes, there are." Dr. Goldberg nodded. "But this isn't quite meningitis. Though it does exhibit many similarities."

"You don't know what it is." Pablo's voice fell to whisper-volume, like he was talking more to himself than to anyone else. It was incomprehensible to him that this highly-equipped, ultra-modern, first-world hospital had no answers.

Later on, Pablo stopped Gloria at the door, unable to resist a question to her in Tagalog. "Have you seen many patients like my daughter? Do they survive?"

Gloria nodded with a solemn air.

"Yes, I have seen them. They are doing a great many things here. Research and experiments. Marge will be out of this sooner than you think. You just have to have faith."

Hearing this, Pablo allowed himself a split-second of hope. What he would give if tomorrow, when they returned, Margie were awake and laughing, waiting for them? Then he saw Gloria's face, smiling with friendly confidence and self-important wisdom, and instantly hated her for knowing nothing. He sensed all these faded moments of hope in the hospital air, just floating there, like invisible dust.

Why had he let Margie travel so far to study in the first place? He remembered the day before she left, when she seemed to be having second thoughts. "Nonsense," Pablo had scolded her. "How can you give up a chance that anyone would jump at?" he asked her. When she cried, he held her tight and then pushed her away. "You'll be all right, *anak*."

The two men walked out of Margie's room in intensive care, and they passed another waiting lounge, one with a television. There was an NBA game on.

"Margie played basketball, you know?" Pablo said, wanting to say her name. Brian said nothing. "She was on the team in high school—she had a great three-point-shot." It pleased him that he could reach for that detail, something he was sure this man did not know, and flaunt it.

But there was no mistaking the delight in Brian's expression, hearing this story.

"Marge can do anything. She tries everything. It's what I love about her."

Pablo fell silent. Absurdly, he also felt jealous and further, angry, that he needed Brian now and had to depend on him. The complex sensation was not new in these past days, and popped up like a little bubble of toxic air that would then ping away.

They had a routine. Brian fetched him in the mornings from Margie's studio apartment. They went to the hospital. They had lunch in the cafeteria. They went back to sit by Margie or in the waiting lounge where the television was. They spoke to Dr. Goldberg. They made small talk about golf, the weather, cars, Brian's family. Already, Pablo knew how Brian took his coffee. That he drank diet soda. That he smoked nervously, around half a pack a day, and persisted, rudely Pablo thought, even in the face of his coughing fits. In the evenings, Brian took Pablo back to Margie's apartment. Later, after Pablo opened himself a can of something he could eat with the rice he cooked in the rice cooker—sardines, luncheon meat—Dulce would telephone. At first, his wife would force herself to be calm, but toward the end of every call, Dulce would give way to shrill hysteria and anxious grief.

"What are you even doing? Why aren't you with Margie?" His wife would accuse him unreasonably.

"No change for the worse. That's something." He had said to her last night. He knew he needed to have something else to say to her today.

"She is stable, the doctor says," Pablo said.

"I'm coming. I will book my ticket right now," Dulce said this, weeping into the phone.

He said no. He promised his wife that they would decide this once they knew more. It just didn't make sense for both of them to be here right, not now. He knew he would not be able to keep it together if Dulce were here.

When their son, Miguel, came on the line, he said, "Tell me the truth, Dad." He knew too well how his father could lie to his mother.

"Just pray very hard, son," was all Pablo could say.

Later that night, Pablo got up from his daughter's bed, unable to sleep. He paced the short length of her bedroom, his cold bare feet on her furry carpet. He made his way by the light streaming into the window from the sidewalk lamp posts. He stared at the pictures she had framed above her bed. Pray. But Pablo could not follow his own advice.

Instead he explored his daughter's room. He opened her bedside drawers, examining their contents. She had pictures, letters, bits and pieces of things he could not see clearly in the dark. And then there was a journal, fabric bound and heavy in his hands. He switched on her desk lamp and leafed through it, pausing at the last page. Her final entry was in Tagalog and it was clearly about Brian. She was realizing just how special he was, what he was starting to mean. Pablo closed the book, not wanting to read more. He settled back in bed and only an hour later fell into restless sleep.

Now the silence in the hospital room was overpowering. Pablo made himself look at Margie again. Her face and her arms had swelled up. Her skin was ghostly white. Her eyes were partially open: slits of red and white. Her very position was unnatural—one arm jutting out, perpendicular to her torso as though it were not her own limb, but some appendage that had been screwed on, taped up, pushed through with a needle, so the fluid that was her tasteless food, drink and medicine could seep into her body. Margie had never been so still. Both as a child and as a woman, she was a boundless wellspring of energy. Even asleep, she was not still. Back from business trips, Pablo would inquire about a bruise on his wife's arm or leg where a thrashing, sleeping Margie sharing her mother's bed, had kicked her in the night.

Pablo sat down by his daughter's bed, glad that Brian was back in the waiting lounge. Finally, he was alone with his daughter. He took her hand. Such a soft, white hand, and it didn't used to be. It used to be brown, strong and even a bit rough. Pablo kissed it and allowed himself to sob in silence. He told his daughter he loved her, thought back upon all those times he recalls being seized with this emotion, like a sudden storm, and wished desperately he had been able to say the words out loud in this manner, each and every time.

But Margie could not hear him. She was dead. Pablo knew it. He could not stop thinking it. Dulce would never forgive him. She wouldn't have it. She'd invoke the saints, recite the novenas. Brian, who bought flowers every day so Margie would see them when she woke, he was the one with the amazing faith. All Pablo could do was sit and think he no longer knew his daughter. He probably would never know her again. And his daughter was dead as surely as he was alive.

Pablo stood, crazed all of a sudden. He rushed back to Brian in the lounge for no reason he could fathom, at once overcome with harrowing regret and blame coursing through him as he ran through the gleaming, white halls. Why had he allowed her to leave? Why had he pushed her? He could feel the time closing in. He could no longer say that the doctors were doing their best, could no longer throw on this blanket of security. Because it was a lie. Looking at the floor as he ran, Pablo bumped into Dr. Goldberg.

"Where is Mr. Jacobs?" She asked with some urgency. Pablo gestured toward the lounge, unable to speak. Together they entered to find Brian smoking and drinking another cardboard cup of coffee.

"There is some news, Mr. Jacobs, Mr. Garcia. I've consulted with a colleague of mine at Cornell. He recommends a combination treatment that they use for encephalitis that, in his experience, has a way of stabilizing these seizures." She pushed her glasses back up the high bridge of her nose. "If we can stop the seizures, we can slowly take her off the sedation. It's an approach we can . . . utilize . . ."

The doctor continued to talk, more to Brian than to him. Pablo stopped listening. He needed all the concentration he could command to fill himself with hope. He almost did not see the way Brian's face had changed. No longer closed and remote. Perhaps this was what he really looked like. This was the face his daughter loved.

"When will you be able to bring her out of the sedation?" Brian asked.

The doctor hesitated, for the first time it seemed.

"Mr. Jacobs, like anything else, there are risks. We can't be sure that there won't be any . . . detrimental effects, on her brain, for example. It's possible there may be damage."

For the first time, this doctor, this woman, looked at Pablo. It was as though she hoped that his age and experience might help her manage the younger man's hopeful expectations.

"Her kidneys are showing signs of failure . . . that's why there is all this inflammation in her limbs and in her face. We also have to do tests on her other vital organs. But I do recommend this treatment, at this point. If the seizures stop, we might be able to pull her out. But you need to be prepared that she may be very different. What I'm saying is, we need your consent."

"Let's do it, then." Brian said. "Bring her back . . . I don't care . . . I need . . ." he trailed off and turned to Pablo. It was a small acknowledgement.

Pablo exhaled. What if Margie came back some kind of vegetable . . . a child who no longer knew who she was or worse, who anyone else was. He let his eyes meet Brian's.

"All right." Pablo heard himself say. "Please, do what you can."

"I will call you back as soon as I know more. Or you can leave now and come back later in the afternoon?" The woman told them to go home, to get something to eat.

It seemed to Pablo a stupid thing to say. He did not want to leave to get something to eat. But Brian said they might as well. It would pass the time.

In the car, Brian whirred the windows open, so fresh air blew on their faces as they drove through the campus. He said he would take Pablo to a diner, *their* favorite place for brunch, his and Marge's. He pointed out a few sights, something he had never done before. These were places that they went to—the steps of the university art museum, the movie theatre where they had seen six movies now, usually a midnight revival of something one of them had already seen, the ice cream parlor on main street, where according to Brian, the line for an ice cream cone wound all the way around the block.

"She always gets the same flavor, mint chocolate, but she always takes a spoonful of mine . . . unless it has nuts."

"She dislikes nuts." Pablo murmured.

Brian sighed.

"Sir, I know this must be hard for you," the white man said slowly, not looking at Pablo but keeping his eyes on the road. "Margie never did have the chance to write. It was sudden for her, I guess . . . even though it wasn't for me. This is not the way I wanted to meet you."

Brian cleared his throat, uncertain what to say. For a split second, Pablo thought Brian was no different from the awkward boys in the sofa in his living room, anxiously waiting for some kind of approval.

"I love her very much. We were going to drive to the West Coast. I was going to take her to Disneyland. Once she gets well, that's the first thing we're doing." Pablo envied and admired Brian for saying "when" instead of "if."

The diner was a small greasy spoon place with a glass door with a bell attached so it rang when you pushed it open. Outside, the glass windows were plastered with white paint spelling out the words: Hamburgers, Pancakes, Omelette, Crepes.

They slid into a booth with ripped and faded red leather seats, and the waitress in pink gingham waited by the counter, allowing them time to see the menu.

"What will you have . . . sir?" Brian asked.

"Anything." Pablo replied, feeling his stomach turn. "It doesn't matter."

"You need to eat, sir. We both do."

The air was heavy with the smell of butter, sugar and bacon that somehow felt nauseating. He did not want American food. Had never cared for it. This was why he never wanted to go to America. Margie had always been the same. Every morning for breakfast, it was dried fish or cured pork with garlic fried rice for both father and daughter. Pablo doubted very much that this place was a favorite of Margie's. When had she changed? And did she really love this American? Pablo's heart ached at the thought that he might never know the answers. The two men sat in silence, not even trying to make conversation. Just days ago, they would at least try—talk sports or politics. Today, their little shared space of quiet was odd, and Pablo suddenly knew what it was he wanted to hear.

"Can you just please tell me what happened that night?" Pablo tried to keep his voice neutral, clear of blame or resentment, but he knew that every word was weighted with both all the same, like too much sugar and milk in a cup of coffee.

Brian took another gulp of his before he finally spoke. Pablo winced at the sound of his swallow. Brian's words were slow as though he was having difficulty finding the right words, like English was for him, all of a sudden, a foreign language.

"She had had the flu. It was going around for a week. Nothing major . . ."

Pablo stifled a sigh.

"I mean, it was a low-grade fever. She was complaining she was tired. Also, it was finals week, and she wanted to take all of them. She wouldn't talk to any of the professors to schedule make-up exams. But when the tests were all over, she said to me, 'Now I can be really sick.'"

Pablo felt tears smart behind his eyes. It was such a Margie thing to say.

"You didn't take her to see a doctor?"

"No. No I didn't." Brian's voice started to get hoarse. "I'm so sorry."

The waitress came with a single plate of waffles and bacon that she laid on the table in front of them. Pablo stared at the food, the squares on the waffles, the heat that still sizzled on the bacon. If it was anyone's fault, it was his fault. Pablo thought so. Dulce would think so.

"It's not your fault," Pablo told him. "You could not have known."

"She said, 'go home.' I stayed with her. Made her soup. She was laughing. I thought she was coming out of it."

Pablo willed the man to talk faster. Talk faster, damn it. There was no more time.

"I waited till she fell asleep, and sat with her. I felt her forehead and it was burning hot—the Tylenol didn't do a thing. That's when I started to worry. I thought, I'll wake her and take her to the emergency room. So I did. Then she opened her eyes, but she didn't see me. Then all of sudden, she sat up. Her eyes were rolling, and she was moaning, and her tongue was out. I called 911. It was a seizure, the doctors told me later on. But the scariest thing . . ."

Brian stopped, and Pablo saw he was gripping his mug so hard, the coffee moved in the cup.

"Marge looked at me, but she had no idea who I was."

Pablo no longer knew what to say or do, and finally, had nowhere else to look but Brian's eyes. The man met his gaze. Brian's eyes were not blue or brown like Pablo assumed they would be. They were clear and dark.

What would it be like, Pablo wondered, not to be 68 with an ulcer and hypertension, not to be a father with his daughter in a coma in the hospital? What would it be like to be 24 and to fall in love and then have it violently wrenched away from you? And what would it be like not to know whether you would ever have it back again? It must be a different, desperate kind of pain.

Brian spoke, "It's only a matter of time now. I just know she's going to get out of this. This new treatment . . ." The certainty in the man's voice made Pablo close his eyes in compassion. It was close to four o'clock now, and they were the only ones left at the diner.

"Can I get you something else?" the waitress asked him. All of a sudden, Pablo was starving.

"Another plate of this, please," Pablo pointed at the waffles.

Pablo had always felt he had a good life, and he was grateful for it. If the line faltered a little—his business went through a bad patch; he had succumbed to the temptations in his marriage—it always went quickly, quickly back on track. That was all he could ask for. But now Pablo was very much afraid that it was, in fact, too much to ask.

When they returned to Margie's room in the hospital ICU, Dr. Goldberg was there waiting for them. "All we can do now is wait," she said.

It must have taken hours, but the hours felt like days. Waiting with Brian for Margie to return was a whole life, it seemed to Pablo. And the life he had had, he and Dulce, raising Margie . . . that was just minutes.

Brian sat in the corner chair in Margie's suite, holding his head in his hands. Pablo paced.

"Are you all right?" he asked the young man.

Brian looked up, his face wet. He shook his head. "She may not know me. She may not remember anything."

"If you weren't here now, where would you be?" Pablo asked.

Brian took a deep breath.

"We would be driving to California."

"You and Margie?"

"That was our plan. She wanted to see America, and driving is the best way. Then from LA, she was going to fly home. She already bought the ticket."

"Wait, Margie was planning to come home?"

"Of course, sir. She missed you all terribly."

Pablo let himself be pleased by this. It was such a small thing. He tucked it away to tell Dulce later. Margie wanted to come home.

"And you? Your plan?"

"I had . . . I have a summer internship in San Francisco. We were going to write, and then, see each other back at school in September. And then . . ." Brian stopped. "I just hope—" The man stopped again and nervously ran his fingers through his hair just like the boys back in the sala in his house in Manila. Pablo joined him in whatever silent hope the man had.

And that's when it happened. It was Margie's voice. Such a small sound. Like the word "Oh" with two syllables. Or it might have been a giggle or a whimper like something had gotten caught, stuck in her throat.

"Marge? Marge?" Brian was at her side within seconds. Her eyes began to move rapidly, blinking fast.

Brian shouted for the doctor, and Dr. Goldberg was there instantly. She started reading the monitor while taking Margie's pulse. Pablo kept his eyes on Margie.

Something was happening. The monitor began to beep rapidly and then even more rapidly. Margie's eyes struggled to open.

"Margie? *Anak*?" Pablo couldn't keep the words from escaping.

And then Margie's eyes were still—just closed shut.

"It's another seizure, I'm afraid, a big one. The plan . . . it didn't work. We were unsuccessful."

"No!" Brian's voice was stuck in his throat.

"The kidneys have failed. I'm afraid the heart is under severe stress."

The words echoed in Pablo's mind. The kidneys. The heart. And then Dr. Goldberg said the only thing she could say.

"Please, do stay with her until she's gone. I'm so very sorry." And then she left the room.

"No . . . no . . . no" Brian kept saying, his voice becoming fainter and fainter. He sat beside the bed, holding one of Margie's hands, burying his face into her side. Pablo just stood there, overcome—he unclenched his fists. He knew Margie was gone. He had known this from the beginning, so it was not a surprise. Pictures flashed in his mind of the girl that she was, the woman she had become. Slowly he walked to the other side of Margie's bed. Then he looked at her. She looked like she was asleep now, like she might even wake up if you touched her. So Pablo did, and felt her hand, still warm. He just stood there and held his daughter's hand. Then he watched as Brian bent his head close to hers. His words were clear and distinct.

"*Mahal kita*, Marge, *Mahal na mahal kita.*"

The man told his daughter he loved her. Margie had taught him this. It was like a surprise, almost like a sign. Still his daughter did not stir.

The man bent to kiss Margie's lips, and then he lay his head by hers and wept anew like a little boy. He could not stop, and Pablo let him. Later on, Pablo placed his hands on Brian's shoulders, pulling him gently away.

"Enough *na*, Brian," he said. It was the first time Pablo had called him by name. It was the right thing to do. As for the rest, it would all just have to wait.

Note how differently "Dreams in English" begins from "The Boat":

In the last letter Pablo remembered from Margie, though he could not say when that was exactly, she told her father she had started to dream in English.

Here, we're brought directly into the consciousness of Pablo and we enter a memory instead of learning what the present holds. Still, we have already started to receive clues. We see that this is a father/daughter story most likely and that their mother tongue is not English. The way in which de Jesus's story moves through time is different from Nam Le's techniques, but no less effective. The flashback lasts nearly a page before we shift to the present. The flashback takes Pablo back to a time when Margie as a child was accused by her teacher of cheating for copying the artwork of another child. But we learn that the class had been in English and Margie only spoke Tagalog—she hadn't understood her teacher, so she just copied her classmate's work. There's a note of pride in Pablo's thoughts as we come back to the present time of the story:

And this little girl that had won herself a scholarship to study art and art history in America was now dreaming in English? It was truly amazing. Pablo wondered what Margie's first dream was about, and wished to God that he could ask her, because if she could answer, he knew she would tell him.

Here is where we first learn of the ostensible conflict of the story. In the next paragraph, we learn that Margie is now lying in a hospital bed. We don't know where, only that it's far from home and she is unconscious. This short paragraph serves only to establish the present moment of the story, which we will later learn is in a Boston ICU unit, where Margie lies comatose. Once de Jesus has established this, she dips back into Pablo's consciousness. The recollection of Margie's letter about her dream triggers a reflection on a dream he had ("it seemed like it happened a thousand years ago") his last night in Manila.

Aha! Consider the slow accrual of information the author is slyly inserting without it seeming like information. If it seemed like a thousand years ago, we can infer that it was a long journey to get to his daughter's bedside. We still don't know she's in Boston at this point, but we know he's travelled far. And we know he's travelled from Manila. Pablo can't recall the dream, only the happy sensation it gave him. As he cycles through the possibilities of what the dream was about, we learn more tidbits about him, that he once had a "mistress" (surely, a secret) and we learn of a sailboat he had built with his own hands. Is this a real sailboat or a dream sailboat? It hardly matters—it says something about his class, a focus on creature comforts, but also a sense of self-reliance. Perhaps these details say something different to you. Again, that doesn't matter. What matters is that de Jesus is building a portrait of Pablo in your mind through this slow and steady *drip drip drip* of details situated firmly in Pablo's point of view.

Thus far, we've only had one brief paragraph in the present. Isn't it time to lay off the dreams and learn what's going on, how and why Margie fell ill and how serious it is? Not quite. The longer you can reasonably postpone filling in *all* the details, the better, whether you're dealing with a stolen canoe, a boat in peril on the high seas, or a daughter in a hospital bed. Generally speaking, you're not postponing this information for long, but long enough for us to get interested in the characters and let them carry us along from that point on. We know that Margie is in a hospital bed and that she's not well even if we don't yet know completely who she is or how she arrived there. So there's time to draw this out, to plant us in Pablo's consciousness and learn about his concerns, his hopes, his fears, and generally what makes him tick.

In the next paragraph we learn about his sense of regret, and we learn of his great affection for his daughter. We've italicized all the words that give us a sense of his feelings, the kinds of feelings a parent might entertain, all adding up to a profound sense of guilt that he couldn't have protected her somehow.

> He **regretted** it wasn't Margie herself that he dreamed of. It might have been of her, as the chubby cherub she once was, leaping into his arms, showering him with kisses as she embraced him, all the while grabbing fistfuls of his hair. The sensation of her solid little body, warmly damp from perspiration, the soles of her feet chalky black with dust. That was a million years ago. Pablo **felt he betrayed her**. There was his little Margie, fallen ill all by herself in this cold country, and Pablo had lain there asleep, **dreaming his own silly, selfish dream.**

Not until the following paragraph do we get to the situation as a whole, when Pablo recalls being awakened out of his pleasant dream by an American voice informing him that his daughter was in a coma. Now we have almost all of the crucial information we need—but not until the third page or so of the story. And remember, we haven't even been introduced yet to Margie's secret, her white American fiancé, Brian. That comes in the next paragraph.

We won't bother to go through the entire story in this way, but we wanted you to slow down in your reading and look at the ways in which both writers go back and forth in time and, in so doing, simultaneously build their characters as well as move the narrative forward. This kind of dance between the past and the present is at the heart of building characters and creating a sense that they didn't take their first fictional breath with the first word of the story. This is especially important when writing about traumatic situations as both stories do. It's hard to keep a dry eye at the end of either, yet neither is sentimental. Each story earns its emotional power through an exploration of humans caring for one another in situations of peril. Imagine reading either "The Boat" or "Dreams in English" if the authors had not dipped back into the past of their characters' lives at all. We'd be left with archetypal situations of loss, but that would be all, and chances are, we wouldn't find either story as moving as they are.

Exercises

1. A powerful theme throughout literary history is that of one person attempting to save another, as is the case in both stories we've examined in this chapter. Write a scene in which your main character's goal is either to bring another person safely somewhere else (it doesn't have to be another country) or an attempt to help someone who is in grave need or danger. Start either in medias res or recalling a specific scene from the character's past, and then try to alternate the paragraphs from either the present to the past or the past to the present.

2. A person takes a trip only to discover that the person they thought they knew well was hiding something from them. Or perhaps not, and they only think this is the case. Write into this situation and discover what that secret is.

3. A person is hiding something from someone close to them whom they haven't seen in a while. Or perhaps the person knew all along what was being hidden from them. Write into this situation and discover what that secret is.

4. The worst thing for a parent is to imagine their child's death. Imagine your worst fear of loss and write a story about that from the point of view of the person who experiences the loss. Remember, such stories need a mix of the characters' past and present in order to be effective. That doesn't mean you need to know everything about them at the outset. You can discover a lot about your characters as you go.

5. Write five first lines with possible Macguffins that will get us interested in reading on. Now give those first lines to a writing partner and receive five first lines from them. Pick a first line that seems most promising and start building a character and a situation from that line, aiming for a bait and switch from that first line. What clues about the character are embedded in your first line and how have you adhered to or subverted those clues?

CHAPTER 8
MYSTERIES

The one thing we wish we could prohibit all writing students from including in their fiction is a crime or mystery that must get solved. Whether the crime is a murder, or a heist, or kidnapping or some other drama, this very much is the influence of movies and television. We are the first to admit our own addiction to mystery and crime dramas: *Law & Order, Sherlock, Elementary, Broadchurch, Criminal Minds, Top of the Lake, The Mentalist, Blue Bloods, Bones, Castle, Poirot, The Blacklist,* and so forth, and as a younger writer would be occasionally prone to killing off characters or writing plots with mysteries to be solved. It was the way to write page turners, right? While it's true that mystery and crime make for great fiction, it is equally true that for books (not TV or movies), this is a very specific genre that has rules and conventions of its own. Just as we previously noted that it's important to do your homework, if you really want to write mystery and crime, make sure you know the demands of the genre.

However, in this chapter we want to focus on mysteries that speak more to human existence than to the requirements of the mystery genre. The real meaning of *mystery* is partly rooted in Christian theology and refers to a religious truth or a doctrine of faith that cannot be solved by human reasoning. The broader, secular meaning is something secret, inexplicable, or even beyond human comprehension. An enigma. To tread the borders of *mystery*'s true meaning is the stuff of some of the most exciting and provocative fiction. The two stories we have chosen for this are both by Chinese writers—"The Door" by the award-winning Hong Kong author Dorothy Tse and "Where Did I Lose You" by Fan Xiaoqing, who is a well-known writer from Suzhou in China. In both stories, a central image repeats and grows into an increasingly inexplicable mystery. As in Chapter 3 on routines, both "Birds" and "We That Summer" dealt with the quotidian and used repetition to heighten the drama; these two stories follow a comparable pattern but with a different dramatic purpose and outcome. Something as ordinary as a door in a home proves to be a portal to the unknown and unexplained. Take some time to read Tse's story and think about why this mysterious door is so significant and what effect it creates for the story.

1 "The Door"

by Dorothy Tse (Hong Kong)

Translated from Chinese (Cantonese) by Natascha Bruce

Dorothy Tse's awards include the Hong Kong Book Prize and Biennial Award for Chinese Literature as well as Taiwan's Unitas New Fiction Writer's Award. She has four story collections and has edited *A Compendium of Hong Kong Fiction from 1919-1941*. Her first collection translated into English is *Snow and Shadow* (2015).

By the time the men arrived, the sky was a swathe of bruise-dark purple; a red and blue concoction that seeped through the air like melting stage make-up. I leaned from a first-floor window to watch them as they swaggered up the main street. They wore baggy, factory-issue windbreakers that puffed in the wind, like balloons ready to take flight. But when they reached the front door, their trapped shadows leaked away, leaving them more like deflated dolls.

They did not remove their shoes, which were caked in dust and mud. Instead, they marched straight inside, treading all over my wife's well-swept floor, and threw themselves onto the sofa and the chairs that encircled the dining table (and, in one case, onto Lily's wooden rocking horse), asking what I had to eat. I fetched a pear tart from the kitchen and sliced through it with a wheel cutter, turning to catch their reactions as I cut. Just as I suspected, they were too absorbed in their own gloomy worlds to have noticed my wife's masterpiece. I couldn't help feeling sad for her and her meticulous efforts—of course her refined gesture had gone to waste, with guests as boorish as these.

She had made the tart the night before, kneading flour and water into a soft skin and pressing it into a circle, then laying on slices of pear in a spiral, working out from the center. When she put it in the oven to cook, the crust rippled like waves and the pears glistened like molten gold.

"There aren't many moments in life as moving as this," I said to her, watching the transformation through the oven door. She was standing beside me and giggled behind her hand, elbowing me in the arm as though I'd made a joke.

The men devoured the tart in an instant, scraping down to the bottom of the dish and coming face to face with my pathetic reflection in its stainless-steel surface. I thought back to the last time my wife made a tart, and felt its lingering sweetness welling in my throat. She and Lily would probably be on the train already, far outside the city. Now only the men were in the flat, with their chewing and belching, their periodic hearty slaps at something or the other, and their constantly jiggling legs. I moved to a far corner of the living room to escape them, sitting down on a low stool near the entrance to the kitchen.

I'd never been fond of these manly get-togethers. Inviting them over had been my wife's idea. A few days holiday were coming up, and she'd put a hand over mine and asked about my plans. I had the idea of building a model castle with Lily (I'd already bought the set and hidden it under the bed, where Lily wouldn't find it). There was also a strip light in the kitchen that hung down at one end, and it was high time I fixed it. But my wife didn't seem to be paying attention to my answers—she went to stretch out on the sofa, closed her eyes, and let out a soft, contented sigh.

"The thing is, I've bought train tickets. I've decided to take Lily away for a couple of days, to give you a bit of freedom. Why don't you invite your friends round?"

And, of course, those "friends" she mentioned were the men I worked with in the furniture factory, fixing and inlaying wood. I didn't have anybody else.

* * *

Several years before, in order to live with my wife in the city center, I'd had to leave the little flat that I shared with my parents in District M, where we relied on one another for everything. At the time, Lily was still inside what I used to think of as my wife's black aquarium. I would spread my fingers across her rounded belly, and feel the faint, rippling motions of a lonely aquatic creature. Perhaps another description could have been a train without a view? When I left, watching from the train as the icy night swallowed row upon row of squeezed-together houses, it struck me that I didn't recognize a single person in the fluorescent-lit carriage. My wife and I had known each other less than six months; she was fast asleep against the darkened window glass, and her illuminated face had taken on the contours of a stranger, shaking with the rhythm of the train. I placed my hand on the high swell of her stomach and tried to imagine the child's face, but Lily didn't have a face yet, or even a name. On public transport, nothing is more permitted than feeling like a stranger. I thought I'd miss the familiar people from back home, but the train entered a tunnel and my parents' voices were crushed by the roar of the engine. Even I changed, turning into the flickers of light and shadow projected into the carriage from outside.

Starting a new life was easier than I imagined. I brought only one suitcase and moved into the flat where my wife had been living all along. Everything was already there. Light fixtures with cloth umbrella shades hung from the ceiling, casting a warm glow over the ripe peaches on the dining table. She had crocheted antimacassars that extended like cobwebs along the length of her sofa, and there was a thriving tropical plant, grown to the same height as me. A coat pattern she was making had spread across the work table in the living room (she dreamed of becoming a fashion designer, but had been drawing up patterns for other designers ever since art school). Pulling back the sunflower-print shower curtain to soak in the tiny bathtub behind it, I had the feeling that I'd become another part of the house. Inside my wife's orderly space, I had come alive.

But after moving into my new home, I was much further from the furniture factory, which was on the outskirts of District M. To arrive at work on time, I had to wake up at the crack of dawn, when even the dust motes were still asleep, and join the flow of commuters feeding into the sea of drab city faces. And once I became a regular passenger, there ceased to be anything charming about trains. Back then, the crush of passengers was rife with resentments, especially between locals and the many others who came from elsewhere. A good number of times, a muttered comment sparked an on-board fist fight. Nothing ever went quite so far as the poison gas attacks reported in other cities, but suspected bombs turned up at the station on more than one occasion. Eventually, they were all dismissed as pranks, but there were always a couple of skulls or shoulders trampled in the preceding panic.

On my days off, I chose to stay at home as much as possible. I read, or fixed furniture, or simply stayed in bed with my wife until Lily pushed through our door, clutching her book of fairytales. She'd climb up and burrow her way between our languid bodies, demanding that we go through those crazy stories yet again: a mother who sold her own child to support her desperate craving for cabbage; a daughter who disguised herself in animal skins to escape the lascivious affections of her father; a blue-bearded monster who killed his wives and kept the corpses locked in a secret room.

Once in a while, I'd go with my wife to meet her friends and, to my surprise, I found I did not dislike these gatherings. My wife refused to believe that I had never really socialized before, because her friends always showered me with praise for my impeccable manners. She didn't understand that it was precisely because I had no history in those situations that I could pull it off—I didn't have to act like "myself," so I simply played the role of her husband.

My wife didn't have the kinds of girlfriends who were always heading out to the beauty salon or comparing the latest shoe styles, though all sorts of people seemed to feel especially drawn to her. The building's cleaning lady, for example, who was always taking her aside to share pieces of neighborhood gossip. Or the man who came to fix the water pipes, who could recognize her from miles away and would wave enthusiastic greetings, even though he'd only been around once in months. Or the solitary old lady who used to sit out on the main street in her wheelchair, taking in the sun, still as a statue; at the sight of my wife, her head would dip and her fingers would suddenly spring to life, rapidly wheeling the chair towards her. My wife never told me what she heard, when she stooped down and pressed her ear to the old lady's mouth. She'd just smile, gripping the Chinese pear that the lady had pressed into her hands. In the evening, once we were home, she'd slide its sweet, juicy flesh into my mouth like a secret, one slice at a time.

As for me, standing behind my wife at parties, all I wanted was to make my presence as unobtrusive as a shadow. With a smile fixed to my face, I carefully remembered her friends' names, spoke very little, nodded at the appropriate moments and, every so often, made sure to place morsels of food in her bowl. That was all it took.

"How come you don't have friends of your own?" my wife would ask me, and I never had an answer. I had her—and later, Lily—and because of her I had all her friends, in a way, and this was enough for me. But when she asked the question, my contentment made me doubly ashamed. I didn't mind not having a social circle of my own. Wasn't it just further proof that my reclusive character was unsuited for mainstream society? Before my marriage, in an attempt to keep up "appropriate" levels of interaction, I sometimes dragged myself along to staff socials at the factory, or joined my parents on low-cost outings with the local community center. Afterwards, I was always exhausted, filled with shame and frustration at the thought of my chameleon-like facial expressions, and all the things I'd said but not meant. At the same time, I found it reassuring to have made the effort, as though I'd fulfilled a duty to act like a human being. Once I was married, I attached myself to the goodwill around my wife, like a cold shadow hitched to a warm human body, and found myself winning the approval of others without any need to struggle at all.

* * *

The men all lived near the factory, and to reach the city center they had to endure the torture of the train ride. I've explained what it was like—they liked to stress that, were it not for our great friendship, they would never put themselves through such torment on a day off. But I didn't believe they would ever have let their dislike for the journey stand in their way. What they declared to be our "friendship" could have been the reason, but there were other possible factors: the exciting buzz of the city, or the table laden with food that my wife prepared for every gathering, accompanied by an endless stream of beer. Perhaps even more to the point, they had bellies chock-full of complaints, and they needed to get far enough from their own homes to vent in peace.

In the furniture factory, I never went near these men. I worked silently and alone, by a window with a view onto a line of cotton trees. If you walked deeper into the factory, passing through the angry sound of hammers banging against wood and steel, you'd encounter men's irate, exhausted eyes, turned a dull grey by the swirling sawdust. But now, enthusiastically recounting their misfortunes from the comforts of my home, their eyes emitted vivid beams of light. Sometimes, their faces would take on the expressions of dictators, lining up their personal tragedies like obedient citizens. Naturally, they would conclude that their wives were the eyes of every storm, or else their wives' parents, or those foreigners who kept coming in to find work, or the tropical climate, or the pollen that filled the streets in springtime. If it hadn't been for all those external factors, the men would have been bolder, and lived entirely different lives.

Listening to their endless, meandering talk, it was hard to stop my mind from wandering. I'd slip away down a little forked alley, losing myself in my thoughts. In this sense, I had to be thankful for their uncouth, oblivious natures, because it meant they were unlikely to notice that my attention was elsewhere. I suspected that even they ended up lost in their chatter; astray in forests they had planted themselves. Then there'd be a few words that struck them like sharp stones, shocking them back to consciousness. Their faces flushed and their ears went hot, and they worked themselves into such aggressive, emotional states that I felt like a wild animal tamer, with a duty to calm them down. I'd keep their drinks topped up and bring more food from the kitchen.

On this occasion, I brought out the last of the comfort food: the chicken my wife had roasted the previous night. Such a beautiful bird, wings clamped tightly against its glistening body and head inclined slightly towards me, with its crest sticking up angrily. The eyes had been shut all morning, but somehow were now wide open and staring fixedly at me, as though sizing me up. I caught sight of my face reflected in the television screen; you couldn't have called it a warm face, but I watched it crack into a winning smile. This was something I'd learned from experience: a facial expression is like any other domesticated life form, it knows when to nod and wag its tail, or when to burst out laughing.

I was surprised to see this same smile reciprocated on the men's faces. Usually, they kept up an uninterrupted litany of grumbles and debates, only stopping after a string of reminders that the last train was due. That day, however, they lost interest in talking ahead of schedule, and had no appetite for the food left on the table. Yet they seemed to have no intention of leaving. I looked away from them, towards the door to the kitchen, thinking of the strip light hanging down at one end, wishing I could go in and fix it. But the men pinned me with their stares. Their silent smiles were like so many nails, keeping my buttocks tacked to my seat. Not knowing what to do, I turned to watch the sky changing color through the window. At first, a big group of black jellyfish-like creatures seemed to be swimming through it, slowly devouring all other colors, but gradually I realised it was the other way around: the other colors were vomiting the black, and this was why it looked so mottled and fractious. And in front of that ominous roll of blackness, faces were pressing in on me, their hands reaching for my arms, clasping me in a brotherly embrace. One of them patted my back and said, "No need to keep your feelings all bottled up, how are things with the wife lately? If there's something going on, you should tell us." Then he poured the second half of a bottle of beer into my glass, filling it to the brim, and cheerily told me that they weren't leaving until I confessed the truth.

I took a sip of beer and, as the bubbles dissolved pleasurably in my mouth, wondered whether this was a rite of passage, and they were welcoming me as one of the guys. But all I could do was shake my head, because what could I tell them about my wife? That late every evening, once our kid was in bed, we huddled under the same sheet, tired but happy, discussing the menu for the next day's dinner? That I liked to go food shopping in the market after work, examining the shape of an aubergine or an onion, contentedly imagining the delicious aroma once it arrived in her hands? That I would bury my head between her thighs and stick out my tongue, tasting her sweet, seaweed flavour? None of those things were suitable for sharing. Not because they were too private, but because they were too close to happiness. Pain and misfortune are the only gifts suitable for friends; only shared tragedy builds friendships. Perhaps because they'd had too much to drink, the men's eyes glowed red and they encircled me like a pack of starving dogs, eager to gnaw on the bones of my hidden sadness. But what did I have to feed them?

* * *

There was nothing in my present life that I could really complain about. I couldn't imagine doing any job other than working in the furniture factory. I loved the scents of the different kinds of wood, and how each had its own distinctive grain—to the point that, every time we shipped out a finished chair or bedframe or, worst of all, big wooden farmer's table, I felt a pang of regret. And my blissfully-happy marriage was surely some mysterious gift of fate, because until I was thirty-eight years old, I'd never even been in love.

It all started with a complimentary ticket to a Christmas party that came attached to my family's new air conditioner, giving the address as a three-star hotel in the city center. My father solemnly pressed the ticket into my hand and I understood that there would be no getting out of this particular assignment (we were not a well-off family and unexpected gifts were bright spots in our lives, certainly not things to be turned down). But when I stepped into the hotel ballroom, which was festooned with streamers and balloons, with my face freshly shaved, dressed in my only white shirt, I immediately regretted that I'd come. I walked into the crowd of men and women I'd never met before and felt their chatter and laughter weighing against my chest, leaving me gasping for breath. I kept walking straight ahead, my eyes trained on the back of the room, where there was a row of long tables covered in white tablecloths. The tables were laden with all kinds of little delicacies—light glinted off the grease of flaky pastry rolls and the grooves in the fresh cream swirled on top of tiny cakes, and this was my salvation. I marched single-mindedly towards them and piled my plate high. Then, selecting an out-of-the-way corner, I settled into an unoccupied chair and promised myself that I could leave once I had eaten all my food.

I must have been too concentrated on the cakes, because until she whipped out a shiny silver fork, I didn't notice my wife (although at that stage she was still just some unknown woman). She sat down in front of me and exclaimed, "There's none of this one left! You don't mind if I have some of yours, do you?"

As though conducting a symphony, she held her shiny fork poised over the mini donuts on my plate (believe it or not, I'd taken two of every kind). I nodded immediately;

in fact, I'm sure I blushed. She grinned, revealing a row of widely-spaced teeth. It thrilled me to discover that the gaps between her teeth were much bigger than other people's; dark and mysterious, like tunnels waiting to be entered.

Her curtains were the gauzy, translucent kind that let light flood in, dispersing the last, muddled dreams of the early morning. I thought she was still in bed, but when I reached for her my fingers clutched at air. I staggered out of the bedroom, calling wildly through the unfamiliar flat, the events of the night before as uncertain as my footsteps. I didn't even know her name. I followed the hallway, peering into another room, which led to another room, whose walls seemed to block the way to another. Confused, I walked back along the hall. She seemed to have vanished, until her face pressed against my shoulder, appearing as suddenly as a snake darting from a cave. "Where have you been hiding?" I asked, and she smiled but said nothing, curling a hand round to pass me a cup of ink-black coffee and a mini donut dusted with icing sugar.

Her mini donut was much better than the ones in the hotel, just as she had promised. I remember that morning vividly, the way we walked out onto the street hand in hand, mouths covered in icing sugar, inviting mockery from passers-by. But I had passed by the kitchen, and there had been no trace of cooking on the gleaming counter tops. I never said anything, but my wife's "disappearance" was not a one-off occurrence; in her flat, the same thing happened again and again. Was there some kind of secret passage, where she could hide without making any sound? Any time I raised these kinds of questions, she would tap me lightly on the forehead and joke about my over-active imagination.

It's true that it was just a small, two-bedroom flat. Walking out of the master bedroom, I was confronted by the gloomy hallway. The first room on the right was Lily's—if I opened the door, I'd see her dolls and wooden building blocks strewn across the floor. To the left was the bathroom, and straight ahead was where we ate dinner every evening, which linked to the living room, which doubled as my wife's studio. The kitchen was to the left of the living room, and at the back of the kitchen was a door. The door seemed like it must lead somewhere, but when I opened it, all that was there was a headless dressmaker's mannequin draped with a coat that hadn't yet had its sleeves sewn on and a few stacked-up boxes stuffed with my wife's yarn and fabrics, along with a few of her older projects. If I shoved all this to one side, there was just a murky white wall, pressing in on me.

Before we married, my wife's flat was like an express train just for us, a place for snatched pleasures and living in the moment, and I never had the chance to explore it properly. She gave me a tour after I moved in. "It used to open out onto an illegal balcony with a view of the street," she told me, "but that had to be dismantled a few years ago."

So why did she fail to mention the door? Later, while cleaning the flat, I discovered that, in the hallway, diagonally across from Lily's room, there was another door; one that I'd never noticed before. It had always been concealed in the shadows, but with the light spilling out from Lily's room I could see its outline. Even in the light, it wasn't an ordinary door. It looked as though it were afraid and trying to hide itself in the wall, like an enormous creature covered in camouflage. There was no handle and, no matter how I pushed, it wouldn't budge. I gently stroked the surface, but it refused to respond. The gap between the door and doorframe was too narrow for my fingers to fit.

My wife shook her head when I mentioned it, asking what crazy thing I was talking about now. I brought her over to look but she played it down, saying it was probably just part of the decoration, because a door in that location wouldn't have anywhere to lead to. Did she think I was some kind of joke? She put her headphones back on, clearly in the middle of listening to something, and started to laugh. I stared at the black gaps between her teeth, now on full display, but couldn't begin to guess what they were hiding.

After Lily was born, I often carried her into the hallway and stood in front of the door, pointing at it, saying, "Look, Lily, don't you want to go and play behind the door?" I would take her hand and try to make her press it into the edges, but she always shook free and threw her arms around my neck, closing her eyes and burying her face in my shoulder. Once, I was firmer about it and forced her fingers into the crack, hoping they'd be able reach past the accumulated dust, but she wailed loudly, as though she'd touched something dangerous. She didn't stop until my wife ran over to ask what had happened, brow furrowed with concern, and carried her away.

* * *

Perhaps my wife was right, and the door was just a figment of my imagination. Maybe it was a repeat of another door, one I'd seen in middle school. I had nothing to hide from my wife, but I'd never told her that once, in middle school, you could almost have said that I fell in love (possibly, I hadn't told her because I thought I'd forgotten all about it).

Was it the very first day of middle school? I had arrived very early. Because of the sultry weather, or else my aversion to groups, I headed straight for a big, leafy acacia tree. I sat beneath it, enjoying the fresh breeze and imagining my face turning unrecognizable in the shadow, while listening attentively to the voices behind me.

Those two girls must have met before, because they exchanged nicknames and code words that only they could understand, excitedly sharing tales of their fathers being "pervy"—they stretched out the word, making it *peeeeervy*, as though it had breath and feelings of its own. There was a pattern to their conversation: they took turns to give examples of "pervy" behavior, and then proceeded to assess it. For example, one girl told the other that when her father went downstairs to buy a paper, she had seen him slipping porn magazines in between the pages. Then the other girl said that father always took the raised walkways to go home, because it meant he could ogle the breasts of women below. Sometimes, the fatherly wrongdoings were deemed suitable only for whispers and I couldn't hear what was said, just the cackles of laughter that followed. After a while, I realized that for them the important thing wasn't the content of what they were saying, but the exaggerated, mutually-affirming way in which they said it. It brought them closer together.

Once I worked this out, I lost interest and stopped listening. Surveying my surroundings, I saw that the playground had broken up into little cliques. All the new students had found themselves companions, aside from a few loners who stood off to one side, emanating the wretched air of abandoned animals.

Of course, back then I thought that I was different. For some people, solitude is a choice; for others, it's something life decides for them. I had actively rejected company, whereas those other students were flawed, and on account of this had been squeezed out and abandoned. There was a girl standing by herself, some distance from the other students, grinning in my direction, and I quickly determined that she was one such creature. I had nothing better to do, and so I looked back at her. A while later, I realized that I couldn't tear my eyes away, and the reason was the wide gaps between her teeth, which made me feel like I knew her. They reminded me of the street market and its line of grinning clowns, lips stretched back so that customers could shoot at their teeth.

When I was younger, there were a few boring streets in District M that would sometimes liven up at night. On the ground, or else on makeshift tables, people would lay out random, messy assortments of cheap clothes, toys, household items, and electric appliances. The goods were dusty and dirty, leaving almost no doubt that they were second-hand, but most of the shoppers had no other choice. And thus, despite their sad appearances, the objects glinted with a desperate kind of life.

For us kids, these rare transformations saw the streets become a fairground. A long queue always snaked from the entrance to the space shuttle ride, which charged two dollars to carry children two meters into the air and back again, and crowds clustered around a game of torturing goldfish with a little net. But I only ever had eyes for the wide, flat faces of the clowns. I had an insatiable passion for shooting at their teeth.

Repeated practice meant that my technique was honed to perfection, but even once I could easily have knocked out every single big clown tooth, I always made sure to leave one standing. My father used to accompany me to the market, and refused to let this go; he'd snatch the gun from my hands and shoot out that last tooth himself, winning me the toy bear jackpot but leaving me in tears. He didn't understand that I couldn't bear to see a completely empty mouth, but found a clown with only one tooth left hilarious.

I don't know why the girl with gaps between her teeth looked at me with such warmth, that first day of school. When the scratchy speaker-system voice started repeating orders for us to line up, the clown-girl followed me, and we walked together into the rank of students. Contrary to what I'd first thought, she wasn't one of the abandoned creatures. As it turned out, she blended easily with all kinds of groups, and was welcomed by everyone. In my case, on the other hand, she was my only friend for the whole of middle school. Perhaps she thought I was the rejected one, and that was why she befriended me? The thought made me want to run away. But then, at lunchtime, when she invited me to sit with her on the old tires on the school slope, and we traded side dishes from our lunch boxes, my resolve crumbled. And (I have to admit) when she laughed, showing those black gaps between her teeth, I felt indescribably happy.

After class one day, she asked whether I wanted to come over to hers. She said her mother had bought a lot of chocolate cake the day before, but there was only her at home and she couldn't finish it by herself. It was the first time I had ever been invited to a friend's house. Too embarrassed to tell my parents, I went home to change my clothes, snuck a few pears out of the fridge and into a plastic bag, and then crept out again.

The clown-girl lived on top of a hill, in a peaceful little neighborhood that I'd never been to before, in what turned out to be a three-story detached house. She came to the door and graciously accepted my bag of unappetizing pears. Then, just like a grown-up, she brewed tea for me and served it in proper tea cups, and placed two slices of chocolate cake on two butterfly-patterned dessert plates. Usually, our interactions felt as natural as breathing, but that day, probably because of the unfamiliar surroundings, I felt awkward. We sat side by side on the sofa. I waited for ages for her to start eating her cake, so that I could follow suit, but she ignored all the refreshments in favor of meaningless chit-chat.

I forget what we talked about; all I remember is that she was wearing a silk nightgown that she must have borrowed (stolen) from her mother's wardrobe. Sitting beside her, every so often I'd glimpse the gentle swell of her still-growing breasts and, whenever she shifted position, feel the heat from her body waft against mine. I don't know how long it was before she announced that she was leaving for a bit, but we still hadn't touched the cake. I watched her walk away, unable to summon a response.

I was all alone in a spotlessly-clean living room. The ceiling was much higher than the one in my house, and the walls were covered in fragile glass and ceramics. At first, I barely dared move for fear that the house would rock and all those expensive-looking ornaments would come crashing down. But the girl was away a long time and, eventually, I couldn't sit any longer and found myself walking out of the room. I passed through a room containing a piano and a collection of musical instruments that I didn't recognize, and then a room lined with what looked to be very serious books, and then another that was entirely empty aside from a red rug spread across the floor. And then I saw her, on the stairs to the first floor. I followed and remember very clearly that when I reached the top of the stairs she was in a hallway not far from me, facing a wall. I called her name, but she didn't answer. Instead, she vanished. I went to where she had been standing and discovered that it wasn't a wall, it was a door, but there was no keyhole or handle to turn, just a thin seam where the door met the doorframe. I tried to shove it open, but it didn't budge. Then I shouted for her again, but the house was silent. The door stood defiantly where it was. I gave it a couple of good hard kicks, but it made no difference at all.

Disheartened, I went back downstairs. I wanted to return to the living room, but I couldn't remember where it was. I walked all over the house looking and kept ending up in the room with the red rug. It was like being trapped in a maze. When I finally made it to the living room, I was pouring with sweat. I went back to the sofa and sat down in the same spot as before, not daring to drink the tea or touch the cake, or even to move a muscle. There was no clock, meaning I had no way of knowing how much time had passed, but the little flowers of hazelnut cream on the cake had collapsed, and the rays of sunlight hitting the wall had moved several inches closer to me. When the girl reappeared, I searched her face, convinced that something must have changed, but said nothing. She pointed to my belly and asked what was going on; I looked down and saw that my trousers were tented like a little mountain over my crotch, and my whole body was shaking.

* * *

I don't quite know why, but that afternoon I found myself telling my boorish guests about the door. Afterwards, they looked at me with excited, dream-filled eyes. "There's no such thing as unsolvable!" they said, assuring me that the world's greatest locksmith was among us.

Giving me no time to think it over or object, the men leapt from their seats. They were like frightened cockroaches, scuttling around the hidden crevices of the flat. The only one I could see was in the hallway, in front of my door (although it hardly qualified as mine). He pressed his nose against it, as if trying to detect its scent. He sniffed up and down all four sides, and then cocked his head and looked thoughtful. Not long after, another man came out of the kitchen with my toolbox. One man—and I have no idea when he'd gone out there—climbed in through the living room window. Another emerged from the bedroom I shared with my wife, hurriedly throwing something on the floor as he left. Surely not the full-length nightgown my wife had been wearing the previous night? Yet another had found Lily's toy wand and was waving it around. The man in front of the door clapped his hands to get everyone's attention, and loudly proclaimed his assessment. Without a doubt, most of this speech was just for show, because he added a quiet line right at the end, about only being able to open the door if he had a very fine wire or some other little thing, such as a hairpin.

By this stage, the men were gathered in front of the door. What was inside? I watched from a distance, undecided as to whether or not I wanted them to succeed (not that I had any real say in the matter). The door looked frailer than usual, as if it was barely existing. One of the men poked a piece of very fine wire into the crack, and the door emitted a piercing shriek, as though it wasn't a door being opened but a living organism being sliced apart. The whole room broke out in goose pimples.

The door opened. The men were delighted; they lined up and marched single file into that place I'd never managed to reach. When the last man had disappeared through the door, I was alone in the flat once again. But I was still sitting on my stool. Strangely, I felt no urge to go through the door myself, and instead just stayed where I was. Sometime later, I finally walked over. Now the opening was right in front of me, but it was still hard to summon the will to enter. The door seemed smaller than it was supposed to be, as though it would be impossible to fit through without stooping. What's more, I'd always assumed it was a standard rectangle, but now that I looked more carefully, it was actually a trapezoid, its sides slanted at bizarre angles. I contorted my body into different shapes, trying to barge my way in, but the door kept forcing me out.

I couldn't work out how the men had done it. From what I remembered, they'd walked in quite naturally. I tried to shout into the door opening, but the moment my voice passed the doorframe it stopped, as though hitting a muffler. Gusts of icy wind kept blowing in from the other side. I tried to stick my head through, hoping to see something, but the view was blocked by some kind of internal structure (almost as though the door were growing on top of another door).

The mists parted, although I couldn't say when, revealing a crescent moon like a razored eyebrow on an infinite expanse of face. There was beer spilled on the table, its bubbles all gone, glowing with a soporific blue light. Minutes ticked past and not a single man came back through the door. What had they found in there? I thought I could hear a distant shrieking. Would my wife and Lily be asleep by now? I was very tired; so tired, I passed out on the sofa.

When I woke up, the sun had restored some reality to the world, including to the roast chicken, which had been stripped of most of its meat. What remained was a wingless, legless, olive-shaped skeleton, with its eyes wearily closed. I went to the door and found it returned to its original state. I traced my fingers along the rim. It was shallow, like a door-shaped shadow, or an imitation of a door. I crooked a finger and rapped with my knuckle, and it made a low, husky noise, like a voice coming from deep in someone's throat.

* * *

After the holiday, aside from her prominent suntan, my wife was the same wife she'd been a few days before, and my daughter the same daughter. I shook the box containing the model castle, and Lily shrieked with excitement outside the front door, immediately letting go of my wife's hand and rushing inside. Without pausing to take off her shoes, she pounced on the box and began tearing it open. At the sight of the fragments of model castle scattered across the floor, my wife gave me a helpless smile, and then announced that she'd bought some squid and a bottle of squid ink to make us squid ink risotto for dinner.

The light in the kitchen was fixed, making the plates and bowls in the drying rack sparkle, and my wife looked extremely pleased. At dinnertime, she served us each a plate of the risotto, and placed a big bowl of peach and rocket salad in the center of the table. As we ate, our mouths turned jet-black. My wife winked and said, "Pretty good to have a couple of days of freedom, then?" Was she hinting at something? I waved the question away, and asked her and Lily about their trip. They looked at one another and smiled but said nothing, as though, inside their inky lips, there was some secret they couldn't tell me.

Lily lay on the floor stacking tiny building blocks one on top of the other, completely absorbed in her castle. While my wife was showering, I knelt beside her and whispered, "Won't you tell Daddy what happened while you were away?" She shook her head, still focused on the construction. I scooped her up and put her on my knees, pressing my face close to hers. "First answer your father's question," I said. "Then you can go back to playing." Lily pouted and burst into tears. My wife strode out of the bathroom and took Lily in her arms, kissing her and saying something into her ear, and then the child was all smiles again. How had she done that? She turned to look at me. I expected her to blame me for upsetting Lily, but she just grinned. I saw the gaps between her teeth, black as black, and couldn't help feeling a stab of resentment.

That evening, I went into the bedroom without waiting for my wife. But in order to reach it, I had to pass by the unopenable door and, when I did so, I heard a faint breathing sound, like a cry for help.

I wasn't sleepy and lay on the bed with my hands behind my head. I thought of how, early the next morning, before the city was awake, I'd have to rejoin the mass of strangers squeezing onto the train. In a city teeming with resentments, who knew what setbacks lay in wait? And in the factory, the air swirling with sawdust, I knew I'd see those men, swaggering past me in their identical windbreakers. I'd lower my gaze and keep on with my work in silence, avoiding their reddened eyes. I loved my work. An advantage to being a carpenter was that you could immerse yourself in voiceless, wordless wood, and a whole day could pass without the need to exchange a single word with anyone.

My wife had not yet come to bed, and Lily had not yet come to kiss me goodnight. I couldn't sleep, so I got up again. Walking out of the master bedroom, I was confronted by the gloomy hallway. The first room on the right was Lily's—if I opened the door, I'd see her dolls and wooden building blocks strewn across the floor. To the left was the bathroom, and straight ahead was where we ate dinner every evening, which linked to the living room, which doubled as my wife's studio. The kitchen was to the left of the living room, and at the back of the kitchen was a door. The door seemed like it must lead somewhere, but there was just a murky white wall, pressing in on me. The house was extremely quiet, and I couldn't find Lily or my wife; it was as though they'd faded into the air. I went back into the hallway and saw the frail door still hiding in the wall, although its outline was blurred. Sitting down with my back against it, I thought I could hear a faint sound coming from the other side. But it could have been the wind rattling a distant window blind, making it chatter like a row of teeth.

Writers love language (which is why we write in the first place), but there is sometimes the temptation to wax overly poetic, especially in the imagery we try to create. Yet the most powerful images often derive from those things that appear in our everyday lives. In the opening of this story, Tse presents an ominous picture of these men arriving as guests at their colleague's front door, and you might initially think that something terrible will follow. The sky, for instance, is a "bruise-dark" purple and the men in their windbreakers are described "like balloons ready to take flight" but once the protagonist opens his door to them, their "trapped shadows leaked away" and they enter his home looking more like "deflated dolls."

What effect does the writer achieve with an opening like this? She definitely creates *mystery*, in that she foreshadows a less-than-normal arrival. Although this very poetic and descriptive image makes a strong statement, most of the language of the story is much more direct and ordinary. Instead, the most memorable image we're left with is that of an inexplicable door, one that appears to be impossible to open or sometimes, even to locate. At every turn in the story, it pops up again, heightening the mystery.

How does Tse create that mystery? As we said earlier, repetition can be a useful technique to use in fiction. In "The Door," Tse repeats the word "door" fifty times (fifty-one if you include the title), either on its own or as part of the compound word "doorframe." Would you have guessed this number when you read the story? We confess that we did not and only knew via a search. While it is evident that the door increases as an obsession of the story for the protagonist, and it clearly is the central image, the very ordinariness of the word makes its repeated use less noticeable until the tension in the story increases. In fact, repetition is very significant as a *literary device* that Tse uses to tell a deeper, psychological tale about the protagonist, while creating a mystery about the wife in whose home the family lives.

But what is the *real* mystery of this story? It's useful to study the way the narrative unfolds because it's not until halfway through (specifically at 49 percent of the word count) that we first encounter this mysterious door. Before that, the story is about the protagonist's anxieties in having these colleagues visit him, something he does only because his wife urges him to do so. We learn that he is quite a solitary person and it is his wife who is much more sociable and that they have a young daughter Lily. In fact, except for a few jarring moments, he seems like a reasonably contented man who says "There was nothing in my present life I could really complain about." Yet by the time we get to the end of the story, we are witness to a mystery so inexplicable that we might ask, why is there this door and what is really going on?

You can decide for yourself what the story really means, but here are a couple of things to think about for your own writing that you can learn from this example. The story is divided almost exactly into two halves—the first as discussed above is a *setup that disarms the reader*. We think nothing much is going to happen because the *situation* described doesn't seem either extraordinary or mysterious (a little like our title and opening paragraph for this chapter). However, in the second half, the story takes a decidedly bizarre turn the moment we are introduced to the mysterious door: "The kitchen was to the left of the living room, and at the back of the kitchen was a door." From that moment on, the mystery heightens with each paragraph and we are also introduced to "the gap between the door and doorframe" that was too narrow for his fingers to fit through. This two-part structure can be a good architecture for a story.

The other useful lesson we glean from this story is the way Tse uses *unexpected language or images or moments to jar our senses*. We've already noted the language of the opening paragraph. Right after the boorish guests arrive, the protagonist reflects on the reason why he's holding this unwanted get together in the first place. It was because of a few days' holiday he had and his expectation was to build a model castle with Lily. However, his wife tells him that she's already bought train tickets and will take Lily away for a few days, which is a surprise both to the character *and* the reader. At this point we also find out he has no friends other than these colleagues, and they are not really friends. Look through the story and see how Tse *injects uncertainty into what we think we're seeing*. Recall also the strip light that hangs down in the kitchen, needing to be fixed, an unexpected image that later repeats.

In the second story, "Where Did I Lose You?," Fan Xiaoqing also uses repetition and the ordinary image of a name card, something that is common in China, in this story about how much we think we know about either ourselves or other people. Unlike "The Door," however, it delves into the motivation of the characters, specifically in how people choose to treat others, and the story is rooted in a realistic place (we know we're in China), whereas "The Door" could be taking place anywhere. Read the story and also think about what the writer appears to be saying about society and its customs.

2 "Where Did I Lose You"

by Fan Xiaoqing (China)

Translated from Chinese (Mandarin) by Paul Harris

Fan Xiaoqing's award-winning fiction includes 18 novels and over 300 novellas and short stories. Her story "A History of City and Villages" won the prestigious Lu Xun Literature Prize. She also authored numerous essays and screenplays. Born in Suzhou City, she currently serves as chair of the Writers Association of Jiangsu Province.

> Wang You had long forgotten when it was that he was first given somebody's name card. Nor had he the faintest recollection of the occasion, whose card it was, their job title, what the person looked like or even whether it was a man or a woman. Try as hard as he might to remember, it was no use.
>
> When he asked people of an older generation if they could recall when name cards first became popular, no-one could say for certain. Some said the late 1980s, others a bit earlier, others a bit later.
>
> But all this is beside the point. The fact is, once there were no such things, but the moment they caught on, they spread incredibly fast. Suddenly the sky seemed to rain name cards.
>
> Nowadays even nannies have cards printed, to hand to potential employers. I even know of a conman who keeps a store of them to distribute to passers-by, in which he

offers to teach them the tricks of the trade. I hear that nursery school children exchange them too.

Like when you're out walking, you see a street-sweeper in his worn-out working clothes. You know immediately from his appearance that he's from the countryside. But while he's sweeping, out comes his mobile and in a moment he's squatting on the ground making a phone call. This is now a common sight. In the same way you now accept anyone pulling out a name card as part of the routine. As a result, the pavements are covered with cards, like fallen leaves. If you accidentally tread on one, you feel a bit guilty, but then you accidentally tread on another. Treading on someone's name card is like treading on their name—it's almost a personal insult. But it's hard to avoid, with so many of them littering the pavements. Apart from being a vital ingredient in China's economic development, for some people the handing-out of a name card has meant a lucky break, set them on the road to riches or maybe marked the beginning of a great romance. Even the pokiest print shop can launch the career of dozens of small business owners.

After name cards took off in a big way, name card holders soon followed. These look rather like photo albums and come in a variety of sizes and styles: large, small, thick, thin, fancy or plain. They usually have an attractive cover and inside a set of plastic pockets—smaller than those in photo albums—of just the right dimensions for a name card, that is, about 9 x 5 1/2 cm. If you're given a name card of a different design by someone (an individualist, in other words), it won't fit your holder. It will either be too big or too long or made of another material, such as bamboo strips, cloth or reed. Then you've got a problem. However, such cards (and such people) are in the minority. Most settle for the standard 9 x 5 1/2 cm job, and any minor variations, such as calligraphic instead of printed characters, a background design, plain name and phone number with no job title, different-colored paper (light green, pink or sky-blue, perhaps) won't affect the basic format. All these alternative versions will fit into your holder which, when opened, does indeed rather resemble a photo album.

And, just as perusing old photos will remind you of the time and place they were taken, so opening your name card holder can start to trigger memories.

As your eyes alight on a succession of names, you will be reminded of past meetings, some interesting, some less so, some pleasant, some not so pleasant, some useful, some totally fruitless, but all part of life's rich tapestry. However, if it all happened too long ago or your memory is not so good, some of them will be difficult to pin down accurately or will just be a hazy memory, while others may have gone out of your mind completely. You'll think "Who was he?" or "Where did I get that card?" or even "How could I possibly have met him?" For example, what are a nuclear weapons manufacturer and a tea-egg salesman doing exchanging cards? But there's no denying it when the cards are in your holder. Some people without the slightest connection with your professional or personal life can appear in your name card holder. Try as you might, you can't come up with a rational explanation and the fact that they're there in your holder is a silent accusation that you've forgotten all about them.

In fact, Wang You had forgotten about quite a number. He had lost the very first card he had ever been given. But there was still the first card in his collection of holders. Wang You's holders were arranged systematically and in each one the cards were stored according to the date on which he had received them. This particular card was in the first pocket of the first page of his first holder. The man's name was Du Zhongtian. He certainly had nothing to do with anything that Wang You was involved in now. Wang You had met him only that once and thereafter there had been no further contact. But Wang You had kept his card. So there must have been something distinguishing him from those whose cards he had thrown away. When he had an idle moment, Wang You would take out his many holders and flip through the cards in chronological order, and there, heading them all, was always Du Zhongtian.

Wang You would sometimes feel tempted to dial the phone number on the card and see who answered. Was it likely, though, that this Du Zhongtian was still on the same number after all these years? Certainly not. The city had changed its phone numbers twice since, first from six to seven digits and then from seven to eight-digit numbers. On the other hand, the adding of an extra digit was always done according to a rule. For example, when the first change was made to seven-digit numbers, they just added a 5 before all existing numbers. The second time, they added a 7. So, Wang You supposed, if he put 75 in front of Du Zhongtian's old number, he might get through. All the same, he never did dial the number, for fear of making a fool of himself.

Actually, there was a reason why he had kept Du's card. One day many years before, Wang You had been eating at a restaurant with a party of people. As is normal at such gatherings, the first thing they did after sitting down was to exchange name cards. This was the established convention even then, and failure to observe it before eating would make people feel uncomfortable, as they wouldn't know why they were there or who was sitting next or opposite to them at table. The atmosphere would be constrained as if something vital was missing, even cold and unfriendly, and the guests wouldn't enjoy themselves. But once cards are exchanged and they know who everyone is, the party can get going. The guests know how to address their neighbors by their proper title and can start getting down to business. There will, of course, most likely be someone without a card, in which case his neighbor always says "Never mind, but here's mine anyway," while the other one is quick to apologize, saying he has just run out of cards, but he'll bring one next time. Actually, this is only a manner of speaking, as there may never be a next time.

At such meals nowadays many of the guests have no idea why they are there. Some will have been dragged along just to make up the numbers. The hardened drinkers will be there to liven up the party. Those with some status in society will be there to add a touch of class to the occasion. There will also be the one who just comes to pay the bill or who attends on behalf of someone else otherwise engaged. The people at such banquets therefore often have almost nothing to do with each other and their presence at the same event is something of an anomaly.

Like the time Wang You had occasion to invite a Communist Party boss to a meal at a restaurant. He was a very busy man, but he at last said yes, and both the restaurant and the room were his choosing. When Wang You got to the restaurant and went to the room, he saw that the Party boss had not yet arrived but there was already a table-full of people, all strangers to one another, their only thing in common being that they all knew the Party boss. At first, everyone felt embarrassed, until he turned up, looked around the table, smiled and said, "I'm the only one here today who knows who you all are," and

Mysteries

so introduced everyone to each other. At which all the guests got up from their seats, started exchanging cards, and the atmosphere immediately relaxed. They all knew the truth was that the Party boss was too busy to meet them individually and so had brought together a whole lot of people who had never met each other before. The meal could well have been torture for all concerned. Instead, it proved a great success, with quite a few leaving in a fair state of intoxication.

By the way, some people you meet at such parties are so vague that, even after a considerable intake of wine and the usual exchange of civilities and mutual compliments, you're none the wiser as to who they are.

In these cases it's always a good idea to exchange cards; then at least you know who you're sitting next to. There are not many people who don't have cards, and only a few will have run out of theirs. There may be the oddball who, when everyone else is handing out theirs, says he doesn't hold with name cards or, if he has them, won't give them out. People will usually overlook this eccentricity or say something in mitigation, like "Celebrities don't need cards."

But to return to the occasion in question. Once Wang You had been given the others' cards, the party could begin in earnest. Things went with a swing, with everyone drinking and chatting away and with a good chance of sorting out the issues that were the main reason for organizing the banquet. When it was all over, everyone said their goodbyes, some already treating their fellows as if they were old friends. Having eaten and drunk their fill, they all filed out, some in front, others behind, with Wang You in the middle. He hadn't gone far before he noticed something white flutter down onto the ground, apparently thrown away by one of those in front of him. He picked it up. It was a name card on which was printed "Du Zhongtian" and had evidently been given out by someone at the party.

Wang You had also been given Du's card, which he now had in his trouser pocket. Wang You said, "Oh!" and someone came up from behind to have a look. This must have been Du Zhongtian himself, for when he saw it was his own name card that Wang You had picked up, he looked rather put out and muttered something. Wang You blushed and quickly pushed forward to the man ahead of him and handed him the card, saying, "I think you dropped something." The man turned his head towards Wang You and Du Zhongtian and, though it would have been too dark to make them out properly, said he hadn't dropped it, but thrown it away, as he had so many cards it wasn't worth keeping them all. This apparent snub evidently upset Du and Wang You hastily said to the man, could he have forgotten that this was Du Zhongtian? However, the other failed to take the hint, but instead said, who was Du Zhongtian? Ashen-faced, Du said it was him and, at that, snatched the card from Wang You's hand, tore it up, tossed the pieces into the air, and the name card floated down in fragments like so many snowflakes. Before the last piece had reached the ground, Du Zhongtian had vanished into the night, leaving behind the impression of a very angry man.

Wang You stood there puzzled. He expected the man who had thrown away Du's card to look suitably abashed. But no, he just said nonchalantly and with a smile "Oh, that was Du Zhongtian, was it? I don't see why he should be so annoyed. What would be the use in keeping his card?" And, as if he felt he still hadn't made his point, he clapped Wang You on the shoulder and said, "Don't you see, old boy? Suppose I kept the card and put it in my card holder at home. I'd come across it after, let's say, six months and be sure to throw it out. So why bother with it in the first place? Might as well get rid of it straightaway." Wang You looked at the pieces scattered on the ground and felt quite unhappy, as if he was the one who had been rude to Du Zhongtian and had thrown his card away. Not that Wang You had never in his life thrown away someone's name card, but he would never have done so in their presence. He would have taken it home, put it in a drawer and, when after a while the drawer had got too full and nothing more could be squeezed in, he would have had a clear-out and disposed of any unwanted cards. But ever since that evening when Du Zhongtian had torn up his own card and made such a public exhibition of his anger, Wang You had never been able to throw away anyone's card.

He placed Du Zhongtian's in the first pocket of the first page of his holder and thereafter kept all the cards anyone ever gave him, finding a place for them in one of his dozen or so tightly-packed holders.

Occasionally he would leaf through his store of cards. This usually happened when so many odds and ends had accumulated in his study that he had to do something about it. As he was tidying up he would, of course, glance at the many cards he had kept over the years. In the early days he was still able to remember some of the people concerned and how he had met them. But as his collection continued to expand, his memory of who these people were and what they did began to fade. Once he noticed a card which said, "Techno Frontiers, General Agent."

Wang You couldn't for the life of him recall what Techno-frontiers was or even what General Agent might mean. After racking his brains, he thought it must have something to do with science. But as he was only editor of a house magazine at a local records office, how on earth could he have met the General Agent of Techno-Frontiers? Try as hard as he could to remember, his mind was a blank. He felt that his memory was packed to capacity, but what he needed to remember eluded him. Name cards have their uses, but they can also cause a lot of unnecessary bother.

Like that time Wang You met a man at some function or other and handed him his card. Thereafter he got a call from the man on his mobile almost every day. He was seeking guidance on a historical novel he was writing.

He'd only just embarked on the novel, he said, and wanted Wang You to look at what he'd written so far and say whether he thought it was worthwhile carrying on. Wang You conscientiously read through a few pages of the manuscript. But before he had time to give an opinion, another instalment arrived, and then a third and fourth in rapid succession. Although the author was only supposed to have started the novel, it already ran to several hundred pages and moreover showed the man to have not a shred of literary talent. Wang You would have liked to have severed relations with the man there and then. But he would not be put off. Wang You stored his phone number in his mobile, so that it would display when the man rang and Wang You could avoid answering. But the man was canny and evidently realized what Wang You was up to—he would simply call from another phone.

Thus Wang You fell into the trap. This battle of wits continued for nearly six months until Wang You could stand it no longer. He told him, "Mr Li, I'm not the editor of a publishing house. I'm in no position to help you." To which Li replied that he wasn't asking for help. He only wanted Wang You to take an interest in what he was doing. He'd been made redundant from his job. He loved history and loved writing. Maybe Wang You didn't appreciate his situation. If so, he'd be happy to explain further. . .

By now Wang You's head was spinning. And it was at this point that a colleague of his came over to his desk, accompanied by an elderly lady. The colleague tapped on his desk and said, "Penny for your thoughts, Wang You?" Only then did he become aware that the elderly lady was standing there smiling at him. Wang You made an effort to smile back. "Are you Wang You?" she said. "Yes," he said.

Because of the nature of his work Wang You often had dealings with amateur historians, especially elderly enthusiasts. They would sometimes turn up of their own accord, with their reminiscences of the city. As old people tend to be rather garrulous, once they start talking there's no stopping them. But actually this was exactly what Wang You needed, for amid their ramblings there might be a precious nugget of lost history. However, this old lady, when he told her he was Wang You, did not launch straight into what she had come about, but instead looked him up and down as if she didn't believe him and said doubtfully, "You really are Wang You?" He assured her he was. She shook her head slightly. Whether this meant that she didn't accept he was Wang You or Wang You was not the person she wanted was unclear. His colleagues standing by laughed and one of them said, "Wang You, she suspects you're not the genuine article. You'd better show her your ID." The old lady's eyes slowly shifted from his hand to his pocket, as if she really was expecting him to produce his ID. But when Wang You said irritably, what good was an ID, that could just as well be a fake, she laughed and said, "All right, I believe you. You are the real Wang You and I've found you."

Wang You said, "I don't think I know you. How come you seem to know me?" She said, "You may not know me, but there is someone I'm sure you do know—Xu Youhong. You know him, don't you? I'm his wife." She could see that Wang You was still in the dark. So she said, "Wang You, why don't you say something? Are you sure you're Wang You?" "Of course, I am," he said. "But I don't recall anyone by the name of Xu Youhong. Who is he?" "You may not remember him," she said. "But he remembers you. He has your name card. That's how I found you." Wang You thought hard, but still could not bring to mind anyone of that name. So he had to say he was really sorry, he gave out a lot of cards and couldn't always recollect who to. "If you really were Wang You," she said, "you would definitely remember Xu Youhong. Anyway, why not come to my house sometime when you're free?" Wang You eyed her uncertainly, but she had already handed him a name card, adding, "You can come whenever you like. I'm always in." And with that she left, leaning on her walking stick.

Wang You stared blankly at the card in his hand, while his colleagues joked, "Wang You, you already have one mother-in-law. And now here comes another to size you up!" Wang You then saw the card the elderly lady had given him was her husband Xu Youhong's card. It just gave his name with no title or indication of his job, no business name or address. But his home address was given in full plus his phone number. Wang You felt there was something odd about the whole affair. Still, he automatically put the card in his desk drawer and for the time being forgot about it.

The following weekend he stayed at home. But there was something at the back of his mind that made him uneasy and unable to relax, and he realized it was the thought of

Xu Youhong's card that was nagging him. He began to regret that he had been so free in handing out his own name cards. He had no idea when this Xu Youhong had got his card or what he wanted from him now. And why hadn't he come himself, instead of getting his wife to come? He searched his memory over and over again but could find no clue to this conundrum. In the end he made up his mind he must go to the man's house. At least that should clear up the mystery. After all, it was only a seventy- or eighty-year-old lady. Even if she was an eccentric, she wouldn't eat him.

So that Sunday afternoon Wang You first called in at the office and retrieved the name card from his desk drawer and, checking the address on the card, went in search of the elderly lady's house. When he got there, he knocked on the door. It seemed she was on the look-out, for she opened the door almost immediately and greeting him with a smile said, "Wang You, I knew you would come."

Once inside he noticed the photo of an old man (evidently now deceased) on the wall and the elderly lady said, "That's Xu Youhong. He's been dead these past six months." Wang You looked more closely at the photo, but was still unable to decide whether or not he had known the man. Nor could he recall any circumstances in which he might have given him his name card. He said to the elderly lady, "I'm afraid I've got a dreadful memory and I give my card to so many people. I could try phoning around. Perhaps someone else will remember." She smiled and pointed to her home telephone, "You can use that." Wang You phoned friends, relations and colleagues, but found no one who had known Xu Youhong. They also found his question a bit strange, and some asked why he wanted to know and what his connection was with this Xu Youhong. One of them said, wasn't Xu Youhong something to do with the stock exchange? In the end, all this fruitless questioning left him thoroughly demoralized. He decided to have one last go, but this time made no attempt to go into details and simply said the name Xu Youhong. The person answering said straightaway, "Xu Youhong? Of course I know him. You do mean Xu Youhong?" Wang You almost jumped with excitement and gabbled, "Yes, I do mean him. Did know him?" "What do you mean 'did'? We're right now enjoying a game of mah-jong together. Do you want to speak to him?" This took Wang You completely off guard, and he just said, "No, it must be a mistake. Xu Youhong died six months ago." His friend at the other end shouted, "What are you talking about? Are you trying to kill off my old friend Xu Youhong?"

Wang You hung up and looked helplessly at the elderly lady, shaking his head, while she nodded and said with a sigh, "People nowadays are so forgetful." She turned to the photo on the wall and said, "Youhong, the others may not remember you, but at long last here is someone who does and he has come to see you." She opened a cupboard and took out a small, thin name card holder, saying, "Wang You, my husband didn't leave behind many cards, only these few, but yours is among them."

Wang You took the holder and there, sure enough, was his card in one of the pockets. He looked again carefully. The card must have been quite a recent addition, as it gave as his job title "Chief Editor," and he'd only been appointed to that position six months before. Had he already forgotten something that had happened such a short time ago? He had no idea when or where he had given Xu Youhong his card.

The elderly lady said that, before he died, Xu Youhong had given her his name card holder and told her that all the people in it were good friends of his and, when anything happened to him, she should get in touch with them if she was in any kind of trouble. He had thrown away the card of anyone who was not a proper friend. But anyone whose card was there would be sure to help. However, after Xu had died, she had phoned each one in turn, but no-one remembered him. A few said the name was vaguely familiar, but as soon as they asked if she could give them a bit more to go on and they learned that he had died, they could no longer remember anything about him. She told Wang You that she knew he didn't entirely believe her, so she suggested he try phoning again, picking a name at random from the card holder, to see whether anyone would come if they still remembered Xu Youhong. Wang You felt that this was getting ridiculous. He couldn't go phoning up complete strangers. And what right had he to interfere and interrogate them as to whether or not they had known Xu Youhong? With a sigh of resignation the elderly lady said all right, but if he didn't try or all of his enquiries ended in a blank, then no-one would come. Then she told him to sit down and thanked him for coming and for paying his respects to the dead man's photo, which she said would be a comfort to his soul in heaven. Wang You absent-mindedly turned again to the photo. Xu Youhong was smiling gently at him as if he really was pleased.

Wang You felt he ought to explain that he had never actually known him, but couldn't bring himself to do so.

The elderly lady began talking about her husband, saying that he often used to mention Wang You. She told a story of how once Wang You had imbibed a large quantity of beer and urgently needed to relieve himself, but couldn't make out which toilet was which and so had sneaked into the ladies'. Fortunately, Xu was going in after him and, when he saw Wang was there, hastily blocked the entrance and told any woman who tried to enter that the toilet was out of order. Then, when Wang You came out having sobered up a little, he took Xu Youhong to task, asking him why he was standing in the doorway of the ladies' and was he trying to have a peep.

Wang You could no more recall this incident than he could Xu Youhong the man. But he didn't let on nor did he offer any further explanation. He just let the lady go on talking. He would even, if she mentioned a particular occasion, try and supply a few extra details. For example, she recounted how Wang You had once been invited to a wedding, but had gone to the wrong place, ending up at the celebrations of another couple. It so happened that Xu was among the guests at this other wedding, so Wang You assumed that he was at the right one, sat down, partook of the food and drink and, even when the time came for everyone to leave, still hadn't realized his mistake. Wang You burst in, "That's right. Later, when the friend who had invited me asked me why I hadn't come after I had accepted the invitation, I felt a bit uncomfortable and said, 'No, I was there. There were just too many people and I didn't manage to get to you. But I gave my wedding present to your nephew.' My friend said, 'Come off it! You weren't there.' I said, 'But Xu Youhong can vouch for me. We were sitting at the same table.' My friend said, 'And who's Xu Youhong when he's at home? I don't know anyone of that name. Why would I ask him to my nephew's wedding?' We went on arguing till at last it dawned on me that I had been at the wrong function. Xu had been at another wedding." The elderly lady went into fits of laughter at this and said, "Yes, yes. My husband told me all about it."

The more Wang You contributed, the more he enjoyed assuming this new role and now he imagined he could remember everything down to the last particular. However, in his eagerness to add corroborative and picturesque details, he sometimes went a bit too far. The lady showed him another card in the holder. The man in question was the manager of a karaoke bar. She said the man had insisted on giving Xu Youhong his card at their first meeting. Xu hadn't wanted to take it, but then the man got annoyed. "My husband was a kindly man," she said, "and when he saw the man was upset, he quickly took the card. He came back and told me the man was a decent chap." Wang You could see that the elderly lady was relishing this story and couldn't resist the temptation of adding a touch of spice to the tale himself. So he said, "Yes, I remember. I was there at the time. We were both singing with the man, and I never knew your husband had such a good voice, especially at his age. And what wonderful breath control! He stole the show. He sang the whole evening, one song after another. In fact, so much so that he made himself hoarse. Did you notice when he got home?" The lady at first said nothing, but after a while looked at Wang You and said, "Wang You, are you sure you've got it right? My husband had a terrible voice. He couldn't sing in tune and never went to karaoke. How could he have sung himself hoarse in a karaoke bar?" Wang You hastily retracted and said, "Yes, of course. I must have been thinking of someone else and got the two mixed up." The lady smiled and said, "You see, you youngsters haven't got as good memories as us old folk."

Wang You was still at a loss as to why she had asked him there. Surely it couldn't be just to invent these fictions about things that had never happened or talk all this nonsense in front of a photo of the dead husband in order to bring solace to his soul in the afterlife. He mumbled something inconsequential and at last felt he should ask the lady whether anyone still owed Xu Youhong any money or was she in any other difficulty. She said no, no-one owed anyone anything. He then said, "Then I'm not sure why you . . ." With a gesture of the hand she cut him short. "Thank you, Wang You," she said. "Thank you for coming here and talking to me so much about my husband. Actually, I know that everything you've said you made up and has nothing to do with him."

This took Wang You completely by surprise. She went on, "In fact, all I told you about my husband I made up too. You never knew him and he never knew you." Still puzzled, Wang You pointed to Xu Youhong's name card holder and said, "But how did he get hold of my name card?" She said, "Oh, name cards don't mean a thing. They must be one of the most pointless inventions, don't you think?" That evening, after Wang You had left Xu Youhong's house, he hadn't gone far when he noticed a name card on the ground, apparently thrown away by someone. He had already passed it, but he stopped, retraced his steps, bent down, picked up the card and put it in his pocket. Just as he was doing this, it suddenly occurred to him that this must have been how his own card came to be in Youhong Xu's holder. His wife must have picked it up. Wang You took the card home with him and carefully put it in his holder. When his wife saw him doing this, she said, "Have you met someone new?" He just smiled, but said nothing.

So a stranger had now come into his home, even become part of it and, who knows, Wang You might one day remember him. His name was Qian Yong—a common enough name. You could probably find thousands of them if you looked on the Internet.

Did you find the story amusing? We know we did, and the *gentle satire* Fan uses is an interesting contrast to the harsher satire in some of the earlier stories in this anthology, such as "An Errand," "Farangs," "Birds," or "All About Skin." Fan's approach is more of one that *pokes fun* at the overuse of name cards that is common not just in China, but also in Japan and much of Asia. It is this very commonplace practice that provides the starting point from which the story springboards.

But the larger question to consider is who the "you" is in the title of this story that the "I" has lost. Is it Xu Youhung, whose wife Wang You visits? Or is it the person whose name card appears first in his cardholder, Du Zhongtian, one who remains a mystery even after the story ends? In the story we do briefly meet a man who *might* be Du when Wang recounts the banquet where he picks up Du's card. But Du's identity is never certain. Also, who is the "I"? We meet a narrator right at the start who tells us about Wang You and the short history of how name cards caught on: "I even know of a con-man who keeps a store of them (name cards) to distribute to passers-by, in which he offers to teach them the tricks of the trade," but that "I" transforms into "you" and remains the second person for the rest of the story.

There is a novel, *Soul Mountain* by Gao Xingjian, the Chinese writer-in-voluntary-exile who was the first Chinese-born and Chinese-language writer to win the Nobel Prize in literature in 2000 (note: China does not recognize him as a Chinese winner, because of his foreign domicile and French nationality; their recognition is reserved for Mo Yan, who won the Nobel in 2012 and is a Chinese citizen in Beijing). One interesting feature of Gao's work is the way pronouns such as you, I, he, she, it become interchangeable. This technique is further enhanced in Chinese, because the characters for all third-person subject pronouns (i.e., he, she, they, it) are homophones or words with the same pronunciation, an effect that is *not* lost in translation. In the novel, this technique is purposefully used to speak to the instability and disintegration of the self.

A similar effect is created by Fan's story, because it's soon apparent that the I is also you, and that you is also him, or Wang You, the protagonist. In fact, we might possibly consider this an example of a kind of autofiction, which we discussed in Chapter 5 about identity. After all, this story is concerned with what we might call the *mystery of who we really are* when reduced to a name card.

Writing fiction is in part an exercise in asking and answering the question of not just who we are but why we exist. Paying attention to the mystery of existence keeps us humble as writers, and we understand that even though we may be "playing god" by creating our fictional worlds with characters, plot, conflict, or mystery, writing good fiction is about something larger than the superficial aspects of such creation. It's not just what happens in a story but *why it happens* that matters. So ask yourself why Xu's wife plays the trick she does on Wang, or why Wang decides to visit her. Or why the narrator tells this story about name cards in the first place.

One final noteworthy aspect of this story is the way it moves between social commentary or explanation and storytelling. For example, after the brief history of name cards and Wang as the protagonist are introduced, the story about the banquet begins and we learn this is the kind of occasion where name cards are routinely exchanged. The voice shifts in the next paragraph: "At such meals nowadays many of the guests have no idea why they are there" and continues in this vein before we return to the story of the specific occasion where Wang acquires Du's card. You can think of such a story as also *wishing to inform the reader about the culture and practices of the place* that is the setting. This can be a useful technique to use if you're writing a story set in a place that may be relatively unknown. The trick of this story is the focus on name cards as an entry point to talk about social practices in China that can be taken to an extreme.

Both these stories deserve re-reading and are open to interpretation. It is in our interest as writers to aim for that level of complexity in our own fiction.

Exercises

1. In "The Door," the mysterious door does not appear till mid-way, whereas in "Where Did I Lose You" the name card problem is presented at the start. Write two different openings with a same item as the image or symbol using these two approaches.
2. Think about an idea or social practice that has always puzzled you. Write a story that makes this the central mystery and let your imagination take you down multiple paths of possibilities.
3. Construct a scene of an ordinary, everyday situation where people behave as you would expect using a single character's POV (either first- or third-person close). Use language for that POV to describe the situation as bizarre or extraordinary even though nothing unusual actually happens.
4. Write an opinion piece that pokes gentle fun at a practice in your social milieu. Then, write a story of a character who takes this practice very seriously and show them in a scene engaging in this practice. Interweave the language of your opinion piece with the story in the way Fan does in "Where Did I Lose You."
5. Come up with a mystery that needs to be solved. Write a story that prevents it being solved.

CHAPTER 9
TABOOS

Discomfort is not always a bad thing, at least when it comes to literary fiction. Some writers show us the world as it might have been or might yet be, for good or ill. Others show us worlds that have never existed. Still others give us intimate glimpses into realistic situations we might consider highly private and sometimes even shocking. We've never believed that shock, for its own sake, is a worthwhile goal for a short story writer. We can hardly count the number of times over the years a student in one of our introductory courses has presented the workshop with a story meant to shock and disturb his (it's usually a "he") classmates and perhaps even his teacher with the scandalous exploits put forth in his latest short story. Almost invariably, these stories are sexually graphic and treat sex as though the author and his generation are the first to discover the amazing activity. Forgive us, please, if we sound a bit jaded, but heaven save us from the young man who has discovered sex and wants to share it and his virility with the rest of us. Maybe he will succeed in shocking and offending some of his classmates, but it's also likely that he will cause injury to the instructor's eyes from excessive rolling and injury to the vocal cords from excessive groaning (rather than moaning). We're not saying that sex is off-limits—but writing a smart and riveting sex scene takes skill and imagination. The short story writer Joy Williams once assigned her class to write a kiss. What simpler exercise could there be? But the class had difficulty because it's not easy to write a kiss that seems anything but a generic and uninteresting gesture. Try it. Write a kiss scene that seems neither generic, clichéd, nor overly sentimental.

We recently watched a Korean comedy in which a young woman starts selling sex toys when she's fired from her job. She doesn't want her boyfriend to know about this, so she does everything to hide this fact from him. But one day, she tries on a strap-on to show a customer, but the customer kicks her out of her home and into the street. The strap-on is faulty and she can't remove it, so she has to find a way home with a bulge under her dress. Guess what? Shortly after she arrives home, her fiancé shows up. She says she wants to take a shower, all the while trying frantically to remove the strap-on. Her fiancé wants to join her. She draws a bubble bath and hides in the bath. Her boyfriend enters the bathroom. He's got a ring for her. He tugs on her hand to put the ring on her, but instead he grabs . . .

This is a classic *snowball effect*. The snowball effect is one of the fundamental comic techniques, and one way to both create tension and also relieve it, especially where sex is concerned. As the name implies, a series of actions, starting out small, go from bad to worse, gathering force until the inevitable crash at the bottom of the mountain. That's one way to write about sex in a manner that complicates it and makes it entertaining.

The three stories we've included in this chapter all involve sex, and if at least one of them doesn't surprise and/or disturb you, you might want to check if you have a pulse. One or two even might offend you, but try to keep in mind that at their heart, they're character studies and the actions of the characters aren't gratuitous but are meant to explore the ways in which communication between humans is helped or hindered by our need to connect physically as well as emotionally with others. We don't write stories to condone or approve human behavior but to explore it, and in order to do so, some brave writers venture into territories that might make even *them* blush.

Let's start with the oldest of the stories, the oldest story in our book, in fact. "The Quilt," written by Ismat Chughtai in 1942, is a kind of coming-of-age story, told from the point of view of a naïve narrator, a young girl who spends an extended period of time with Begum Jaan, an aristocrat married to the local Nawab, or Viceroy. Nawabs in India before independence were often, though not exclusively, Muslim, the counterpart of the term, Maharaja, originating during the Mughal Empire and lasting through the British empire. When the story was originally published, it definitely created a stir. Chughtai was put on trial on obscenity charges and asked to apologize. On trial in a court in Lahore, she not only refused to apologize but also won her case. Here, ambiguity saved the day. Her lawyer pointed out that the story contained no obscene words and that there were no overt references to sex acts. For this book, we commissioned a new translation from Urdu by Gopika Jadeja, and when we taught the story not long ago in the United States, we learned that the story still has the power to offend. One student, one of the strongest in terms of class participation, was disturbed by the story because she considered Begum Jaan and her lover/employee as little more than would-be pedophiles. That gave us pause. While the young girl is the protagonist of the story, we'd argue that the focus is on the Begum and Rabbo.

As you read the story, consider on what basis you're making judgments about the characters, taking into account the historical context in which it was written, the ensuing controversy of the story's publication, the difference in culture (if there *is* a difference) between your own and the culture depicted here, and if your judgment of the characters (if you have one) opens up or discourages discussion of the story and its techniques, themes, and characters.

Often, in such discussions, we tend to focus on content rather than technique, and that seems to us a missed opportunity. As we've discussed previously, stories create tension. The moment you release the tension of a story, it's over. That's why a lot of stories never release the tension, never let the reader relax. As you read "the Quilt" and the other two stories in this chapter, be mindful of the ways in which the authors create tension in the character(s) and by extension, in the reader. In "The Quilt," you'll notice that there's a big gap between the tension the young protagonist feels in comparison to Begum Jaan and Rabbo. In what other ways does the author increase the tension and use the naiveite of the protagonist to heighten this tension? What about Chughtai's choice to make this a retrospective story, told by an older narrator, ostensibly many years distant from the events she's recounting? What are the advantages and/or disadvantages of choosing this type of narration? Look through the story and note when and why the older narrator intrudes with an observation. Why has Chughtai chosen these moments to intrude on her younger protagonist? Also, note that while this story is told as a kind of memoir, it's fiction.

Let's take a look at it now.

1 "The Quilt"

by Ismat Chughtai

Translated from Urdu by Gopika Jadeja

Ismat Chughtai (August 21, 1915–October 24, 1991) was an Indian Urdu novelist, short story writer, and filmmaker. Beginning in the 1930s, she wrote extensively on themes including female sexuality, class conflict, and middle-class morality. One of her most enduring works remains the short story, *Lihaaf (The Quilt)*.

When I cover myself with a quilt in the winter, its shadow on the wall looks like an elephant swaying. My mind awakens to the veiled past, thoughts running through my head.

Forgive me, for I am not going to tell you a romantic tale about my quilt. Nor can I attach any idea of romance to the quilt. I think a blanket may be more comfortable than a quilt but its shadow is not as terrifying as that of a quilt, when it wobbles on the wall. This is a story about the time when I was a little girl, spending my days fighting with my brothers and their friends. Sometimes I wonder why I was so aggressive! At that age when my sisters were busy gathering admirers, I would fight, shoes flying, with all the children in our family, and others besides.

This is why when Amma went to Agra she left me with a dear friend, who was like a sister to her. She knew that there was no one there I could get into a fight with, not even a mouse. This was my punishment. So Amma left me with Begum Jaan. The same Begum Jaan whose quilt has been etched in my memory like the brand of a flaming iron. Begum Jaan's poor parents had given her away in marriage to the Nawab because he was said to be virtuous, if mature in years. No one had seen prostitutes or loose women going to his house. A haji himself, he had also helped others go on Haj.

But the Nawab had a very strange obsession. Some people have a passion for breeding pigeons or quail fighting. Some enjoy watching cockfights. But the Nawab was dead against such frivolous sports. Students frequented his house. Young, fair, slim-waisted boys whose upkeep the Nawab paid.

He married Begum Jaan, brought her to the house with all its possessions, and forgot her. The poor fragile little Begum wasted away in her loneliness. Who knows where her life begins? At the moment when she made the mistake of being born, or when she married the Nawab and began to spend her days lying on a bed? Or perhaps it was when delicacies began to stream from the kitchen to the drawing room and through the chinks in the screen she caught glimpses of the slender-waisted young men with shapely calves dressed in sheer kurtas, sending her into raging fits of jealousy.

Or did it begin when she was tired of the praying and seeking of blessings, of the futility of charms, amulets and nightlong vigils? But how do you melt a heart of stone? The Nawab remained unmoved. Heart broken and desperate Begum Jaan turned to books for succour. Here too she found no relief. Reading romantic novels and sentimental verse pulled her deeper into depression. She could not sleep. Her longing turned slowly into indolence.

She lost all interest in clothes and jewelry. One dresses to impress. But neither could the Nawab take his gaze off the boys in gossamer kurtas to look at the Begum, nor did he allow her to leave the house. From the time Begum Jaan arrived as a bride, relatives would visit and stay for months at a time. But Begum Jaan remained imprisoned.

Watching the relatives angered her even more. They enjoyed themselves, ate ghee and had warm clothes made—all at the expense of the Nawab—while the Begum remained cold and stiff in the winter night despite the fluffy new cotton in her quilt. Each time she turned in her bed, the quilt made new faces, casting shadows on the wall. Not one of the shadows inspired any hope for life. It seemed like Begam Jaan was not destined to live a good life, yet she began to live and live to the fullest!

Rabbo was the one who held her as she fell down the abyss. Soon her withered body filled out. Her cheeks began to glow and she blossomed. A unique and mysterious oil massage made the Begum come alive. No, you won't find the recipe for that oil even in the best of magazines.

When I saw Begum Jaan for the first time she must have been about forty. How magnificent she looked reclining on the daybed, her back resting against Rabbo who sat massaging her waist. A pair of purple pashmina shawls covered her feet. She looked like a maharani! I loved her face. I was so fascinated; I could sit by her for hours just looking at her. She was fair, without a trace of red on her skin. Her ink dark hair was always well oiled and combed. I had never seen a strand out of place. Her eyes were black. Her eyebrows shaped like drawn bows made her eyes look intense. She had heavy drooping eyelids and thick, dense eye lashes. However, the most striking feature on her face was her lips. They were always painted red. There was a trace of a moustache over her lips and long hair over her temples. Sometimes even as you watched, her face took on a strange look, like that of a young boy.

The skin on the rest of Begum Jaan's body was also white and taut, as if it had been stitched tightly onto her body. When she stretched her calves to scratch herself, I would steal a look at the glowing skin. Begum Jaan was very tall and well-built with large, smooth hands. She had a shapely waist. Rabbo used to rub her back. I mean for hours on end. As if a back-rub were one of the necessities of life. Maybe even more of than the necessities of life.

Rabbo had no other household duties. She would sit on the bed, massaging Begum Jaan's feet, head or other parts of her body. Whenever you looked Rabbo was massaging some part of Begum Jaan's body. Speaking for myself, if someone were to touch my body so much it would wither and rot away.

Even this everyday massage was not enough. When Begun Jaan took a bath, Rabbo would massage her body with perfumed oils and scrubs for a full two hours before the bath. Just thinking about it made me turn away. After the bath, the doors of her room were closed and *angeethis* (braziers) were lit. Then another round of massages. Only Rabbo attended to Begun Jaan, the other maid servants would mutter under their breath, bringing necessary items at the door.

You see, Begum Jaan suffered from a persistent itch. No amount of oil massages or rubbing of unctions gave her relief from the itch. Doctors and Hakims said there was no disease, her body was unblemished. There may be some infection under the skin, they thought. Rabbo brushed these remarks away saying, "These doctors are crazy! There's nothing the matter with you. Let your enemies be sick! It is just the heat of your blood." She would smile, making eyes at Begum Jaan. Rabbo! She was as dark as Begum Jaan was fair, as red as the other was white. Glowing like heated iron! Her face was pock-marked and her body firm and solid. She had a small, taut paunch and her hands were nimble. She had full lips that were always moist and a strange nauseating smell emanated from her body. How nimble those small, swollen hands were! At times on the waist, then sliding they would go to the hips! From there to the thighs and running to the ankles! When I sat next to Begum Jaan I would follow the movements of Rabbo's hands.

Summer or winter, Begum Jaan wore muslin kurtas of Hyderabadi Jaali Karga[1]; white as foam kurtas paired with brightly coloured pajamas. Even when it was hot and the fan was on, she covered herself with a light shawl. Begum Jaan loved winters. I also enjoyed being in her house in the winter. She did not move around much. Lying on the rug, she would munch on dry fruits as Rabbo rubbed her back. All the other maid servants were jealous of Rabbo. That witch ate, sat and—o god!—slept with the Begum! I discovered later that Rabbo and Begun Jaan were a topic of juicy gossip during celebrations and gatherings. Any mention of their names led to peals of laughter. What tales people told at their expense! But Begum Jaan was oblivious. Her existence revolved around herself and her itch.

As I said, I was little at the time and quite enamoured with Begum Jaan. She was also fond of me. Amma went to Agra, leaving me with Begum Jaan. She knew that alone at home with my brothers, I would fight with them. This arrangement pleased me. Begum Jaan was also happy. After all, she was Amma's dearest friend!

The question arose—where was I to sleep? Of course, in Begum Jaan's room. A small bed was placed next to her bed for me. We talked till ten or eleven in the night and played chance. Then I went to my bed to sleep. Till I fell asleep, I saw Rabbo sitting in the same position rubbing Begum Jaan's back. "Dirty woman," I thought. Suddenly, I woke up in the middle of the night, strangely frightened. It was pitch dark. And in the darkness, Begum Jaan's quilt shook as if there were an elephant trapped inside.

"Begum Jaan!" I said, scared. The elephant stopped moving and the quilt lay flat.

"What is it? Go to sleep," Begum Jaan's voice seemed to say from somewhere.

"I am scared," I squeaked, mouse-like.

"Go to sleep," she said, "What is there to be afraid of? Recite the Ayat-ul-kursi."

"Accha."

Quickly, I began to recite the Ayat-ul-kursi. But each time I got stuck at "Ya'lamu ma bian," even though at the time I knew the ayat by heart.

"Can I come to you, Begam Jaan?"

"No beti, sleep," she said firmly.

Then I heard the sound of two people whispering. "Oh no! Who else was there in the room?" I wondered, frightened even more.

"Begum Jaan, what if it is a thief or robber?"

"Sleep, beta. What thief?" This was Rabbo's voice.

I buried my head in my quilt and slept.

When I woke up, I had completely forgotten the frightening spectacle of the night before. I have always been superstitious—to be frightened at night, to wake up and run out of bed, to mutter in my sleep were common occurrences in my childhood. Everyone said I was under the influence of some evil spirit. So, by morning I had no recollection of what came to pass. The quilt looked completely innocent in the morning. The next night when my eyes opened, I could hear Begum Jaan and Rabbo arguing quietly in bed. I

---

[1] A short top with a keyhole neck opening traditionally made of white muslin. The kurta may be covered with net (jaali), the combination called *jaali karga*. It is worn both by men and women.

could not hear what they were saying, but I heard Rabbo crying convulsively. Then there were the slurping sounds, like a saucer being licked. Oh! Scared, I went back to sleep.

One day Rabbo had gone to meet her son, a belligerent young man. Begum Jaan had done much for him. She helped him start a store, found him a job in the village, but he refused to consider his responsibilities. He even stayed with the Nawab Saheb for some time, receiving new clothes and gifts. But he ran away such that he did not come to Nawab Saheb's house even to see his mother. So Rabbo went to a relative's place to meet him. Begum Jaan was loath to let her go, but Rabbo was also helpless in this situation. She went anyway.

Begum Jaan was restless all day. She complained of aches in all her joints, but she could not bear anyone touching her. She did not eat and lay listless all day.

"Shall I rub your back, Begum Jaan," I asked as I enthusiastically shuffled a deck of cards. She looked at me keenly.

"Shall I? Really?"

I set the cards down and rubbed her back for some time as Begum Jaan lay there quietly.

Rabbo was to return the next day, but she did not make an appearance. Begum Jaan grew increasingly irritable. She drank tea all day and developed a headache.

Again, I began rubbing her back—smooth as the top of a table. I rubbed gently, happy to be of service to her.

"Rub harder. Open the straps," Begum Jaan said, "Here . . . below the shoulder . . . yes . . . that's good." She took deep breaths, expressing her pleasure.

"And there . . ." she said. She could have reached the spot herself, but she wanted me to rub it for her. I felt so proud then! "Here . . . hey . . . you are tickling me!" she laughed. I was talking as I rubbed.

"I will send you to the bazaar tomorrow. What do you want? A doll that sleeps and wakes up?"

"No, Begum Jaan, I don't buy dolls. Am I still a child?"

"So, you are an old woman then?" she laughed. "If you don't want a doll, I will get you a babua, a real baby. You can dress it up. I will give you lots of clothes. You hear," she said, rolling over.

"Accha," I responded.

"Here . . ." she took my hand and placed it where she was itching. She would move my hand to wherever it was itching. And I, lost in thoughts of a babua, kept rubbing mechanically as she continued talking.

"Listen, you need some more frocks. I will ask the tailor tomorrow to make some new ones. Your Amma left some material."

"I don't want any made from that red material. It looks cheap." I continued to speak without thinking where my hands went. Begum Jaan lay still. "Arrey!" I exclaimed in surprise and jerked my hand away.

"Hey! Watch where you are rubbing! You crushed my ribs." She smiled mischievously and I was embarrassed.

"Come and lie down next to me." She made me lie down, my head on her arm. "You are so skinny! Your ribs are showing," she said and began to count my ribs.

"Umm," I protested.

"What? You think I will eat you up? Your sweater is too tight . . . you aren't even wearing a warm vest." Uncomfortable, I wriggled.

"How many ribs do we have?" she asked, changing the topic.

"Nine on one side and ten on the other," I said, relying on my memory of the hygiene class in school. Absurd.

"Move your hand . . . yes, one . . . two . . . three . . ."

I felt like running away . . . but she held me tightly. "Uumm," I wriggled out of her grasp. She burst into laughter.

Even today, when I remember her face as it looked then, I feel uncomfortable. Her heavy eyelids drooped. There was a dark shadow on her upper lip. In spite of the cold, beads of sweat glistened on her lips and nose. Her hands cold, but soft—as if their skin had peeled off. She had removed her shawl and her body shone like a ball of white dough through her sheer kurta. Her heavy gold jadau buttons hung towards the side of her collar. Evening had fallen and the shadows in the room deepened. I was overwhelmed by a strange, unnamed fear. Begum Jaan looked at me with her dark eyes. My heart was crying. She was pressing me like a clay toy. Her warm body made me panic. But she was as if possessed. My mind was so gripped with fear, I could neither scream nor cry.

After a while, she lay down, exhausted. Her face pale and dull, she was taking deep breaths. I thought she was dying, and ran out of the room.

Thankfully, Rabbo returned that night. Still scared, I covered myself with the quilt and went to sleep. I lay there for hours, but could not fall asleep.

For some reason, Amma had not returned from Agra yet. I was so scared of Begum Jaan, I would sit all day with the servants. I was terrified of stepping into her room, yet what could I tell anybody? That I was afraid of Begum Jaan who was so fond of me . . .?

That day, there was another argument between Rabbo and Begum Jaan. I feared any discord between them. Call it my misfortune, or whatever else, because it drew Begum Jaan's attention to me. She saw that I was wandering outside in the cold and could catch pneumonia.

"Girl, will you bring shame to me? How would I answer for it if something happened to you?"

She made me sit next to her and washed her hands and face in the basin. The tea was kept on a table nearby.

"Make some tea, please, and give me a cup too," she said wiping her face with a towel. "I will change my clothes while you make tea." She was changing her clothes, and I was drinking tea. If she sent for me when having a massage, I would keep my face turned away and run away as soon as I could. Now as she was changing her clothes, I sat squirming. I kept my face turned away and sipped my tea.

"Oh Amma," I thought to myself, "is this the punishment I deserve for fighting with my brothers?"

Amma never approved of my playing with boys. Some asked, are boys the tigers or cheetahs that they will swallow her daughter? And who are these boys? Her brothers and their puny little friends! But Amma was convinced that women should be segregated, protected with seven layers of locks. And here, I was more terrified of Begum Jaan than all the goondas in the world. If I could, I would have run out into the street, and not stayed a moment longer. But I was helpless. I stayed there despite myself.

Begum Jaan had changed and was made up. Laden with ornaments and doused in the warm, heavy scents of attar she seemed even more passionate. She began to shower me with her affection.

"I want to go home," I said in reply to all her suggestions and started to cry.

"Come to me. I will take you to the bazaar . . . listen."

I dug my heels in. "I want to go home," I repeated to all her offers for new toys and sweets. "I want to go home," the refrain continued.

"There your brothers will hit you, you little witch," she said slapping me affectionately.

"Well, let them!" I thought to myself and sat stiff and unmoved.

"Raw mangoes are sour, Begum Jaan," Rabbo gave her opinion from the sidelines, hurt and jealous.

And then Begum Jaan had a fit. The gold necklace she had offered me a little while ago lay in pieces on the floor, her fine muslin dupatta was in shreds. And the parting in her hair, which was always flawless, was lost under a tangled mess.

"Oh! Oh! Oh! Oh!" She screamed as her body convulsed. I ran out.

Begum Jaan finally came to her senses after many ministrations. When I tiptoed to the room to sleep and peeked in, I saw Rabbo nestled against Begum Jaan's waist, rubbing her body.

"Take your shoes off," Rabbo said, rubbing Begum Jaan's side. Mouse-like, I slipped under my quilt.

Srrr ssrrrr fftttt khch. More peculiar noises.

In the dark, Begum Jaan's quilt was swaying again like an elephant.

"Allah! Ah!" I moaned.

Under the quilt the elephant flipped and sat down. I was also quiet. The elephant rolled and swayed again. Every cell in my body shivered. That night I had resolved to gather my courage and flip on the bedside light. The elephant flopped around, as if trying to kneel down. Chapad chapad. That slurping sound again, as if someone were smacking their lips, enjoying a delicious chutney. Now I understood! Begum Jaan had not eaten anything all day. And Rabbo was a glutton! She must be gorging on some good food! I flared my nostrils and sniffed the air. I could smell only attar, sandalwood and the warm scent of henna. Nothing else.

The quilt began swinging again. I tried very hard to lie still and quiet, but the quilt began to make such strange shapes that I was shaken. It seemed as if a huge toad were croaking and inflating itself, ready to spring, and now would leap on me!

"Aa . . . no . . . Amma!" I picked up my courage and cried out, but no one paid any attention. The quilt crept into my mind and there it began to grow. Still scared, I put my feet down on the other side of the bed and groped for the light switch. The elephant somersaulted under the quilt and lay flat. As it somersaulted, a corner of the quilt rose by a foot—

"Allah!" I gasped as I dived back into my bed.

The year 1942 was a year of great upheaval, not only the Second World War but the Indian nation asserting itself and striving to assert its independence from Great Britain. Deepika

Marya, writing in the *South Asian Review*, argues that this is a story of agency. In such a tumultuous time, it represented not only something shocking sexually to many conservative readers, but a political shock too in its rejection and resistance to the Patriarchy. Chughtai's grandniece, Dr. Zoovia Hamiduddin, likewise a story writer, thinks the story is read too narrowly if it's only considered in a sexual context and not in terms of its larger cultural and historical context. She sees it as a story about the effects of Patriarchy AND Colonialism on the lives of these women. Both women are trapped in a prison-like set of colonial and sexist structures that make their encounter one of "prison sex." To read the story only as a pioneering piece of LGBTQ literature is to misread it, as she suggests the filmmakers who adapted the story to the screen for the 2018 feature *Lihaaf: The Quilt* have done. Chughtai herself, who wrote the story as a twenty-something-year-old, came to dislike the story for all the trouble it gave her and because she thought it would be the only thing she'd be remembered for. "I wish I had never written it," she wrote. "Nobody understood it anyway." Still, as we know, literature can sometimes effect social change. "The Quilt" was based on a real story about a Begum and her masseuse that Chughtai had heard. Several years after the story was published, the person on whom it was based approached her. Chughtai was worried about the woman's reaction, but the former Begum thanked Chughtai for writing the story—it had given her the courage she needed to divorce her husband.

Let's look at another story of agency and rebellion, *Video* by Meera Nair. The twists in this story might seem particularly troubling to some, but again let's look at it as an examination of agency in a marriage between a man and a woman in a traditional society. Even the most shocking stories can be full of nuance and irony. Again, the content might be shocking, but let's focus on the way the story is told and how the author reveals the narrative through the obsession/compulsion of the point of view of the character, Naseer. It's his desire that drives the story, at least halfway through it. The author turns the story upside down after Naseer fulfills his compulsion, and then it's Rasheeda who takes the reins of the narrative, though it's still from Naseer's point of view. Through the actions of the two partner/adversaries, the story becomes a tug of war of power and the different ways in which power is enacted.

Let's read it now.

2 "Video"

by Meera Nair (USA)

Meera Nair's debut collection, *Video* (Pantheon, 2002), won the Asian-American Literary Award and was a *Washington Post* Best Book of the Year. Her stories, articles, and essays have appeared in the *New York Times Magazine*, in anthologies, and on National Public Radio's Selected Shorts, among other places.

> Naseer lay beside his wife in the dark and wished he had never seen that video. He blamed it for all the trouble they had been having lately. He knew Rasheeda was angrier than she had ever been in all their years of marriage. Ever since he first asked her the question, she had flung her silence at him. But that was only during the day, in front of the rest of the family. At night, after the children were asleep, she hadn't been so quiet.

Now, with his blood cooling, he thought of mollifying her as he had done for many nights lately, and making her understand with clear, logical, unemotional explanations why he needed her to do this for him. She was his wife, for God's sake. He had rights, didn't he?

"Rasheeda! Listen—" he began.

"Fifteen years we've been married and now you want me to do this—this thing!" His wife sat up abruptly, reached for her nightgown, and thrust her head into it.

Oh God, here she goes again.

"Allah, please put some sense into this man. Is this a good thing to ask your wife to do? I've had three of his children and now he asks me for this . . ." Her voice was muffled but the aggrieved tone came through loud and clear.

She acts as if she has a Star TV channel blasting directly into Allah's living room. As if He's just waiting there, eager to listen to Madam Rasheeda. Naseer knew the situation was serious, but he couldn't help smiling in the dark.

"Allah, he has gone mad. His body's noise is louder than any voice of reason," Rasheeda continued.

Why does she talk so loud? Naseer twisted his head around to make sure the door to the children's bedroom was closed. She will probably wake the children and his brothers and their wives and his mother the way she's carrying on. Surely his brothers didn't have troubles like his: a recalcitrant wife who sat up in bed at night and belligerently talked to her God.

He looked at her now as she sat marooned in the middle of the bed. The light from the streetlamp filtered through the cotton curtains, turning her broad back pale blue. It was hot and still and Naseer shivered involuntarily as the sweat on his legs dried.

A few nights ago, he had even cited the teachings of the mullahs exhorting Muslim wives to listen to their husbands in all things. But then she was hardly the sort to be frightened by the mullahs, not with her direct line to Allah.

"But Allah, I'll tell you one thing. Never shall I submit to this man's whims. I'll do my duty as a wife, but where is it written that I have to do such things?" Rasheeda's monologue showed no signs of flagging.

That last bit was for his benefit, not Allah's, thought Naseer as he reached for his pajamas at the foot of the bed. And what was this about doing her duty as a wife? When she was in bed with him, she didn't just lie there hating it like some other women he had heard about. He should know. She liked the stroking and rubbing all right. Not that there had been too much of that lately. Take tonight. He hadn't cared to slip his hand down her body and finish her off. He'd asked her right in the middle of it all, gasping the question at her, shameless in his need. But once again she said no, shaking her head from side to side, her eyes tightly closed. So he had ended it quickly and not bothered with her at all. But it wasn't right, and he didn't like it. Naseer shifted uncomfortably on the far side of the bed. He liked his fingers being swallowed up in her slopes and ridges and bumps, in that hidden, miniature landscape all her own. He liked having her face turned up at him, her eyes gone far away to the place where her feeling was building. He liked her giggling, embarrassed because she thrashed about so much. She'd always giggled, ever since the first time, a few months after their wedding when he had finally stumbled on how to pull her across the threshold of fear and nervousness to pleasure.

Her complaints to Allah done at last, Rasheeda lay down, taking care to not brush against him in the muggy dark. Everything had been fine right until the moment he sat down on the black rattan chair in Khaleel's shadowed living room and the video player was turned on.

Naseer had gone over to his cousin Khaleel's place to ask his opinion about a new van he wanted to buy. He'd use it to deliver hardware supplies from his store to customers who phoned in their orders. One had to move with the times. Khaleel had his own auto repair shop and could pick out a bad vehicle from a good one by merely listening to the sound of its engine, like a doctor to a patient's chest. Nusrat, his second brother's wife, had called loudly after him from the kitchen window as he opened the gate and stepped out into the street. "It's kababs tonight, so don't be late. You know how Rasheeda won't eat without you."

Adnan, thin and gangly, with Rasheeda's fine, flyaway hair, was playing cricket in the street in front of the house. After a quick sideways glance confirming that his father had stopped to watch him, he gazed seriously at the ball. Old Janaki Ram was sitting on his stoop in his striped undershorts, customary teacup in hand.

"Your boy is hitting four after four today," he said. Naseer smiled and rubbed at his beard to hide his pride.

A few minutes into Adnan's turn at the wicket, Naseer started down the street and Adnan lifted his hand off the bat for a second in farewell. Naseer fought an impulse to tell Adnan to go home before it got too dark. He was fourteen and Naseer didn't want to embarrass him in front of his friends.

The street barely managed to squeeze between the buildings that lined its length. The houses scrunched up against each other and in the shadows of the late evening they seemed to draw closer together, huddling over the street like gossipy old women. The houses around here had hardly changed from when his father's father had first moved in here. Naseer looked up affectionately at the lacy wooden balconies, their curlicued railings still overhung with the saris housewives had forgotten to take inside from the sun. As he walked he greeted the men resting from the heat on the porches, old men who, with the memories of his father still fresh in them, expected him to stop and inquire respectfully about the gout or kidney stones or unemployed son they suffered from.

Here and there transistor radios played softly, the tinny voice of Lata Mangeshkar singing a song about being stricken sleepless by love. One stanza flowed into another, accompanying him from porch to porch all the way down until he turned the corner onto Khaleel's street.

Here the houses around him were newer. Bright white-washed walls shouldered up against worn stone flared and dimmed in the light of passing cars. A shiny black Fiat jutted out of a gate, taking up street space. Khaleel's place was the last one, just before the street curved away at an angle.

When Naseer got to the door the house was dark, yet he could see the TV's staccato flicker in the living room through the opaque windowpane. At his knock the TV was switched off. Khaleel took his time to answer the door.

"Oh! It's you. I thought it was Baba come back from Madras early," Khaleel said, wiping his palm down the front of his shirt.

Khaleel's father had a twenty-year-old property dispute that came up for a hearing every few years and took him away from home. The old man's tenacity had become a joke in the family. "I rented a VCR for the day—thought I'd watch some films.

You know how Baba is so strict and all, not allowing us to do anything." Khaleel moved aside to let Naseer in.

"All the women kissing men in broad daylight in front of the children, this TV sheevee will destroy the country yet . . ." Naseer mimicked his uncle's disgruntled old man's voice.

Khaleel didn't laugh as he usually did.

Looking at his cousin now, Naseer thought, as he had many times before, how strange it was that all the men in his family were short and wiry and bearded.

"So what're you watching? Anything with Amitabh in it?" Naseer loved the actor. When *Sholay* had been released, he had seen it five times.

"No," Khaleel said. "Come on in and see for yourself." When Khaleel switched on the VCR, there were two foreigners on the screen—a woman and a man. The man lay on the bed and the woman knelt between his legs. White skin, golden hair, smooth nakedness. She bent down. Then she opened her mouth over him. After one frozen minute of in-credulity, everything inside Naseer contracted. He put his hands over his stomach as if to contain the faint tremors he felt starting. He watched the woman, her movements sometimes languid, sometimes frenzied, her cheeks working. It was unbelievable that any woman would admit a man inside her face, to touch her tongue and her teeth and the inside of her cheeks. The two of them seemed bound together in some extreme ecstasy, the man watching the woman looking at him. They took a long time to finish. Watching the man as he arched on the bed, Naseer felt as if he was about to lose control and slide off the chair trembling and moaning—right there in Khaleel's mother's living room with its bright blue carpet and showcase filled with the ceramic dogs her daughter had sent from Dubai. Naseer got up abruptly and mumbled something to Khaleel about coming back another time. Moving toward the door, Naseer saw himself reflected indistinctly on the TV screen, his shadowy form moving closer as he neared the set. Khaleel barely acknowledged his departure, and his eyes, glittering in the blue light, remained riveted on the screen.

Outside, Naseer leaned against the wall and breathed deeply. He could feel the rough stubble of its surface pressing against his shoulder blades and back through the thin muslin of his kurta. The wall was uncomfortably warm.

He couldn't bring himself to walk just yet, not with this hot weight in him, as if everything inside had descended to settle around his lower stomach and thighs. It was almost pain but not quite, he thought, shocked at the great scrabbling need that stretched down his middle. There had been a time when he was twenty-three and just married to Rasheeda when he could go four times a night. The greediness of a recent virgin—that's what it had been. The need had been a constant unfulfilled thrum in him. Now here it was again, as if someone had plucked hard at a taut string that ran from his head down to his toes.

When he finally pushed himself away from the wall and started walking home, he felt grateful that the old men on the stoops had gone inside to their dinners. He had heard the boys who hung around the college cafeteria snicker about things like this a long time ago, but it had always remained some mythic thing that occurred elsewhere, not in a home, not on an ordinary bed.

Back at home he found Rasheeda in the bedroom getting fresh nappies for the baby.

"Oof, oh! Husband! Stop it! Everybody's waiting for their dinner downstairs and you're doing nonsense things," she laughed, brushing him aside, a little surprised at his sudden ardor. Then she hurried away, the cloth triangles swinging from her hands.

He stood in the middle of the bedroom, reluctant to go down and face the clattering crockery and noisy children in the dining room. What if he rented a VCR and the film himself and got Rasheeda to watch it with him? No. It was impossible—the only TV they owned was in the living room and his mother watched *Understanding the Koran* on it in the afternoons, her silver head nodding sleepily, her fingers slipping now and then off her prayer beads.

At dinner Rasheeda caught him looking at her as she returned from the kitchen with a refill of the kabobs and smiled absently in his direction. The oil from the biryani had left her lips slick and shiny. The older children, who had been fed earlier and sent into the living room, fought for control over the TV. Today was Wednesday and that meant *Baywatch*. Naseer knew his brothers would join the kids to watch the serial after dinner.

"Bhai-jaan must have snacked at Khaleel's—he's hardly eating anything at all," Nusrat announced archly. Everyone turned to look at Naseer and he had to nod yes and scramble to name a snack. He got up hurriedly from the table. Farhana stumbled up behind him and stood clutching desperately at his legs for an instant before plopping down onto her behind. She drew breath to wail. He picked her up and went into the living room to order his sons up to bed—he didn't want them watching half-naked women cavort on the beach.

The children bribed and nagged into going to bed and alone with his wife at last, Naseer could feel Rasheeda's pleased astonishment at his impatience.

"Wait, wait, let me turn off the light," she said, reaching for the lamp.

"No. Wait," he said. He put his hands on her hips and pulled her down with him on their bed. Then he pushed himself away from her and took a deep breath. "I saw this video at Khaleel's"; he began and stopped. He wanted to say the words carefully, lucidly, even though whole sentences and phrases had jostled in his head all through dinner and the interminable conversation with his brothers afterward. "It was foreign and they were, you know, doing it." He felt embarrassed but determined. This had to be said.

"Allah! Cheee! Toba toba, so *this* is what you were doing," Rasheeda looked at him, her mouth contracting in disgust.

"Listen, I have never seen anything like this . . ." He pressed on. He told her about the video, about the woman and what she had done for the man. Just saying the words excited him. He felt relieved. Now she knew too. The knowledge of this disturbing, fascinating new thing was no longer in his head alone.

Rasheeda moved away and watched him gravely, warily, as he struggled on, trying to explain the moment, the things he'd felt.

In the end, his telling ragged at the edges, he blurted out what he wanted. He knew, even as he stumbled over the words "me" and "mouth," that they came out all wrong, as if they were not meant to be said aloud between them there in their bedroom of fifteen years.

Rasheeda's face contorted in shock and she jumped off the bed as if the sheets were on fire. After a first strangled sound of surprise she stood silent.

"No." She said it quietly. Just that one word, thrown down firmly in front of him without any explanation attached. "No," she said again as she lay down heavily and turned her back to him, her nightdress rustling in the dark. Then, after a long silence in which he willed himself to calmness and was about to fall asleep—"Never."

From then on it had been the same story—every night a repetition of tonight. Her "no" was all-encompassing, leaving him without space to maneuver or argue. All she gave him was that word, and it stood steadfast against all his attempts to wear it down, as unassailable as a mountain made of glass.

Yet every day in his head the blonde woman's mouth stretched itself wide and pink over him and would not let him rest.

Sitting behind his counter in the hardware store, Naseer looked at the men who came in asking for hinges and light fixtures and wondered if he was the only man in the world who had spent all these years so pathetically ignorant of this pleasure. Surely all sophisticated men enjoyed it. It was his father's fault for forcing him to marry at twenty-three.

Naseer had wanted other things. Nodding over his college books through the long, humid nights, he had imagined himself, standing bareheaded under a pitiless blue sky, building the dam that would put sweet water in the earthen pots of the villagers and green their fields. Just like Dilip Kumar in the movie *Naya Daur*. But he was the eldest son, ordained to carry on the family business, and Naseer couldn't bring himself to break his father's heart. So, instead of Naseer, his brothers had become engineers. They were the ones who sat in high-ceilinged government offices, dusty with stacks of forgotten files, and approved plans to build other buildings exactly like the ones they worked in. Now, with his father gone, they accorded him the respect they would have given his father. It made him more distant than ever from them.

Naseer told himself he was deeply unhappy. The craving wouldn't let him be and he felt betrayed by this discontent. He had struggled to be pleased with his lot over the years. Even when he was forced to take on the business, he had taught himself to find satisfaction in the idea of some unknown house, somewhere in the city, growing older, held together by his hinges and latches and nails, the doorknobs pushed open day after day by children and the children's children, the curtains pulled back on his curtain rings. There was a kind of immortality in it. Now Rasheeda had spoiled it all. Why couldn't she behave as wives should?

Rasheeda started sending his breakfast out of the kitchen with Aliyeh, the youngest sister-in-law, who kept her sari-covered head bowed respectfully as she quickly set his omelet down on the table, poured his tea, and scuttled back into the kitchen. As if he was a guest who had overstayed his welcome, thought Naseer.

Ever since his mother had ceremoniously handed over the keys to her after Siddiq was born, Rasheeda had run the household. She had slid expertly into the role of matriarch, although she'd been barely thirty-one, as if she had practiced running a household of seven adults, five children, and three maids secretly over the years.

Nowadays, as she walked past him pretending to be busy with the children, he resented that she could always find things to do in the confused bustle of communal living. With his brothers, their wives, or the children always around, he could never get her alone. At night, he was usually asleep by the time she finished ironing school uniforms or discussing tomorrow's menu or whatever it was she did down there to delay coming upstairs.

Some nights he stayed awake, fighting sleep. But the more he tried to persuade her, the more adamantly she condemned this ungodly practice, vociferously calling upon Allah to intervene. Naseer couldn't stop asking either, couldn't just let it be. It's like an unending game, he thought. Only whatever move he made Rasheeda was already there, anticipating him, ready with her defense.

At mealtimes, Naseer imagined he could feel the eyes of the other women on him. Could Rasheeda have dared tell them about what was going on between them? She wouldn't, would she? Violate the quiet yellow warmth of their bed, throw it open for all to peer and comment? His thoughts brought on a great, bursting pressure in his chest.

Yet in the evenings he couldn't wait to get back home. It was a relief just to have Rasheeda somewhere nearby where he could at least watch her face. And her mouth.

When his parents had found him Rasheeda, he had said yes without a demur. It was his mother who had asked the marriage broker, "Do we really want such a highly educated daughter-in-law?" She had been uneasy with the fact that Rasheeda had passed high school. But his father had surprised him by insisting on the match.

Naseer saw Rasheeda on the evening of their wedding only after the Kazi, his interminable mumbling incantations finally done, decreed he could see the bride.

He had gone into the zenana, the women's hall, where she sat surrounded by her relatives and friends, the women whispering and shimmering around him in their yellow and green silks. One of Rasheeda's oldest aunts held a long-handled mirror under her bowed head, carefully angling it inside her dupatta so that he would see only her face and nothing else. He never forgot that first glimpse of her face framed by the veil, the mirror filled suddenly with large sloping eyes and pale pink mouth. Clumsy as he bent over to peer at the mirror, he had stepped on her skirt, and she had put her hand out quickly to tug the material away. Her hand had lain there for an instant, white and forlorn, before it retreated under her heavy, embroidered shawl. A faint, damp mark was left behind on the rose silk where she had touched it, and he was overwhelmed by a sudden compassion. He had wanted to tell her then not to worry—everything would be all right.

Sometime during the all-important first night, Naseer asked her to stand next to him and was surprised to discover that he was only half an inch taller than she was. In spite of her nervousness, she had laughed. The rest had come slowly, in awkward fits and starts. He was gentle with her and she patient with him. Just as he mapped her body, he cataloged her peculiarities—the faint, fair down on her legs, the way her arm pressed the pillow to her face in the morning, shutting out the day for a few minutes more.

Then the children arrived. First Adnan, then Siddiq, and the last one, Farhana, a wriggling, big-bottomed baby girl. Over the years they fit into each other. Now when he reached for her at night it was like driving down the road to the store. He knew when to take the curve, which pothole to avoid, and where to stop. He hadn't wanted much more. Until the woman in the video opened her glistening mouth.

It was the twelfth of June and Rasheeda's birthday. It was time they solved this impasse, he decided. He called in the afternoon and told her he had tickets to the latest Aamir Khan movie.

"How many?" she asked, her voice unsmiling on the telephone.

"Just you and me," he said firmly. On the rare occasions they went out to the movies or a restaurant, all the brothers and their wives would go together, piling into the old green van, everyone teasing Aliyeh, the youngest sister-in-law, forcing her onto her husband's lap.

When he went home to pick Rasheeda up, there were giggles from the kitchen. She sat quietly by him until he finished his tea and samosas. A woman's love can be measured by how many samosas she urges you to eat, he thought. She did not force any upon him this time.

"Good samosas. Okay. Let's go, the movie begins at six thirty," he said, all bluff and hearty, hoping she would play along, at least in front of the sisters-in-law, who looked over at them from time to time.

"Why this sudden good mood? This movie and everything?" Rasheeda didn't smile back.

She must know that he was trying to get back to where they were, before she'd stopped talking to him, he thought.

"Well, it is your birthday, isn't it?" he said. He had bought her a present but didn't want to give it to her in front of the other women. Nusrat would have had something catty to say for sure.

Rasheeda didn't answer, but she didn't argue either, just got dressed quickly and walked out with him, flinging a stream of instructions over her shoulder on what to give each of the children for dinner. On her silk sari, flowers spread over her breasts like purple hands.

The entire family came out, crowding around the gate to see them off. Farhana began to cry.

"Enjoy yourselves," Nusrat smirked. Aliyeh bent down and smoothed Rasheeda's sari over her calves one final time.

"It's not as if we're going away for three years, is it?" Naseer grumbled.

"Shh, it's okay. We don't go out alone together every night," Rasheeda said.

Back from the movie, Naseer stood in front of the mirror in their bedroom and drew Rasheeda to him.

"We still look nice, don't we?" he said. In her high heels, she was slightly taller than he was.

"I like your shorter beard," she said, so he rubbed it against her cheek. His hands stroked her wide hips and pulled her against him.

"I must do something about my weight," Rasheeda said, but he shook his head.

"Imagine if you were thin and bony like that heroine in the movie. I like large portions." He slipped his hands under her breasts and hefted them in the mirror. Rasheeda's hands came up to pull his away, but she was laughing, her face soft and forgiving.

Later, Naseer did all the things she liked: rubbing her back in widening circles, dragging his thumb slowly across her armpit. He took his time, teasing her, starting her up and slowing her down and starting her up again, until she was desperate and insistent against his palm.

Naseer lay awake for two hours after Rasheeda fell asleep. He felt hollow and dissatisfied. The lovemaking between them had been decent. But he couldn't help wondering how much better it might have been if she had lowered her mouth to him, taken him slowly into her mouth. He hadn't brought it up this time because he was afraid she'd stop talking to him again.

Next to him Rasheeda shifted onto her back. A few minutes later she started snoring softly. Naseer smiled. She was always indignant when he told her she snored, as if it were somehow his fault for even bringing it up. He put his hand on her shoulder. A push onto her side always made her stop. Not that she'd know or wake up. His mother liked to say that Rasheeda could sleep through an earthquake. Yet when Farhana was younger, she'd scramble up even when the baby just burped in her sleep. It was amazing how women could switch themselves off and on like that.

Rasheeda smacked loudly in her sleep and her mouth fell open. Watching her, Naseer felt himself become hard even before the thought was fully formed in his head.

He slid off the bed, his heart pounding. He walked around to Rasheeda's side, fumbling with the string of his pyjamas. Her mouth was slack and agape and she did not wake up even when he knelt awkwardly with his knees next to her face. He leaned far over her head and tried to direct his cock safely inside her mouth. His knees were trembling so hard that he had to grip the headboard with his other hand—even then he slid off the edge of the bed a few times. Then he was in. Was he touching the roof of her mouth?

Just then Rasheeda woke up and stared at him looming over her, his crotch in her face. In her shock Rasheeda's lips closed automatically over him. She made a strangled sound. He thought confusedly of pulling out, but he could not. Not then. Afterward, he couldn't remember when he thought she wouldn't mind or how he held her sleep-dazed head still and ignored her struggling. It was all over in seconds anyway. She got up, ran into the bathroom, and didn't come out for a long time.

I could have touched her brain if I'd wanted to, he thought, feeling excited and mellow at the same time. I was so close to where she lives, not somewhere down there far away; I was more inside her than I've ever been. Then he fell asleep even as he was thinking that he would never be able to sleep.

Rasheeda was still in the bathroom when he woke up in the morning. She hadn't come out even when he left for the store, three hours later. When he came back in the evening, Nusrat, who over the years had developed a certain degree of familiarity with him, took it upon herself to have a word with him. Rasheeda had stayed in the bathroom the whole day.

"She refuses to go to a doctor, says there's nothing wrong with her," she said, looking genuinely worried.

Rasheeda went to the bathroom twelve times the next day.

Ten times the third. She did not stop frequenting the bathroom even after a week yet she refused to see a doctor. Naseer, frightened for her life, even brought one to the house. The doctor, a small, skinny man who looked as if he'd received his degree only months ago, stood nervously in their bedroom, clutching his brown leather medicine bag to his crotch.

"I am fine, Doctor-saab, please go away," Rasheeda yelled from the bathroom.

"Get a *peer*. They know about these strange afflictions, this nonstop diarrhea and suchlike things," the doctor stuttered and fled.

Naseer couldn't bring himself to summon any sorcerers with their magic cures into the house. Maybe she would get better on her own, he thought.

But Rasheeda wouldn't stop. She claimed the outside bathroom for herself. It stood next to the small vegetable garden in the backyard and had been abandoned after the new bathrooms with concealed plumbing were built. She gave herself up to its white-tiled interior at regular intervals. Every hour on the hour, like the BBC. Right in the middle of tying bows in Farhana's hair, she would set her comb down and hurry to the bathroom. Halfway to the greengrocer's down the road, she would stop and head back to the house, overcome by her colon.

Yet nothing else seemed to be the matter with her.

Naseer could hear the sisters-in-law talking and laughing in the kitchen as he ate his breakfast alone. "The whole day she's in the bathroom, but she doesn't look sick or lose weight," they would say. "It is sort of unnatural, don't you think?"

He had to admit it was true. Rasheeda's plump white arms and open luminous face still looked as desirable as ever as she pushed past him, hurrying toward the bathroom.

Since Rasheeda didn't get any sicker, the household adapted quickly, resilient as always. This peculiar new bump was absorbed quickly and ironed flat into its texture. Rasheeda's vigils in the bathroom soon ceased to be an event and became part of her Rasheedaness, protected from comment by their very familiarity and repetitiveness. Even the children tired of shouting "She went ten times today" at him the minute he returned from work. His brothers didn't offer their irritating commiseration anymore.

The children came home from school and went straight to the outdoor bathroom, confident of finding Rasheeda there. They stood outside the door to talk to her.

"Gunjan stole my orange. I hate him," Siddiq would say. He hoarded complaints like sweets.

"The math teacher is horrible. You come and tell the principal that he shouldn't give us so much homework." Farida, Nusrat's little princess, could appeal only to Rasheeda, since her mother didn't believe in coddling children.

"I need ten rupees to pay the PT fees tomorrow." Even Adnan, his initial embarrassment forgotten, leaned against the outer wall of the bathroom and held shouted conversations with her.

"Never mind, I'll give you another orange tomorrow . . . Don't talk about your teacher like that. Have you no respect . . . Adi ask your father for the money." She'd answer each of them, serene and inviolate, firmly embedded in their world.

Gradually, as the days became weeks, even the vegetable sellers and fishmongers pushed their handcarts to the back gate near the bathroom and Rasheeda. They would lean over the gate and make their appeals.

"Fresh tomatoes, four rupees, Bibiji. Ekdum fresh!" the vegetable wallah would shout.

"Three is quite enough," Rasheeda would bargain with zest, and they'd give in easily, bemused by this new method of commerce.

"Only for you, Bibiji, don't tell anyone else, only for you three rupees." The transaction concluded, the vegetable wallah or fish wallah would go up to the kitchen and get the payment from Aliyeh or Nusrat.

For a time there was the problem of the keys. As the eldest daughter-in-law, only Rasheeda had the honor of carrying the keys to the pantry and the cupboards. Since the doors were kept carefully locked against the pilfering servants, Aliyeh and Nusrat had to trek down to the bathroom and Rasheeda every time they needed supplies.

One day Naseer saw Nusrat standing outside the bathroom door, tapping her foot impatiently. When she saw him, she muttered under her breath. The next morning Naseer sent a carpenter he knew to cut a small door in the center of the larger one. Rasheeda, temporarily out of the bathroom, said nothing, but she came out from the kitchen to watch him as he planed the sides of the small square of wood and attached hinges and a latch. She offered him tea when he was done, the carpenter reported when Naseer asked him, his voice as studiously casual as Naseer's. Naseer almost started to say that now all Rasheeda had to do was pass the key through the hinged door to whoever came knocking, but he caught himself in time. No need to add to the gossip that was surely circulating already. That evening Rasheeda brought Naseer his tea and set it on the table before him silently. He raised his head eagerly but she walked away before he could say a word.

One Sunday afternoon, when Rasheeda was taking her siesta, Naseer walked around the vegetable garden and, after making sure no one was watching, peered into the bathroom. It was hot inside the dingy room, with a thick, spongy heat that reflected down from the tin roof. On the ledge beside the commode were seashells, a bottle of glue and some pasteboard, someone's half-finished math homework, a recipe in Urdu, and the small transistor radio he had given her. She's destroying our marriage because she wants to listen to Hindi songs in the toilet, he thought. She had metamorphosed even as he watched, like the women in the fairy tales of his childhood, who turned into houris or winged ponies if a man dared to spy on them. Only he was dislodged. Everything else went on as normal. The TV was loud in the living room—the entire family was watching *Star Trek*. He couldn't understand the fascination with weird-looking space travelers. His life was in shambles; there were objects collapsing inside him, shivering apart like a dilapidated house struck by a cannonball, and they were watching TV.

Rasheeda had left his bed the second day after her visits to the bathroom began and now slept with the children, who were delighted; within minutes she had turned it all into an exciting game. Some nights he would hear them giggling behind the door in the other room.

Lying awake at night, he stared at the faintly luminescent square of the window and struggled to form the sentences he wanted to say to her in the morning. He would wake up and she would be gone, sucked into the everyday chaos of the household. He imagined himself marching into the kitchen to drag her out and confront her with the state of their marriage. But the thought of his sisters-in-law looking up aghast at him— the omnipotent, respected elder—made him cringe at the potential embarrassment of it all. In the meantime, Rasheeda continued to orbit around the toilet like a penitent devotee seeking absolution.

As the days passed, even the ladies of the neighborhood resumed their customary afternoon visits. They sat with their teacups in the shade of the tamarind tree in front of the bathroom and talked about other housewives who weren't there. Rasheeda would go in and out of the toilet, and the conversations would continue uninterrupted. Naseer had had the roof of the outhouse tarred so now it was a lot cooler inside.

Miriam, one of the young women down the road, had started dropping in more frequently than the other housewives. Her brand-new husband listened more to his parents than to her, she pouted, the color rising in her cheeks.

"It's as if I am nobody, just someone he can . . . you know . . . and then ignore." She caught the end of her blue dupatta between her teeth and stopped. The listening women sighed sympathetically. They knew.

One afternoon, Rasheeda called Miriam close to the door of the bathroom. Miriam smoothed a few strands of hair away and pressed her ear to the door. All the straining women could hear was a low mutter from inside. Miriam had a secret smile when she left. A few days later Miriam was back—all glow and giggles. Whatever Rasheeda had advised had worked like a charm. He's my little puppy dog now, Miriam crowed.

That was the beginning of it. Later, when there were lines of young women waiting to talk to Rasheeda in the bathroom, the original story was repeated proudly by Miriam. I was the first, she'd say, walking importantly through the small knots of women waiting to recount their troubles to Rasheeda. They told her things they wouldn't tell their best friends. Most of the talk was about husbands and in-laws, the trials and tribulations of living in joint families. Sometimes all some embattled girl wanted to hear was her own voice. They called Rasheeda *Sandaz Begum—Madam* Bathroom—affectionately. All she did was dispense commonsense advice. But the women kept coming back.

To Naseer this meant that he saw Rasheeda even less than before. She spent even more time in the bathroom. There were even more people who demanded her attention now. His mother, disgusted by the goings-on in the backyard, called him into her room and said some sharp words to him.

"Who does your wife think she is? Some kind of guru or what? What is all this khoospoos whispering with women in the backyard? Would your father have tolerated all this nonsense?" She spat a thick brown stream of tobacco into the silver spittoon beside her bed.

One Saturday, after he had spent an hour watching the women murmur in front of the bathroom from behind the curtains of his bedroom window, Naseer realized that each of these women had probably spoken longer with Rasheeda than he, her husband in the eyes of Allah, had in the past few weeks. Rasheeda banned consultations on Sunday so she could do whatever she did in the bathroom in peace. When she came out to prepare the evening meal, he cut a four-inch-square out of one of the bathroom's wooden walls and covered the opening with steel mesh.

"It will make it easier for you to hear the women's complaints," he told Rasheeda the next day, putting his mouth close to the mesh. He had stood in line behind the women for twenty minutes. When they saw him, they hurriedly veiled their heads and shifted in embarrassment at having this man in their midst, not knowing whether to stay or leave. But he didn't move, not even when his brothers and their wives peeked out at him from the windows of the house. Now the children took their places, some standing on tiptoe to look over the balcony wall. Except Adnan. He had left the house the moment Naseer stepped into the back garden. As he got closer to the mesh, Naseer imagined Rasheeda looking at his face framed in the square, open and naked to her gaze in the sunlight. When he finally peered in, blinking from the sun, he could see only her dim form and little else in the gloom. She turned toward him abruptly, startled by his voice.

"Just wanted to make it easy for you to hear the women's complaints," Naseer repeated. She looked at him and said nothing. He thought he saw her nod. After a few moments Naseer left his place in the line and walked back to the house.

At dinner that night, Rasheeda reached across the table and heaped a ladleful of rice onto his plate. When Naseer looked up at her, she was looking back at him. Before she turned her face away to answer one of the children, he was quite sure he saw her mouth twitch gently at the corners.

Imagine if the author had ended the story two thirds of the way through with the line, "Then he fell asleep even as he imagined he would never be able to sleep." How would the story be different in its effect on you? In many ways, it would be a completely different story, wouldn't it? Perhaps you're as baffled as Naseer by Rasheeda's actions in that they're not only surprising but even counter-intuitive. After being assaulted by her husband while she slept, we might want her to do any number of things instead of locking herself in the bathroom. Maybe she should move out completely and go to a shelter or to relatives? Maybe she should get a restraining order. Or maybe she should just castrate him. If you're thinking that any of these solutions are good ones for Rasheeda, from lawful reactions to vigilante justice, then you're reflecting your own cultural values and your own reactions, not those that are open to Rasheeda, who lives in a traditional society. Likewise, if she had reacted in any of these ways, the story would lose all or most of its tension because it would have ended in a predictable manner. The moment she goes to the police or leaves with the children, the story becomes moralistic, the author wagging her finger at Naseer, and by extension, those reading the story, as if to tell us what we should already know about right and wrong. This notion of writing counter-intuitively is one method of making a story come alive. Consider writing such a story yourself in which something happens that suggests an aggressive response, but instead of going down that path, you allow your characters to have a counter-intuitive reaction. Imagine, for instance, a story in which someone discovers a burglar in the process of robbing their home. Instead of calling the police, fleeing in terror, shooting the burglar or being shot or otherwise harmed by them, what if the home owner invites the burglar in? Those other reactions or outcomes are kind of boring, aren't they? The scenario in which the protagonist invites the burglar in and says, "Sure, take whatever you want. I have no problem with that. In fact, let me give you a hand," that's intriguing. It makes us curious. Why would someone do something so foolhardy? It's your job as a writer to find out. Don't necessarily solve the mystery right away, or not in a way that completely satisfies our curiosity, consequently lessening the tension. There are many directions in which you can take this, but try not to make the answer to the question, "Why?" too pointed or gimmicky. Again, think counter-intuitively. A potential explanation:

The protagonist is seventeen years old and is furious that they have been grounded and not allowed to go to a Harry Stiles concert they have been looking forward to all year. And so when the burglar starts breaking in, the son/daughter of the owners thinks this is a perfect revenge.

With every subsequent choice the character makes, we learn something more about them. As a writer, you're constantly trying to answer questions about your characters' motivations. Our next question might be, does the narrator know the burglar? Perhaps it's a friend or acquaintance at school who they have invited over to rob the house. That's one possibility, but how well does the protagonist know this person they've invited over to burgle their parents' place? Another possibility is that the burglar is a complete stranger. That's certainly the most counter-intuitive possibility, but not necessarily the right choice for you as a writer. The most counter-intuitive possibility isn't always the best choice for the story you want to tell. The point is to start thinking in such a manner to lead you away from other more standard and lackluster paths your story might otherwise take.

Our final taboo story is likewise about some counter-intuitive actions on the part of the protagonist. In Ploi Pirapokin's story, a novice Buddhist monk recalls an act of kindness from a now-suffering man and returns it in an unusual manner.

To understand this story in context, it's important to know a little bit about Buddhism in Thailand, where the story is set. Theravada Buddhism is the national religion of Thailand, practiced by 95 percent of the population. Practically all males spend some time as monks, generally around the age of twenty, but sometimes earlier. Theravada Buddhism is also widely practiced in other parts of Southeast Asia, such as Laos and Myanmar. Once, in Myanmar, we were approached by a monk in one of the temples who wanted to practice English with us. Perhaps in his mid-twenties, he was full of stories, including a rather shocking one in which he told of a kind of prostitution ring run out of the one of the central temples by some corrupt monks, whom he condemned. We can't really vouch for the truth of his story, and we wondered why he was telling us this. Of course, we don't intend in any way to disparage Buddhism by recounting his story. We're just suggesting that counter-intuitive things happen in real life about as often as they do in stories. In any case, we should remind ourselves that in the Western tradition, priests, pastors, preachers, and monks don't always have the best record when it comes to upholding the moral standards they supposedly adhere to, especially where sex is concerned.

The young monk had been with us the entire afternoon by this time and we wondered whether there was some kind of financial angle on his part. We knew that monks are typically impoverished and this wouldn't have been the first time that a stranger, though never before a monk, had approached us in an engaging manner that eventually became an appeal for money. We asked as politely as possible if he wanted us to make a donation, but this suggestion seemed to offend him slightly, and we wound up parting ways not long after, though he gave us his email address. Apparently, he really just wanted to practice English, as he said, and didn't want anything from us other than that. The point here is that we are always making calculations about the intentions of others and the baggage we bring to any interaction, our past experiences or lack of experiences with the person in front of us influences our behavior and the degree of selfishness, generosity, cynicism, and so forth that we bring to play. The whole spectrum of human interplay guides people in robes and other spiritual garments as much as it guides those of us in secular endeavors. With that in mind, let's take a look at "Prayer in Training."

3 "Prayer in Training"

by Ploi Pirapokin (USA)

Ploi Pirapokin co-edited *The Greenest Gecko: An Anthology of New Asian Fantasy* (2021) and is the nonfiction editor of *Newfound Journal*. Her work appears in *Tor.com, Pleiades, Literature* in *Context, Apogee Journal, The Offing, Bellingham Review*, and more. She has received several grants and fellowships for her writing.

Buddham saranam gacchami
He remembers; Khun Tim, the village pharmacist, thrusting a paper packet of herbs to give his mother. "I'll pay you next week," Ruey said, a small boy again, embalmed by the fear of losing his only parent. Khun Tim shook his head and this act of kindness became their little secret.

The wrinkly, crumpled man Ruey saw in front of Siep Drugs those three years ago now sits on the temple floor, his thighs two thick stumps where his legs once were. Khun Tim waits for the monks to stop chanting.

dhammam saranam gacchami
Like joss paper, Ruey's face burns when Khun Tim makes his request out loud: He wants a lover. He deserves one for standing between the gun and his oldest son. For standing up to policemen who made quotas needlessly executing drug users. Against Thaksin's war on meth.

There is nothing left for the old man: his youngest joined the temple, the house is empty. All he owns is a dusty plateau, a dirt playground no longer inhabited by grains.

Ruey thinks Khun Tim is too bold. He is not the only one in the temple who wants to be loved, who wants to be taken in by a warm hug, and to feel a hot body pressed up against his stomach.

There were thirty monks in training, small boys like Ruey in their teens, too thin to work on the farms and too old to stay inside classrooms. Given to the temple as charity, their parents believed this new life would give them a chance to grow, to have a shot at an education, and eventually leave.

sangham saranam gacchami
"I want you to pray for him," Father Mana announces from the front. He touches Khun Tim's elbow, a kind gesture. "Pray that somewhere in one of these women's hearts, that one will see Khun Tim the way we do."

Khun Tim donates a large basket of dragon fruit, as though the larger the basket meant the more likely Buddha would answer his prayers.

dutiyampi Buddham saranam gacchami
"Pray for Khun Tim, for his dead muscles, and for the doctors who could not fish the bullet out of his legs."

Ruey thinks of his sister, and forgives her, and forgives himself for being envious of her. He followed her everywhere. He followed her back to Khun Tim's tractor, with Khun Tim's sons Art and Vic. She only did what she wanted, telling Ruey he was her chaperone, that he had to watch out for her, never thinking of how she changed him. There, she took off her clothes, and laid across the cabin. Art went in the passenger seat, while Vic kissed between her legs. Ruey heard her laughing and begging one of them to enter her.

He had wanted to trade places, to spread his legs and have one of their mouths on him, to close his eyes and laugh. He wondered who Father Mana had to forgive before he chose a life of yellow robes. Before he gave up his desires.

dutiyampi dhammam saranam gacchami
At the temple, their voices spun, accumulating merit, even though nothing drove them but the air from their lungs, the wind. Does Buddha really care how much you paid for your prayers? Does He care how many monks speak on your behalf?

Ruey prays too, in the morning, before the rooster crowed and they were called in to sweep the main temple floor. He wishes he made boys like Art and Vic laugh. He imagines he could make many boys happy with long wanting glances, with simple smiles, with quick kisses. He thinks, a prayer can put a crippled man at ease, but so can a smile—and the latter costs nothing. He wonders if he could make the man who made his mother happy smile, even for just a few minutes.

tatiyampi dhammam saranam gacchami
Ruey is tired of playing robot-Buddha. He is tired of being a prayer in training for the giant prayer machine. His words washed nothing away, nor did it give legs, sons, and mothers back.

Monks cast a thin veil over clear eyes, set to believe that there's no more to life than what's being lived. He is tired of saying "So be it." Who do you consult with for kisses? How do you say, I deserve to be loved too? How does Buddha answer your prayers?

Praying calmed heartbeats meant to tick and nothing else.

The monks stand up and start clearing their mats. Ruey helps Art carry Khun Tim into his wheelchair.

tatiyampi sangham saranam gacchami
Ruey takes Khun Tim to the outhouse. He tilts the wheelchair forward a little so that Khun Tim can unzip his pants. Ruey wraps his arms around him so that he does not fall. A yellow stream shoots into the urinal, then the force weakens and Ruey knows it is his time to help Khun Tim wipe off.

Art runs to get toilet paper. Ruey holds Khun Tim's cock in his hand to not let urine dribble on his pants. The old man in his arms keeps his eyes closed, humiliated.

Ruey remembers that this is the village pharmacist, the one who had given his mother herbs as charity. They shoved away chemotherapy, made her light-headed with happiness.

Ruey grips his hand a little harder, Khun Tim's cock hardening in his hold.

The old man flushes red, embarrassed that a boy's touch arouses him. But Ruey starts slowing pulling on it, a new kind of charity. Ruey knows that this act of kindness is fleeting, this kind of love temporary. This is better than praying. When Khun Thim gasps, Ruey bends close to his left ear and says, "This can be our little secret."

Once again, we have a situation that ends in a somewhat counter-intuitive way. How you react to Ruey's "prayer" is your own business, as it were. Whether or not you would have acted as he did, or whether you approve, is not so much at issue here, though of course it's something worthy of discussion. But that's a matter of content, not technique, and we're primarily concerned with technique here. Ask yourself how the author subverts your expectations. What does she do that seems counter-intuitive? Why does she include the Thai prayer, interspersed in italics throughout the story? What is the effect of this? If you know Thai, perhaps the answer will be different, but if you don't know Thai, what does the Thai do, technically speaking, to enhance the reader's experience of the story? These are the kinds of questions a writer asks—what can I borrow or steal from this person's technique to use in my own story? If you're at least as concerned with these technical questions as you are with content, then congratulations. You're thinking like a writer.

Exercises

1. A burglar is surprised by someone in the house being burgled, and even more surprised when the burglar is invited to rob as much as they please. Take this counter-intuitive premise and turn it into a story. Try to make it as plausible as possible but don't explain so much that it loses all its tension.

2. Write a comic kiss or a sex scene that goes from bad to worse using the snowball effect.

3. Write a story in which a sheltered person is introduced to something they had never before seen or considered, and they become obsessed with it (this doesn't have to be sexual, of course). It can be a food, an activity, a type of music. The challenge here is to create some obstacle in the way of this obsession and make at least some of their choices counter-intuitive.

4. Think of several societal taboos and write them down. Next, don't write a story about any of them. Spare us and yourself the embarrassment please. Now, write down several activities that you consider normal and not taboo at all. Choose one and write about it as though it were as forbidden a taboo as the ones on your first list.

5. Write a story with the structure of one of the taboo stories we've read in this chapter. A child visits the home of a close friend of their parent and is shocked by what they see. A married woman or man visits the home of a relative and sees something on their laptop or TV that they can't unsee, and it starts to drive them crazy. A figure of authority takes pity on someone who once helped them out. They do something for that person that has to remain a secret between them. Make the situation your own and just use the structure as a template for the story you decide to tell.

CHAPTER 10
HISTORIES

A song released in 1960 by Sam Cooke that begins with the line *Don't know much about history* ("Wonderful World") became extremely popular, and especially so in Asia during our teenage years. It was a song that spoke to our desire to get out of all the homework we hated, especially in history, which was not exactly our favorite subject back then.

Today history, especially recent history, can feel dauntingly impossible, given the rapid and unceasing flow of information about what is happening everywhere that so quickly becomes "history." In writing fiction, we sometimes would rather escape all that reality in favor of writing fantasy or stories about private lives, and forget about world or national events that are, after all, beyond our control. Yet historical reality contributes to who we are in our moment of time. In the two stories here, historical incidents and personalities give the writers an entry into the inner lives and conflicts of their protagonist, and offer a way to tell a larger story that embraces the real world without feeling like a history lesson of names, places, and dates. In "Bee Honey," Japanese writer Yoshimoto Banana transports her protagonist to Buenos Aires, where she encounters a procession recalling Argentina's coup d'état, one that led to a harsh rule under the military junta; this encounter of "time passing" forces her to confront her own "color of sorrow." By contrast, in "Lee Kuan Yew Is Not Always the Answer," Inez Tan's futuristic story set in 2039, her protagonist, a twenty-four-year-old social studies schoolteacher, confronts her own emotional history through a history class about Singapore's founder, Lee Kuan Yew, who, even in death, rises from the grave to shake up her present life.

What can historical events contribute to the writing of fiction? For one thing, it can take us closer to self-understanding, as evidenced in these two stories. While we might feel, as the lyrics of "Wonderful World" suggest, that love is all we need, rather than boring classes in biology, algebra, or history, those same boring subjects made the song a hit. Also, for those of us who dreaded history (as we certainly did) because it was such a chore to memorize all those presidents, dates, wars, treaties, and the myriad historical incidents we were expected to know and regurgitate in our awful public exams, the *real* meaning of history for the writer is how it affects the lives of ordinary people. When used with insight, and even humor, history can lift a story beyond that of just one man or one woman in their own place and time, and resonate for readers in many parts of the world.

Read "Bee Honey" by Yoshimoto Banana, and as you do, ask yourself what the historical event presented in the story has to do with the protagonist's personal story, during this trip she makes to Argentina.

The Art and Craft of Asian Stories

1 "Bee Honey"

by Yoshimoto Banana (Japan)

Translated from Japanese by Michael Emmerich

Yoshimoto Banana is one of Japan's most well-known writers internationally whose twelve novels and seven essay collections are worldwide bestsellers. Her work is concerned with urban existentialism and the problems faced by Japanese youth, as well as the way trauma shapes a person's life.

I was sitting in the plaza in front of La Casa de Gobierno, not feeling much of anything. There were a few men standing around, acting so suspiciously that it was obvious at a glance they were pickpockets. To my surprise, once I had indicated that I was on to them, giving each man a look that said, "Yes, I can see you're a pickpocket," they kept their distance. Now whenever my gaze met one of theirs he looked right back at me, as if we were acquainted. Was it that hard to make ends meet here, or were people just very laid back? I didn't get it . . . an odd city, Buenos Aires.

I had taken a seat at the edge of a bed of flowers to watch the pigeons and an old lady selling pigeon food. She didn't seem to have anything weighing on her mind. She had simply come to spend the day selling pigeon food. I guess that was more or less how I felt myself.

At the far side of the plaza, I could see the pink walls of La Casa de Gobierno—"The Government House." Madonna sang there in *Evita,* didn't she . . . God, how did I ever end up seeing a movie like that? . . . No sooner had this question occurred to me than I found myself remembering, once again. The rainy night when I rented the video and watched it in the living room. He came home in the middle of that awful movie. His right side was drenched—he said the wind had broken his umbrella. I brought a bath towel and gave his head and body a casual rubbing down, the way you might dry off a dog or a cat, then flopped back on to the sofa. The place smelled like rain, just from him having come in. Clear beads of water streamed down the windowpane. The road outside was quietly, blackly wet. It was an ordinary night, like all nights. He made a pot of coffee and handed me a cup. The cup itself we had bought together one Sunday, at an antique shop nearby. We had to make a lot of turns to get there, and . . . that's right, there were flowers blooming, tons of them, all different colors, and the road looked white in the sunlight, so I felt I was in heaven. Orange, yellow and pink flowers. Green grass swishing in the wind. I had way too many memories—like standing between two mirrors, staring into their distance. Our history together, his and mine, had the near-infinite expanse of a world in miniature, and now I was cut off from all of it.

I had come to visit a friend who lived in this city.

My friend was learning to tango when she and her dance instructor, an Argentinian, fell in love and got married. Now she had a sort of business showing around visitors from Japan. She wasn't an official guide or anything, but she seemed busy enough. She said she got paid at the end, after the tour was over, like a tip. Her husband was away just then, touring with some of his dance students, so I stayed at their house. My friend had to take some people around during the daytime, and it was night by the time she got back. I took it easy until she finished, day after day. It was fun to be so free; I wished I could live that way forever. Recoleta was especially nice, the part of town where she and her husband had their house—lots of trees and grass—and I felt great just wandering around. I walked and walked, trying to keep myself from thinking. Only when my legs began to ache and my mind grew numb did I feel I was finally myself again. A little wine at night was all it took to send me tumbling into bed. For the time being this is fine, this is enough, I told myself night after night, sprawled out on an uncomfortable sofa bed in a house that wasn't mine, the unfamiliar sounds of an unfamiliar city ringing in my ears. I have to give myself time, that's all I can do. Like a wild animal lying very still in the darkness, licking its wounds, waiting, just waiting, nothing else, to give its feverish body time to heal. The best thing for me right now is to go on doing nothing like this, to let my spirit recover, little by little, until I learn how to breathe again and can think seriously about what to do.

"There's a procession of mothers wearing white scarves in the Plaza de Mayo today, starting at two," my friend said on her way out that morning. "Watching it isn't exactly pleasant, but it makes me think about all kinds of things every time. All kinds of things, really. I mean, this is recent history we're talking about. I think you'll understand when you see them. You'll think about your own parents, too, back at home."

So I made my way to this plaza, to witness the procession. Soon the mothers—old enough by now to be grandmothers—began to gather, arriving alone or in little groups, their white scarves tied over their heads. A few journalists were there to cover the event, and a few policemen. The pink walls of La Casa de Gobierno looked blurry under the cloudy sky. They mixed ox's blood into the paint to get that color. Suddenly a tremendous flock of pigeons fluttered into the air, and the dozen or so old women in white scarves began slowly circling the plaza. Some old men walked with them, and there were a few others, presumably relatives. The women cradled old pictures in their arms. Photographs of grinning young men, young women dressed in their finest. Expressions so sweet and ordinary it was almost impossible to believe they had been swept up in something so terrible.

"Are you from Japan?" asked a middle-aged woman standing next to me. She looked as if she might be Japanese, and spoke in Japanese.

"Yes, I am."

"I came to this country as an immigrant. We live in the suburbs. It was awful back then. All of a sudden we found ourselves living under the junta, just like that. Many people vanished. Students who had once dabbled in leftist politics, Peronists. Participating in a demonstration, little things—that was all it took. Hardly any of them returned."

She was Japanese, that was clear, but something about the way she was dressed, something in her expression and her make-up, gave me the sense that she had been away from Japan for a long time.

"I saw a movie about it once."

How did I end up seeing such a disturbing movie? There were images of kidnapped students being corralled, half naked; students being raped; having hoses turned on them; being abandoned, blindfolded. Those parents walking in the plaza in front of me must have been at their wits' end then, unable to sleep at night; and yet they were living in their own homes as usual. During that period, these people lost something extraordinarily important, a sense of something, forever. Their sons and daughters lost their lives; they lost part of themselves.

"A military truck drove into the forest near our house one night," the woman said. "We were so scared we wouldn't even go outside. Soon we heard a horrible barrage of gunshots, people screaming and groaning, then another large truck came and it was quiet again. When we went into the forest the next morning, there was blood on the ground, all over. That's how thirty thousand people disappeared."

I nodded without speaking, watching the procession.

It occurred to me that the pigeons and the pickpockets, the immigrant beside me, the tourists, we were all just *here*. You could tell, looking at them ambling around the plaza in their white scarves, that those mothers no longer thought their children might come home. Maybe this was their way of expressing the constant, unending frustration they carried in their hearts, of giving form to the time they had lived through, of refusing to let what had happened get lost in the oblivion of simply being here, like this, right now. Cradling pictures of their daughters and sons, the old women chatted among themselves. That made me feel the reality of it all the more. That's how it goes, I thought. This is time passing. This is the color of sorrow.

Sorrow never heals. We simply take comfort in the fact that our pain seems to fade. How flimsy my own sorrow is, compared with what these parents feel. It has no real basis, none of this outrageous injustice to support it. It just keeps drifting on in its indistinct way. And yet that doesn't mean one is more valuable than the other, or deeper. We are all in this plaza together. I let myself imagine.

One morning, her son, at the height of his teenage cockiness, goes off to school as always, hardly taking a sip of coffee, long and lanky in his favorite jeans. To his mother, he looks the same as he always has, ever since he was a boy. That look is where all her memories reside—it's only natural. He never mentioned to her that he once participated in a demonstration, just for a little while, and maybe just because his friends were going. He never comes back. What would that feel like? No one can say for certain what happened until after the rash of political upheavals that follow in the wake of the coup d'état. No one tries to help, because everyone is too scared. Terrible rumors keep circulating, throwing her into confusion; there are no good rumors. Those fortunate enough to make it back from the internment camps live in terror, and the stories they tell make her hair stand on end . . . I was at high school when it happened, but it's too far away. This isn't a story of the Inca Empire. It didn't even take place during wartime. I was living in Japan then, living at home with my parents, rebelling against them, staying out until morning, doing things, when this happened, here, on this earth. It's too big, too much—I felt as if I might faint.

I thought.

Why, right now, here under this languid, overcast sky, are all these afternoons we live, theirs and mine, intersecting in this way, in this unremarkable plaza?

I noticed a plump woman among the circling mothers who looked like my own mother. The longer I looked at her, the more similar she seemed, except for the color of her eyes. As I stared, I began to think she moved in the same way, too.

Whenever I caught a cold, my mother would mix up a drink for me, dissolving honey in hot water, adding a splash of whisky, squeezing in the juice of a lemon. She was still doing that for me when I was at high school. On one of those evenings when children were bleeding and being tortured here, I was being pampered by her. Maybe that is what this world is? Precisely *that*? For some reason, my mother called her drink "bee honey." No matter how many times I pointed out that it was really more like "honey lemon," she said her name was better and kept it. I seemed to feel the hot, sweet taste of it filling my mouth. It's the same all around the world. A mother's scent. A whiff of the female body, and something heavy, sweet, endlessly deep. That scent was here now, filling the plaza, circling it, because there was no other outlet, going around and around.

"It's ridiculous! You can't break up over something like that!" My mother cried on the other end of the line. "Married life lasts a long time, all kinds of things happen. Even if you do break up in the end, at least give it two or three more years."

"I won't have a second chance if I get any older than I am now," I replied. "At your age, two or three years doesn't matter," my mother said.

An unrelated scene came to mind: me pressing my face into the sofa, wailing, after our cat died; my mother running her hands roughly, but with a gentleness in the tips of her fingers, through my hair.

If only my husband no longer loved me! If only his love would simply vanish! If only his lover were a nasty, unpleasant woman! But in real life, things don't work out so neatly. He conveyed his love by calling me here every night since my arrival. He sounded unsure of himself, had none of the casualness of my mother's hands—was that the distance between us? I thought we had become a family, but in reality we were just two strangers doing our best to compromise. And yet I had a feeling I would back down that night, finally, urged on by all the years we had spent together.

I would start wanting to tell him, when we talked on the phone, about the feelings that were churning inside me after seeing these mothers. It was so confusing . . . Tonight, holding this confusion inside, I would lie down once more on that sofa bed, in my friend's house. I had the feeling, though, having seen these mothers with my own eyes, not in a movie, not reading about them in a book, but seeing them, hearing their voices and noticing how their skirts swayed in the breeze, seeing how they laughed as they chatted—all that had come together inside me to form a core, something that could change me, just a little. Suddenly I saw myself, what I was like as a human being, from a place very, very far away.

A few other mothers, also dressed in black and wearing white scarves, had set up a stall on the far side of the plaza. I walked over. They were selling videos, pamphlets, postcards, T-shirts. A sign explained that the profits went to support their activities. I had picked up a T-shirt, planning to buy it, when one of the white-scarved mothers started talking to me. I wasn't sure what to do, since I don't speak Spanish, but a young woman nearby, probably a journalist, translated into English for me.

"She's saying that an 'S' size might be better. People are wearing T-shirts kind of small these days."

I couldn't help smiling. Such strength, and of course she had once had a child of her own . . . Mothers are mothers no matter what country they come from, after all, and that's a very sad thing to be. Will I ever become a mother myself? Will I ever be able to see these people, to think of them, in a different light? With nothing decided, everything seemed oddly renewed. I bought the T-shirt, said thank you and left the plaza behind.

While it is helpful to know that the coup d'état Yoshimoto references is the 1976 one where the Peronists were ousted by a military junta, it is not absolutely needed to appreciate the story. The first historical reference in the story is the musical "Evita," which is likely better known to you than Argentina's history, one that is fraught with multiple coup d'états. If anything, history feels almost too big to the protagonist who wants, in part, to dismiss it because it all seems so impossible. In fact, she thinks of history as the "disturbing movie" about Argentina that she doesn't fully understand why she ever chose to watch.

However, the unnamed protagonist does witness the procession of mothers wearing white scarves, in part because her friend has encouraged her to see it, saying, "I think you'll understand when you see them. You'll think about your own parents, too, back at home." This foreign coup, one that is not immediately relevant to the protagonist's life, becomes the emotional edge of Yoshimoto's story. The magnitude of this national trauma becomes apparent when she talks to a Japanese woman in the plaza who tells her about the many protesters (mostly college students) who were arrested and never heard from again. The mothers arose as a grassroots movement of grieving women who demanded to know the fates of their children. History tells us that many women were raped in prison, and their children given away as "gifts" to right-wing military families, and that hundreds of those who disappeared were simply shoved out of helicopters or planes over the sea. That the procession is a protest against what occurred in recent history elicits the protagonist's response because, as she realizes: "I was living in Japan then, living at home with my parents . . . when this happened, here, on this earth." The protagonist cannot ignore the facts, summed up by the woman who says: "That's how thirty thousand people disappeared." In fact, this historical incident was the one that transformed "disappeared" into a transitive verb meaning to kill and wipe from the face of the earth.

As we said in Chapter 9 on "Taboos," disturbing material is not a bad thing in our fiction. We all know bits of recent histories from our homes and other parts of the world, especially traumatic or difficult events that shape or change our worlds, and these find their way into our fiction, both directly and indirectly. In earlier chapters, "Boondocks" is set against the Second World War, and "The Boat" is a result of the Vietnam War and stories such as "My Mother Pattu" (Malaysia) or "A Clerk's Story" (India) are infused with hints of their historical British colonial reality. In fact, it is almost impossible to ignore history, since as we do know, rulers rise and fall, war is followed by peace, genocide happens, and even if we might prefer to we really cannot ignore the realities of history, however horrifying.

How do we respond when what's going on in our world feels too disturbing? One response is to retreat from the bigness of that feeling while other people throw themselves into the mosh pit, so to speak, reveling in the heightened sensations of energy and sound. The worldwide Covid-19 pandemic that began in 2019 is a case in point, because some people isolate themselves, unwilling to take any risks, while others party in large groups, despite warnings and laws, perhaps because the idea of control seems almost absurd in the face of how little is still really known about the disease. History repeats itself in this instance, as the bubonic plague or "Black Death" in the fourteenth century appears often in literature. At this writing, there already are numerous poems and stories that reference Covid-19 as a historical moment.

Yet "Bee Honey" is not about the historical coup, or even Buenos Aires which is where the protagonist is, but is instead about the sorrow that hasn't healed for her, unlike the comfort she recalls when her mother would make her bee honey, a honey and lemon drink to alleviate a cold. So if you do write a story that references Covid-19 (or any other historical incident), you might consider how someone reading it twenty years later might respond. When you try to break down this story, ask yourself what the story is really about? The answer is not history.

Our second story takes on the historical figure of Lee Kuan Yew, and Inez Tan uses Singapore's history much more directly than Yashimoto does in "Bee Honey." Read Tan's story and as you do, ask yourself why she uses as much historical information as she does in the story and what purpose it serves.

2 "Lee Kuan Yew Is Not Always the Answer"

by Inez Tan (Singapore)

Inez Tan is the author of *This Is Where I Won't Be Alone: Stories*, which was a national bestseller in Singapore. In 2018, she won the Academy of American Poets Prize, and she holds an MFA in Fiction from the University of Michigan and an MFA in Poetry from UC-Irvine.

I was passing by class 4J during recess time when two girls rushed out, saying, "Miss Lim, Miss Lim, can we show you something? Miss Lim, Miss Lim!"

This can't be good, I thought. I made a big show of looking at my watch. I could have looked at my chipfeed, but like many other teachers, I still wore a watch so students could see when I was keeping an eye on the time. "I have to teach another class in five minutes," I said.

"It'll be very fast, Miss Lim! Please, please. *Please.*"

Reluctantly, I followed them into the classroom. As Primary Four students, they still sat with their desks pushed together in groups of five, forming little islands. The desks were only separated when they had to take exams in strictly spaced rows to prevent cheating. Today, they'd rearranged their desks to create space in the center of the room, where they had placed three desks in a row. One student, Lola Pang, lay giggling on the floor beneath them. Lola was always in the thick of things like this.

"Girls, the floor is dirty. Your uniforms are white," I said ruefully, but really they were drain-water grey, and this explained why.

"Are you watching, Miss Lim?" asked one girl breathlessly.

"Yes," I sighed.

"And action!"

Lola crossed her arms over her chest and closed her eyes. Three other girls stepped up onto the desks, hands to their foreheads, and delivered dramatic recitations:

"Oh no! Singapore is under attack! Our total defense has been breached!"

"Oh no! The economy just crashed! We are losing our competitive advantage!"

"Oh no! The opposition party just won the general election by a landslide victory!"

"What!" cried Lola, startling awake. She kicked her knees up towards her, rolled out from under the desks and jumped to her feet. "I will get up!"

"Gasp! It's Lee Kuan Yew!"

"Lee Kuan Yew?"

"Lee Kuan who?"

"It's me, Lee Kuan Yew!" shouted Lola. "I will save you, Singapore!"

She raised one fist in the air, like Superman, and pretended to knock each of the other girls off the desks. Each girl jumped down and did the death they did best: one staggered around holding her head, one pretended to choke, the third lay on the floor and thrashed energetically about.

"Lee Kuan Yew, he's our hero, he's saved us!" chorused the other girls from the sidelines.

"Just remember, Singapore," said Lola importantly. "Even if you are going to lower me into the grave and I feel that something is going wrong, I . . . will . . . get up!" With that, she rolled under the desks again and resumed her former position, mummy-like.

All the girls stood, bowing and clapping for themselves. "Miss Lim, Miss Lim, what do you think?" they asked.

"I hope you put just as much effort into studying for your exam this Friday," I said. They started whining and groaning, the usual. "See you in class tomorrow," I said, blinking through my chipfeed on the way out. The feed showed that I still had 22 minutes before my next class, and it suggested a list of tasks I could complete in that time. There's always work to do. I dismissed the feed and kept walking.

It was important to show the students that you weren't amused by them. That made them work harder. People need to work hard if they want to survive. At least the girls were using key terms, like "landslide victory." They'd need that for question 32 on their upcoming exam: "Explain the significance of the 1959 legislative assembly general election." Was it too much to hope they would all remember that the People's Action Party won 43 out of 51 contested seats?

As I headed down the corridor, I could hear them restarting the game: "I will get up! I will rrrrrise from the grave!" Already I could hear them amending the script, elaborating where fiction better served their purposes. They are the future of our nation.

I teach Social Studies. The girls call it Propaganda, as in, "Sorry, Miss Lim, I forgot to bring my Propaganda homework today." They are very proud that they learnt the word. My Primary Four students are ten years old. Some of them are beginning to wear junior bras. More of them need to be told about deodorant. It's a tender and baffling age.

Lola and her gang are always coming up with something ridiculous. They're full of nonsense, I might say if I were over forty. When I became a teacher I promised myself that I'd try to remember what it was like to be my students' age, and sadly, that isn't hard for me. Well, I'm only 24. Also I'm *still* wearing some of my own junior bras. My mum makes snide remarks about them when she goes to hang them up on the bamboo poles outside our flat. "Why still no boyfriend?" is another thing she says.

But back to the little skit the girls put on, "I will get up," etc. The next week, as they were filling in the blanks of a difficult worksheet on their tablets, I heard Lola say: commandingly to her group members, "Just put Lee Kuan Yew. It's usually Lee Kuan Yew."

When they passed up the worksheets, I saw that some of them really had written Lee Kuan Yew's name down more times than was reasonable. I marked them wrong; they were wrong. I thought that'd be the last of it.

But then I collected their exams on Friday and found more:

11. The name "Singa-pura" derives from the story of Sang Nila Utama catching sight of a wild <u>Lee Kuan Yew</u>.

48a. In 2032, Singapore became the first country in the world to implement <u>Lee Kuan Yew</u> throughout the entire public transportation system.

56c. The treaty between Chief Minister David Marshall and the British colonial government granting Singapore partial internal self-governance was signed on <u>Lee Kuan Yew</u>.

79. The five stars on the Singapore flag represent <u>Lee Kuan Yew</u>, <u>Lee Kuan Yew</u>, <u>Lee Kuan Yew</u>, <u>Lee Kuan Yew</u> and <u>Lee Kuan Yew</u>.

I was sitting at my desk, making extra big Xs in red when my friend Sharifah came by my desk, holding her tablet. "Have you been putting them up to this?" she asked.

14. The process by which a solid turns into a gas is called <u>Lee Kuan Yew</u>.

18. In the following experiment, one possible explanation for why the metal ball bearing was not attracted to the nail is <u>Lee Kuan Yew</u>.

23. Digestion begins at <u>Lee Kuan Yew</u>.

"How curious," I said.

"And did they perform that ridiculous skit for you? 'I will get up'?"

"It's based on an actual speech he delivered over forty years ago," I said. They deserved a bit of credit for that. "In 1998, when he was defending his decision to continue on in Parliament after he'd stepped down as prime minister, he said, 'Even from my sickbed, even if you are going to lower me into the grave and I feel that something is going wrong, I will get up!'" We'd watched the video together in class. Grey-haired, but throbbing with energy, the man had also said, "Those who believe that after I have left the government as prime minister, I will go into a permanent retirement, really should have their heads examined."

"He's certainly made an impression on them," said Sharifah. "When I walked into class today, they said, 'Miss Sharifah, Miss Sharifah! Do you how many languages he learnt so he could speak to his constituencies? Miss Sharifah, did you know that he donated ten million dollars to help children learn both English and their mother tongue?' Those cheeky monkeys. I know they're just trying to waste time at the beginning of class."

"They're acting out to vie for your approval," I said.

"How else do they know to relate to authority?"

"You're as bad as they are."

"It's for their own good."

Another colleague, Joseph, stomped over, tablet in hand. His large square glasses had fogged up in the air-con, which made him look even more impassive than usual. Sharifah says he and I should date because we have so much in common. It's hard to tell when she's being sarcastic. The girls think we're meant to be. Two of them are writing a play about it. Whenever they see me come into the classroom, they throw themselves over a ragged notebook on their desks, convulsing with laughter. I saw the notebook one day when I was waiting in their classroom for them to come back from science lab. I'm pretty sure they left it out on purpose, open to a particularly juicy scene:

MR JOSEPH WEE: Cheryl, there's something I've wanted to say to you for a long time. I'm madly in love with you. From the moment we met, I knew I wanted to stay forever by your side.

MISS CHERYL LIM: Oh, Joseph!

MR JOSEPH WEE: *(sings)* Every word I say is true. This I promise you.
(They fall into each other's arms. Curtain. END OF ACT II!)

We actually have gone on two dates. Both were horrible. On the first, we saw a movie. On the second, we saw a movie and ventured to grab a bite at Toast Box. A mistake. We awkwardly gossiped about the principal for a while, and then Joseph leaned forward and said, "I like how passionate you are about your subject. I've always felt that way about mine. When I was our students' age, I was solving quadratic equations for *fun*."

"My God, you're damaged," I said, and an uncomfortable pause hung in the air while both of us waited to see if the other was going to laugh. "Okay," I said after a minute. "When I was their age, I cut out photographs from my Social Studies textbook and pasted them into my diary. I remember I had Maria Hertogh with her adoptive mother, Che Aminah binte Mohamed, families relocating after the Bukit Ho Swee fire, a British nurse ladling out soup to a line of local children during World War II, and Zubir Said, the guy who wrote the national anthem."

"And that's what you loved doing?"

I hesitated. I spend so much time with my mum that I forget what it's like to talk to someone candidly. I could have said that our country's history meant so much more to me than a few afternoons of girlish scrapbooking. I'd always wanted to know the people who'd been here before me, shaping the world I found myself in today. I felt I owed them something. Beyond that, I felt it would be a terrible thing to forget them. I didn't even know who "they" were—they were as much the collage of faces from the cover of my P4 Social Studies textbook as the ones who weren't pictured at all—and I knew I was being irrational. Still, I wondered what they would have thought of me. Not even my mother knew I still had those photos tucked away, and I wasn't sure why I'd told Joseph about them. I chickened out and deflected. "I just saved them because they looked nice. I remember admiring Zubir Said's smart white shirt."

Joseph raised an eyebrow at me. I returned his gaze. He backed down first, with a self-conscious glance down at his own shirt, which was blue. Both of us picked up our pork floss toast and looked away.

I suppose those dates weren't that bad. At most, they were inconclusive. *Dear Diary, I might have written, he's what I most detest, but he also sees right through what I most detest about myself (the evasiveness, the cute act). Sometimes I can't stand him. Other times I think his influence is just what I need. So maybe I do like him??? It's like seeing a mirror image of myself and not knowing if I'm repulsed or entranced.* But I never think things like that. Never.

Now Joseph leaned over my desk to show me his students' latest exams. In the space provided for the students to work out a problem sum, one had written a mini essay: *Lee Kuan Yew was called in to solve the case of the missing x. Who could have a motive for committing such a horrid crime? Did any of the suspects have an alibi? Was no one above suspicion? Was it even possible that x had wanted to disappear all along?* "I will get to the bottom of this," swore Lee Kuan Yew. "I will not stand for any crimes to be committed in our harmonious and meritocratic society!" *He called on Singapore's best detective, Inspector Lola Pang* . . .

So Lola was behind this too. Of course the others would follow her lead.

"Well?" said Joseph.

"It's quite creative," I said.

"They're not supposed to be creative. They're supposed to solve for x. Besides, it's disrespectful to the man."

"Is it? They've been singing his praises. You should see what they do to people they don't like." Sir Stamford Raffles had really gotten it this year.

Joseph scowled. "Don't fool yourself, Cheryl. You know they're mocking him. You're always too soft on them. You shouldn't be encouraging them to put down something they know is wrong just to be funny."

"I'm not encouraging them to do it."

"Regardless," he said crabbily, "you need to tell them to stop."

"That will certainly encourage them," said Sharifah, trying not to smile.

"Shall I arrest them for sedition while I'm at it?" I asked.

"You're their teacher," he said humorlessly. "You think of something."

That night, my mum and I went out for dinner. We fought our way to the front of the queue for the bus, and we fought our way to get into the queue for the restaurant. None of this was strictly necessary, but whatever we do, my mum has to lock horns with other people to get any satisfaction. It makes her feel alive. She got to complain some more about how slow the flying food service robots were and how small the portions had become, which put her in quite a good mood. For the grand finale, we fought aggressively over the bill. "I'm working now, Mum," I said loudly. "Let me get it."

"Save your money," she snapped. "Your children may need it for their education."

At home, my mum presented me with a small durian cake and I acted surprised, as though I hadn't seen the box appear in the refrigerator yesterday or smelled it every time I opened the refrigerator door. It was a wonderfully pungent cake—our open carton of milk had already absorbed some of its flavor just by proximity. She cut us a finger-thin slice each. "I appreciate you spending your birthday with your old mum," she said. In the same neutral tone of voice, she added, "I suppose you didn't have a date or anything else planned."

"I was thinking of watching this year's Lee Kuan Yew special on Channel 5."

"Aiyoh," she said, despondently. "Even my friends don't watch those."

"My students have been fascinated by him." I use my students as an excuse for a lot of what I do. Being tired, being lazy, being busy, being childish. In fact, they probably make me better than I would be otherwise. I expected a sharp retort from my mum along those very lines, but instead she looked deep in thought. We sat on the sofa and I projected the documentary onto the wall. My mum also unfolded the ironing board and did the ironing, because she always has to outdo me.

The authorities made a different documentary each year, for release each March 23. Yes, I was born the very day Lee Kuan Yew died—23 March 2015. I don't mean to imply that I feel a special connection to his ghost or anything like that, just that I've always been conscious of having been born into a different era. In the past, our leaders fought their battles to determine what we were not. We were not a British colony. We were not a communist state. We were not part of Malaysia. The struggle now has been to define what we are. Adolescence—we can relate to that, especially those of us who haven't quite figured our way out of it yet.

The program covered all the major milestones: his education at Cambridge; the formation of the PAP in 1954; winning every election; banners of the familiar red lightning bolt set in a blue circle; his cabinet all dressed in white, to symbolize their freedom from corruption; his tears on national television when Singapore separated from Malaysia; delivering the annual National Day Rally. There were clips of him shaking hands with Richard Nixon, Ronald Reagan, Kofi Annan, Hu Jintao, Angela Merkel. That all seems so long ago—before China annexed Taiwan and Japan, before self-driving cars, before the first chipfeed was implanted in a live human subject, right here in Singapore. The girls complain endlessly about having to memorize dates and facts; when they turn 21 and their brains have stabilized enough for their chipfeeds to be implanted, they'll be able to look up anything they want just by thinking of it. I tell them that there's a difference between retrieving information and knowing how to use it, and that's why they're in school. Another thing they complain about is that what they learn in Social Studies doesn't affect their daily lives, and therefore it must be irrelevant. They think they are their own little individuals who sprang forth from nothing and made a new world, at their birth. But they are absolutely a product of their history. None of us is exempt from that. And the sooner they learn to accept it, the better.

The documentary, nearing the end, reviewed Lee Kuan Yew's retirement from the position of Minister Mentor in 2011, a post he'd created for himself. He voluntarily stepped down from every position he ever held; no one could have made him go. Then the programme jumped ahead to his death. Crowds gathered at the Padang and around Marina Bay. Some people queued for over 12 hours to leave cards, flowers and stuffed animals at the designated memorial sites. More attended his funeral than the camera could capture, a slow procession in heavy rain.

My mum was getting emotional, which she rarely did. She didn't look particularly sad, but it was as though an invisible wall had been lowered for a while, enough for you to feel what she was feeling instead of having to deduce it from conflicting signals. I asked, "Did you find out before or after I was born?"

"Before," she said, briskly running the iron across one of my skirts. "I was in the hospital by then. The nurse I like came in. I remember the look of shock on her face. She said 'Lee Kuan Yew just passed away.' That's when I felt that I was going into labor." She gave a short laugh. "Or so I thought. Actually you didn't come out for another few hours. But you felt what had happened. I felt you feel it."

She cleared her throat.

"When I was younger," she continued, "I was very angry at him. In his early days, he tried to make less-educated women have fewer babies, because he felt that their children would contaminate the breeding pool. He didn't believe people were equal. He did a lot of good anyway. But so did every person who worked hard to make a better life for their family and themselves. Every single person."

"Thanks, mum," I said, before things could get really soggy. "I love you too."

"Good," she said. "Enough of this. Let's watch something else."

We put on *Gone with the Wind* and ate the rest of the cake together. She patted my hair. "You're still young, you know. And pretty. You'd be even prettier if you put a little effort into your appearance, like Scarlett."

"You don't have to be nice just because it's my birthday," I said. My mum believes in being tough on me. She'd wanted me to win a scholarship to Oxbridge or an Ivy League school. Doctor, lawyer, Indian chief, so the children's rhyme goes, but all I managed was to gain admission to the National Institute of Education. Each night that I received a rejection letter, she steamed a pomfret—my favorite—clearly meant for the celebration of better news. I remember looking down at one round expressionless eye. The pomfret lay flat on one side, its underbelly a dull white gleam, its fins like tattered grey sails hung stiffly over the edge of the dish, bent by the pot my mother had cooked it in. Her cooking was never bad, but those were the worst meals I'd ever eaten. I've hated pomfret ever since; it's just as well she's never prepared it for us again. Eventually I was happy enough about my results, but wasn't enough for her. Nothing ever was. Her displays of kindness, even the passive-aggressive ones, weren't the real her. But I liked it when she was nice, all the same.

On Monday morning in 4J, I had a speech prepared. "Girls," I began, "there is something we need to address." About half of them looked scared. But a handful were grinning at one another, having already guessed what I was going to say. "I have been hearing from other teachers that you have been writing 'Lee Kuan Yew' as an answer on your exams, even outside of Social Studies."

"That's because Lee Kuan Yew is always the answer," said Lola.

I fought the urge to reply, "Lee Kuan Yew is not always the answer." Never accept a fight on their terms. "Well," I said, "it just so happens that that's something we're going to question in today's lesson."

I sent worksheets to their tablets. "Close your textbooks, you don't need to look at them. I want you to answer the following questions *without* mentioning Lee Kuan Yew or the government." I gave Lola a hard stare, but she missed it, looking down at her tablet, seemingly befuddled. "Everyone's answers will be different," I went on. "Write down the right answers for you."

My name is:
In Singapore, the most important people to me are:
My favorite place in Singapore is:
My favorite food in Singapore is:
My passions are:
One day I hope to work as: because:
I have a part to play in helping Singapore because:
One historical event that affects my life today is: because:
I am proud to be a Singaporean because:

The girls were making confused noises. They are quite funny when they get like that. I walked around the room, checking on them. Lola raised her hand.

"Yes, Lola?"

"Miss Lim, what if I have to put the government for one of my answers?"

"Which one?" I said, humoring her.

Lola pushed back her chair, stood up, held up her tablet with both hands and read, "One day, I hope to work in the government of Singapore because I have strong leadership skills, I want to make a difference, and I think it is time that Singapore had our first female prime minister."

Every girl turned to look at her. She held their gaze unwaveringly. There was almost an aura coming off her, from her messy ponytail down to her battered canvas shoes. She was serious. And I felt a twinge of sadness. Someone like Lola would never be prime minister. She was a free spirit. She had not yet learnt to dream within her means.

"You can put that down if you really mean it," I told her.

"I do," she said matter-of-factly, and went back to her work.

Towards the end of class, the girls projected their responses onto the back wall. I told them to spend the last few minutes reading what they'd all written, and recording similarities and differences. I stood behind them, reading too. I was still taller than most of them, though that would change before they left this school. Their answers were good, if occasionally rote or sanctimonious, but they had the rest of their lives to work on them. A few responses were rather creative, to use Joseph's much maligned word. Was I just afraid of his being right, or was this really an improper use of class time? Was I too soft on my students? A good buzz of conversation filled the room, with everyone orderly and on task. As it was in this place we lived. But maybe I was fooling myself again. There was always something stirring: the growing disparity among income groups, anti-immigration murmurs and constant spillover from the unrest in other countries, near and far. Maybe we lived in more radical times than I was willing to acknowledge. Maybe it would be time, soon, for another dramatically decisive leader. Someone cut from a new kind of cloth. As I looked at the girls, I had the strangest feeling suddenly. I was afraid to turn around in case Lee Kuan Yew was behind us, watching. Of course, he wasn't.

Before you read this story, how much did you know about Singapore or Lee Kuan Yew? Chances are, unless you happen to be from Southeast Asia or have lived in Singapore, you probably know very little. There is no musical about Singapore comparable to "Evita" that Tan can reference that would garner much international recognition. Perhaps the movie "Crazy Rich Asians" comes close, but that is not rooted in a historical figure the way "Evita" is. Instead, Tan references a classic Hollywood movie that many readers everywhere would recognize, "Gone with the Wind," an epic historical romance set during the American Civil War and Reconstruction era. Until "Lee Kuan Yew, the Musical" comes to Broadway, it's unlikely that most readers would know very much about postcolonial, independent Singapore's first leader. So Tan's inclusion of Lee's name as part of the title is a very good way to make that history memorable. And we suspect you now also know more about Singapore's history and Lee Kuan Yew than you might ever have expected to learn from a short story. It is a history, we must confess, that we find fascinating, given how technologically advanced, crime-free, and well designed in terms of urban development Singapore is today.

What else does Tan do to build the world of her story? At first, we do not necessarily know this is set in the future. The reference to the "chipfeed," which is slipped into the second paragraph, is the first hint that we may not be in the present as we know it. This is a useful technique which avoids the melodrama that a futuristic setting can evoke, when too much attention is paid to the bells and whistles of technology. Instead, what Tan achieves is a way to criticize the benignly repressive government that is the reality of Singapore, both historically and in the present. By setting the story in the near future, she suggests that nothing will change, that history is destined to repeat itself.

But is that really what the story is about and is that what the author wants to say? How does Tan make this story more than just a satirical jab at Singapore's first leader or the private story of a young Singaporean teacher still subject to her mother's oppressively unreasonable judgment? While Tan does poke fun at Lee Kuan Yew through the games her ten-year-old students play with his name, the narrative never underestimates or distorts Lee's historical importance.

Much of the story's strength comes down to how Tan uses history to make her protagonist, Cheryl Lim, come alive. First, "Miss Lim," which is how we meet her, is a passionate teacher who loves history, one who cares a great deal about teaching her ten-year-old charges who, like most children that age, can be naughty, over-energetic, and needy for attention. Miss Lim is a teacher who exercises control: she is not easily swayed by their rambunctious drama, noting that "It was important to show the students that you weren't amused by them. That made them work harder. People need to work hard if they want to survive." This is both in keeping with a character who is a teacher, but also provides an entry into her inner life. We immediately suspect that her own life might have been one of hard work and that survival might not have been so easy for her. Lim's response to her students' play that satisfies her is that at least they got some of the terminology correct, such as "landslide victory," and she thinks instead about the exam question they will have to answer, because it is her job to teach them to do so successfully.

Go through the story and find how bits of history are used in scenes to show us more about who Cheryl Lim is. In every scene where she interacts with others—her friend Sharifah, the science teacher; Joseph Wee, the math teacher with whom she goes on two, unsuccessful dates; her mother at home—a little more of her own story unfolds. Singapore's history parallels her own personal and emotional history, and this makes us see her as someone who is complex, caught between a desire to please her mother who wants greater achievements from Cheryl, as well as marriage, and grandchildren for herself, but understanding increasingly more about who she is and how she is or isn't able to fulfill those expectations. That this is tied to what Singapore might be able to achieve in the future—for example, will Lola or another girl one day grow up to become the first female prime minister—leaves her with a "twinge of sadness." By taking us through this story in Cheryl's POV, one that *naturally* thinks about history, we discover the emotions that Cheryl herself isn't always able to confront, and see why that might be so.

One important technique Tan uses is to *tie one significant historical fact directly to her protagonist*—she is born the day Lee Kuan Yew dies—in order to make her almost like a *"chosen one"* whose story *deserves* to be told. This is an aspect of fiction writing that we need to uncover in our own stories which is to ask ourselves—why is *this* character the protagonist and not *that* other one. For instance, if Cheryl's mother were the POV instead of Cheryl, what role would history play? Would history be the right entry point for her mother's story? Would Lee Kuan Yew? We think probably not. Likewise, if the math teacher Joseph Wee were the protagonist, the story might instead be titled "Solve X, Forget Creative Writing." It's more than just making someone a history teacher that gives a writer the right to use history as the entry into that person's story; it's how that history echoes the conflict, despair, or uncertainty that is rooted in the character's story. An added benefit is that by stating the date and year of Lee's death—2015—Tan tells us exactly when in the future this occurs, since we already know Cheryl is twenty-four, without breaking the fictional dreamscape of the story.

One last point to note in Tan's use of history is the sly humor she injects into the narrative. By putting the words about Lee Kuan Yew into the mouths of ten-year-old schoolgirls, she gets away with saying outrageous things about Singapore's first leader in ways that would not be nearly as effective in straight narrative or through an older character. For instance, the students call their history studies "Propaganda homework" or in their "creative" story about the case of the missing x, they have Lee Kuan Yew saying that he "will not stand for any crimes to be committed in our harmonious and meritocratic society!" The satire is clear, but it's entirely written into the drama of these fictional characters.

It's important, however, in using history for your fiction, not to simply juxtapose a personal pain or anxiety to a historical trauma. A story that trivializes a historical trauma (or figure) runs the risk of trivializing history. For example, to juxtapose the sadness a character experiences over the death of a pet against the Rwandan genocide would run that risk, or to write about a visit to Auschwitz in a story that is mostly about how much someone is overcharged at the beer hall next door hardly does history justice. Yoshimoto's protagonist in "Bee Honey" remains unresolved about her husband's infidelity that made her take the trip to Argentina, but her seeing those mothers "with my own eyes"—victims of a much greater injustice—she is forced to recognize herself as a "human being," just like all those who disappeared whom the country continues to mourn. Similarly, Cheryl in Tan's story feels the specter of Lee Kuan Yew hovering, as the past continues to cast a shadow over her and her country's future.

So challenge yourself to research and explore historical incidents or figures that intrigue you as another technique in your toolbox as a writer. But make sure that you recognize the meaning of that history vis-à-vis your own fiction. You *do* want to know as much as you can about history, even if what you really want to write about is love or the absence of love.

Exercises

1. Find an incident from where you live that was in the news fifteen to twenty years earlier that had a lasting impact on your community. This could be an environmental disaster, a terrible fire, a scandal involving a local celebrity or politician, and so forth. Research the story through news archives. Outline a chronology of the major events and create a fictional character who was there at the time and have them tell the story of the incident.

2. Choose a historical figure who incites your curiosity and research their life. Locate two or three key accomplishments, failures, or significant life events that serve as a framework for a contemporary character's story. Write that story.

3. Place a character in a foreign country, as in "Bee Honey" and write a story of that character's encounter with some aspect of the country's history that resonates with their own life.

4. Write a fictional historical incident in a real place—this could be a village, town, city, or country—use real geographical locations, but make up an incident that occurs there. Write a story of a first-person character who has left that place for many years and must return in search of something to do with that fictional incident.

CHAPTER 11
FUTURE TENSE

The two stories we're going to learn from in our final chapter are both set in the future (or perhaps in an alternate reality in the case of "Pink") and both in some sense deal directly or tangentially with geopolitics. A professor of ours in grad school once asserted that all stories are political whether the writer is aware of the politics of the story or not, and we still believe this to be true. Stories uphold or subvert the societal norms of their times, but not in the same way as editorials. They do so ambiguously, or at least the successful ones do. That's not to say that one can't glean a moral, political, and/or ethical stand from a story, but heavy-handed moral lessons are the stuff of propaganda, not of fiction. If your reader feels they are being led by the nose to your political beliefs, they might feel their intelligence is being insulted. Still, anyone who knows about the Hong Kong protests in the recent years won't be able to read the story "Learning Curve" without understanding its political implications. As we've stated earlier, we don't really like that word, "message" when it comes to stories. Ask yourself when you read a story such as "Learning Curve" what it implies, not what its message is. Implication leaves some wiggle room while "message" doesn't. Nonetheless, it's no wonder that writers of all kinds are often the first to be locked up by authoritarian regimes, if the authorities are smart enough to understand what they're reading. That's why, for centuries, Chinese poets couched their criticism of the government in poetry. What bureaucrat is going to be interested enough to analyze a poem? The same is true of fiction. The Soviet-era writer, Yuri Olesha, wrote a brilliant novella in the late 1920s, titled *Envy*, about a Soviet industrialist who creates a kind of cheap sausage to feed the masses. The industrialist is portrayed throughout as a cheerful populist oaf with few thoughts other than sausage occupying his mind. The book was at first hailed as a masterpiece of Soviet literature and even the Communist Party paper, *Pravda*, reviewed it favorably. It took several years before bureaucrats smart enough to understand tone, metaphor, and symbolism realized that in fact, *Envy* was a sly satire of the Soviet system, and the book was banned along with the rest of Olesha's works. Unlike many of his contemporaries, at least he wasn't shot.

Part of *Envy* is a kind of surreal fantasy in which the main character, Nikolai, a man envious of the industrialist Babichev, teams up with Babichev's bitter brother Ivan to undo the industrialist with a giant robot-creature meant to smash Babichev and his factory to bits. The robot seems completely a delusion, but it's also possibly in part what confounded the Soviet authorities so thoroughly that they didn't want to admit they had no clue what the story was finally about. Officials and propagandists, unlike story writers, want their messages loud and clear.

When writing with a conscious political agenda, some writers, like Olesha, wrap their tales in *allegory* and likewise either add an element of fantasy (as in *Envy*) or set their tales in the future (*1984* and *A Handmaid's Tale*). Often, we can consider these *cautionary tales*, a warning to be vigilant or that current belief and tendencies will lead to a dystopian future. Of course, not all stories of the future are overtly political, while others actually do predict the future pretty well. For instance, Ray Bradbury's classic story, "The Veldt," does a chilling job of predicting virtual reality, but the story's power comes from its exploration of the alienation between parents and children that has likely always existed. The future will continue to yield technological innovations for better or worse, but the basic conflicts in human and societal relationships will likely stay more or less the same. *1984* was in many ways an allegory about the Soviet Union and the police state, and Orwell settled on the title by flipping the date it was written: 1948. The great writers are always saying as much about the present as they are about the future. Sometimes it's a warning. Sometimes it's a stark acknowledgment. One thing for certain is that the authorities never approve—the more you are saying about the present when writing about the future, the more dangerous you're perceived to be.

Let's take a look now at "Pink." This is a story that really should be read twice. Do us and yourself a favor and read it twice.

1 "Pink"

by Hoshino Tomoyuki (Japan)

Translated from Japanese by Brian Bergstrom

Hoshino Tomoyuki's many novels and novellas have won most of Japan's major literary awards. *Ore Ore* (2010) won the Kenzaburō Ōe Prize and was published in English as *ME* (2017). He has also authored numerous short stories; some were translated for the English collection *We, the Children of Cats* (2012).

> The sixth of August marked the start of the nine-day streak of blistering heat. Just after one in the afternoon, Tokyo registered forty degrees Celsius. It was the highest temperature on record, and the heat kept rising, reaching 42.7 degrees two hours later. The humidity never dropped below 80 per cent, and the sky, though cloudless, was thick with a pale mist. Older people greeted each other, laughing, with lines like *Next week is the Bon festival, but the dead might go back early—it's too hot even for them*. Perhaps because age had numbed their senses, they seemed unbothered by the heat, and several of these very senior citizens were content to stand talking in the sunshine that beat down on Tokyo's Kaki-no-ike Park. It seemed to Naomi, as she listened to two old biddies go on while she watched her niece play in the sandpit, that it might be a good idea if they thought about their own welfare rather than that of the dead. Or maybe they *were* the dead, having returned for Bon, but without realizing it they were chattering away thinking they were still alive. Though why the dead would want to come back to this prison called life—just because it was that time of year again—was beyond her. *If I had the chance to end it all*, muttered Naomi to herself, *I'd leave this world in an instant and never look back*. What was her problem? Why was she so irritated, she didn't even know these women, why was she getting so carried away? It was the heat, the goddamn heat, and it was her goddamn stupid sister, who insisted that Naomi take her daughter outside to play at least once a day—for her health—even in this toxic weather. *Why don't you take her outside?* thought Naomi, but she nonetheless did as her sister asked, the promise of a thousand yen for her trouble pushing her out the door.

Naomi's two-year-old niece Pink *(what a stupid name to give a kid)* was absorbed with her playmates in some sort of sandpit public-works project, and so, seeing that other mothers were keeping an eye on things, Naomi left the play area and walked over to the edge of the pond to have a smoke. There were no trees to filter the sunlight, which poured down from the yellow sun like sulphureous gas. Even the cicadas, whose tinny drone was usually inescapable, were silent. The hot air oozed with humidity, sticking to Naomi like a swarm of insects. It felt less as though she was sweating than that her skin was melting and running down her body. Everything around her seemed not entirely solid, a series of colors running together like so many abandoned scoops of ice cream. *When the temperature gets high enough, even the landscape melts,* thought Naomi.

Little bodies began to fall one by one from above. They were birds, dropping down for a dip in the pond. They gathered at the edge, splashing themselves with water. Sparrows and white-eyes, starlings and bulbuls: there were so many of them. A few birds actually immersed themselves in the water—ducks, Naomi thought, but when they broke the surface, she could see they were sparrows. She saw some dive straight into the water. Naomi counted the seconds—one . . . two . . .—and then, flapping their wings, the birds emerged and flew up into the sky.

It wasn't just sparrows. The white-eyes, the bulbuls, the starlings: they all began to dive into the water, as if imitating the sparrows. At one point, the oversized body of a crow crashed into the water, causing the smaller birds to fly off. Only the pigeons, perhaps unable to dive, scuttled back and forth at the water's edge.

The crow finally left, and the sparrows returned. They dived into the water again and again, twisting their bodies and spinning in the air. Had sparrows always been waterfowl? It began to seem so to Naomi. As they emerged from the pond, water spraying, the wet sparrows gleamed in the sun. Suddenly, in their midst, shiny things began to leap from the pond. They were fish! Similar in color and size to the sparrows, the fish were flying alongside the birds just above the surface of the water.

Naomi crouched down and dipped a finger into the pond. As expected, the water was warm—too warm. The fish were suffering. They were throwing themselves into the air for the same reason the birds were plunging into the water. Seeming to follow the sparrows' lead, the fish twisted and somersaulted in the air. Were they trying to fan themselves? Birds have wings; humans have hands; fish have only their bodies to twist and turn if they want to generate a breeze.

Fish were jumping and twirling all across the surface of the pond. The pond was alive with the spray they produced, a silver mist that, carried by the hot wind, cooled Naomi's face.

Naomi was gripped with a sudden joy. This place was a living hell. No creatures were dead, but they felt closer to death than the dead. Assaulted by such unbearable conditions, they longed to flee their existence. Birds wished to stop being birds and become fish, fish longed to stop being fish and become birds, cats wanted to be people, people longed to become anything but people. And so they all went crazy, flailing and flopping, spinning and twirling. But wasn't it fun too? To spin, to twirl?

A crowd gathered to watch the leaping fish, but Naomi broke away from them and began twirling slowly by herself, arms outstretched like a ballerina. She spun clockwise as viewed from above, her body the axis of the clock, arms tracing a circle parallel to the ground. The soft breeze produced by her twirling touched the sweat on her skin, cooling it. Slowly, gently, so as not to get dizzy, she twirled her way back to the sandpit where Pink was playing.

Naomi raised her head to look up, which gave her the illusion the sky was drawing closer, as if she were floating up into space as she spun. Spiraling like a drill or a shuttlecock, she bored her way upwards through the layers of air. To spin and spin until you moved like the wind itself—would that make her a tornado? Well, nothing so strong as a tornado—a whirlwind? That's it, I'm a whirlwind. If she became a whirlwind, she'd stay cool. Light. She could fly.

Naomi lost track of where her feet were carrying her. She brought her eyes down from the sky and stopped spinning. She was near the sandpit, and just about to run into a metal post. Now the heat pressed in on her from all sides, and sweat poured from her like water from a spring. She felt wobbly, and her head ached. She should never have done this. Once you start to twirl, you can't stop, because if you do, it'll be even worse than before you began. The only way out was to spin and spin forever.

Naomi walked over to Pink, saying, "Time to go home!" as she grabbed the child's hands. The moment she did this, she was struck by a feeling that something wasn't right. Naomi looked around, inspected Pink from head to toe, but nothing seemed out of place. Still, Naomi couldn't shake the feeling that some unknown had been introduced into the world around her, something that created a subtle but inescapable dissonance. It was as if everything around her had been replaced by an exquisite fake.

In order to collect herself, Naomi, still hand in hand with Pink, spread her arms to create a circle between them and began to spin with the child, singing softly. *Bird in the cage, bird in the ca-a-age . . .* Pink danced happily even when her legs tangled up as they spun. Naomi didn't want Pink to get dizzy, so every few spins they would walk side by side for a bit until Pink said, "Let's play bird-in-the-cage again!" They'd re-form the circle between them, repeating the pattern again and again until they reached home. Exhausted by the heat and the excitement, Pink fell asleep at once. Not long after, Naomi was asleep too.

That evening, they watched the television news over dinner; it was all about the heatwave. Not only Tokyo but all of Japan had seen temperatures exceeding forty degrees, with 392 people hospitalized and 56 dead, mostly elderly. But the story that really grabbed people's attention was that of a seventeen-year-old schoolgirl in Fukui who'd spun and spun under the blazing sun until she succumbed to heatstroke and died. According to friends who were with her, the girl had said, *Hey, what if we spin like fans—wouldn't that cool us off?* And so she tried it, and it worked so well she invited her friends to join her—*Oh, it feels so good! Try it, try it!*—and they did, but soon, dizzy and nauseated, they lay down to rest, and, after a while, the girl lay down beside them; when it came time to get up, she was still, and when they tried to rouse her they realized she was gone. A so-called expert compared her to someone trapped on the top floor of a burning high-rise choosing to jump out of a window rather than face the flames; it was a perfectly logical choice for that person, not abnormal in the least.

"Things are so fucking awful they're going to die either way. Let's not beat about the bush," Naomi carped at the television.

"Could you not use that kind of language in front of Pink?" her sister objected. "As it is, all she does is imitate everything you do."

"It's only natural. I'm the daddy around here. She's a daddy's girl."

"No one asked you to be her daddy. She's better off without one. All I asked was for you to be her big sister."

Appalled at the utter immaturity of Pink's father, Naomi's sister had dumped him and kept Pink. It was like throwing away a box of sweets and keeping the prize that came with it. She was working at a nursing home to make ends meet, and had invited Naomi, who had graduated from university but was without a job, to look after Pink in exchange for a place to live. Naomi had accepted the invitation without a moment's hesitation. She'd been stuck in the couch-surfing life and, nearing the limits of her friends' patience, she'd been on the verge of signing up with the Self-Defense Forces anyway. The truth was that Naomi had been fixated on the SDF since she was little; she had the feeling that her sister's offer was, at least in part, an effort to stop her from enlisting.

After he was dumped by Naomi's sister, Pink's father thought he would "toughen himself up" by participating in right-wing demonstrations, and about a year later he showed up on her doorstep, the fashionable street style that had been his sole redeeming feature replaced by a tired old kimono that clung to his thickening frame. *I'm an adult now. Give me another chance!* When Naomi's sister had asked what he meant by "adult," he replied that he could now state his beliefs without fear even as the world looked unkindly upon him, that he could remain cool and resolute even as he was blasted by the harsh winds of public opinion, that he had learned how to stand his ground even if it meant putting his body on the line and that he would put everything on the line to protect himself and his family. Naomi's sister had heard enough, and she told him to get out. But he refused, saying that he was no longer the weakling who gives up and leaves just because a woman tells him to.

As the confrontation escalated, Naomi returned with Pink from one of their customary trips to the park and couldn't help breaking in. She'd once seen Pink's father in action—on a street corner with a group yelling into megaphones for revival of the colonial policy of Five Races Under One Union. "You joined the right-wingers to find yourself—what do you think you're going to find here? There's nothing for you here, not yourself or anything else."

Enraged by Naomi's ridicule, Pink's father began yelling, though it wasn't clear exactly what he was saying. Naomi cut him off: "This is you being an adult? All you've done is learned how to yell! Everything else is the same; you're still a little boy begging for attention: *Mummy, Mummy, listen to me, Mummy, please!* A real adult would start by asking my sister what she needs!" Pink's father slunk away, swearing they would get what was coming to them.

Naomi's sister was left feeling uneasy, worried that he would try to get revenge. But ever since then, Pink had stuck to Naomi like glue, from the beginning of every day to its end.

"Naomi was smoking!"

"Telltale!"

Naomi took Pink's cheeks in her hands and squeezed them, rubbing them up and down. Delighted, Pink shouted, "You were smoking! You were smoking!" in the hope of prolonging the cheek squeezing. As she dutifully complied, Naomi noticed that the small bruise Pink had got earlier in the day—she'd bumped into the doorknob while playing around as they got ready to go to the park—had disappeared without a trace.

Starting the next day, Naomi's sister insisted that Pink be out of the house so she could have some time to herself, if only in the morning or evening when the temperature fell below forty degrees. Each day, Pink would rush to the door, ready to start playing bird-in-the-cage. Her body plastered with cooling patches, Naomi would do as she was told.

There were now—several days into the heatwave—endless reports of people sustaining burn injuries from cars and rocks that had heated up during the day. What with streets and buildings and the humid air holding stored-up heat, the temperature failed to dip below thirty-five at night, and hot winds blew continuously from the outdoor units of cranked-up air conditioners as if they were clothes dryers. Day after day, the number of people dying from the heat reached triple digits, and anywhere you went, you'd encounter the corpses of small animals. On the fifth day of the heatwave, the city of Kofu saw temperatures reach 50.2 degrees. It was a new record for the country. Where Naomi lived with her sister and niece, the temperature soared above forty-five by noon. When things "cooled off," dropping down to forty in the late afternoon, Naomi would leave the house with Pink. Almost no one was outside, the area a ghost town, the streets like vacant sets. Pink and Naomi made their way to the park, spinning and sweating all the while. Naomi drank bottles of Pocari Sweat in an attempt to replace the liquid draining from her body. By the time they reached the park, she looked as if she'd emerged from a soak in a hot spring.

All signs of life had disappeared from Kaki-no-ike Park, and a terrible stench rose from the pond. The water level was low, the surface oily and lumpy with dead fish. Not just dead fish—dead birds were mixed in with them—and some sort of larger striped animal, part of its bulk sticking up out of the water. Naomi didn't want to know what it might be.

She took Pink into the shade beneath a huge zelkova tree, and they began to play bird-in-the-cage. The ground was pitted and uneven, not only because the earth had hardened and cracked in the heat, but also because the tree's roots, seeking water, were extending crazily in all directions. If a tree concentrates its energy in its roots, it can displace the earth. Most plants in conditions like these might wither and die, but a tree that was strong enough could fight for what water there was.

On the other side of the pond was a large camphor tree. Someone over there had tied a rope around a branch and was twirling in mid-air from it. *So, somebody else had the same idea!* Naomi thought appreciatively as she and Pink went to take a closer look.

"It doesn't hurt, hanging like that?" Naomi asked the young man.

"Not at all, it's nice and cool!" he replied. "Gives me goosebumps."

"So you're doing what the fish do?"

"Fish? No, no. I saw it on TV! You can spin like this and feel cool—and you can get dizzy enough to forget everything!"

"The other day the fish in the pond were jumping and spinning in the air, trying to get cool too."

"But they're all dead now, right?"

The young man grabbed the rope and nimbly pulled himself up its length to sit on the branch. "I'm not just cooling off, you know," he said as he untied the rope from his waist. "I discovered that if I really let myself spin, it was like I was getting . . . purified. If I was feeling depressed, I'd feel better, as if the depression flew off somewhere while

I was going around and around. Like I was in a salad spinner. So I began to spin faster and faster. Pushing the limit, you know? I would get sick and vomit. And I would sweat, really sweat. It was like detox. Like bidding farewell to parts of me that were bad. And as *I* got rid of more and more toxins, I could spin as much as *I* wanted without getting sick. It was the most amazing feeling. Like it wasn't me who was spinning, but some larger force that was spinning me. It felt good giving myself up to this great force I'd never noticed before. I don't know how to put it. Maybe it's like life taking over, so you can just go with it, naturally. Like letting go and feeling easy, feeling . . . peace."

The young man had descended from the tree and was now standing in front of Naomi and Pink.

"Huh. Well," Naomi said, "I've been spinning a little these days, but I've never felt anything like that."

"It's not just me. I mean, there're a lot of people who feel this way. They begin by just spinning, but then they have some kind of awakening. And they realize that the spinning is really a kind of prayer."

Naomi felt irritation bubble up within her. "Prayer?" she said, her voice rising. "To whom? For what? I don't get it."

"A prayer to a larger force, or power, kind of. Asking it to make us suffer less. Like a prayer to the heat, even. Or a prayer for rain."

"I take it this *larger power* hasn't heard our prayers yet?"

"Maybe the prayer isn't powerful enough yet. I believe that if enough people come together and unite their feelings, something will happen. It's like a prophecy."

"So, after prayer comes a prophecy?"

"It's not just wishful thinking on my part. There's really something to this, I know it. And I'm not the only one. When you're spinning, you get this feeling that, I don't know, you're getting stronger, you're growing. You really feel it. Everyone feels this way, so we've started to believe that if we can gather all this power together, we can really make something happen."

"I've never felt anything like that."

"Maybe it's rude of me to say, but I think your spinning must be inadequate. You have to do it more, devote half a day or more to it, and you'll see. The feeling will come, and it will be real."

"I haven't been spinning all day every day or anything, but I've been doing it pretty regularly for five days now, and all I've noticed is that it feels good while I'm going around and around, but once I stop I feel exhausted. Isn't that normal?"

"Five days? You're more experienced than me! You started the first day of the heatwave then, right? That makes you one of the first to be enlightened! Don't you think it's strange? That so many people began spinning that day—not just you but people all over Japan? Nobody was copying anybody else—they just started doing it naturally."

"You mean like that girl who died?"

"Yes! Our first martyr. I myself only began spinning when I heard about her on the news—I'm just a wannabe! Who am I to say anything to you—you're the real deal, starting spontaneously like that. What made *you* do it?"

"I told you, I was watching the fish jump and twist in the air and imitated them. It wasn't some revelation from above."

"If you see fish jumping and twisting, do you always start doing it too? Did anyone else watching the fish start spinning?"

Naomi shook her head. All she knew was that she had separated herself from the crowd that had gathered around the pond and started twirling, off on her own. She had separated herself from the others because she knew she'd be behaving differently from them.

"So I'm right. The fish might have been the inspiration, but it was a larger force that moved you."

Naomi was shaken. She began to doubt that her spinning was a result of her own intention. But she didn't agree with the young man that some higher force had possessed her, either. That wasn't how it felt. It just seemed as if the only way to respond to such crazy heat was to do something she would never normally do.

"What about tornadoes or whirlwinds? They're touched off by forces larger than themselves, right? Natural forces, like gravity and atmospheric pressure. But no matter how hard you pray to the atmosphere or to gravity, they won't make the heat go down."

"Do you think it was gravity or the atmosphere that made you start spinning?"

"Well, no, but—"

"Were all the people who started spinning that day moved by the same force that produces a whirlwind?"

"I don't know anything about anybody else. All I know is that I thought if I became a whirlwind I might cool off."

"Most of the people who started spinning that day describe it like that. They thought if they could become a whirlwind, or become a breeze, or become a fan, then they'd finally get cool."

"It doesn't seem so strange that people who are all subjected to the same unusual heat would end up having similar thoughts."

"We could stand here and debate all day, but what's the point? We should go where the others are and see for ourselves. Even if you don't end up agreeing with me, you'll at least see what I'm talking about."

"Where the others are? Where's that?"

"Just over this way, at Kumano Shrine."

The young man spun around as he led the way to the shrine. Naomi and Pink began to spin too. Before long, the three of them formed a big circle as they continued on their way. Pink shrank shyly away from the young man at first, but gradually relaxed and began to return his smiles. Even before they entered the grounds of Kumano Shrine, they could sense a force emanating from inside. And once they passed through the torii gate, they found the place packed with people, their body heat and moisture rising like steam from an internal combustion engine. They were twirling, all of them, as if intoxicated. All in the same direction too: clockwise. Completely silent, their heads slightly tilted, staring into space through half-lidded eyes as if near sleep, their arms spread like butterfly wings, they spun around and around in the same direction at the same speed. It was so quiet, as if the shrine were sucking the sound from the air, while the energy the twirling crowd exuded was so strong it seemed able to blast any onlooker into the air.

The first to join them was Pink. She began awkwardly, losing her footing and bumping into one of the twirlers. As if drawn in by Pink, Naomi too started to move. Out of the corner of her eye, she saw the young man walking away.

Naomi closed her eyes completely and felt her own self-generated wave of energy coursing through her body. If she could just ride that wave, she could spin and spin forever. She let herself go with it, her arms rising of their own accord, like the wings of a bird. She tried to spin a bit faster and felt resistance in her body, as if it were putting on brakes. Before long, she realized that this resistance, like walking against a strong wind, came from the wave of energy produced by the people spinning around her. The wave she was riding came not just from her own movements but everyone else's too. The waves produced by the spinning of each individual interacted in complex ways, rippling the air within the shrine's grounds, and Naomi rode the waves with great skill. Everyone around her was riding these complex rippling waves, moving with them and putting up not the least resistance, lost in the motion. It was like music. Like dancing to music. Soon Naomi felt her consciousness on the verge of leaving her completely. She had the feeling that if she passed out, she would ascend to another level and be able to spin furiously, on and on, even unconsciously. Her insides would grow transparent, herself subsumed entirely by the trance. Surely more than half the people around her were spinning in such a state. *I might as well let go completely,* thought Naomi, but as she did she became aware that the crowd had thinned significantly, and that there was only a smattering of fellow spinners left around her. The wave grew weak, depriving Naomi of the force that had been driving her, and she stopped. The heat descended once again upon her, and, pouring with sweat, Naomi took Pink by the hand and headed away from the shrine. "It hurts, I said! Why aren't you listening to me?" yelled Pink, pulling her hand from Naomi's grasp. It was only then that Naomi realized she had been yanking Pink along. "You're not respecting my will!"

What? Naomi looked hard at Pink. *Why is she talking like that?* Pink was clearly parroting the exact words that Naomi said to her sister all the time. But this was the first time Pink had said anything like that herself.

"I'm so sorry. Do you still feel sick?"

"My legs hurt."

"We spun around too much, huh? That guy really got us going . . ." This last bit was addressed more to herself, but Pink replied nonetheless. "Yeah, he's really cool."

Pink kept complaining that her knees hurt, so they stopped to rest again and again as they made their way home, finally arriving only after night had fallen.

As soon as they walked into the house, Naomi's sister glared at Pink and sighed, "Those clothes are already too tight for you, aren't they? We're going to have to get you some new ones." Shaking her head, she added, "It would be nice if you could take a break from growing once in a while, you know."

Naomi, who didn't remember Pink's clothes being too small when she'd helped her get dressed that morning, dubiously pulled at a sleeve. It was indeed tight as a drum.

The next evening, Pink and Naomi found the young man spinning from the camphor tree again.

"I didn't think I'd see you here today!" he exclaimed.

"The kid kept pestering me, saying she wanted to go back to the shrine," Naomi said, pointing at Pink.

"So why aren't you there?"

"I wanted to spin by myself," Naomi replied, almost angrily.

The young man looked intently at Naomi from where he hung suspended in mid-air. "Every day more people show up, so it's getting a bit hard to find room over at Kumano—maybe we should try Sampin Temple. It has bigger grounds."

"I told you—I want to spin by myself. And anyway, why are *you* out here all by yourself?"

"I can't really handle crowds."

"What? You were the one going on and on about everyone uniting in feeling and all that crap! Do as you say and not as you do—is that it?"

"I can pray here all by myself and still be united in feeling with everyone else."

"There's a term for that, you know. Delusion."

"It's like I said yesterday. It's a real feeling I have. And so I'm just fine out here all alone. But it's different for people like you. I really am someone who can't handle crowds, and so I know how people are when they truly want to be left alone. They're not like you. It's so obvious to me that all you really want is to melt completely into a crowd. Besides, I saw how you were yesterday."

There was no denying it. Naomi hadn't gone back to the shrine because she was afraid of her desire to do it all again. Maybe this guy had her figured out, and that's why he was tempting her now with Sampin.

"But enough about me. What I want to know is why you can't stand being around other people."

The young man clambered easily back up his rope and, standing on the branch, undid the knot at his waist before shimmying down to the ground.

"Have you heard of the Greater East Asian Friendship Society?"

"Yeah. They're the Five Races Under One Union guys."

This was the right-wing group Naomi's sister's ex had joined. Their idea was that, instead of East Asian countries squabbling all the time, they'd form an East Asian Union—like the European Union—and that East Asia would become a free economic zone. The headquarters would be in northern Kyushu, and a free-trade zone would be established in Kyushu or Okinawa or Hokkaido, where people from the union would be able to move in and out freely. The standard currency would be the Japanese yen and the standard language would be Japanese, with a major effort to spread the study of Japanese to all nations that were likely to participate. The government would strive to establish harmony with neighboring countries and promote the doctrine of the Five Races Under One Union, in addition to which they would establish a strong military. Even now the society was staging monthly demonstrations advocating these positions.

"I wasn't bright enough to get into anything but a local vocational school no matter how hard I studied," the young man said. "I wasn't the kind to join a gang, so I wasn't popular with girls. My sport was gymnastics, and while I got pretty good at the rings and parallel bars, I was never better than anyone else who practiced a lot. In other words, I was completely unremarkable—maybe below average. I never thought I'd be able to find a good job when I graduated, and sure enough, I didn't. Objectively speaking, I was disposable. But I wanted to improve myself, even just a little, and ended up getting interested in history. I joined a history group. Groups studying Japanese history, they're full of losers like me. Below average, socially awkward: they don't fit in anywhere and they're desperate not to feel like losers. These groups are hangouts for the serious-minded but mediocre. I joined one, and then, along with another guy from the group, joined the Greater East Asian Friendship Society."

Naomi had seen enough of her sister's ex to understand exactly the kind of feeling the young man was describing. Come to think of it, this story wasn't so different from her own trajectory either, graduating from a third-rate university and applying to 108 companies only to be hired by none.

"And you know, I felt great when I did things with them. I could respect myself. We were serious, maybe not so bright, but committed to debating important things and doing something about them, unlike the thoughtless, lazy people all around us who went about their lives with no sense of urgency. That this pride might lead to arrogance was maybe inevitable; after all, I was only about twenty. But I had a strong sense that I was working on behalf of Japan. The group gave me responsibilities, I worked with the police and got permits, I was put in charge of a platoon of demonstrators."

"Platoon?"

"Yeah, the society was organized into different levels, and each level had its captains and lieutenants and other borrowed military titles. They made me a sergeant major, and I led a platoon. The idea was that if the Japanese military did get re-established as the society hoped, a period of military experience was going to be required for membership."

"Why?"

"So that we could defend ourselves without help. Self-reliance was a big thing in the society. We had slogans like *Rely not on others—let others rely on you!* Anyway, one day one of the demonstrations I was leading got into a clash with some anti-foreign group. Those guys are idiots—they think that Japan will benefit by picking fights with its neighbors. The basest, most thuggish way of thinking. The Greater East Asian Friendship Society was about establishing Japan's leadership of East Asia at a much higher level—we didn't want to dwell on petty differences. They never understood that. So they saw us as the enemy, and they targeted us that day. They were screaming stuff like *You want to sell out Japan! You're just a bunch of Koreans!* Some of my guys wanted to rise to their challenge, but I tried to keep everyone calm. The police trusted me, so they were on our side too. But the rookies in our group who wanted to fight started shouting me down and yelling that there was a government mole in the society. The anti-foreign idiots joined in, and soon all hell broke loose. Later, at a society meeting, I tried to explain what happened as calmly and clearly as I could. I thought that in a group focused on the big picture, reason would prevail over tough-guy talk, and so I couldn't believe what happened next. I was accused of being the mole, a traitor working for a government that was selling out its people, an agent provocateur causing division within the group, an enemy of the Japan that was to be, an anti-patriot. I was kicked out of the society. And you know who the leader of the charge against me was? My friend from the history group! To see friends turn on me before my eyes, willing to string me up in front of a group I was devoted to—it was like I died, really died, in that moment."

"And so now crowds are a source of trauma for you."

"That all these believers in self-reliance could suddenly turn into a mob like that . . . but now I understand what it was about. We thought we were using reason to bring about a revolution in society, but all we really wanted was to feel that our lives weren't useless, that we had purpose, had value; we were each trying to find ourselves but instead we ended up finding an 'us'. The content of the things we said or did didn't really matter. What was important was the feeling of 'us'."

"You said it was obvious I wanted to melt into a crowd. Are you telling me I'm a candidate for something like the Greater East Asian Friendship Society?"

"I might have said that before. But not now. Because this 'tornado dance' thing is pure. You don't do it to please anyone, even yourself. The joy and satisfaction are in the spinning itself, and all the unnecessary parts of the self fall away. There's no gap between one dancer's intentions and another's. That's why it's a kind of prayer. It's different from an ideology or a political position. It's a shared suffering and a shared attempt to overcome that suffering. A plea, from the simple basis of being alive. There's no difference between people at that level. Of course, some might not experience this suffering. But they're relatively few; most begin spinning purely from a desire to ease their discomfort, and everything else just flows from that."

Naomi remembered the curious joy that had burst within her as she watched the fish leap and spin in the pond. They had spun in the air because their world had become a living hell, because they wanted to become anything else besides what they were, as if they believed that to spin was to be reborn. If that joy was what this young man meant by "purity," she understood what he was saying perfectly.

"You called it a 'tornado dance'?"

"Yeah, I heard it on the news yesterday. They call it that."

"Who does?"

"There's supposedly a little village up north of Tokyo that had a traditional dance they called the 'tornado dance'. Tornadoes would hit the area every few years, killing villagers and destroying crops, and so, to contain the tornado god's wrath, the whole village began whirling themselves around in the opposite direction, clockwise. The area became depopulated over the years, and the tradition disappeared, and now the people left there say that's why the whole Tokyo area has had all these tornadoes lately."

"Well, do you want to come with us to tornado-dance over at Sampin Temple, then? But if you're going to slip away again, you might as well stay here. Pink and I will be fine on our own."

"All right, I'll stay." The young man began to climb back up his rope to the tree branch.

"I wonder—do you think there are more people like you, spinning and spinning on their own somewhere?"

"I bet there are. There must be plenty of people around with stories like mine." The young man said this with a smile that seemed to come from the bottom of his heart.

"Scary!" It was Pink who said this. Naomi looked back at the young man. He was concentrating on suspending himself from the tree again, now that Naomi and Pink were out of sight and thus, it seemed, out of mind. "Let's go," said Naomi, tugging Pink by the hand.

Sampin Temple turned out to be already filled to bursting with spinners. All was silent, even the cicadas; the air held only the smell of hot bodies, wafting from the temple in clouds. If Pink hadn't been there to lead her by the hand, Naomi might not have ventured in. But sure enough, her hesitation and unease faded away as she began to move. Surprisingly, Pink no longer clung to her as they spun, but rather went off to twirl alone. She took rests from time to time, but she spun just fine by herself, becoming as intoxicated in the trance as anyone else. She didn't seem to be stifling any nausea either.

An hour passed this way, and Naomi could no longer deny it. Pink was growing, and quickly. Her body was getting bigger, and the look in her eyes showed that her mind was maturing as well. Which meant that Naomi had to be ageing faster too. If she didn't want to chew up the time she had left, she had to stop spinning, right? But she didn't have the impression that time grew slower when she stopped. In fact, it was during her twirling that it seemed to slow down. Enough that it was a reason she kept spinning.

A chill went through Naomi. This unseen larger power, was it deceiving them, compelling them towards unspeakable acts? Were they unknowingly speeding time up? Was it a conspiracy? Was the young man in the tree sending people to these shrines and temples to do this "tornado dance" for him? He said there were others like him all over. Were they a coordinated group inciting a movement? Were people like her, who longed to become one with something larger than herself, unwittingly becoming slaves?

Don't be stupid! I started spinning all on my own. It was only after however many days of it that I met that guy, there's no reason to think there's a conspiracy. Conspiracy theories are just illusions conjured by uneasy hearts. I'm totally at ease when I spin. If I do feel uneasy, all I have to do to feel better is spin more. Spinning makes all that is illusory fall away. The things that remain—those are the things that are real. That are true. Things like Pink growing up so quickly, for instance.

Naomi began to spin faster. She twirled fast enough that the landscape around her melted into a colorful blur. Now she was so good at spinning that no matter how fast she went around, she didn't feel sick. Spurred on by her, the dancers around Naomi began spinning faster as well. At this speed, it seemed as if they would be lifting off the ground before long. She could feel her consciousness begin to detach itself again, somewhere in the back of her mind. *Let go*, she thought. *It's time.*

She spun. She flew. Gravity disappeared, and she floated in the air for a moment, only to gently come back down to earth when it returned. Her body still felt light. The rush of grey in front of her resolved into distinct shapes. She concentrated her gaze. A figure began to rise before her. The grey became transparent. The figure was Pink. Now a teenager, she had become pretty, even sexy. She was spinning as fast as Naomi, but she appeared still as she returned her aunt's gaze. And not just Pink. Everyone around Naomi moved so fast that the movement disappeared, leaving their still figures to emerge from the blur. It was like a zoetrope or the frames of a film, images revealed through high-speed revolution. But they were not just images; she could reach out and touch them. "It's getting late, we should get back before dark," said Pink, but when Naomi took her by the hand, Pink shook her off. "I'm not a kid anymore."

Even as they continued to spin at such high speeds, they found that they could walk normally as they made their way home, as if it were a day like any other. When they reached the house, Naomi's sister greeted them at the door waving an envelope watermarked with cherry blossoms. "It arrived!" she exclaimed. The back of the envelope bore a Ministry of Defense insignia, and the letter informed Naomi that although she was just finishing the last vacation period of her military service, she was being deployed; and so, in the time it took to say, *Off I go!*, Naomi became a crew member on the destroyer *Sakimori*. Because it was a battle to defend some islands, the fighting took place almost entirely at sea, with threats and displays of force exchanged almost as if choreographed in advance, but Naomi's unit, under cover of the crossfire, was commanded to make a landing using ultra-mini, single-passenger submarines, and just as Naomi was thinking she'd succeeded, it turned out to be a trap, torpedoes coming at them from three sides within the confines of the bay, and while she managed to eject herself from the submarine right away, she was hit in the back by shrapnel from the explosion, which immobilized her, and she drifted out to sea, only to be picked up by a passing cruiser and given a hero's welcome upon her return home, but even as she spent her time in the hospital working diligently at rehabilitation, she never rid herself of a lingering paralysis in her arms and legs, and she grew depressed with the passage of day after listless day, while her sister, who was a nurse after all, did her best to take care of her; her depression expressed itself as resentment, resentment spewed at her sister and the world. *It can just go to hell for all I care!* she would say and say again, and soon the islands were all snatched away, Japan's supposed allies declaring that they wouldn't intervene, and thus the East Asian Union dissolved, leaving Japan isolated, its food supply rapidly diminishing, the country finally paying the price for opening its food markets so completely to foreign goods, the dome agricultural industry woefully behind the times, unable to increase promotion to meet demand, and even in Naomi's household, meals dwindled two servings of thin potato gruel a day, and Pink, having once so idolized Naomi and being now so disgusted by her current state, left home to live in a dormitory while she attended technical college, volunteering for the army right after graduation and ending up on the front lines near Kyushu, where she became a casualty of war at twenty-one, taken out by an unmanned stealth-fighter strike, leaving Naomi overwhelmed with guilt as if she had been the one to do the killing, the heaviness of her heart paralyzing the rest of her body completely, but even as she imagined her own death again and again, she couldn't bring herself to abandon her sister to what had become a life dark with tragedy, a life her sister strove every day to keep herself from abandoning completely, and thus it was that August came again as rumors swirled that the war had reached Japan's main island at last, and the sun, as if driven mad, poured heat mercilessly down upon the land, Tokyo's temperatures breaking forty for the first time in nineteen years. Weakened and hungry, the residents of the archipelago, reduced to mere shimmers in the hot air, winked out one by one, and it dawned on Naomi as she watched her sister unable to cope, languishing before her on the tatami, that she could become a fan herself and create a breeze to revive her, and so, taking a small fan in each hand, she wrestled with her stiffened body, forcing it into motion, and as she slowly began to revolve, she remembered how she had spun like this to battle the heat nineteen years before, how Pink, so young then, had clamored to play bird-in-the-cage and spin, and as she shared these memories with her sister, they revitalized her enough that she joined Naomi in her spinning, a spinning that somehow made them both feel newly strong, and newly hungry too, enough to want to leave the house for food, and so out they went as the sun went down, and in the park they encountered a crowd of people gathered at the edge of the pond, spinning slowly all in unison, and Naomi found herself joining them, looking up into the sky just as she had before, but this time she felt she was falling, and she noticed she was spinning left, counter to the clockwise revolutions of nineteen years ago, perhaps this meant that time could reverse direction too, could unbind her from this past that so entangled and constrained her, and perhaps Pink could come back to life as well, and together they could go back to before they'd twisted their bodies in wicked prayer and find some other way to free themselves from a world become a living hell, and so she vowed that once they'd wound the world back a full nineteen years, they would take it in their hands again and make it theirs at last; on and on she spun, every revolution a prayer in reverse.

In your second reading, did you notice any discrepancies? We did. For instance, Pink dies when she's twenty-one but Naomi says the spinning event happened nineteen years earlier, which would have made Pink two. It's possible, but at her youngest in the story Pink had seemed older than two. And then there's the matter of Pink aging before Naomi's eyes. We also learn in the beginning of the story that Naomi had wanted to sign up for the National Defense Forces, but didn't, though we later learn that a letter arrives for her with her enlistment orders.

There are a number of such contradictions in the story that would either lead us to believe that the author is a sloppy writer or that he knows exactly what he's doing and has a reason for doing this. We believe the latter, but will leave it to you to sort out what you think the reasons are.

There's also the matter of the spinning. While this aspect of the story might strike you as pure fantasy, there are historical precedents for such behavior. There have been incidents throughout history of people dancing or twirling themselves for days at a time, often to the point of exhaustion or death, as in the Strasbourg Dancing Plague of 1518, when a woman started twirling silently in the middle of town. Before long, others had joined her and soon there were over 400 "victims." The best part of this episode was the town's response. They built a stage and hired musicians to accompany the dancers. Eventually, the town carted the dancers off to the mountains to pray for absolution. Yes, there are possible rational explanations, such as moldy rye bread that can cause people to hallucinate and behave strangely (rye bread mold is also a possible culprit for the mass hallucinations that might have brought on the famous witch trials) but rational explanations are no fun. A scientist or historian looks for explanations while a story writer looks for the answer to the question, "And then what happened?"

To us, odder than the twirling/praying of Naomi and the others is the stranger they encounter, the man who belongs to a right-wing defense group. What's strange isn't the existence of such a group—they exist in Japan as in most other parts of the world. In Japan's case, the country can call its Defense Force an army because of its anti-militaristic constitution drafted in the wake of the Second World War and the devastating toll Japan's Imperial Army took on Asia. What's remarkable is that this aspect of the story takes up a fair amount of space when it would seem to have little to do with the main thrust of the events. Or so it might seem. Again, think of the perspective from which the story is told. This is Naomi's story and her concerns are the story's concerns. We'll leave it at that and let you sort it out.

Let's revise what we stated previously. While rational explanations can be a bit disappointing, interpretations can be a lot of fun. That's why we engage in discussions about stories.

But what can we learn from this story? That's the question you should always ask yourself when you're examining a story with a writer's eye.

Notice how the tone and rhythm of the story match the situation—this is a story about the world heating up, and yes, we are going to be reminded of global warming, but is this a story *about* global warming per se and its dire results for humanity? Perhaps on some level that's an aspect of it, but on the character level, this is a personal story as the heat takes over Naomi and the others and becomes a kind of delirium. The story itself starts out rationally enough but becomes itself a kind of delirium, almost a fever dream of a story. The last several pages are one long paragraph in which a series of cataclysmic events happen in quick succession. Of course, we must remember that this is a translation and it invariably looks different in Japanese, but one of the tasks of the translator is to capture the feel of the original as much as possible. The point here is that when you write a story, the rhythm and diction of a story should reflect its content as much as possible. The way words look on a page, the length of your sentences, the ways in which you vary sentences—all of this contributes to the reader's experience.

In the case of "Learning Curve," this story is without a doubt as much about the present and the recent past as it is about the future. Set in Hong Kong of the near future, around 2034, the story centers on the interactions between Lana (the point of view character), her husband Michael, and their son Dave. The conflict is largely between Michael and Dave, who we learn quickly, sets out nightly for anti-government protests. If you happen to be a Chinese government official reading these words, or a Chinese nationalist, it's likely you will want to read no further. You'll either want to cut this story from the Chinese edition of this book or more likely, make certain there is no Chinese edition. We do not write these words with bitterness or to mock said Chinese officials and nationalists, only to show that even fiction can have real-world consequences. Do we want a Mainland Chinese edition of this book? Of course we do. Do we imagine taking the story out of this book to make it more palatable to officialdom and nationalists who see the Hong Kong protests of the recent past as treasonous? Our answer is self-evident, but we should also state this is why we have left this story for the last. In any case, we hope that any potential official censors have at least learned something new about fiction writing by reading through this text to this point.

Let's back up and give a brief history of the "Umbrella Movement," an understanding of which is central to this story. The Umbrella Movement began in Hong Kong in September of 2014 as a protest against Beijing's increasing encroachment against free elections in Hong Kong, which had been one of the cornerstones of the handover agreement between China and the UK. A treaty between the two countries established Hong Kong as an autonomous zone within greater China, but in recent years, China has rolled back Hong Kong's autonomy. The Umbrella Movement started in reaction to one of these rollbacks, Beijing's insistence on approving the slate of candidates who could run for office and making sure that only pro-Beijing officials would be in the upper echelons of power.

Go ahead and read the story with the understanding that you are reading it from the past, that Michael and Lana are, as you read the story of their future, in their early twenties, living in Hong Kong, married already and with an infant son, Dave, to take care of now.

2 "Learning Curve"

by Yeung Chak Yan (Hong Kong)

Yeung Chak Yan's story "Make Believe" appears in the anthology *The Queen of Statue Square: New Short Fiction from Hong Kong* (2014). Her doctoral scholarly work in computational linguistics combines her dual interests in language and information technology. She holds a MA in Creative Writing from Bath Spa University.

It was one of those weeks again.

Lana tapped her tablet to pause the latest episode of *Why So Serious* when her son came out of his room. Dave was dressed in black. He moved about the flat quickly, going into the bathroom, heading to the kitchen to fill up his water bottle, and now rummaging the snack cupboard at the corner of the living room.

On the other side of the couch, Michael gave a quiet snort. The tablet in his hands was filled with text—the Sunday morning paper, most likely—though his attention was on their son, who had so far been wisely ignoring his father's attempt to reignite their argument last night. Dave took two energy bars from the cupboard and hurried back into his room. When he emerged again, he was carrying his brown backpack.

Michael shifted. Lana wondered if he, too, had realized that Dave always used this particular backpack when he went and did his "things." Probably not. Men seldom noticed this kind of detail.

"Don't you have schoolwork to do?" asked Michael, his voice too loud in the room.

A hint of irritation crossed Dave's face, but he managed to rein it in and walked over to the front door. Michael lowered his tablet.

"Don't come back too late," said Lana before her husband could say another word. "And be careful."

Dave nodded and left. Michael shook his head and returned to his news. Lana started up her comedy again, but the sound did nothing to mask the sudden silence in the flat. She glanced over at Michael. He was still reading—no, he was staring at a screen that had darkened from inactivity, deep in thought. She didn't like the look on his face.

"Seems like it'll just be you and me this morning, Michael," she said.

He did not look up. "Yes, seems like it."

"How about we go to that new restaurant in the mall?" she asked. "I have a coupon for a two-person set and it's about to expire."

He remained silent for a while longer, then let out a loud breath and gave her a tired smile. "Well, we can't have that now, can we?"

* * *

It was seven when Lana returned home on Monday, though her good mood at managing to finish her work on time did not last long. As soon as she stepped out of the lift, she could hear Michael's voice. It got louder as she approached their flat.

"Responsibility?" he bellowed. "You are breaking the law and you are telling me this is your *responsibility*?"

And then there was her son's voice, equally loud.

"We have the right to protest when the government is wrong! If we don't speak out now, soon we won't be able to say anything at all, just like the people in China. Is that what you want?"

A moment later, the front door opened and Dave walked out, carrying his brown backpack. He paused when he saw her, his gaze darting from her to the still opened door and back.

Lana's first thought was to tell Dave to listen to his father—there were rumors on the Internet that the police were about to clear the protest site—but she couldn't bring herself to say it. Dave left through the fire exit instead of waiting for the lift, as though he couldn't wait to get as far away from them as he could.

For a long time Lana stood there, between her fleeing son and her silent husband in the flat. *This is unfair*, she thought. They shouldn't have to deal with this. She shouldn't have to come home after a day of work to find her husband and son shouting at each other again. Dave should be at home playing video games, not spending all his free time sitting outside the Government Complex. And Michael . . .

She entered the flat and closed the door. Michael was standing rigid with his hands clenched at his sides. She took a few steps towards him and stopped when he turned to her.

"You let him go," he said.

She did. "He'll go either way. It's not as if I can stop him."

"I don't understand you sometimes."

She didn't understand him sometimes. He was acting as though he had no idea why Dave was heading to the protests, as though they had not done the same years ago, when they were young enough to believe they could change the future.

"He will learn," she said. "He's a smart boy."

* * *

She left her office at eight-thirty on Tuesday. One of her staff had sent a wrong document to a client, leaving her to clean up the mess. By the time she returned home, Michael had finished cooking dinner and was waiting for her. Their son was nowhere to be seen.

"Dave?" she asked and immediately regretted it. She was usually more careful.

"Where else?" said Michael, his voice tight.

She took her seat opposite from him at the dining table. The pork chops were burnt and the dish of steamed eggs was overcooked. She ate them without complaint; now was not the time to tease him about making what he would normally call "amateur mistakes."

Five minutes passed by, then ten. For a moment Lana thought they might make it through dinner without incident. Naturally, this was also when Michael lost his patience and slammed his hand on the table.

"Foolish boy!"

"He will learn," she insisted.

"At what cost?" he snapped.

She reached over and held his hand. She hadn't realized he was still so—

But of course he was still bitter. She had been with him when he was denied entry into Guangzhou, and when he was fired for no apparent reason a week after his old company had been bought by a mainland competitor. He had looked so angry then, so . . . disillusioned.

He withdrew his hand and turned away. Neither of them managed to finish their bowl of rice that night.

* * *

Dave was home for dinner the next day. He was restless and returned to his room soon afterwards. Through the half-opened door, Lana could see him typing furiously on his phone while the screen of his laptop kept refreshing with new messages and photos.

Part of her was tempted to go in and talk to him, to let him know that she did understand what he was going through. She had walked the same path before, and their opinions on their government were not as different as he thought.

It had been almost twenty years since she had last been to a protest, but she still remembered what it had been like, being out there on the streets, sweating in the heat, and waiting—yearning—to be heard. The high-speed rail controversy in 2009. The fight against the implementation of the so-called "Moral and National Education" in 2012. She was no stranger to sitting outside the Government Complex day after day. Then the Umbrella Movement happened, and ended it all for her.

Most people were calling it the "928 Incident" now. The government had started using the new name about five years after the occupy movement. Soon, the media began to adopt it, then the general public. Lana herself had clung to the old term Umbrella Movement. Not that she ever said the name out loud anymore, or had any reason to. What was there to talk about? They had failed. All they had done was prove how futile it was to fight against Beijing's will, and how naive they were to think Hong Kong stood a chance. They had blocked the streets for weeks, yes, but so what? They had no real leverage and China still held all the cards. They could keep throwing themselves against the Government Complex in Admiralty, but their voices, even if they were loud enough to reach the impenetrable fortress up north, would always be nothing but mere annoyance.

She stopped going to protests afterwards. Perhaps she was too pessimistic—or realistic—but she never understood why some people regarded the Umbrella Movement as a beacon of hope for the future of Hong Kong. For her, it always felt like a final, desperate gamble, one that came to be because no one knew what to expect, not the police, not the government, and not the people who had been shaken into action. A protest this big would never happen in Hong Kong again; everyone knew it, and she suspected it was in part why so many had joined in. If they couldn't win this time, they never could.

They lost. They were utterly ignored by Beijing. And as the tents vanished from Admiralty, so did Lana's will to fight. She couldn't help it. She was too much of a Hong Konger to continue investing in a fruitless pursuit when she could use the time and effort on her own career.

Inside the room, Dave was still typing on his phone, and not for the first time Lana wondered what her son saw in this city that made him want to fight for it. She had at least seen it in its better days; he had been born after the Umbrella Movement. But he was at home tonight, and Lana knew her son well enough to guess what was happening.

Dave was learning. He was starting to see the reality of the situation, as she had years ago. It was as she had told Michael. The problem would solve itself. All they had to do was to wait it out.

She forced herself to turn away and walked back to her room. There was no need for her to say anything now. And no, there was no reason at all to be disappointed.

* * *

Dave was out again on Thursday. He had not even come back home after school, likely choosing to head straight to Admiralty and avoid another confrontation with his father.

"One day, he will find himself blocked off everywhere. No schools will take him. No companies will hire him," muttered Michael as he paced the living room. "And then he will understand."

"He knows to be careful," said Lana. "I've told him not to go to the front. He's a smart boy."

"How can you act as if nothing's wrong?" said Michael.

"Act as if nothing's wrong?" she repeated, louder than she intended to. "Of course I'm worried, but what can I possibly say? We have done it too, Michael."

He paused at the reminder, then shook his head. "All the more reason for us to stop him from making the same—"

The unspoken word hung in the air. He couldn't say it, Lana realized. He couldn't bring himself to admit that he—that they—had been wrong. He bowed his head, looking tired and resigned. She stepped forward and held him, like she had years ago on the last day of the Umbrella Movement, when everyone knew the police were about to clear out the tents.

They had only known each other for seventy-nine days then—for just as long as the Umbrella Movement had lasted. It was a canister of tear gas that brought them together—the first one that the police fired at the beginning of the protest. She found him at the side of the road, bent over with his eyes shut, struggling to breathe. She followed the instructions the people on the streets were shouting out and rinsed his eyes with water, trembling and crying the whole way, so much so that he asked if she was all right, as if she was the one in pain—or maybe she was, but at least not physically. He thanked her for helping him and rushed back towards where the police were as soon as his breathing returned to normal. She watched him go, and suddenly the decision of leaving or staying became an easy one—maybe it was because he made her feel useful, or because she could tell he was as terrified as she was.

It was *yun fan*, she supposed, that made them run into each other again two days later. There were a lot of people in Admiralty, after all. He thanked her for a second time and then they started talking, about Hong Kong, about themselves, and about the future. They were so hopeful then, certain that they could make a difference.

"Do you really . . . regret it?" she asked.

He had paid for it, years later, while she had got lucky. No one knew how the government compiled the name list, only that there was one.

His gaze softened and he pulled her closer. "Don't be ridiculous."

* * *

Friday. Michael spent the evening watching news. Lana took the time to do laundry. She kept the bathroom door closed, but she could still hear the television. She didn't need to look to know what the police were doing.

At ten, when Dave still had not returned, she asked Michael to change the channel. He switched off the television instead and took out his tablet. Fifteen minutes later, he put it down, grabbed his wallet, and headed out, saying he had forgotten to buy something. A few cans of Tsingtao at Seven-Eleven, no doubt. He would then take a long walk in the park and return hours later. She was well aware of his habit.

Dave came home about ten minutes after Michael had left. He closed the front door and leaned against it. He looked unharmed, but his eyes were red. Was it pepper spray?

Lana approached him. "Dave?"

"I left when the police showed up," he murmured, "like you told me to."

Not pepper spray then. "What happened?" she asked.

"The police came and said they were about to take action, but . . . there weren't enough people at the site tonight. I heard the police have brought two water cannons and—" He ducked his head. "It's not that I think the government is right. It's just—"

He did not think it was worth getting hurt or arrested over. Shouting slogans while being protected by the safety in numbers was one thing, paying a personal price for it was another. Lana understood. She, too, would have fled on the first day of the Umbrella Movement had she not run into Michael.

Maybe that was why she had taken its failure so hard; she had given her all, and expected something to come of it. She had always been the pragmatic one. She had pulled back as soon as she saw the sign of defeat. She had even deleted all the photos and comments about the Umbrella Movement on her Facebook in case they would be used as evidence against her. As it turned out, it paid to be careful.

But at what cost?

She watched as Dave left for his room with his head bowed in shame, and once again found herself cursing this city, where teenagers had to fight to protect their home, and where parents had to tell their children that it was fine to be selfish, that acting on one's belief was not necessarily the best course of action. After all, justice, democracy and the common good were but abstract concepts that could not fill one's stomach.

She shook her head. How insufferably Chinese.

Could things have been different? If she had not given up all those years ago, if she had tried harder, would Dave's Hong Kong have been a better place?

* * *

On Saturday, Lana came home after her half-day work to find Michael on the couch, sitting with his arms crossed and Dave's brown backpack on the floor by his side.

"Found it in the bin outside," he said. "The boy's throwing it away. Waste of a perfectly good bag."

"He left when the police arrived," said Lana. "He . . . came to realize there was only so far he was willing go for what he believed in. It upset him."

Michael said nothing. She could only guess what he was thinking, or why he had brought the bag back.

"Do you think it's our fault?" he asked.

"I don't know," she said. It was impossible to tell what he was referring to.

A moment later, Michael stood up and walked towards Dave's room with the backpack, his disapproval evident on his face. Lana chuckled, and something inside her seemed to have loosened up.

Perhaps it was not a total loss, after all. Something of those very special seventy-nine days had remained—something that still made them act foolishly on occasion, and made them want to believe in a happy ending for those willing to fight for it. And maybe that was enough. Maybe that was the best they could hope to accomplish.

You might think that you've caught us out—here is a story with a definite message, no? Does it really have a message? We'd argue that it doesn't. True, where the characters and, by inference, the author, stand on the issue of Hong Kong's autonomy from the Central Communist Party in Beijing, is not in doubt, but that's not the same as conveying a definite message. You could read the story and come to the conclusion that protesting against overwhelming odds is not worth the personal cost, or you could come to the opposite conclusion, or neither. Like many stories, it presents a conundrum, not a problem with a definite solution. It asks the question, How do we balance our individual happiness and security with our hopes and dreams for the society we want to live in? If we make no difference at all, what is the point of our suffering? How can an older generation refuse to let a new generation make its own difficult choices one way or the other? You could say that at its heart, this is a family story about wanting to protect their children.

As you can see, this story is not only relevant to the people of Hong Kong, but to anyone protesting injustice as they see it. It's likely that parents or grandparents have the same worries about their children participating in Black Lives Matter protests as their parents or grandparents had about their protests against the Vietnam War or in favor of Civil Rights.

If you decide to set a story in the future, know that you are saying at least as much about the present as you are about the future, likely more. You're not going to get the future right, so don't worry about that. In "Learning Curve," we can already see that real events have outpaced the events depicted in the story. Since the story was written, the Umbrella Movement has been eclipsed by massive demonstrations against a law to allow Hong Kong residents to be tried in Mainland China. Protesters largely saw this as their last hope to retain some semblance of autonomy. The protests were quashed finally when Beijing imposed a broad law that allowed authorities to arrest anyone they saw as anti-Beijing and charge them with sedition. Perhaps twenty years from now, Dave will be joining street protests up to a point, but perhaps not. What's indisputable, however, is that somewhere in the world, parents and children will be having difficult conversations twenty years from now, much like the one depicted here.

Exercises

1. Research some legendary or real event that took place centuries ago, such as the Dancing Plague of Strasbourg, and set it in the present or the future. Set it in your own country with people you know or those who might know.

2. Write a scene in which a character starts an action and can't stop. Others join in and they can't stop either.

3. Think about a pressing political issue (voter suppression, global warming, racism, state-sponsored brutality) and imagine setting a story about this issue twenty years in the future, fifty years, 100 years, and then 1,000. The conflict might be an internal/external one, such as Xu Xi's "All About Skin," or it might be a family conflict, but if it's only a societal conflict and the message is loud and clear (e.g., racism is bad), you'd be better off writing an editorial. Instead, make the backdrop a political/societal one, but make the conflict more personal and affecting fewer people. Don't worry. We'll get it.

4. Think about a personal problem you've faced recently or a problem you're really worried about and let someone 100 years from now worry about that same problem. Change only one thing about the world of 100 years from now, nothing else. It could be big or it could be small, but we as readers shouldn't realize the story is set in the future until page two or three.

5. Write a version of "Pink" in which some big natural event occurs. Instead of a heat wave, temperatures have dipped down to historic lows and your main character has an unusual response. Or maybe all the leaves have fallen from the trees and won't sprout again. Or maybe a mysterious purple spray mists the earth. Or lawns start growing an inch an hour. Don't worry about what it means, but let the story go where it wants, even if you're not sure what it means to you. After you've written as far as you can go with the character's response, introduce a character who sees the world differently from your main character. See where it takes you. Perhaps you will have an "aha" moment when you realize that what seemed like nonsense to you initially now makes *a lot* of sense as an allegory.

INDEX

Abu Dhabi   57, 65–7
action, significance of   16, 26, 44
agency, significance of   205
Ahmed, Michael Mohammed   36
alienation   70, 80, 81, 95, 240
"All About Skin" (Xu Xi)   99–105
   significance of   105–6
allegory   113, 239, 240
All Nippon Cutis   102–5
alter ego   106, 113
ambiguity   5, 30, 113, 198, 239
American, idea of   99–105
antagonist   25
anxiety   50, 56, 58, 133, 164, 166, 185, 238
Apogee Journal   219
archetypes   115, 129–30
Asia   1–3, 50, 65, 69, 80, 106, 115, 126, 127, 195, 218, 223, 236, 248, 249, 252
attraction
   "Convince Me" and   31–6
   No Toes and   37–44
Australia   1, 2, 37
authenticity   25, 30, 95, 99
   of lived experience   17
authoritarian   3, 239
authority   113, 129, 144, 233, 239, 240, 260
autobiografiction   99
autobiographical fiction, significance of   98
autobiographication, significance of   98
autobiography, significance of   98
autofiction   195
   American   99
   significance of   98–9
   types of   98–9

Baguio (Philippines)   88
Bait and Switch   157
Barth, John   99
Bass, Ellen   29
bathos   125–6, 129
"Bee Honey" (Yoshimoto Banana)   223–7
   significance of   228–9
Bellingham Review   219
Bergstrom, Brian   240
betrayal, significance of   18, 160, 170, 210
biographical autofiction (*autofiction biografique*)   98
biography, significance of   98
"Birds" (Unnikrishnan)   45, 57–65
   significance of   65–7
Blood: Collected Stories (de Jesus)   159

"Boat, The" (Nam Le)   131–57
   significance of   132, 157–9
"Boondocks" (Hemley)   115, 127–9
Borderline Citizen (Hemley)   127
Bradbury, Ray   239
Britain/British/United Kingdom (UK)   1, 2, 106, 116, 198, 204, 228, 232, 254
Brothers, The (Tenorio)   5–16
   significance of   16–18
Bruce, Natascha   173

Camus, Albert   2
Cantonese   106
Cat in the Agraharam and Other Stories (Kumar)   70
cautionary tales   239
central image   30, 36
Cheever, John   80
China   2, 254
China cutis, significance of   100–1
Chinese Lives (Zhang Xinxin)   107
Chughtai, Ismat   2, 198–9, 205
"Clerk's Story, A" (Kumar)   70–8, 87
   significance of   78–9
Colonna, Vince   98
Compendium of Hong Kong Fiction from 1919-1941, A (Tse)   173
conflict   80, 106, 115, 132, 170, 195, 199
   attraction and   29, 36
   as building block of fiction   26
   family, causes of   5, 16, 18, 25
   future tense and   240, 254
   histories and   223, 234, 237
   intercultural   3
   routines and   45, 67
   turmoil and   78–9
"Convince Me" (Jiang Yitan)   29, 31–6
   significance of   36–7
Cooke, Sam   223
corporate rung   101, 103
corpus-ceiling glass   100, 101, 103
cosmopol, significance of   101–3
counter-intuitiveness   217–18, 220
"Counterpoints" (Joyce)   37
"Crystal River" (Smith)   157
cultural attitude, significance of   126
culture   3, 113, 195, 205, 217
   attraction and   35, 44
   clash of   115
   diasporas and   132, 157, 158
   invaders and   115, 126, 128–9

Index

Little Fish and 70, 79, 88, 94
Cursed and Other Stories (de Jesus) 159
Cusset, Catherine 98

day-in-the-life-story 70
de Jesus, Noelle Q. 2, 131, 159
Derma 100–5
description, significance of 16, 26, 44, 98
dialogue, significance of 2, 16, 26, 66, 95, 98, 126
    attraction and 43, 44
    as stylized 95
diasporas
    "Boat, The" and 131–59
    "Dreams in English" and 159–70
dictum 69
disturbing material, significance of 228
Domino Effect 131
"Door, The" (Tse) 173–85
    significance of 185–6
Doubrovsky, Serge 98
"Dragon Menu" (Zhang Xinxin) 106–13
    significance of 113–14
drama/dramatic 66, 115, 126, 173
    family and 16, 18, 26
    histories and 229, 236, 237
dramatization 69, 129
dream 5, 102, 111
    diasporas and 152, 157, 158, 170
    future tense and 254, 260
    histories and 235, 237
    mysteries and 175, 179, 182
    routines and 63, 65, 67
"Dreams in English" (de Jesus) 131, 159–69
    significance of 169–70
Dungeonquest game 50, 56, 57

embarrassment 9, 11, 60, 81, 103, 120, 122
    attraction and 39, 43
    diasporas and 132, 153, 161, 162
    mysteries and 181, 188
    taboos and 202, 206, 207, 209, 214–16, 220
Emmerich, Michael 224
empathy 35, 130
English 2, 3, 19, 23, 173, 218, 227, 231, 240
    diasporas and 160, 161, 167, 169
    invaders and 115, 118–20, 122, 124, 126, 127, 129
    Little Fish and 80, 81, 85, 87, 92, 95
    skins and 98, 99, 106
enigma 173
Envy (Olesha) 239
Epiderm International 102–5
episode/episodic 6, 16, 66, 80, 124, 253
"Errand, An" (Lacuesta) 88–93, 105
    significance of 93–5
exposition 25, 43, 131–2, 157–8

fabulist 66, 67
face 31, 40, 97, 108, 234

diasporas and 133–41, 143, 144, 146–56, 163–6, 168, 169
family and 6, 7, 9, 10, 14–16, 20, 22–4
future tense and 241, 255, 260
invaders and 118, 122, 125
Little Fish and 71, 73, 75, 76, 79, 85, 87, 91–4
mysteries and 175–80, 183, 184
routines and 48, 52, 63, 65
taboos and 200, 203, 206, 209, 211–14, 216, 219
fallen worker, theme of 58–65
    heat and 60–1, 66
fallible narrator 37
family 5
    "Brothers, The" and 5–17
    "My Mother Pattu" and 18–27
fantastical autofiction (*autofiction fantastique*) 98
Fan Xiaoqing 173, 186, 194
"Farangs" (Lapcharoensap) 115–25, 129
    significance of 125–6
Fast and the Furious, The (film) 42
Faulkner, William 95
feuds and conflicts 16
Filipino 2, 3, 6, 8–11, 129, 159
Fils (Doubrovsky) 98
first-person narrative 37, 45, 80, 87, 97
flashback 66, 94, 157, 158, 169
Forgive You and Forgive Myself (Love Poems) (Jiang Yitan) 31
fun 36, 40, 97, 102, 129, 254
    family and 19, 24, 25
    histories and 225, 232
    Little Fish and 84, 88
    poking 194, 236
    routines and 49, 60, 61
funeral, Filipino 8–11, 14–15
future tense 239
    "Learning Curve" and 254–60
    "Pink" and 240–54

Gao Xingjian 2, 195
gaze 38, 41, 80, 184
    diasporas and 137, 144, 147, 154, 167
    future tense and 251, 256, 259
    histories and 224, 232, 235
    routines and 49, 52
    taboos and 199, 207, 216
gender 16, 113, 128, 157
generalization 44
Greenest Gecko, The (Pirapokin) 218
guilt 20, 26, 32, 36, 170, 187, 252

Hamiduddin, Zoovia 205
Hand, Philip 31
Handmaid's Tale, A 239
Han Yujoo 45–6, 55, 56
Harris, Paul 186
heavy-handed 25, 30, 37, 67, 69, 70, 95, 239
Hemley, Robin 115, 127, 129

Index

Hepburn, Oh Hepburn (Jiang Yitan) 31
historical trauma, significance of 238
histories 3, 79, 95, 115, 190, 198, 205, 223, 253
    "Bee Honey" and 223–9
    "Lee Kuan Yew Is Not Always the Answer" and 229–37
"History of City and Villages, A" (Fan Xiaoqing) 186
Ho Chi Minh 131
homesickness 81
Hong, Janet 45
Hong Kong 2, 3, 106, 254
Hoshino Tomoyuki 240

image/imagery 88, 112, 115, 129, 185, 225, 251
    attraction and 29–30, 44
    repetition of 30, 43, 173, 186
Impossible Fairy Tale, The (Han Yujoo) 45
India 2, 3, 70
Indonesia 106
in medias res (the middle of things) 132, 133
Integume 100–2, 105
internal logic 67, 113
Ionesco, Eugene 113
It Never Rains on National Day (Tiang) 80, 81

Jadeja, Gopika 198
James, Henry 69
Japan 19–20, 49, 64, 115, 116, 127–9, 195, 224–6, 228, 234, 240, 242, 248, 249, 252–4
Jiang Yitan 31
journey narrative 80
Journey to the West (Monkey) 80
Joyce, James 37, 69, 80, 95
juxtaposition 88, 131, 238

Kafka, Franz 105, 113
Karthick, Arun 70
Korea 2, 45, 51–2, 56, 67, 197
Kumar, Dilip 70–1

Lacuesta, Angelo R. 88, 105
lady don juan 101, 103
language 3, 16, 35, 98, 248
    diasporas and 160, 167
    invaders and 115, 116, 118, 124, 126–9
    Little Fish and 67, 70, 79–81, 87, 94
    mysteries and 185, 186
    significance of 115
    unexpected 186
Laos 218
Lapcharoensap, Rattawut 115, 116
Le, Nam 2
"Learning Curve" (Yeung Chak Yan) 239, 254–9
    significance of 260
Lebs, The (Ahmed) 37
"Lebz Rule" 42
Lee Kuan Yew 236

"Lee Kuan Yew Is Not Always the Answer" (Tan) 223, 229–36
    significance of 236–7
Leung, Brian 128
life writing, modes of 98
literary device 185
Literature in Context 219
Little Fish
    "Clerk's Story, A" and 70–9
    "Errand, An" and 88–95
    "National Day" and 80–8
local color 70, 95
loneliness 58, 66, 75, 84, 199
Long, John Luther 115
Lu Xun 1
Lu Xun's Mustache (Jiang Yitan) 31

Macguffin 157
Madame Butterfly (opera) 115
Malaysia 18–19, 139, 228, 234
Mandarin 31, 107, 186
Manickam, Saraswathy M. (Saras) 18–19
Manila (Philippines) 88
Marya, Deepika 204–5
meaning 129
    attraction and 29–30, 43
    histories and 223, 228, 238
    Little Fish and 69, 80, 94
    mysteries and 173, 181, 182
    routines and 45, 54, 56
melodrama 18, 236
memoir, significance of 25, 96, 98, 198
metafiction 98, 106
Metamorphosis (Kafka) 113
migrant workers 45, 57, 65–7, 110, 129
"Modest Proposal, A" (Swift) 97
Monkey 80
monologue 75, 206
Monstress (Tenorio) 5
moral tale 66
motif 57
motivations 18, 25
    of character 26, 37, 186, 217
Mo Yan 2, 195
Murakami 2
Myanmar 218
"My Mother Pattu" (Manickam) 18–25
    significance of 25–7
mysteries 173
    "Door, The" and 173–86
    "Where Did I Lose You" and 186–95

Nair, Meera 205
Name Le 131–3, 157–9
Narayanan, Padma 70
narrative 2, 5, 36, 129, 185, 205
    diasporas and 157, 159, 171
    histories and 236, 237

Index

Little Fish and   69, 78–80, 87
routines and   45, 66, 67
narrator   157, 195, 198, 217
   attraction and   36, 37, 43
   invaders and   125, 126, 129
   Little Fish and   69, 80, 87
   routines and   45, 55–7, 67
   skins and   97, 106, 113
Nasir (film)   70
"National Day" (Tiang)   80–7
   significance of   80, 87–8
Neon Genesis Evangelion (anime)   49
Newfound Journal   218
New York Times Magazine (newspaper)   205
1984 (Owell)   239, 240
"No Toes" (Ahmed)   29, 36–43, 97
   significance of   43–4
nuance   17, 26, 30, 115, 205

obsession   43, 70, 79, 97, 140, 185, 199, 205
O'Connor, Flannery   2, 80
Offing, The   219
Olesha, Yuri   239
omniscience   69, 70, 79, 80, 88, 94, 95
Ore (Hoshino Tomoyuki)   240
organic symbol   30, 43
Orwell, George   240

pathos   126
pattern   25, 57, 80, 108, 147, 242
   attraction and   30, 43
   mysteries and   173, 175, 180, 181
People's PiFu   102, 104, 105
perspective   45, 93, 100, 115, 126, 253. *See also* points of view (POV)
Philippines   2, 5, 88. *See also* Filipino
physicality, obsession with   43–4
physical violence, significance of   18
"Pink" (Hoshino Tomoyuki)   240–53
   significance of   253–4
Pirapokin, Ploi   218–19
Pleiades   218
Poe, Edgar Allen   3
points of view (POV)   2, 45, 87, 93, 95, 129, 237
   collective   55–6
   omniscient   69, 70, 79, 80, 88, 95
   second-person   70, 79
   shift of   56
   third-person   66–7, 93
politics/political   2, 3, 16, 45, 167, 205
   future tense and   239, 250
   histories and   225, 226
   Little Fish and   69, 70, 79, 91, 96
Pound, Ezra   1
"Prayer in Training" (Pirapokin)   218–20
   significance of   220
Producers, The (film)   97
propaganda   230, 237, 239

protagonist   37, 43, 66, 126, 130, 131, 185, 195
   alter ego and   106
   author and   97–8
   family and   25, 26
   histories and   223, 228
   Little Fish and   69, 70, 80
protest   203, 228, 239, 254, 256–8, 260
protest fiction   45
Puccini   115

Queen of Statue Square, The (Moore and Xu Xi)   255
"Quilt, The" (Chughtai)   198–204
   significance of   205

realism   67, 69, 95, 105, 186, 197, 257
   autofiction and   98–9
red herrings   57
repetition   43–4, 54, 57, 173, 186, 214
   of image   30
   as literary device   185
   of routine   56
"Report to an Academy, A" (Kafka)   105
resolution   5, 17–18, 27, 105, 155, 243
Reynolds, Stephen   99
rhetorical questions   45
Rhinoceros (Ionesco)   113
Romeo and Juliet (Shakespeare)   29
routine
   "Birds" and   57–67
   repetitiveness of   56
   "We That Summer" and   45–57, 66, 67
rule of three   30, 43

San Francisco Chronicle (newspaper)   5
Sang Ye   107
satire   45, 55, 57, 69, 236, 237, 239
   callousness and   97
   gentle   194
   moral tale and   66
Saunders, Max   99
Secret Life of Walter Mitty, The (Thurber)   106
secrets, significance of   159
Self-Impressions (Saunders)   99
semi-autobiography   27
sentimentality   17, 95, 126, 161, 197, 199
sentimental resolution   17–18
setting, significance of   1–3, 16, 195
   futuristic   236
   sense of   157
   special occasions as   79
Sightseeing (Lapcharoensap)   116
Singapore   3, 70, 80, 82, 87–8, 96, 129, 223, 229, 231, 234–7
skins, shedding
   All About Skin and   99–106
   Dragon Menu and   106–14
Smith, Charlie   157
Snow and Shadow (Tse)   173

266

Index

snowball effect   197
societal critique   55
Son of Good Fortune, The (Tenorio)   5
Soul Mountain (Gao Xingjian)   195
Sound of Music, The (film)   22, 23, 25, 26
South Asian Review (newspaper)   205
Spencer, Brent   97
Springtime for Hitler   97
State of Emergency (Tiang)   81
Statue of Clint Eastwood, The (Jiang Yitan)   31
Stay (Lacuesta)   88
stereotype   125, 129, 130, 157
Stevenson, Robert Louis   106
Strange Case of Dr. Jekyll and Mr. Hyde
    (Stevenson)   106
Strasbourg Dancing Plague (1518)   253
stream of consciousness   95
SubCutis   101, 103, 105
sub-four seas   101, 103
suicide, idea of   45, 46, 48–9, 51–4, 56, 57, 67
Sukenick, Ronald   99
surrealism   95
    fantasy and   239
Swift, Jonathan   97
Sydney Morning Herald (newspaper)   37
symbolism   16, 26, 57, 67, 131, 234, 239
    attraction and   29, 30, 35, 43
    dream   67
sympathy   18, 115, 121, 130, 157, 216
    attraction and   36–7, 41
    imagination and   95

taboos   197
    "Prayer in Training" and   218–21
    "Quilt, The" and   198–205
    Video and   205–17
Tagalog   10, 17, 95, 129, 160, 162–4, 169
Tan, Inez   223, 229, 236–7
Temporary People (Unnikrishnan)   57
Tenorio, Lysley   5, 16, 17
tension   80, 87, 185
    attraction and   29, 43
    building of   26
    diasporas and   132, 152, 159
    family and   5, 16–18, 25
    psychological   17
    taboos and   197, 198, 217
Thailand   2, 218
theme   1, 2, 16, 29, 115, 198
Theravada Buddhism   218
third-person narrative   66, 93, 195
This Is Where I Won't Be Alone (Inez Tan)   229
thoughts   16, 26, 43, 52, 67, 78, 97
    disorderliness of   95
Thurber, James   106

Tiang, Jeremy   80, 81
tone   16, 70, 92, 153, 206, 233, 239, 254
    attraction and   30, 41
    routines and   45, 55, 66
    skins and   97, 106, 113
Tor.com   218
transitions   159
Tribe, The (Ahmed)   37
Tse, Dorothy   173, 185

Ulysses (Joyce)   80
Umbrella Movement   254, 260
uncertainty   85, 139, 166, 237
    mysteries and   179, 186, 191
    routines and   53, 55, 64
underwired g-strung   101, 103
United Arab Emirates (UAE)   45, 65
United Kingdom. *See* Britain/British/United Kingdom
United States   2, 106, 107, 129, 131, 157, 198
universal   31, 69
Unnikrishnan, Deepak   45, 57, 66
unrealistic   18
uselessness, sense of   56

"Veldt, The" (Bradbury)   239
Video (Nair)   205–17
    significance of   217
Vietnam   2, 119, 131, 133, 136, 158, 228, 260
"Vietnam War, The"   131
Vonnegut, Kurt   99
vulnerability   37, 43, 44

Wall Street Journal   104
Wang, Helen   107
Washington Post (newspaper)   205
We, the Children of Cats (Hoshino Tomoyuki)
    240
"We That Summer" (Han Yujoo)   45–55, 66, 87
    significance of   55–7, 67
What Maisie Knew (James)   69
"Where Did I Lose You" (Fan Xiaoqing)   186–94
    significance of   194–5
white space, significance of   158
Williams, Joy   197
"Wonderful World" (Cooke) (song)   223
Woolf, Virginia   1, 95
Worthington, Marjorie   99
"Wrysons, The" (Cheever)   80

Xu Xi, Jenny Wai   99, 106, 113

Yeung Chak Yan   255
Yoshimoto Banana   223, 224, 228

Zhang Xinxin   107

www.ingramcontent.com/pod-product-compliance
Lightning Source LLC
Chambersburg PA
CBHW081803300426
44116CB00014B/2223